"This book is very effective in explaining the operations of the Belt and Road initiative in terms of sustainable development goals whole also considering the Digital Silk Road and the overall effect of all activity upon sustainability. It does so with detailed explanations before going on to assess the effects. It does so through a rigorous assessment of the CSR reporting of the companies involved and their effects upon the respective locales. But do not take my word for this – read and assess yourself!"

Professor Dr David Crowther, *President, Social Responsibility Research Network*

CSR Reporting and the Belt and Road Initiative

The Belt and Road Initiative (BRI) is a major development strategy launched by the Chinese government with the goal of fostering economic cooperation among countries along the proposed routes. The BRI marks a new era in which multinational enterprises (MNEs) from developing countries are beginning to take primary responsibility for driving global flows of outward foreign direct investment (OFDI). Among hotly debated topics on how the BRI is reshaping the global competitive landscape, corporate social responsibility (CSR) reporting practices of Chinese MNEs along the Belt and Road are noteworthy but relatively less discussed.

This book investigates how do Chinese MNEs engage with, define, and implement CSR under such an enormous cooperative initiative through analyzing their CSR reporting practices in the BRI host countries. Besides this, opportunities and challenges of the BRI investments for sustainable development in host countries are examined. The book provides critical insights into the current institutional architecture for CSR reporting to promote sustainable development. It also highlights the importance of stakeholders' capacities to sustain, enact, and execute strict CSR disclosure laws and regulations.

The findings mark important implications, particularly in view of growing concerns about international reputational damage of unsustainable OFDI. The book is suitable for researchers, undergraduate and postgraduate students in the fields of CSR, sustainability development, accounting, and international business; as well as others who are keen on the latest development of the BRI in relation to other developing and least-developed countries.

Ruopiao Zhang is Assistant Professor in the Department of Accounting and Finance at the School of Business, Macau University of Science and Technology. Dr. Zhang obtained her Ph.D. degree in Accounting from the University of Macau. Dr. Zhang is an early career researcher in the field of social and environmental accounting with specialization in corporate social responsibility and sustainability, biodiversity and extinction accounting.

Carlos Noronha is Associate Professor in the Department of Accounting and Information Management, Faculty of Business Administration, University of Macau. Dr. Noronha researches and publishes in the area of social accounting, especially in corporate disclosure. Currently, he is collaborating with his research team in the development of the Phenomenon *Grande*, a theoretical perspective to look into inter-related and multi-disciplinary social phenomena through a critical lens.

Jieqi Guan is Assistant Professor in the School of Hospitality Management, Macao Institute for Tourism Studies. She obtained her Ph.D. degree from the University of Macau. Her research areas are mainly related to social accounting and reporting, corporate social responsibility and sustainability.

Routledge Advances in Management and Business Studies

126. Digital Entrepreneurship and the Global Economy
Edited by J. Mark Munoz

127. Cross-cultural Knowledge Management
Cultural Influences in China and Brazil
Jacky Hong and Jorge Muniz Jr.

128. Human Resource Management and Internal Marketing
Teena Mishra

129. Human Resources Management in Multinational Companies
A Central European Perspective
Marzena Stor

130. Corporate Culture and Globalization
Ideology and Identity in a Global Fashion Retailer
Yi Zhu

131. Corporate Compliance and Conformity
A Convenience Theory Approach to Executive Deviance
Petter Gottschalk

132. CSR Reporting and the Belt and Road Initiative
Implementation by Chinese Multinational Enterprises
Ruopiao Zhang, Carlos Noronha and Jieqi Guan

133. Corporate Social Hypocrisy
CSR in the Era of Global Crises
Dalia Streimikiene, Asta Mikalauskiene and Gabija Stanislovaityte

134. Information, Security and Society in the COVID-19 Pandemic
Edited by Natalia Moch, Wioletta Wereda and Jerzy Stańczyk

For more information about this series, please visit: www.routledge.com/Routledge-Advances-in-Management-and-Business-Studies/book-series/SE0305

CSR Reporting and the Belt and Road Initiative

Implementation by Chinese Multinational Enterprises

Ruopiao Zhang, Carlos Noronha and Jieqi Guan

LONDON AND NEW YORK

First published 2023
by Routledge
4 Park Square, Milton Park, Abingdon, Oxon OX14 4RN

and by Routledge
605 Third Avenue, New York, NY 10158

Routledge is an imprint of the Taylor & Francis Group, an informa business

© 2023 Ruopiao Zhang, Carlos Noronha and Jieqi Guan

The right of Ruopiao Zhang, Carlos Noronha and Jieqi Guan to be identified as authors of this work has been asserted in accordance with sections 77 and 78 of the Copyright, Designs and Patents Act 1988.

All rights reserved. No part of this book may be reprinted or reproduced or utilised in any form or by any electronic, mechanical, or other means, now known or hereafter invented, including photocopying and recording, or in any information storage or retrieval system, without permission in writing from the publishers.

Trademark notice: Product or corporate names may be trademarks or registered trademarks, and are used only for identification and explanation without intent to infringe.

British Library Cataloguing-in-Publication Data
A catalogue record for this book is available from the British Library

ISBN: 978-1-032-29868-9 (hbk)
ISBN: 978-1-032-29869-6 (pbk)
ISBN: 978-1-003-30244-5 (ebk)

DOI: 10.4324/9781003302445

Typeset in Galliard
by KnowledgeWorks Global Ltd.

Contents

List of figures — xi
List of tables — xii
Foreword — xiii
Acknowledgment — xvi
List of abbreviations — xvii

1 Globalization, CSR, and Multinational Enterprises from Emerging Economies (EMNEs) — 1

   Introduction 1
   Why go abroad? 3
   Challenges and opportunities 6
   CSR of EMNEs 9
   CSR is not a panacea 11
   Current challenges 12
   References 13

2 The Rise of China's Economy and the Chinese MNEs — 19

   Introduction 19
   Concepts of internationalization 19
   Stages of internationalization 20
   Motivations of Chinese MNEs 23
   Competitive advantages of Chinese MNEs 26
   Chinese MNEs as a starting point 28
   Note 30
   References 30

3 The Belt and Road Initiative and CSR — 33

   The political economy background of the BRI 33
   CSR and BRI: Some underlying theories 35
     Stakeholders and the BRI CSR 35
     Legitimacy, isomorphism, and the BRI CSR 36

viii *Contents*

    Social contract, norms, and the BRI CSR 39
    Resource dependency and the BRI CSR 40
A theoretical framework of CSR and BRI 42
Notes 44
References 45

4 CSR Reporting and Chinese MNEs   50

China as a latecomer and quick learner of CSR 50
Institutional CSR governing Chinese MNEs 57
Pressures on Chinese MNEs' CSR reporting 61
Notes 63
References 65

5 CSR Reporting in BRI Countries   69

Theoretical basis of Chinese MNEs' CSR reporting
  in BRI countries 69
    Stakeholder theory 70
    Institutional theory 71
    Legitimacy theory 73
    Social contract theory 75
    Resource dependency theory 76
    International strategic theory 78
Why is CSR reporting along the BRI
  worth exploring? 79
Situational factors affecting CSR reporting along
  the Belt and Road 83
Notes 85
References 86

6 Assessment of CSR Reporting Quality along the Belt
   and Road   96

Assessment of CSR reporting quality 96
Assessment of CSR reporting quality
  of Chinese MNEs 97
Appendix 111
  Appendix 1: List of BRI host countries 111
  Appendix 2: Sample firm list 112

Notes 116
References 116

Contents ix

7 CSR Reporting Contents of Chinese MNEs in BRI
  Host Countries   120
  Top ten CSR reporting topics related to BRI
    host countries 120
    Economic impacts along the BRI 120
    Maximizing local people's livelihoods 124
    Unifying environmental safeguards 125
    Human-oriented principle in overseas
      employment 127
  Top ten emerging CSR reporting topics related
    to BRI host countries 127
  CSR reporting quality in BRI host countries 132
  Notes 137
  References 137

8 The Impact of Ownership Types on CSR Reporting
  Contents and Quality   143
  The influence of ownership type on CSR reporting
    of Chinese MNEs 143
  Topical analysis of CSR reporting of Chinese MNEs 147
  A new political-economy basis for developing
    CSR reporting by Chinese MNEs 151
    State ownership 152
    Discretionary reporting for reputation 153
    Reporting transparency and humanization 154
    Honors and awards as mimetic forces 155
    Reporting influenced by party directives 156
  Notes 160
  References 160

9 Industry-specific CSR Reporting Contents in BRI
  Host Countries   164
  Highlighted industries along the Belt and Road 164
    Land connectively through transportation
      infrastructure: Construction industry 167
    Green finance and sustainable BRI: Banking
      and finance industry 171
    Digital Silk Road: Information and
      communication technology (ICT) industry 176

    Challenges ahead 180
    Notes 182
    References 183

10 CSR of Chinese MNEs in Developing Countries under the BRI Context: Through the Lens of Africa   186

    Footprints of Chinese MNEs in Africa 186
    Africa for the BRI or the BRI for Africa:
      A mixed blessing? 188
    CSR threats of the BRI in Africa 190
    How does CSR assist companies in gaining
      legitimacy in Africa? 190
        Environmental and biodiversity conservation 193
        Empowerment of women 195
        Fair education 196
        Community welfare 197
        Anti-corruption 198
        Promotion of employment 199
    The BRI and the SDGs: The way forward
      for Africa 200
    Notes 202
    References 202

11 How China's Belt and Road Initiative Is Faring: Implications and Outlooks for Corporate Social Responsibility   207

    A review of CSR and the BRI in this study 207
    The BRI at the crossroad of a world full of
      difficulties 214
    Concluding remarks 216
    Notes 219
    References 219

Index   222

Figures

3.1	The theoretical framework incorporating CSR into the BRI	43
5.1	Theoretical framework of CSR reporting in the BRI countries	80
6.1	Research methodology process	98
8.1	Top ten CSR reporting topics of CEs in the BRI host countries	149
8.2	Top ten CSR reporting topics of SOEs in the BRI host countries	150
8.3	Top ten CSR reporting topics of PEs in the BRI host countries	150
9.1	External factors influencing the CSR reporting contents of Chinese MNEs in the ICT industry	181

Tables

3.1	Guidelines and action plans governing the Chinese MNEs participating in the BRI	34
3.2	Overseas CSR actions vis-à-vis key stakeholders along the Belt and Road	36
4.1	Various forces affecting overseas CSR practices of Chinese MNEs	55
4.2	CSR regulations for Chinese MNEs	59
5.1	Overseas CSR actions vis-à-vis key stakeholders based on the BRI's two main policy documents	71
6.1	CSR report screening process	99
6.2	References for the establishment of the evaluation framework of CSR reporting quality of Chinese MNEs along the BRI	100
6.3	Evaluation framework of CSR reporting quality of Chinese MNEs along the BRI	101
6.4	Illustration of assigning scores in content analysis	107
6.5	Descriptive statistics	110
7.1	Top ten CSR reporting topics related to the BRI host countries	121
7.2	Top ten emerging CSR reporting topics in the BRI countries	128
7.3	Overseas CSR (OCSR) disclosure quality by year	133
7.4	Score distribution of different CSR reporting topics (raw score)	134
8.1	CSR disclosure quality by firm types	144
8.2	Comparisons of overseas CSR disclosure quality by firm types	146
8.3	CSR topic-level one-way ANOVA results	148
8.4	2021 Sustainability honors and awards of Huawei	156
9.1	Sample list in case studies	166
9.2	Social and environmental risks of different types of land transportation projects	168
9.3	Related policies for green finance in China	173
9.4	Green bond issued by major Chinese multinational banks	174
10.1	The BRI threats and related CSR crisis	191

Foreword

There can be no doubt that the Belt and Road initiative of China is having an effect upon the world and changing economic and trading relationships. Equally there can no longer be any uncertainty that this is being complemented by the Digital Silk Road (Hillman, 2021) and that the effect of these will increase over time. Some have characterised this as a competition between China and the United States for influence in the developing parts of the world and consider the effects. Of far greater significance though than the relationship between these two superpowers is the effect that these initiatives will have upon the people and countries affected by the developments which are taking place as a part of these initiatives. After all, despite what is often stated, it is at the local level of individuals and societies where the effects of actions are usually felt. For example, it is amongst individuals where the effects of climate change and other such threats are actually felt. This therefore is a suitable lens to investigate that is happening as a result of the Belt and Road initiative.

It is apparent that a significant amount of investment is being undertaken by Chinese companies in a wide range of countries as part of the initiative and that this investment will have a great impact upon the host countries. Much of this investment is focused upon Africa and involves a significant amount of the building of infrastructure in these countries. Of course, it can be argued that trade cannot take place until the appropriate infrastructure exists but equally it can be argued that these countries will not be able to develop internally without this infrastructure. Of equal importance it must be recognised that one of the platforms of sustainability is equity and that this investment in infrastructure development is assisting to ensure that this equity exists throughout the world. Thus, it is possible to argue that the Belt and Road initiative, coupled with the development of the Digital Silk Road, is actually resulting in greater sustainability in the world. And we would all want to laud this action when interpreted in this way. It is of course equally possible to interpret these actions differently and construe them as a threat to the established world order. But all actions can be interpreted in multiple ways depending upon the interests of the interpreter. I would argue that the effects upon sustainability for the world overrides all other interpretations and this can clearly be seen in this light.

In recent times, many man-made problems have increasingly become manifest. Thus, pollution caused by plastic has recently entered popular consciousness (see Crowther, 2019; Moghaddam & Crowther, 2021) in a major way, not just for its effects upon wildlife and sea life (Eriksen et al., 2013) but also for the effects it is having upon human health (Wright & Kelly, 2017). The issue is not of course new (see, e.g., Carson, 1962) and has been discussed extensively over several decades. Public reaction has, however, been extreme and the danger is that plastic is being cast as universally bad and undesirable – with ire being directed in particular at 'single use plastic' which is commonly used for packaging. It is necessary therefore to set the record straight and to consider use made of plastic and its desirability, or otherwise.

There seems to be a general assumption that there is no need to worry because future developments will enable the problems which have been caused in the present to be solved. In other words, we do not need to worry about causing problems for our descendants because we expect that they will be able to sort them out. After all, we are managing to sort out the problems caused by our ancestors. The difference is though that our ancestors did not realise that they were causing problems and genuinely thought that they were attempting to leave a better future for us. We can no longer hide behind such an assumption as we understand that we are damaging the future. Thus, this assumption cannot be considered to be an ethical choice – only a lazy one! Hence the importance of assessing the effects of these initiatives.

It is, as already stated, the effects upon people and local society which is of greatest importance and the question therefore becomes one of assessing the effects of these initiatives. After all, it is insufficient to invest in these infrastructure developments if this is done at the expense of the destruction of the environment or effects upon people and their local culture and society. Obviously, these things need to be balanced as it is not always possible to ensure that a benefit in one area has no adverse consequences elsewhere. But such is life. In the main, the actions taken in the development of infrastructure are being undertaken by Chinese companies and the question therefore becomes one of assessing the effect these firms are having upon the environment (social, environmental, and economic) in which they are operating. Clearly, one way of assessing the effect of corporate activity is by looking at the corporate social responsibility of their actions. This can be assessed by investigating the CSR reporting practices of these companies and the effects which they are having in the various countries involved.

This book is very effective in explaining the operations of the Belt and Road initiative in terms of sustainable development goals whole also considering the Digital Silk Road and the overall effect of all activity upon sustainability. It does so with detailed explanations before going on to assess the effects. It does so through a rigorous assessment of the CSR reporting of the companies involved and their effects upon the respective locales. But do not take my word for this – read and assess yourself!

Professor Dr David Crowther
President
Social Responsibility Research Network
www.srrnet.org

References

Carson, R. (1962). *Silent spring*. Houghton Mifflin.
Crowther, D. (2019). Plastic tuendae (in defence of plastic). *JOJ Internal Medicine*, *1*(2), 1–2.
Eriksen, M., Maximenko, N., Thiel, M., Cummins, A., Lattin, G., Wilson, S., … & Rifman, S. (2013). Plastic pollution in the South pacific subtropical gyre. *Marine Pollution Bulletin, 68*(1–2), 71–76.
Hillman, J. E. (2021). *The digital silk road: China's quest to wire the world and win the future*. Profile Books.
Moghaddam, A., & Crowther, D. (2021). Sustainable plastic and corporate social responsibility. In D. Crowther & S. Seifi (Eds.), *Palgrave handbook of corporate social responsibility* (pp. 333–353). Palgrave.
Wright, S. L., & Kelly, F. J. (2017). Plastic and human health: A micro issue. *Environmental Science & Technology, 51*(12), 6634–6647.

Acknowledgment

Having an idea and turning it into a book is as hard as it sounds. However, the experience is both challenging and rewarding. We would like to express our very great appreciation to Prof. Mike Tayles for his valuable and constructive suggestions during the planning and development of this research work. This endeavour would not have been possible without the enlightening café conversation during his visit to Macau in 2019.

We would like to express our deepest gratitude to Prof. Rute Abreu, Prof. David Crowther, Prof. Ming Liu, Prof. Xu Zhang, Prof. Endong Yang, Prof. Teresa Chu, and Prof. Simon So for advices, encouragements, and immensely valuable and motivational feedbacks for an early draft of this book.

Words cannot express our gratitude to Prof. David Crowther who wrote a constructive and thought-provoking foreword for this book. His willingness to give his time so generously has been very much appreciated.

Thanks to everyone on the Routledge publishing team who helped us so much. Special thanks to Kendrick Loo and Yongling Lam. Without the assistance and support from the editorial team at the Taylor & Francis Group, this book would not come to fruition.

Last but not least, we are indebted to our families and friends for their unfailing love and unconditional support.

R.Z.
C.N.
J.G.

Abbreviations

ACFIC	All-China Federation of Industry and Commerce
BRI	Belt and Road Initiative
CAFC	China Association of Foreign Contractors
CASS	Chinese Academy of Social Sciences
CBRC	China Banking Regulatory Commission
CCCMC	China Chamber of Commerce for Import and Export of Metals, Minerals and Chemicals
CE	Central Enterprise
CHINCA	China International Contractors Association
CIRC	China Insurance Regulatory Commission
CSR	Corporate Social Responsibility
CSRC	China Securities Regulatory Commission
EIA	Environmental Impact Assessment
EM-MNEs	Emerging-economy Multinational Enterprises
FDI	Foreign Direct Investment
GAC	General Administration of Customs
GDP	Gross Domestic Product
GRI	Global Reporting Initiative
ICT	Information and Communication Technology
ISO	International Organization for Standardization
LOF	Liability of Foreignness
MEP	Ministry of Environmental Protection
MNE	Multinational Enterprise
MOF	Ministry of Finance
MOFA	Ministry of Foreign Affairs
MOFCOM	Ministry of Commerce
MOTI	Ministry of Trade and Industry
MPS	Ministry of Public Security
NDRC	National Development and Reform Commission
NEB	National Energy Board
NGO	Non-Governmental Organization
OFDI	Outward Foreign Direct Investment
PBOC	People's Bank of China

PE	Private Enterprise
SAFE	State Administration of Foreign Exchange
SASAC	State-owned Assets Supervision and Administration Commission
SAT	State Administration of Taxation
SAWS	State Administration of Work Safety
SDGs	Sustainable Development Goals
SFA	State Forestry Administration
SOA	State Oceanic Administration
SOE	State-owned Enterprise
WBCSD	World Business Council for Sustainable Development

1 Globalization, CSR, and Multinational Enterprises from Emerging Economies (EMNEs)

Introduction

Globalization, characterized by industrial advancements, technology transfer, and the prominence of multinational enterprises (MNEs), has been increasing in the past few decades. On the other hand, the rise of emerging economies, such as BRIC: Brazil, Russia, India, and China; MITS: Mexico, Indonesia, Turkey, and South Africa as well as numerous other economies in Africa, East Asia, South Asia, Latin America, and the Middle East, is possibly today's most significant international business (IB) phenomenon. According to prior studies, emerging economies are defined as those economies which have undergone profound transformations during their transition from communism to capitalism regimes that they are also categorized as transition economies (Meyer & Peng, 2005; Roth & Kostova, 2003). By contrasting emerging economies with advanced or developed economies, Meyer (2018) further defines emerging economies as markets which are less efficient, and the governments and businesses with ties to the governments are active participants in the market. Furthermore, network-based behaviors are widespread, and there is a large risk of uncertainty due to volatility. Emerging economies include the features of burgeoning middle classes; large and relatively low-cost but well-educated labor forces, growing entrepreneurial classes with relatively high technological and managerial skills (Bruton et al., 2013). As emerging and transition economies have opened to the global economy in recent years, a number of local firms have expanded worldwide through exports and outward foreign direct investment (FDI) (OFDI) to become nascent MNEs in their own right (Sun, 2009). The OFDI of MNEs from emerging economies (EMNEs) such as Huawei, Lenovo, Tata, Haier, Cemex has already outpaced those of their counterparts from developed economies, reversing the decades-long OFDI trends in the past.

The study of EMNEs could be traced back to the late 1970s and early 1980s (e.g., Ghymn, 1980; Kumar & McLeod, 1981; Lecraw, 1977; Wells, 1983) and accelerated in the 2000s (e.g., Khanna et al., 2006; Meyer, 2004; Narula, 2012; Sheth, 2011). There are also plenty of special issues of academic journals (such as *Emerging Markets Review* and *Emerging Markets Finance and Trade*) dedicated to the research on EMNEs. However, studies of EMNEs still remain

DOI: 10.4324/9781003302445-1

underdeveloped. As early as more than a decade ago, leading IB magazines, such as *Business Week* and *The Economist*, began to trumpet this trend with cover stories about "emerging giants" or "the offspring of globalization" and illustrated the disruptive impact of EMNEs on established MNEs from developed countries. It is believed that the growth of EMNEs, which began in the early 2000s, is a long-term trend with significant effects on the world economy rather than a passing fad. This tendency is primarily motivated by the growing confidence that emerging countries are reshaping the landscape of global trade as their indigenous EMNEs outperform rivals from more economically developed economies, both domestically and internationally (Bhattacharya & Michael, 2008; Cuervo-Cazurra & Genc, 2008). Many of them are able to leapfrog several development stages and compete head-to-head with MNEs from developed economies. In fact, all it takes to see that EMNEs are rapidly developing a strong and unheard-of foothold in the global economy is to glance at the recent evolution of the Worldwide Fortune 500 or Financial Times 500 lists of the most powerful global firms. By 2025, MNEs from emerging and developing economies are expected to account for around 50 of the Fortune Global 500, up from 25 in 2000 (McKinsey Global Institute, 2015). For instance, the rapid increase in the size of the Chinese economy is reflected by the fact that 143 Chinese companies were listed on the Fortune 500 list released by *Fortune* magazine in 2021. Given their growing importance in the global economy, it is not surprising that they have garnered considerable attention in contemporary IB studies.

OFDI was historically undertaken mostly by MNEs from advanced economies investing in other developed economies or in emerging economies (Dunning, 1998). A sizeable and well-publicized portion of OFDI from emerging economies has been invested in places more developed than their country of origin, even though many of these investments have been in other emerging economies (Hennart, 2012). As more EMNEs entered the global capitalist system, the role of business became increasingly important at all levels of society. The way that various communities handle and respond to economic change, however, is extremely essential due to the fact that the global economy is becoming more and more intertwined. Sustainable production, labor standards, or even the cultural and social effects of development cannot be assumed to be converging to a "global norm" or left up to the market alone as trade barriers fall, industrial investment becomes more globalized, and national governments experience a corresponding decline in power (Ramamurti, 2012). On the other hand, the notion of corporate social responsibility (CSR) is founded on the idea that businesses are inextricably linked to social, economic, cultural, and environmental issues, and that they have an impact on businesses and businesses also have a reciprocal impact on them. CSR is viewed as a globally legitimate practice that should be adopted by MNEs to demonstrate to the firm's global legitimacy-granting stakeholders that the organization adheres to metanorms and expectations (KPMG, 2013). Reporting on CSR also offers the host-country and global stakeholders with additional information for evaluating EMNEs in a more reasonable manner, which can counter negative stereotypes based on inadequate institutional conditions in the emerging economies (Kostova et al., 2008). This chapter attempts to appraise and provide the specifics regarding this complex relationship in the context of EMNEs, a topic that is understudied and undervalued within the highly regarded field of CSR.

Prior until now, the CSR discussion of MNEs has been dominated by US and European perspectives, while including the perspectives of developing countries to reflect the "on-the-ground" reality in the global South. However, EMNEs, like their developed-market counterparts, can have significant and potentially transformative effects in their home and host countries. Critical questions about appropriate legal and policy mechanisms to regulate their activities are thus raised. Topics hotly debated by scholars include what competitive advantages do they leverage as they internationalize? Are they unique in any way since they are from emerging economies? How do home-country conditions of EMNEs affect their global performance and CSR strategies? How do their business operations in host countries differ from those from developed countries? Bearing these questions in mind, this chapter will present a clear and comprehensive introduction of globalization and EMNEs as well as their influence on the global business landscape, particularly through the lens of CSR.

Why go abroad?

Most OFDI in the post-World War II era moved from one advanced economy to another. Beginning from the 1970s, IB scholars and development economists were drawn to the strategies of Western MNEs in developing nations and their intense interactions with host governments which occasionally resulted in direct expropriation by host countries (e.g., Kobrin & Hendershot, 1977). The first substantial wave of FDI from developing countries occurred in the late 1970s (Wells, 1977). At least two-thirds of that FDI, often known as South-South investment (Wells, 1983, p. 4), flowed to other developing markets. Even at its peak, however, external FDI from developing nations in the 1970s constituted a negligible portion of global FDI flows (UNCTAD, 2008). It is well known that, over the past two decades, the phenomenon of the internationalization of EMNEs and their international expansion – primarily through OFDI and, especially, by means of cross-border acquisitions of firms as a way to gain access to critical resources, to promote strategic renovation, or to create shareholder value – has become increasingly prevalent globally. The newest kids on the block are EMNEs and the growth of the new multinationals has astonished observers, decision-makers, and academics. A decade ago, many of these companies were minor rivals; today, in a range of markets and industries, they are competing with some of the most accomplished and well-known international corporations. The US, Japan, and Britain dominated the list of the 500 largest corporations in the world when *Forbes* first published its list in 2003. Currently, companies from China and other emerging economies are extensively included in the most recent "Global 500" list. For instance, 67 of the world's top 500 companies are from China.

In stereotypes, EMNEs use comparatively older technologies, labor-intensive procedures as opposed to technology-intensive ones, and their brands have limited popularity outside of their home countries. Furthermore, due to their relatively short history of international operations, they have not yet developed management capabilities and management skills sufficiently learned from experiences in managing operations globally in a range of host nations. According to traditional MNE theories, MNEs engage in FDI to transfer and exploit their capabilities (Buckley & Casson, 2009; Narula & Verbeke, 2015). The recent influx of EMNEs, however, lacks the well-known brands and cutting-edge technology that are typically considered the primary forces behind MNE's international expansion (e.g., Kim et al., 2020; Klossek et al., 2012; Mathews, 2006). Guillèn and Garcia-Canal (2009) suggest that EMNEs are an entirely new form of MNEs and have pursued entirely different internationalization strategies than MNEs.

Stereotypes believe that EMNEs typically have not yet developed international management skills based on knowledge of conducting business abroad in a range of host economies. In contrast, EMNEs are latecomers that are essentially catching up with developed economies as they are more experienced in dealing with institutional voids (Khanna & Palepu, 2005). The majority of the literature concurs that the sets of competitive advantages held by EMNEs and MNEs from developed economies differ significantly from one another. MNEs from developed economies are more likely to possess advantages based on ownership of critical assets such as technologies, brands, and other intellectual properties, whereas EMNEs rely more on production capabilities, home-country social networks (such as Chinese *guanxi* networks), and access to financial capital (UNCTAD, 2008). The advantages enjoyed by MNEs from developed economies are stronger since they have had more time to accumulate skills, but IB scholars expect that EMNEs are bolstering their ownership advantages over time, thereby narrowing the gap with MNEs from developed economies (Lessard & Lucea, 2009). EMNEs have reaped many benefits on the road to investing abroad. The benefits of OFDI can be compared to spillover advantages of internationalization and inverse advantages of host nations' spillovers. For instance, Cozza et al. (2015) attest to the existence of spillover effects from Chinese companies' OFDI into nations in Europe. They discover that a few years after their initial investment, Chinese EMNEs' productivity increases significantly. They further argue that such increase in productivity could be resulted from transfer of knowledge, an improved allocation of firm's production activities as well as managerial best practices. A large of EMNEs originate from countries with insufficient legal protection, political unpredictability, and technological and infrastructure constraints. The EMNEs pursue solutions to get more out of less, improve ways to deal with uncertainty, and develop an obsession with lifelong learning. As a result, EMNEs use their international expansion into developed countries as a platform to acquire vital new resources (such as technology, skills, or other resources) that they desired in order to compete more successfully against their global competitors and in order to get around domestic technological or infrastructure limitations.

There are several drivers that motivate the internationalization of EMNEs. First the inability to increase production or take advantage of economies of scale, as well as the challenges brought on by the existence of trade restrictions or shaky international links with customers, could be motivators for EMNEs to invest abroad. Specifically, EMNEs which have already possessed a certain level of innovation capabilities are going abroad to seek lower production costs and supply chain savings. For example, Huawei and Samsung have established subsidiaries in multiple and diversified locations where they could be embedded into more R&D as well as the arbitrage differences in input costs and prices. Second, many EMNEs already have well-known brands in their home countries and want to escape from the limitations of being caught in the middle of the value chain, where production and assembly are relatively low profit-making compared to the higher profit-making inventions and brand names (Mudambi, 2008). Local business conditions not only can produce stimulating competitive pressures that lead to internationalization, but they can also lead to corporations looking for possibilities elsewhere when they create challenges with infrastructure, labor, security, or corruption. In terms of production cost, lower labor costs could be achieved by moving offshore to locations with lower labor costs as a result of rising production costs and domestic labor shortages in some of the emerging economies (such as China and Vietnam). In order to continuously seek new avenues for economic development, EMNEs have also made efforts to expand outward under the policy incentive. Third, the majority of EMNEs view internationalization as a way to expand their competitive advantages across a wider range of markets as well as a way to gain access to new resources and knowledge. In other words, learning is also an important objective of internationalization for the majority of EMNEs apart from market exploitation. The learning potential of globalization is frequently, at least initially, the more essential objective. This stands in stark contrast with the overseas expansion strategy of traditional developed-market MNEs, which was primarily motivated by the desire to capitalize on domestic competitive advantage (Doz et al., 2001). That to say, some EMNEs base their competitive strengths not merely on the efficient or low-cost value added, but also their abilities to interface with the more complex needs of their customers. Fourth, as discussed before, one of the advantages of EMNEs is their familiarity of doing businesses in similar emerging economies by replicating their business operations. Thus, replications of business operations in other emerging economies are regarded as one of the most important reasons explaining the internationalization of EMNEs (Khanna & Palepu, 2005). Last but not least, seeking more secured natural resources is another factor that motivate the OFDI of EMNEs. For example, infrastructure construction projects and extractive projects are typical topics of OFDI by Chinese EMNEs, which will be discussed in detail in our chapters later.

Challenges and opportunities

Compared to developed economies, emerging economies have lower levels of economic development, institutional quality, and/or living standards. They have also undergone major institutional and market reforms (Sullivan & Sheffrin, 2003). Earlier studies have argued that country of origin positively influences MNEs' internationalization. In other words, there is a phenomenon of "advantage of origin" (Dunning, 1988; Gertler et al., 2000). For example, high-tech companies from the Silicon Valley (e.g., Google, Apple) are more likely to expand to overseas markets due to the well-developed institutional, technological, and human resources environment there which are conducive to fostering ownership advantages and promoting OFDI (Chen et al., 2019). Many studies have shown that MNEs from developed countries are able to enjoy many advantages in the host country when investing in OFDI simply because of their "country of origin" (Elango & Sethi, 2007; Insch & Miller, 2005; Nachum, 2010).

Emerging countries have distinctive institutional environments compared to more developed countries (Bartlett & Ghoshal, 2000). Unlike MNEs from developed economies, EMNEs bear the "liability of origin" when they are going global on a large scale. Specifically, the extra burden that emerges specifically from being an emerging-economy firm has been described as the "liability of emergingness" (LOE) (Ramachandran & Pant, 2010; Madhok & Keyhani, 2012). This refers to the additional disadvantages that emerging-market MNEs appear to suffer when investing abroad compared with advanced-country multinationals. For example, compared with developed countries, emerging economies generally have institutional voids such as imperfect market mechanisms, weak intellectual property protection, and low legal enforcement, which make it difficult for firms to cultivate ownership advantages (e.g., leading technology, brand, and management capabilities) necessary for international expansion in the institutional environment of their home countries, and thus putting them at a competitive disadvantage. Furthermore, stakeholders in host countries (especially developed economies) often "spontaneously" or even "rightfully" apply negative labels such as low-end products, government involvement, unfair competition, backward technology, and poor corporate governance structures to EMNEs, leading to serious legitimacy challenges and credibility deficits for internationalization. In particular, the challenges and opportunities that home-country institutional voids for these enterprises have received significant attention from IB academics. The term "institutional voids" refers to the lack or underdevelopment of institutions that facilitate effective markets, such as governance mechanisms that prevent corruption, safeguard property rights, uphold the rule of law, and establish public investments and infrastructure (Gao et al., 2017). Thus, EMNEs need to employ aggressive internationalization strategies to enter into more competitive and advanced international markets due to institutional deficiencies at home.

Bias is everywhere. When going abroad, EMNEs encounter specific hurdles coming from the same home-country institutional voids that they are attempting to fill through internationalization. For instance, they may face legitimacy challenges in host countries, particularly the more developed ones, because their home-country institutional environments are characterized by weak corporate governance and, consequently, do not provide host-country stakeholders with sufficient information for evaluating these firms. Legitimacy refers to "a generalized perception or assumption that the actions of an entity are desirable, proper, or appropriate within some socially constructed system of norms, values, beliefs, and definitions" (Suchman, 1995, p. 571). For MNEs, legitimacy encompasses their ability to meet social expectations of a range of constituents including shareholders, supplies, customers, governments, and NGOs in home countries as MNEs depend on these actors for the social license to survive (Marano et al., 2017). As a consequence of this, international legitimating actors may form adverse attitudes about these companies due to unfavorable prejudices toward the countries from where these enterprises originate. According to a survey conducted by Edelman Trust Barometer with over 27,000 respondents across 27 countries, when it comes to trust, a company's headquarters location is absolutely critical. Enterprises with headquarters in BRIC nations continue to rank among the least trusted of companies, continuing a trend from prior years. The trust challenge is particularly acute for MNEs from emerging economies seeking to do business in a developed country. In sharp contrast to countries like Sweden, Canada, Germany, and Switzerland, which recorded trust levels as high as 76%, Brazil (38%), China (36%), Russia (35%), India (34%), and Mexico (31%) all had trust levels that were significantly lower than their developed counterparts. Biases resulting from institutional weaknesses of their countries of origins inhibit the generation and circulation of information and other resources and limit the economic potential due to social, regulatory, and political unpredictability (Khanna & Palepu, 1997).

When evaluating the legitimacy of EMNEs, foreign stakeholders may use "adverse institutional attribution" (Ramachandran & Pant, 2010, p. 247) because poor business conditions at home result in weak corporate governance disclosure and a lack of incentive to engage in corporate citizenship (Ghemawat, 2007). Customers in the host country might assume that the subsidiaries of EMNEs offer lower quality goods and services as a result of institutional deficiencies at home (Klein, 2002). Furthermore, host-country governments might assume that the lack of transparency and corruption in the emerging economies affects these companies' international operations (Cuervo-Cazurra & Genc, 2008). Because of the weak labor or environmental laws in their home countries, host-country civil societies may be skeptical of the subsidiaries of EMNEs. Finally, investors in the host country may also perceive poor corporate governance practices because weak institutional environment in emerging economies is unable to enforce or enable good governance (Cuervo-Cazurra & Ramamurti, 2014). Such negative stakeholder perceptions illustrate the wide range of legitimacy challenges faced by EMNEs.

Prior research has demonstrated that EMNEs may have certain advantages over those from developed economies, such as lower cost structures (Ghemawat & Hout, 2008), the ability to leapfrog outdated business practices (Eccles & Krzus, 2010), and expertise in dealing with other countries with comparable institutional conditions (Cuervo-Cazurra & Genc, 2008). That is to say, what appears to be a liability in certain situations may be an asset in others, and disadvantages may change over time to become advantages. It is for this reason that "emerging giants" from the BRIC (Khanna et al., 2006), "homegrown champions" (Bhattacharya & Michael, 2008), and "global challengers" who grew up in developing markets (Aulakh, 2007) are no longer just successful in defending their home markets. They are also venturing into and gaining market share in other developing, developed, and least-developed economies.

On the one hand, many EMNEs outperform their domestic rivals, mostly due to their expertise with local market dynamics, which enables them to capitalize on local institutional frameworks (Dawar & Frost, 1999). They are also adept at dealing with weak institutions in developing nations (Aulakh, 2007) and exploiting institutional gaps to their benefits. While expanding in their home countries, EMNEs may have acquired the ability to deal with inadequate institutional settings, which may be useful in markets with comparable institutional conditions. However, MNEs from developed economies could find it challenging to manage, let alone to take advantage of the unfamiliar institutional frameworks of emerging economies. EMNEs are more likely to enter into least-developed markets (Cuervo-Cazurra & Genc, 2008). They are able to recognize chances to package ancillary services and goods (Ghemawat & Hout, 2008) in order to reduce the potential challenges posed by new MNEs from developed economies because they are familiar with the specific institutional circumstances of emerging markets. On the other hand, making the most of niche markets that traditional multinationals have abandoned is no longer sufficient for some EMNEs (Wells, 1983).

EMNEs also have the audacity to conduct extensive and aggressive FDI activities (Aulakh, 2007; Luo & Tung, 2007). Actually, EMNEs' success in developing and least-developed economies creates prospects for even more success in established markets. In fact, many of the EMNEs innovate and provide high-quality goods and services in their home markets in addition to overcoming regional institutional shortcomings and tailoring their tactics to regional markets. As a result, their products are becoming increasingly competitive in developed nations as a response to the increasing requirements of increasingly demanding clients in developing markets, particularly the pressures for greater quality. EMNEs build cross-border teams, standardize their capabilities, and eventually integrate into developing markets as their level of multinationality rises. The ability of EMNEs to maintain the comparative advantages they have gained through their experience in developing markets may therefore decline, either as a result of the evolution of the institutional and economic legacies of their home country or as a result of their own experience with internationalization and global integration.

CSR of EMNEs

Unquestionably grounded in context, CSR is founded on national business society traditions and reflects various institutional, legal, and ethical traditions (Matten & Moon, 2008; Moon & Shen, 2010). But in the post-globalization era, when big businesses are moving their operations and supply chains across international borders, these traditions become entwined. Additionally, the new sectoral difficulties must ensure that each milieu is dynamic in and of itself, even at the level of the company. These developments will undoubtedly be the subject of discussion when national and international CSR arrangements are made, taking into account that growth and expansion represent new settings and overlays. By engaging in CSR, businesses demonstrate their dedication to promoting sustainable economic growth and collaborating with employees, their families, the community, and society at large to improve quality of life (World Business Council for Sustainable Development, 2004). Thus, acknowledgment from a variety of stakeholders, including shareholders, customers, employees, suppliers, management, and local communities, is one of the key drivers for businesses to invest resources in CSR projects (McWilliams & Siegel, 2001).

MNEs have additionally been cited as "the fundamental cause of political and economic inequities worldwide" (Klein et al., 2001, p. 338). To overcome negative attributes, EMNEs adopt a variety of actions to mitigate the effects of legitimacy deficits (Reimann et al., 2012). EMNEs opt for CSR to align with norms and expectations of global stakeholders, addressing the legitimacy challenges (Fiaschi et al., 2017). Bowen's (1953) *Social Responsibility of the Businessman* is regarded as the beginning of the modern age of the CSR discussion. He remarked that "social responsibility is based on the concept that a firm should operate with an awareness of how its actions affect the achievement of desired social goals". In addition, he presented a list of goals, including "community improvement, security, justice, personal integrity, freedom, and individual development". For decades, academics have debated the issue of businesses' social concerns (Bowen, 1953; Carroll, 1999). Without a doubt, it keeps changing in shape as many authors provide different conceptualizations for CSR. For example, Carroll (1991) defines CSR as an organization's emphasis on and fulfillment of obligations to several stakeholders in numerous contexts, including economics, law, ethics, and philanthropy. Governments, investors, political parties, customers, communities, workers, trade associations, and suppliers are among the influential stakeholders (Donaldson & Preston, 1995). According to Carroll (1991), CSR compels organizations to have not only economic and legal responsibilities to society, but also ethical and discretionary responsibilities. These four elements – economic, legal, ethical, and discretionary obligations – are represented as a pyramid, with "economic" serving as the base upon which the others depend.

MNEs frequently fail to address important concerns in their host nations in an effective manner (Logsdon & Wood, 2005). Authors, such as Bendell (2005) and Newell (2005) address the issue of legitimacy, asking who is authorized to speak and advocate for communities that are affected by MNEs. They contest the right of self-appointed institutions like NGOs to speak for communities. The main thesis is that diverse stakeholders and conflicting value systems necessitate a complex CSR approach. In some circumstances, CSR obligations and stakeholder demands force MNEs to act on both global and local issues (Logsdon & Wood, 2005). Due to the fact that they must establish, maintain, and protect their legitimacy across various institutional environments with probably different or even competing expectations, MNEs generally find it more challenging to attain legitimacy than domestic enterprises (Kostova & Zaheer, 1999). Stakeholders in the host country may interpret EMNEs based on misconceptions about the deficient institutional environments in their home countries. In light of these difficulties, EMNEs may employ "alternative legitimating mechanisms" (Kostova et al., 2008, p. 1001) to meet the institutional standards of their home countries in an effort to reduce the likelihood of legitimacy spillovers brought on by unfavorable home-country institutional attribution.

Although MNEs are advocates and implementers of CSR, their behavior in host countries is still bound and restricted by the principle of "profit-maximization". However, in host countries, especially in some developing countries or less-developed countries, there is a lack of effective and CSR management systems. For instance, China Zijin Mining received a hefty penalty in 2011 for failing to disclose the significant environmental and social hazards associated with the RioBlanco mine project. Additionally, due to the harm done to the local ecology, PetroChina and Sinopec's projects in Mongolia, Indonesia, Mexico, and Gabon had to be immediately suspended. All of these incidents have presented difficulties for MNE investments in host countries. Particularly, two international organizations, namely the Global Reporting Initiative (GRI) and the Organization for Economic Co-operation and Development (OECD), have composed comprehensive regulations for MNEs, though voluntary in basis. Through their sustainability standards and multi-stakeholder networks, the GRI aims to enable decision-makers everywhere to take proactive steps toward a more sustainable society and economy. Sustainability Reporting Guidelines on Economic, Environmental, and Social Performance, the first global framework for thorough sustainability reporting, was introduced by the GRI in June 2000. Its goal was to foster international agreement on the inclusion of the triple bottom line of economic, environmental, and social performance in businesses' sustainability reporting. The significance of the GRI reporting guidelines is that they have broadened the definition of CSR to include corporate governance, economic, environmental, and social imperatives in addition to environmental challenges. The triple bottom line became the accepted modern definition of CSR shortly after that. The OECD Guidelines for MNEs provide voluntary principles and standards for responsible business conduct consistent with applicable laws, ensuring that the operations of MNEs are in harmony with government policies. Except for the GRI and OECD guidelines, the United Nations (UN) Global Compact, the International Labor Organization (ILO) Conventions, and the International Standard Organization's (ISO) principles of non-financial reporting are followed by many MNEs (Chen & Bouvain, 2009; Fortanier et al., 2011).

CSR is not a panacea

MNEs are leading the way in the transition to a more sustainable economy, and the UN Environmental Program (UNEP) has acknowledged the importance of MNEs in reaching the UN's Sustainable Development Goals (SDGs). Therefore, it is vital to comprehend how MNEs approach issues related to CSR. However, CSR is not a panacea for the legitimacy challenges faced by MNEs from emerging economies. Philanthropy and community development predominate in the application of CSR in emerging economies (Azmat & Samaratunge, 2009; Matten & Moon, 2008). These manifestations of CSR can be attributed to highly ingrained and long-standing cultural expectations and norms (Jamali & Neville, 2011; Muthuri & Gilbert, 2011), ingrained religious values and beliefs (Jamali et al., 2009), and the pressing socio-economic demands of the area (Frynas, 2005). Prior studies indicate that, with the exception of Japan, the level of CSR in Asian nations is lower than that in their Western counterparts (Baughn et al., 2007; Chapple & Moon, 2005; Welford, 2005). CSR in Asian countries tends to be related to localized issues and cultural traditions, emphasizing the significance of context uniqueness for CSR, especially of the national and regional systems and their institutional capacity in which enterprises are placed (Chapple & Moon, 2007). CSR is inextricably linked to opinions of the benefits and risks of economic globalization in many developing countries (Fox, 2004).

In recent decades, the instrumental deployment of green and social claims by corporations has risen to the forefront of the public discourse on CSR. In this context, a growing number of corporations have been accused of "talking the talk but not walking the walk", which implies their CSR claims on environmental or social issues have not been supported or followed by actual corporate actions (Walker & Wan, 2012). "Greenwashing" is the term used to describe this separation between socially responsible messages and practices. In this instance, MNEs utilize the benefit of information asymmetry to broadcast helpful information to the outside and conceal damaging environmental information in order to obtain the favor of stakeholders. EMNEs must overcome potential legitimacy issues brought on by the negative logic of the institutions in the home country, as was previously addressed, in order to embed global institutions during the process of internationalization. On the other hand, international economic activities expose EMNEs to knowledge of social and environmental practices that are prevalent in host countries but absent in local markets. These "exchanges" impose new institutional pressures on environmental responsibility practices, compelling businesses to adopt "appropriate" and "suitable" CSR activities in order to satisfy the needs of different institutional legitimacy.

Lastly, the shift from the notion of CSR as an internal management tool toward a more comprehensive understanding of the link between business and society is implied by the new definition of CSR "as a kind of regulation" (Sheehy, 2015) put out by institutional theorists (Gatti et al., 2019). This shift in viewpoint has implications on both theoretical and practical levels. Companies should be prepared to take their CSR efforts beyond standard corporate communication or impression management strategies. CSR initiatives should increasingly be viewed as legal obligations rather than merely marketing-related endeavors. Therefore, legal professionals should work with PR and communication specialists to facilitate CSR's evolution into a legitimate form of oversight. The transformation of CSR toward regulation also entails a change in the capabilities of CSR experts at a scholarly level. EMNEs are complex organizations whose operations are managed at various levels and locations and across various contexts (headquarters vs. subsidiary). EMNEs are being urged to act responsibly more and more due to their extensive reach and significant footprints, as well as growing stakeholder concerns for the welfare of the environment and people. EMNEs are particularly interested in social issues because they interact with a wide range of stakeholders with various CSR demands and requirements. EMNEs need to balance demands from their home and host countries, making it difficult to identify and meet stakeholders' social expectations (Jamali, 2008). Additionally, the CSR measures that EMNEs must undertake to meet more educated stakeholders' expectations vary between developed and developing nations. The CSR approaches of EMNEs toward various stakeholders aid in their ability to establish legitimacy both in their home and host nations as well as internationally (Sethi & Rovenpor, 2016). Despite the difficulties brought by COVID-19, CSR is evolving (Carroll, 2021). The SDGs offer a practical strategy for addressing this issue in this situation and a mechanism to help societies get through the COVID-19 pandemic (van Zanten & van Tudor, 2021). Thus, COVID-19 also offers MNEs the "opportunity" to set the example during lockdowns and setbacks and to continue implementing the SDGs at various scales and as part of their CSR strategy.

Current challenges

In 2013, Chinese President Xi Jinping proposed the cooperation initiatives to build the "New Silk Road Economic Belt" and the "21st Century Maritime Silk Road". Relying on the existing bilateral and multilateral mechanisms between China and relevant countries, and with the help of existing and effective regional cooperation platforms, the Belt and Road Initiative (BRI) aims to borrow the historical symbols of the ancient Silk Road, hold high the banner of peaceful development, and actively develop cooperation with countries along the route. In addition, this initiative is also with the objective to jointly build a community of interests, a community of destiny, and a community of responsibilities featuring political mutual trust, economic integration, and cultural inclusiveness (Li et al., 2019).

Chinese MNEs incorporate the fulfillment of CSR into their strategic value chain and attach importance to the mutual development with host BRI countries.

Besides, Chinese MNEs' commitment to internationalization and localization has positive impacts on their overseas subsidiaries' fulfillment of CSR (Hong & Shuai, 2020). However, the definition of "multinational CSR" remains to be clarified. Although some scholars have tried to conceptualize the model of multinational CSR, these studies are not based on the normative definition (Aguilera-Caraculs et al., 2017). The unclear definition has limited the development of research in this field. MNEs are a special kind of enterprise. The particularity of MNEs increases the difficulty of defining multinational CSR. The more important reason is that there are still many differences in the definition of CSR itself. On the one hand, CSR is itself a multidisciplinary field for research. Scholars and institutions with different disciplinary backgrounds stand in different research perspectives, have different understandings of social responsibility, and put forward concepts of social responsibility in different dimensions. On the other hand, in order to facilitate research, some scholars show an obvious tendency of "pragmatism" in their definitions (Wang & Zhang, 2022).

Besides, a number of studies have been conducted in the related field as aforementioned. Among the literature, there is a need for the analytical frameworks of CSR environment for MNEs to be integrated and unified. Although some scholars have devoted themselves to the research on the operating environment of MNEs (Rosenzweig & Singh, 1991), the description of environmental factors in the existing research is still fragmented, and a relatively systematic framework for environmental analysis has not been formed. The possible reason is that social responsibility is related to the "environments" in all aspects of the enterprise, including the natural and social, the explicit institutional and the implicit cultural, as well as the national. In addition to environmental diversity, environmental differences between MNEs' home and host countries are also important. The remaining chapters of this book will fill in the gaps identified above and analyze the CSR performance of Chinese EMNE's in overseas countries, taking the rising Chinese MNEs as the entry point.

References

Aguilera-Caracuel, J., Guerrero-Villegas, J., & García-Sánchez, E. (2017). Reputation of multinational companies: Corporate social responsibility and internationalization. *European Journal of Management and Business Economics, 26*(3), 329–346.

Aulakh, P. S. (2007). Emerging multinationals from developing economies: Motivations, paths, and performance. *Journal of International Management, 3*(13), 235–240.

Azmat, F., & Samaratunge, R. (2009). Responsible entrepreneurship in developing countries: Understanding the realities and complexities. *Journal of Business Ethics, 90*(3), 437–452.

Bartlett, C. A., & Ghoshal, S. (2000). Going global: Lessons from late movers. *Reading, 1*(3), 75–84.

Baughn, C. C., Bodie, N. L., & McIntosh, J. C. (2007). Corporate social and environmental responsibility in Asian countries and other geographical regions. *Corporate Social Responsibility and Environmental Management, 14*(4), 189–205.

Bendell, J. (2005). In whose name? The accountability of corporate social responsibility. *Development in Practice*, *15*(3–4), 362–374.

Bhattacharya, A. K., & Michael, D. C. (2008). How local companies keep multinationals at bay. *Harvard Business Review*, *86*(3), 20–33.

Bowen, H. R. (1953). *Social responsibilities of the businessman*. University of Iowa Press.

Bruton, G. D., Filatotchev, I., Si, S., & Wright, M. (2013). Entrepreneurship and strategy in emerging economies. *Strategic Entrepreneurship Journal*, *7*(3), 169–180.

Buckley, P., & Casson, M. (2009). *The multinational enterprise revisited: The essential Buckley and Casson*. Springer.

Campbell, J. T., Eden, L., & Miller, S. R. (2012). Multinationals and corporate social responsibility in host countries: *Does distance matter?*. *Journal of International Business Studies*, *43*, 84–106.

Carroll, A. B. (1991). The pyramid of corporate social responsibility: Toward the moral management of organizational stakeholders. *Business Horizons*, *34*(4), 39–48.

Carroll, A. B. (1999). Corporate social responsibility: Evolution of a definitional construct. *Business & Society*, *38*(3), 268–295.

Carroll, A. B. (2021). Corporate social responsibility: Perspectives on the CSR construct's development and future. *Business & Society*, *60*(6), 1258–1278.

Chapple, W., & Moon, J. (2005). Corporate social responsibility (CSR) in Asia: A seven-country study of CSR web site reporting. *Business & Society*, *44*(4), 415–441.

Chapple, W., & Moon, J. (2007). CSR agendas for Asia. *Corporate Social Responsibility and Environmental Management*, *14*(4), 183–188.

Chen, S., & Bouvain, P. (2009). Is corporate responsibility converging? A comparison of corporate responsibility reporting in the USA, UK, Australia, and Germany. *Journal of Business Ethics*, *87*(1), 299–317.

Chen, D. H., Yu, X., & Zhang, Z. (2019). Foreign direct investment comovement and home country institutions. *Journal of Business Research*, *95*, 220–231.

Chen, K., Zhang, Y., & Fu, X. (2019). International research collaboration: An emerging domain of innovation studies? *Research Policy*, *48*(1), 149–168.

Cozza, C., Rabellotti, R., & Sanfilippo, M. (2015). The impact of outward FDI on the performance of Chinese firms. *China Economic Review*, *36*, 42–57.

Cuervo-Cazurra, A., & Genc, M. (2008). Transforming disadvantages into advantages: Developing-country MNEs in the least developed countries. *Journal of International Business Studies*, *39*(6), 957–979.

Cuervo-Cazurra, A., & Ramamurti, R. (Eds.) (2014). *Understanding multinationals from emerging markets*. Cambridge University Press.

Dawar, N., & Frost, T. (1999). Competing with giants: Survival strategies for local companies in emerging markets. *Harvard Business Review*, *77*, 119–132.

Donaldson, T., & Preston, L. E. (1995). The stakeholder theory of the corporation: Concepts, evidence, and implications. *Academy of Management Review*, *20*(1), 65–91.

Doz, Y., Santos, J., & Williamson, P. (2001). *From global to metanational*. Harvard Business School Press.

Dunning, J. (1988). The theory of international production. *The International Trade Journal*, *3*(1), 21–66.

Dunning, J. H. (1998). Location and the multinational enterprise: A neglected factor? *Journal of International Business Studies*, *29*(1), 45–66.

Eccles, R. G., & Krzus, M. P. (2010). *One report: Integrated reporting for a sustainable strategy*. John Wiley & Sons.

Elango, B., & Sethi, S. P. (2007). An exploration of the relationship between country of origin (COE) and the internationalization-performance paradigm. *Management International Review, 47*(3), 369–392.

Fiaschi, D., Giuliani, E., & Nieri, F. (2017). Overcoming the liability of origin by doing no-harm: Emerging country firms' social irresponsibility as they go global. *Journal of World Business, 52*(4), 546–563.

Fortanier, F., Kolk, A., & Pinkse, J. (2011). Harmonization in CSR reporting. *Management International Review, 51*(5), 665–696.

Fox, T. (2004). Corporate social responsibility and development: In quest of an agenda. *Development, 47*(3), 29–36.

Frynas, J. G. (2005). The false developmental promise of corporate social responsibility: Evidence from multinational oil companies. *International Affairs, 81*(3), 581–598.

Gao, C., Zuzul, T., Jones, G., & Khanna, T. (2017). Overcoming institutional voids: A reputation-based view of long-run survival. *Strategic Management Journal, 38*(11), 2147–2167.

Gatti, L., Seele, P., & Rademacher, L. (2019). Grey zone in – Greenwash out. A review of greenwashing research and implications for the voluntary-mandatory transition of CSR. *International Journal of Corporate Social Responsibility, 4*(1), 1–15.

Gertler, M. S., Wolfe, D. A., & Garkut, D. (2000). No place like home? The embeddedness of innovation in a regional economy. *Review of International Political Economy, 7*(4), 688–718.

Ghemawat, P. (2007). Managing differences: The central challenge of global strategy. *Harvard Business Review, 85*(3), 58–68.

Ghemawat, P., & Hout, T. (2008). Tomorrows global giants: Not the usual suspects. *Harvard Business Review, 86*(11). https://hbr.org/2008/11/tomorrows-global-giants-not-the-usual-suspects.

Ghymn, K. I. (1980). Multinational enterprises from the third world. *Journal of International Business Studies, 11*(2), 118–122.

Guillén, M. F., & García-Canal, E. (2009). The American model of the multinational firm and the "new" multinationals from emerging economies. *The Academy of Management Perspectives, 23*(2), 23-35.

Hennart, J. F. (2012). Emerging market multinationals and the theory of the multinational enterprise. *Global Strategy Journal, 2*(3), 168–187.

Hong, W., & Shuai, D. (2020). Research on the social responsibility of Chinese enterprises along the "Belt and Road". In D. Crowther, & F. Quoquab (Eds.), *CSR in an age of isolationism (Developments in corporate governance and responsibility* (vol. 16, pp. 181–203). Emerald Publishing Limited.

Insch, G. S., & Miller, S. R. (2005). Perception of foreignness: Benefit or liability? *Journal of Managerial Issues, 17*(4), 423–438.

Jamali, D. (2008). A stakeholder approach to corporate social responsibility: A fresh perspective into theory and practice. *Journal of Business Ethics, 82*(1), 213–231.

Jamali, D., & Neville, B. (2011). Convergence versus divergence of CSR in developing countries: An embedded multi-layered institutional lens. *Journal of Business Ethics, 102*(4), 599–621.

Jamali, D., Zanhour, M., & Keshishian, T. (2009). Peculiar strengths and relational attributes of SMEs in the context of CSR. *Journal of Business Ethics, 87*(3), 355–377.

Khanna, T., Kogan, J., & Palepu, K. (2006). Globalization and similarities in corporate governance: A cross-country analysis. *Review of Economics and Statistics, 88*(1), 69–90.

Khanna, T., & Palepu, K. (1997). Why focused strategies. *Harvard Business Review, 75*(4), 41–51.

Khanna, T., & Palepu, K. (2005). The evolution of concentrated ownership in India: Broad patterns and a history of the Indian software industry. In *A history of corporate governance around the world: Family business groups to professional managers* (pp. 283–324). University of Chicago press.

Kim, H., Wu, J., Schuler, D. A., & Hoskisson, R. E. (2020). Chinese multinationals' fast internationalization: Financial performance advantage in one region, disadvantage in another. *Journal of International Business Studies, 51*(7), 1076–1106.

Klein, A. (2002). Audit committee, board of director characteristics, and earnings management. *Journal of Accounting and Economics, 33*(3), 375–400.

Klein, M. U., Aaron, C., & Hadjimichael, B. (2001). *Foreign direct investment and poverty reduction* (vol. 2613). World Bank Publications.

Klossek, A., Linke, B. M., & Nippa, M. (2012). Chinese enterprises in Germany: Establishment modes and strategies to mitigate the liability of foreignness. *Journal of World Business, 47*(1), 35–44.

Kobrin, F. E., & Hendershot, G. E. (1977). Do family ties reduce mortality? Evidence from the United States, 1966-1968. *Journal of Marriage and the Family, 39*(1) 737–745.

Kostova, T., Roth, K., & Dacin, M. T. (2008). Institutional theory in the study of multinational corporations: A critique and new directions. *Academy of Management Review, 33*(4), 994–1006.

Kostova, T., & Zaheer, S. (1999). Organizational legitimacy under conditions of complexity: The case of the multinational enterprise. *Academy of Management Review, 24*(1), 64–81.

KPMG. (2013). *The KPMG Survey of Corporate Social Responsibility Reporting, 2013.* https://www.kpmg.com/Global/en/Issues AndInsights/ArticlesPublications/corporate-responsibility/Documents/corporate-responsibility-reporting-survey-2013-execsummary.pdf

Kumar, K., & McLeod, M. G. (1981). *Multinationals from developing countries.* DC Heath, Lexington Books.

Lecraw, D. (1977). Direct investment by firms from less developed countries. *Oxford Economic Papers, 29*(3), 442–457.

Lessard, D., & Lucea, R. (2009). Embracing risk as a core competence: The case of CEMEX. *Journal of International Management, 15*(3), 296–305.

Li, J., Liu, B., & Qian, G. (2019). The Belt and Road Initiative, cultural friction and ethnicity: Their effects on the export performance of SMEs in China. *Journal of World Business, 54*(4), 350–359.

Logsdon, J. M., & Wood, D. J. (2005). Global business citizenship and voluntary codes of ethical conduct. *Journal of Business Ethics, 59*(1), 55–67.

Luo, Y., & Tung, R. L. (2007). International expansion of emerging market enterprises: A springboard perspective. *Journal of International Business Studies, 38*(4), 481–498.

Madhok, A., & Keyhani, M. (2012). Acquisitions as entrepreneurship: Asymmetries, opportunities, and the internationalization of multinationals from emerging economies. *Global Strategy Journal*, *2*(1), 26–40.

Marano, V., Tashman, P., & Kostova, T. (2017). Escaping the iron cage: Liabilities of origin and CSR reporting of emerging market multinational enterprises. *Journal of International Business Studies*, *48*(3), 386–408.

Mathews, J. A. (2006). Dragon multinationals: New players in 21st century globalization. *Asia Pacific Journal of Management*, *23*(1), 5–27.

Matten, D., & Moon, J. (2008). "Implicit" and "explicit" CSR: A conceptual framework for a comparative understanding of corporate social responsibility. *Academy of Management Review*, *33*(2), 404–424.

McKinsey Global Institute. (2015). *The new global competition for corporate profits and Urban world: The shifting global business landscape.* https://www.mckinsey.com/~/media/McKinsey/Featured%20Insights/Urbanization/Urban%20world%20The%20shifting%20global%20business%20landscape/MGI_Urban_world3_Full_report_Oct2013.pdf

McWilliams, A., & Siegel, D. (2001). Corporate social responsibility: A theory of the firm perspective. *Academy of Management Review*, *26*(1), 117–127.

Meyer, K. E. (2004). Perspectives on multinational enterprises in emerging economies. *Journal of International Business Studies*, *35*(4), 259–276.

Meyer, K. E. (2018). Catch-up and leapfrogging: Emerging economy multinational enterprises on the global stage. *International Journal of the Economics of Business*, *25*(1), 19–30.

Meyer, K. E., & Peng, M. W. (2005). Probing theoretically into Central and Eastern Europe: Transactions, resources, and institutions. *Journal of International Business Studies*, *36*(6), 600–621.

Moon, J., & Shen, X. (2010). CSR in China research: Salience, focus and nature. *Journal of Business Ethics*, *94*(4), 613–629.

Mudambi, R. (2008). Location, control and innovation in knowledge-intensive industries. *Journal of Economic Geography*, *8*(5), 699–725.

Muthuri, J. N., & Gilbert, V. (2011). An institutional analysis of corporate social responsibility in Kenya. *Journal of Business Ethics*, *98*(3), 467–483.

Nachum, L. (2010). When is foreignness an asset or a liability? Explaining the performance differential between foreign and local firms. *Journal of Management*, *36*(3), 714–739.

Narula, R. (2012). Do we need different frameworks to explain infant MNEs from developing countries. *Global Strategy Journal*, *2*(3), 188–204.

Narula, R., & Verbeke, A. (2015). Making internalization theory good for practice: The essence of Alan Rugman's contributions to international business. *Journal of World Business*, *50*(4), 612–622.

Newell, P. (2005). Citizenship, accountability and community: The limits of the CSR agenda. *International Affairs*, *81*(3), 541–557.

Ramachandran, J., & Pant, A. (2010). The liabilities of origin: An emerging economy perspective on the costs of doing business abroad. In *The past, present and future of international business & management*. Emerald Group Publishing Limited.

Ramamurti, R. (2012). Competing with emerging market multinationals. *Business Horizons*, *55*(3), 241–249.

Reimann, F., Ehrgott, M., Kaufmann, L., & Carter, C. R. (2012). Local stakeholders and local legitimacy: MNEs' social strategies in emerging economies. *Journal of International Management*, 18(1), 1–17.

Rosenzweig, P. M., & Singh, J. V. (1991). Organizational environments and the multinational enterprise. *Academy of Management Review*, 16(2), 340–361.

Roth, K., & Kostova, T. (2003). Organizational coping with institutional upheaval in transition economies. *Journal of World Business*, 38(4), 314–330.

Sethi, S. P., & Rovenpor, J. L. (2016). The role of NGOs in ameliorating sweatshop-like conditions in the global supply chain: The case of fair labor association (FLA), and social accountability international (SAI). *Business and Society Review*, 121(1), 5–36.

Sheehy, B. (2015). Defining CSR: Problems and solutions. *Journal of Business Ethics*, 131(3), 625–648.

Sheth, J. N. (2011). Impact of emerging markets on marketing: Rethinking existing perspectives and practices. *Journal of Marketing*, 75(4), 166–182.

Suchman, M. C. (1995). Managing legitimacy: Strategic and institutional approaches. *Academy of Management Review*, 20(3), 571–610.

Sullivan, A., & Sheffrin, S. M. (2003). *Economics: Principles in action*. Pearson Prentice Hall.

Sun, S. L. (2009). Internationalization strategy of MNEs from emerging economies: The case of Huawei. *Multinational Business Review*, 17(2), 129–156.

UNCTAD (2008). *World Investment Report, TNCs and the infrastructural challenge*.

van Zanten, J. A., & van Tulder, R. (2021). Towards nexus-based governance: Defining interactions between economic activities and sustainable development goals (SDGs). *International Journal of Sustainable Development & World Ecology*, 28(3), 210–226.

Walker, K., & Wan, F. (2012). The harm of symbolic actions and green-washing: Corporate actions and communications on environmental performance and their financial implications. *Journal of Business Ethics*, 109(2), 227–242.

Wang, L., & Zhang, G. (2022). Has multinational corporate social responsibility been fulfilled to promote their own growth? *Enterprise Economy*, 2022(4), 43–52.

Welford, R. (2005). Corporate social responsibility in Europe, North America and Asia. *Journal of Corporate Citizenship*, 17, 33–52.

Wells, K. D. (1977). The social behaviour of anuran amphibians. *Animal Behaviour*, 25, 666–693.

Wells, L. T. (1983). *Third world multinationals: The rise of foreign investment from developing countries*. The MIT Press.

World Business Council for Sustainable Development. (2004). *Mobility 2030: Meeting the challenges to sustainability: The Sustainable Mobility Project*. www.wbcsd.org/web/publications/mobility/mobility-full.pdf

2 The Rise of China's Economy and the Chinese MNEs

Introduction

The term "globalization" did not enter common usage until the 1990s, coinciding with what *The Economist* has termed the "Golden Age of Globalization". As the cost of transporting goods around the world decreased, communications got less expensive, trade barriers were eliminated, and the global financial system was liberalized, trade flourished, and MNEs grew globally. It was also the time when China reemerged as a worldwide economic powerhouse. Since implementing its reform and opening-up program in 1978, China has experienced substantial economic growth. For the last 40 years, the Chinese economy has grown by an average of 9.5% annually, well above the global average of 2.9% (Oxford Analytica, 2021). Its gross domestic product (GDP) increased from 367.9 billion yuan in 1978 to 99,086.5 billion yuan in 2019, elevating it from a low-income to middle-income nation (Oxford Analytica, 2021), and in 2010, China overtook Japan and became the world's second-largest economy (Landry et al., 2018). Chinese businesses have made a significant amount of outward foreign direct investment (OFDI) abroad over the past two decades, making China one of the top foreign investors in the world. However, the phenomenon has not been well explored from a business research standpoint. After introducing the wave of globalization and EMNEs in Chapter 1, this chapter will introduce the rise of China's economy and the Chinese MNEs. This chapter will also look into China's growing global economic influence and its trade policies. Besides, theories and motivations for the globalization of Chinese MNEs are presented in this chapter.

Concepts of internationalization

Internationalization refers to the process in which an enterprise actively participates in the international business activities and develops from a domestic enterprise into a multinational company. Internationalization is a two-way process, including inward internationalization and outward internationalization (Vernon, 1996). The forms of outward internationalization mainly refer to direct or indirect export, technology transfer, various foreign contractual arrangements,

DOI: 10.4324/9781003302445-2

foreign joint ventures, overseas subsidiaries and branches; while inward internationalization activities mainly include import, purchase of technology patents, domestic joint ventures, subsidiaries, or branches of foreign companies.

An important branch of internationalization research is the research on its development process. Some studies believe that the internationalization of a company is an evolving process, gradually developing from inward internationalization to outward internationalization (Hammer & Champy, 1993). For example, the product life cycle theory believes that a new product has to go through three stages, namely innovation, maturity, and standardization. At different stages, the performance of the product in terms of technology, market, cost, and competition will be different. When exporting to foreign markets, the main reason is that after the competition intensifies, there is pressure to reduce costs by seeking locations with low production costs (Cassiman & Golovko, 2011). Johanson and Wiedersheim-Paul (1975) conducted a case study of four Swedish manufacturing companies. They found that these companies are very similar in their overseas business strategy steps. The initial contact with foreign markets started with occasional and sporadic product exports; as export activities continued to increase, the parent company had more information and contact channels in overseas markets, and the export market began to stabilize through foreign agents. With the increase in market demand and the expansion of overseas business, the parent company began to establish its own overseas company. When the market conditions were mature, the parent company began to make overseas direct investment and establish overseas manufacturing bases. The findings of the studies discussed above are more suitable for the situation of developed countries and cannot fully reflect the special features of developing countries. Kang (1996) and Zhu (2017) put forward a similar growth route suitable for multinational corporations in developing countries based on the actual situation in China. In their research, the internationalization of the enterprise is classified into pre-development type and post-development type. The former is further divided into technology-oriented type and natural resource type. For post-development multinational companies, they are further grouped into conventional, open, and transitional types.

Stages of internationalization

Since the late 1970s, China's OFDI has seen significant modification. This was particularly true in the late 1990s, when the government announced the "go global" policy to boost global competitiveness and guarantee a supply of essential resources. China became one of the major suppliers of OFDI in both developed and developing countries since the beginning of the 21st century. Previous studies have identified several stages in the economic growth associated with the country's opening-up (Garnaut et al., 2018). The first stage (1978–1991) was largely experimental, characterized by strict state regulations and weak capital conditions. When the Chinese government implemented its Open Door policy in the late 1970s, OFDI began to flourish.[1] Nevertheless, in the early years of its outward-looking approach, China's foreign investment was very low. In fact, political considerations meant that almost all OFDI ventures were carried out by state-owned commercial firms (Wang et al., 2004). Although OFDI flows increased modestly after 1985, the amounts of investment were negligible during that period, with average annual flows of USD451 million and stocks of around USD5 billion by the end of 1991 (Garnaut et al., 2018). During this stage, Chinese MNEs were mostly huge state-owned firms operating in monopolized industries, such as financial services, transportation, international trading, and natural resources (UNCTAD, 2006). CITIC Group, COSCO, China State Construction Engineering Corporation, CNPC, Sinochem, CNOOC, China Minmetals, and COFCO were a few of them. These Chinese businesses typically selected Hong Kong as their initial stop on the road to globalization, capitalizing on its cross-cultural links.

From 1992 to 2002, the second stage saw a wave of Chinese multinational companies making significant overseas investments for the first time. OFDI reached over USD4 billion per annum between 1992 and 1993, and nearly USD7 billion per annum in 2001. By the end of 2002, the stock value had risen to USD37.2 billion. Changes in the domestic and international economic and political settings were mirrored in the period's volatile OFDI flows during this period. Among these changes were Deng Xiaoping's southern tour in 1992, which kicked off a more liberalized OFDI policy, as well as the Asian financial crisis in 1997 and China's entry into the World Trade Organization (WTO) in 2001 (Liu & Tian, 2021). However, during this stage, Chinese MNEs appeared to lack innovative technologies, successful marketing campaigns, established brand names, and advantageous business practices. Furthermore, their competitors were mainly well-known multinational corporations from developed countries (Barro, 2016). However, in the process of globalization, Chinese MNEs have experienced numerous obstacles. Inadequate ability to manage risks, such as those coming from law and politics, poor participation in the formation of international standards, impediments to the internationalization of business brands, and the restricted internationalization of company talents are a few examples (Ramamurti & Hillemann, 2018; Zhang, 2009)

OFDI performance in the third stage starting from 2003 has been described as a "miracle" with rising economic growth coupled with sharp increases in OFDI, both in terms of absolute numbers and growth rates. After becoming an active member of the WTO, China's GDP per capita rose from USD1148 in 2002 to USD6767 in 2013 (Barro, 2016). China has redrawn the map of the world economy in its process of integration to become a veritable "world factory", and "Made in China" products are now sold all over the world (Barro, 2016). Although the scale of OFDI development should not be exaggerated, its pace is remarkable. China's globalization policy has played a major role in its transformation into a global economic powerhouse. As the centerpiece of this globalization strategy, OFDI has gradually been promoted by disseminating information about international locations, providing incentives, and gradually relaxing foreign exchange controls. To promote OFDI in projects for natural resources discovery, export operations, overseas R&D centers, and mergers and acquisitions to acquire valuable international assets such as brand names and technologies, a selective support policy has been introduced. Aside from large state-owned MNEs, the second and third stages saw the emergence of a new generation of Chinese MNEs in competitive manufacturing industries, relating especially to electronics and information and communication technologies. For instance, Gree, Haier, and TCL started to play major roles in global consumer electronics markets, Lenovo has surpassed IBM as the world's third-largest personal computer (PC) manufacturer, and ZTE and Huawei are excelling in the global telecom equipment market (Child & Rodrigues, 2005). During the subsequent decades, the leading Chinese state-owned MNEs that were formed in the first phase grew steadily. CITIC Group, a diverse financial and industrial conglomerate, has become one of the top 100 multinational corporations in the world. Aiming to gain control of these resources abroad, CNPC, CNOOC, and China Minmetals have become major participants in the world of natural resources. A growing number of relatively small-sized MNEs across a variety of industries, as well as diversified ownership structures (private ownership, local government ownership, and foreign participation), are further hallmarks of the current generation of Chinese MNEs.

Chinese MNEs gathered experience, skills, and technology, as well as a deeper understanding of international management techniques, as their investments and activities abroad grew. After the global financial crisis, the extent and scope of Chinese MNEs' international operations expanded. In order to develop capabilities and establish presence in new markets, they looked for other routes toward globalization, shifting from exports, projects with foreign contractors, and labor collaboration to greenfield investments and outbound M&A. Over the past four decades, Chinese MNEs have risen rapidly. However, both the internal and external environments have shifted, posing new obstacles as they go forward. China is no longer the labor-rich, impoverished nation that made it the factory of the world. First-tier cities resemble those in industrialized economies to a great extent. Wages and environmental requirements have increased, thus cost competitiveness and domestic growth potential have declined. The pandemic has now worsened these difficulties, and scrutiny of foreign investments has grown.

Despite their extraordinary success, Chinese MNEs are now undergoing the critical process from "product globalization" to "brand globalization". Currently, Chinese MNEs have a strong global presence, with 145 firms (124 for the United States) on the 2022 Fortune Global 500 list; this is up from zero on the magazine's first Global 500 list released in 1990. Although Chinese MNEs have grown substantially in size, their profitability is still unimpressive. In 2022, the average revenue of companies in mainland China (including the Hong Kong SAR) reached USD80.98 billion, which is a significant increase compared to the previous year's figures. The companies' average total assets amounted to USD358 billion and their average net assets of USD43.18 billion exceeded the average level of that of the world's top 500 firms. However, the gap between the profitability of Chinese companies and the average profitability of the Fortune Global 500 firms has widened. The average profit of the 145 Chinese companies on the list was about USD4.1 billion, which is an improvement, though the average profit of the Global 500 rose to USD6.2 billion in the same period. For example, the average profit of German companies on the list was USD4.4 billion; that of British companies was USD6.96 billion. The figures for Canadian, French, and Brazilian companies were USD4.75 billion, USD4.85 billion, and USD8.48 billion, respectively. These numbers are all higher than those of Chinese companies. The profit gap is even more pronounced with the US companies on the list. In 2022, the 124 US companies on the Fortune 500 list had average profits of USD10.05 billion, almost 2.5 times as much as Chinese firms. The profits of Chinese companies on the list and their growth rate were much lower than those of the US firms and the world averages. Furthermore, based on the above data, the average return on sales for mainland Chinese companies on the list was 5.1%; their return on total assets was 1.15%, and the return on net assets was 9.5%. All three indicators lag behind the Fortune Global 500 averages. Furthermore, the figures for these three indicators for the 124 US companies on the list were 11%, 3.21%, and 21.9%, respectively, which show that these firms operate significantly better than their Chinese counterparts.

From a frontier industry perspective, there were six internet companies on the list in 2022, namely Amazon, Alphabet Inc., and Meta Platforms Inc. from the United States, and Jingdong Group, Alibaba Group, and Tencent Holdings Ltd from China. The rankings of these major US and Chinese internet companies have all improved from the previous year. Continuing 2021's focus on information and communication technology (ICT) companies, the United States had 19 companies on the list with average revenues of USD126.2 billion and average profits of USD23.7 billion in this most competitive, high-tech industry sector. China had 12 ICT firms on the list, with average revenues of USD78.7 billion and average profits of USD7.7 billion. Although these Chinese companies have made significant progress in their business performance, the average profit of the US firms in this category was three times of that of China. Considering that the United States and other developed countries hold the core components and key technologies of the industry and that regulations on Chinese companies continue to be tightened, Chinese ICT firms need to make continuous efforts to reduce the profitability gap with the US companies. Overall, the number of Chinese firms on the Fortune Global 500 list in 2022 has increased and expanded. However, as the global industrial chain is being reorganized and the rules of international corporate competition are being reconfigured, Chinese MNEs will certainly face tougher challenges in the future.

Motivations of Chinese MNEs

Dunning's eclectic theory (1995) offers a systematic approach to explaining FDI practices, stating that firms' FDI behavior is determined by ownership, location, and internalization advantages (OLI). In the case of China, the government is said to have had a significant impact on Chinese MNEs' OFDI (Buckley et al., 2002). State-controlled corporations are the primary sources of outward FDI, and many of the largest FDI players are the most profitable state-owned enterprises (Buckley et al., 2007; Morck et al., 2008). Since the "opening-up", the government's position on OFDI legislation has shifted from strict supervision to active sponsorship and even direct support (Buckley et al., 2007). Furthermore, Chinese MNEs have received strong support from domestic institutions, allowing them to accelerate their internationalization efforts and catch up with MNEs from developed countries (Voss et al., 2009).

Chinese MNEs have firm-specific advantages that are similar to those of their counterparts in industrialized countries but different in magnitude. China's MNEs rely much more on advantages related to production process capabilities, affordable resources (in particular labor), institutional and organizational structures, and institutional advantages, whereas the latter are most likely to have superiority based on ownership of key assets, such as technologies, brands, and other intellectual properties. There are, without a doubt, considerable differences from one industry and area to the next. For instance, MNEs in the manufacturing industry are more likely to have advantages in their ability to control the production process. The institutional structure of the Chinese government-controlled SOEs, which have monopolistic strength in home markets and are rather competitive abroad, provides MNEs in the services and primary sectors with a number of advantages. Some of the incentives for Chinese OFDI are comparable to those for OFDI from developed and developing nations. However, other motivations may be unique due to the country's distinctive characteristics in terms of economic development. Market-seeking, resource-seeking, strategic asset-seeking, and efficiency-seeking appear to be the four main drivers of Chinese OFDI (Buckley et al., 2018; Huang, 2016; Huang & Wang, 2011).

The first two are relevant to a wide variety of MNEs that have an interest in expanding their operations to a global scale, while the latter two are more directly connected to specific concerns faced by Chinese MNEs. The fundamental reason why many Chinese businesses venture abroad is to find, keep, or develop export markets. Due to a variety of factors, Chinese businesses have become more reliant on foreign markets during the past three decades. These include trade impediments, particularly possible protectionism in many countries, severe competition from local businesses, especially international MNEs in China, and the modest size of the domestic market relative to the capabilities and goals of Chinese firms. As a result, more and more Chinese businesses are being pushed to open up branches or factories abroad. To assure access to natural resources, mainly oil, gas, and mining, is the second reason for Chinese OFDI. The Chinese government has been concerned about the possibility of running out of essential resources and inputs for economic expansion due to the country's decades-long rapid economic growth. Chinese businesses frequently cite the security of having access to raw materials as their justification for investing abroad. This is due to the fact that, although having abundant natural resources of its own, China has a very low per capita resource availability, especially for materials like iron ore, aluminum, copper, petroleum, lumber, and seafood, which are in high demand. This is reflected in the strategic and political drivers behind some OFDI by sizable MNEs under the supervision of the central government. For instance, an IMF analysis (Jackson & Horwitz, 2018) reveals that 8 of the 12 African economies with the greatest growth rates are not dependent on natural resources. Scholars hypothesize that the interests and motivations of MNEs in general, and Chinese MNEs in Africa in particular, are predominantly resource-driven due to the continent's abundant minerals, commodities, and oil (Biggeri & Sanfilippo, 2009; Cooke et al., 2015). On the other hand, in a number of industries, the Chinese market has already reached its maximum demand level. In areas such as textiles and apparel, bicycles, footwear, and electrical appliances, there exists a large excess of production capacity. Moreover, the above-mentioned are industries in which Chinese enterprises have a competitive advantage that can be utilized in nations with similar or lower economic development.

EMNEs are most likely to invest in advanced technology in developed countries, compensating for their competitive disadvantages. Chinese MNEs are increasingly interested in gaining innovative technology and manufacturing expertise in several markets, particularly in the United States. In this manner, not only is the technology itself shared, but also the capability to implement it in a commercial setting can be created. In particular, Parmentola (2011) contends that Chinese MNEs internationalize to acquire strategic assets and strengthen competitive advantage. Wei (2013) also indicates that the interests of the majority of Chinese MNEs and investors extend beyond natural resources to market scale and the possibilities for further commercial endeavors in the value chain. Some Chinese MNEs employ OFDI as a promising strategy to acquire ownership benefits, including foreign technology and managerial skills, in contrast to developed-country MNEs that already have such advantages prior to making investments abroad. In this respect, OFDI by MNEs from developed countries is driven by the exploitation of assets, whereas some OFDI from Chinese MNEs is driven by asset-seeking or asset-augmenting investments (Child & Rodrigues, 2005). One well-known instance is Lenovo, which benefited from IBM's brand name by purchasing IBM's PC division. In this way, Chinese MNEs could catch up with their developed-country competitors by acquiring assets that are not available in their home nation. Liberalization in potential host economies creates opportunities abroad. As China has become more connected with the global economy, the Chinese government and businesses have developed a global perspective. There is a growing awareness that they operate in a global economy rather than a domestic one. The structural shift toward earlier and greater OFDI by China's MNEs is largely attributable to the motivation to protect and expand export markets, ensure the availability of essential resources, acquire advanced technology and management skills, and capitalize on increased opportunities abroad.

As a short summary, OFDI by Chinese MNEs has been primarily driven by the desire to secure supplies of key natural resources, increase foreign exchange income, circumvent trade barriers in the host country, penetrate new markets, acquire advanced technology and management expertise, and seek strategic assets. Chinese business-seeking OFDI is linked with the host economy's market openness. According to international business theory, economically orientated host countries are more appealing to foreign investors as they blend more seamlessly into global production and trade trends (Buckley & Lessard, 2005; Rugman & Verbeke, 2003). The growth of tariff and non-tariff trade barriers to Chinese exporters, such as export quotas and other "anti-dumping" measures, has prompted some Chinese companies to build offshore manufacturing plants to gain access to foreign markets (Taylor, 2002). In most cases, this form of FDI has been used to serve established markets in overseas countries such as the United States and the European Union. As a result, the host economy's capacity to export is a key factor in attracting Chinese OFDI. Market openness, representing an economy's competitiveness and export orientation, satisfies Chinese investing firms' market-seeking motive (Hennart, 2014). The large concentration of Chinese investment in industrialized countries in general, and the United States in particular, demonstrates the emphasis on generating hard-currency earnings and gaining access to patented technologies. The influx of considerable capital into resource-rich nations such as Australia, Canada, Peru, and Zambia, on the other hand, highlights the importance of exploiting natural resources and minerals. Gill et al. (2007) also offer a more balanced perspective on the motivations of Chinese MNEs. They contend that China needs more overseas countries for a variety of reasons, including resources to support its development objectives; markets to support its expanding economy; and political alliances to support its aspirations to be a global influence. Thus, the idea of "political-seeking" investment is considered to be the fifth motivation for Chinese OFDI. For instance, according to China-Africa Cooperation Vision 2035, "China and Africa hold high the banner of peace, development, cooperation and win-win results, and unswervingly deepen the comprehensive strategic partnership to realize the high-quality development of China-Africa practical cooperation" (Ministry of Commerce of China, 2021). That is to say, the structure of Chinese OFDI has, to a large extent, been significantly shaped by the government. Since the 1980s, overseas subsidiaries have been obliged to reach one of four objectives, namely advanced technology transfer, raw material access, foreign exchange earnings, and export expansion. China has also utilized overseas investments to develop its links with other economies, such as those in Africa and Southeast Asia, and to preserve the prosperity of Hong Kong and Macao throughout their transition to Chinese rule in the late 1990s. China is still a state-controlled economy, which explains why the government plays such a significant role in determining the pattern of Chinese outbound investment.

Competitive advantages of Chinese MNEs

China's increase in OFDI is a structural phenomenon that is directly related to its expanding influence in the global economy over the past few decades. As China attains greater levels of development and becomes a leading trade nation, the advantages of firm ownership are anticipated to expand. In response to the necessity to access markets or resources and, consequently, to lower production and transaction costs by coordinating their regional and global activities, OFDI is a natural extension of China's internationalization drive along with its export boom. Prior studies argue that Chinese MNEs have purportedly overcome their low international experience and established well-known brands thanks to the government's substantial assistance. Additional benefits include sales channel strength (monopolistic posture), size and financial resources, human talent, and technology.

The foundation of China's economic reform is its relationship with its government and firms. The extensive governmental participation in the overseas activities of Chinese MNEs enables them to maintain a symbiotic connection with the government that transcends business activities. It is intertwined with other important aspects such as the Chinese government's ability to control its domestic economy, improve state stability, and seek economic significance in the international arena. In certain situations, companies such as CNOOC (China National Offshore Oil Corporation) possess monopolistic operating advantages in vital industries. In addition, the Chinese government plays a notable role by deploying a number of state-owned financial institutions to support Chinese enterprises, particularly those seeking resources. Included in preferential arrangements are financial aids, managerial autonomy, profit retention, low-interest financing, favorable use of the native currency for exchange, and lower taxes.

According to traditional viewpoints, the comparative advantages of Chinese OFDI arise mostly from the adaption of existing technology to more labor-intensive settings and local raw materials. Chinese MNEs have developed their competitive edge from one of three possible sources. First, the possession of technologies so mature that developed-country firms have phased them out, but which have not yet been mastered by countries lower on the industrialization scale. Second, an advantage gained by downscaling the technology (to smaller markets), making production more labor-intensive (to match lower wage rates), or adapting it to local preferences. Dunning and Lundan (2008) also propose that the success of MNEs from emerging countries resides in the capacity to link firm-specific and country-specific institutional distances, such as environmental and social responsibility. OFDI from emerging markets with relation to localization might potentially in the future mirror FDI of MNEs of developed countries (Dunning & Lundan, 2008). It is also pointed out that the technology of Chinese MNEs is regarded as available, affordable, maintainable, and unavoidable. Advantages of Chinese MNEs include, for instance, lower labor costs in home and host countries combined with exceptional talents to produce great products at affordable prices (Luo et al., 2010). In addition, Chinese MNEs (especially state-owned MNEs) are global leaders in infrastructure development and have successfully bidden for many overseas investments. For example, the decision or agreement to join forces with the Nigerian government to increase the quality of supporting facilities that will enable access to natural resources in the country creates a sort of advantage for Chinese enterprises seeking access to its natural resources. This finding provides factual support that the Chinese government-business ties have been manifested in the parent organization's lax regulations. For instance, financial backing, preferential treatments, and management autonomy gave significant benefits for Chinese MNEs in emerging markets over their competitors. It is noted that the relationship between Chinese MNEs and their government is central to China's economic reform, which is the result of their long-standing ownership structure – a deliberate weapon for achieving political and economic gains (Lattemann & Alon, 2015; Luo et al., 2010).

The impact of government policies on Chinese MNEs' internationalization initiatives is one of their defining characteristics. The government is not just another institution; it is a significant institution that shapes many other institutions in the nation and develops national assets and a business climate that affects the international competitiveness of enterprises. This is particularly true in China, where the government exerts a great deal of control. Specifically, the support of the Chinese government has taken several significant forms. It has entailed using the country's natural endowments of land, people, location, and resources, together with complementary state investments, to accelerate growth, hence enhancing China's negotiating position vis-à-vis foreign enterprises and nations. The Chinese government has made huge investments in physical, human, and institutional assets to increase China's attractiveness as a site for manufacturing goods and providing services (Ramamurti & Hillemann, 2018). China is one of the world's largest and fastest growing economies, with significant exports, trade surpluses, foreign exchange reserves, and geopolitical power, as a result of the country's macroeconomic plan to transition itself into a market economy. China's bargaining leverage with MNEs was bolstered by its economic and political might, which also boosted the growth possibilities of local businesses. In turn, this led to distinctive internationalization patterns among Chinese MNEs, such as the tendency of Chinese firms to "go out to bring in", i.e., to seek strategic assets abroad, particularly in developed countries, primarily to improve their competitiveness in their large domestic market, and to use this as a stepping stone for gaining international competitiveness. On this basis, a variety of policy instruments and state-owned financial institutions are utilized to financially assist Chinese MNEs (Liu & Scott-Kennel, 2011). Therefore, the performance of some Chinese MNEs in overseas host countries reflects dramatically such country-specific advantages.

Chinese MNEs as a starting point

The rise of emerging economies is one of the main features of economic and political development and change in the world today. As the world's largest emerging economy, the rise of China is even more remarkable. At the same time, it has become a hot topic of discussion in the international community as to what changes will China's rise bring to the world in the future. This chapter introduces the stages of Chinese MNEs' internationalization, their motivations to invest abroad, and their unique competitive advantages.

While emerging economies have become increasingly important for almost all international business research, the literature on sustainability and corporate social responsibility (CSR) practices of EMNEs has paid only scant attention to their dynamics in this part of the world. When considering Chinese MNEs' engagement with global CSR governance, researchers have pointed out both challenges and progress. Many have worried that China's rapid development poses significant challenges to protecting our planet (Albert & Xu, 2016). For a very long time, the country has emphasized economic expansion over environmental conservation and social fairness. More recently, its expanding quest for resources across the globe has led to a number of harmful effects on the global environment. Researchers who share this concern frequently blame China's fragmented and authoritarian political structure for the country's weak environmental governance, contending that it undermines transparency, official accountability, and the rule of law in the relevant policy-making processes (Economy, 2014). Overseas investors are concerned that these Chinese parent companies are bringing this philosophy to their overseas subsidiaries. Nevertheless, environmental politics researchers have argued that China has been steadily evolving into a global leader in the struggle to rescue the planet by spearheading a worldwide clean energy revolution, phasing out coal usage, reducing pollution, and creating a system of green finance (Cao, 2018). For instance, in 2014, the national government declared a "war on pollution" and employed a number of policy measures across the nation, such as administrative restrictions, stringent laws, financial incentives, and public awareness campaigns (Wong & Karplus, 2017). Additionally, the concept of "ecological civilization" has been strongly endorsed by President Xi Jinping and the government has identified ecological civilization as a long-term project which is deemed as critical to the future development of China. Chinese MNEs are still "young" and immature comparing with developed ones and are inexperienced in managing complex businesses, let alone global ones. According to a global survey conducted by Brunswick Group (involving 9700 members of the public and 300 Chinese business leaders in 23 countries), respondents in emerging markets have an 80% trust in Chinese MNEs, and the words most often used to describe Chinese MNEs are: excellent service, innovation, and technologically advanced. Respondents in developed countries, on the other hand, have a 51% favorable perception of Chinese MNEs, and the adjectives used to describe Chinese MNEs are: cheap, untrustworthy, and poor quality. However, respondents from all countries believe that Chinese MNEs need to improve their ESG (Environmental, Social, and Governance) performance. Differences in perceptions of Chinese multinationals between developed and emerging-market countries are widening. Compared to developed countries such as Europe and the United States, emerging-market countries, especially those with which China has long-standing trade relations, are more receptive to Chinese investment and engagement activities. The task of Chinese companies to better demonstrate their commitment in these areas will become more urgent after the COVID-19 outbreak. On the other hand, the slowdowns in growth and export speed, as well as the country's ongoing fight to contain the virus which has resulted in frequent lockdowns, are the present challenges faced by Chinese MNEs.

The world's landscape has already undergone profound changes due to globalization. The declaration of "Community of Human Destiny" indicates that China will firmly open up and go global, and more and more Chinese companies will become multinational and global enterprises. Under President Xi Jinping's thought on "socialism with Chinese characteristics for the new era", China's open economy has reached a new level of development. Xi launched the Belt and Road Initiative (BRI) in 2013 to increase regional and transcontinental cooperation and connectivity through investment, trade, and infrastructure projects (Ramasamy & Yeung, 2019). In the past few years, an increasing number of Chinese companies with global operations have possessed competitive advantages that enable them to overcome the inherent disadvantages and high costs of foreign operations. China is investing in Eurasian, Asian, and African transportation and energy infrastructures, including railways, bridges, ports, airports, and pipelines under the auspices of the BRI (Huang, 2016). Chapter 3 will introduce the BRI in a comprehensive manner, including its general framework, geographical coverage, assessment of the opportunities and risks, priorities for cooperation and key policy mechanisms as well as new challenges faced by Chinese MNEs from the perspective of CSR.

Note

1 Along with the economic reforms of the late 1970s, in December 1978, Deng Xiaoping, Vice Prime Minister of the PRC, announced its Open Door policy to welcome foreign businesses wanting to set up in China. For the first time since the Kuomintang era, the country was opened up to foreign investment. Deng also created a series of Special Economic Zones for foreign investment, including Shenzhen, Zhuhai, and Xiamen, which were relatively free from bureaucratic regulations and interventions that hampered economic growth.

References

Albert, E., & Xu, B. (2016). *China's environmental crisis* (Vol. 18). Council on Foreign Relations.

Barro, R. J. (2016). Economic growth and convergence, applied to China. *China & World Economy, 24*(5), 5–19.

Biggeri, M., & Sanfilippo, M. (2009). Understanding China's move into Africa: An empirical analysis. *Journal of Chinese Economic and Business Studies, 7*(1), 31–54.

Buckley, P. J., Clegg, L. J., Cross, A. R., Liu, X., Voss, H., & Zheng, P. (2007). The determinants of Chinese outward foreign direct investment. *Journal of International Business Studies, 38*(4), 499–518.

Buckley, P. J., Clegg, L. J., Voss, H., Cross, A. R., Liu, X., & Zheng, P. (2018). A retrospective and agenda for future research on Chinese outward foreign direct investment. *Journal of International Business Studies, 49*(1), 4–23.

Buckley, P. J., Clegg, J., & Wang, C. (2002). The impact of inward FDI on the performance of Chinese manufacturing firms. *Journal of International Business Studies, 33*(4), 637–655.

Buckley, P. J., & Lessard, D. R. (2005). Regaining the edge for international business research. *Journal of International Business Studies*, *36*(6), 595–599.

Cao, C. (2018). Will China save the planet? By Barbara Finamore. *China Review International*, *25*(2), 126–128.

Cassiman, B., & Golovko, E. (2011). Innovation and internationalization through exports. *Journal of International Business Studies*, *42*(1), 56–75.

Child, J., & Rodrigues, S. B. (2005). The internationalization of Chinese firms: A case for theoretical extension? *Management and Organization Review*, *1*(3), 381–410.

Cooke, F. L., Wood, G., & Horwitz, F. (2015). Multinational firms from emerging economies in Africa: Implications for research and practice in human Resource management. *The International Journal of Human Resource Management*, *26*(21), 2653–2675.

Dunning, J. H. (1995). Reappraising the Eclectic Paradigm in an Age of Alliance Capitalism. *Journal of International Business Studies*, *26*, 461–491.

Dunning, J. H., & Lundan, S. M. (2008). Institutions and the OLI paradigm of the multinational Enterprise. *Asia Pacific Journal of Management*, *25*(4), 573–593.

Economy, E. (2014). Environmental governance in China: State control to crisis management. *Daedalus*, *143*(2), 184–197.

Garnaut, R., Song, L., & Fang, C. (2018). *China's 40 years of reform and development: 1978–2018*. ANU Press.

Gill, B., Huang, C. H., & Morrison, J. S. (2007). Assessing China's growing influence in Africa. *China Security*, *3*(3), 3–21.

Hammer, M., & Champy, J. (1993). *Reengineering the corporation-a manifesto for business revolution*. Harper Business.

Hennart, J. F. (2014). The accidental internationalists: A theory of born globals. *Entrepreneurship Theory and Practice*, *38*(1), 117–135. https://www.brunswickgroup.com/media/7175/%E5%8D%9A%E7%84%B6%E6%80%9D%E7%BB%B4_%E5%9B%BD%E9%99%85%E8%A7%86%E9%87%8E%E4%B8%AD%E7%9A%84%E4%B8%AD%E5%9B%BD%E4%BC%81%E4%B8%9A-2020%E5%B9%B45%E6%9C%88.pdf

Huang, Y. (2016). Understanding China's belt & road initiative: Motivation, framework and assessment. *China Economic Review*, *40*, 314–321.

Huang, Y., & Wang, B. (2011). Chinese outward direct investment: Is there a China model. *China & World Economy*, *19*(4), 1–21.

Jackson, T., & Horwitz, F. M. (2018). Expatriation in Chinese MNEs in Africa: An agenda for research. *International Journal of Human Resource Management*, *29*(11), 1856–1878.

Johanson, J., & Wiedersheim-Paul, F. (1975). The internationalization of the firm – Four Swedish cases. *Journal of Management Studies*, *12*(3), 305–323.

Kang, R. (1996). *Transnational operation of Chinese enterprises: Case study, theoretical exploration*. Economic Science Press.

Landry, P. F., Lü, X., & Duan, H. (2018). Does performance matter? Evaluating political selection along the Chinese administrative ladder. *Comparative Political Studies*, *51*(8), 1074–1105.

Lattemann, C., & Alon, I. (2015). The rise of Chinese multinationals: A strategic threat or an economic opportunity? *Georgetown Journal of International Affairs*, *16*(1), 172–179.

Liu, J. J., & Scott-Kennel, J. (2011). Asset-seeking investment by Chinese multinationals: Firm ownership, location, and entry mode. *Asia Pacific and Globalization Review*, *1*(1), 16–36.

Liu, L., & Tian, G. G. (2021). Mandatory CSR disclosure, monitoring and investment efficiency: Evidence from China. *Accounting & Finance*, 61(1), 595–644.

Luo, Y., Xue, Q., & Han, B. (2010). How emerging market governments promote outward FDI: Experience from China. *Journal of World Business*, 45(1), 68–79.

Ministry of Commerce of China. (2021). *China-Africa cooperation vision 2035*. Retrieved from http://www.focac.org/eng/zywx_1/zywj/202201/t20220124_10632442.htm (July 12, 2022).

Morck, R., Yeung, B., & Zhao, M. (2008). Perspectives on China's outward foreign direct investment. *Journal of International Business Studies*, 39(3), 337–350.

Oxford Analytica. (2021). *China's GDP is carrying strong momentum into 2021*. Expert Briefings. https://doi.org/10.1108/OXAN-ES258861

Parmentola, A. (2011). The internationalization strategy of new Chinese multinationals: Determinants and evolution. *International Journal of Management*, 28(1), 369.

Ramamurti, R., & Hillemann, J. (2018). What is "Chinese" about Chinese multinationals? *Journal of International Business Studies*, 49(1), 34–48.

Ramasamy, B., & Yeung, M. C. (2019). China's one belt one road initiative: The impact of trade facilitation versus physical infrastructure on exports. *The World Economy*, 42(6), 1673–1694.

Rugman, A. M., & Verbeke, A. (2003). Extending the theory of the multinational enterprise: Internalization and strategic management perspectives. *Journal of International Business Studies*, 34(2), 125–137.

Taylor, B. (2002). Privatization, markets and industrial relations in China. *British Journal of Industrial Relations*, 40(2), 249–272.

UNCTAD. (2006). *World investment report 2006: FDI from developing and transition economies: Implications for development*. United Nation.

Vernon, R. (1996). International investment and international trade in the product cycle. *Quarterly Journal of Economics*, 80(2), 190–207.

Voss, H., Buckley, P., & Cross, A. (2009). An assessment of effects of institutional change on Chinese outward direct investment activity. In I. Alon, J. Chang, M. Fetscherin, C. Lattemann, & J. R. McIntyre (Eds.), *China rules: Globalisation and political transformation* (pp. 135–165). Palgrave Macmillan.

Wang, X., Xu, L. C., & Zhu, T. (2004). State-owned enterprises going public the case of China. *Economics of Transition*, 12(3), 467–487.

Wei, W. X. (2013). Chinese trade and investment in Africa. *Journal of African Business*, 14(2), 72–74.

Wong, C., & Karplus, V. J. (2017). China's war on air pollution: Can existing governance structures support new ambitions? *The China Quarterly*, 231, 662–684.

Zhang, K. H. (2009). Rise of Chinese multinational firms. *Chinese Economy*, 42(6), 81–96.

Zhu, S. (2017). Research on the international business model and strategy of Chinese enterprises. *China Business Update*, 2007(9), 40–42.

3 The Belt and Road Initiative and CSR

The political economy background of the BRI

In September 2013, President Xi Jinping announced the "Silk Road Economic Belt" strategy during an official visit to Kazakhstan. In October of the same year, President Xi proposed the joint construction of the "21st Century Maritime Silk Road" in his speech to the Indonesian parliament. In November 2013, the Silk Road Economic Belt strategy and the 21st Century Maritime Silk Road were upgraded to a national strategy as the "Belt and Road Initiative" (BRI) at the Third Plenary Session of the 18th Central Committee of the Chinese Communist Party. The term "Belt" of the BRI refers to the projected overland routes for road and rail transit through landlocked Central Asia along the legendary Western Regions' historical trade routes, and "Road" of the BRI refers to the Indo-Pacific maritime routes connecting Southeast Asia to South Asia, the Middle East, and Africa. The "Office of the Leading Group on Promoting the Implementation of Belt and Road Initiatives" serves as the BRI's supervisory body, which is housed within the National Development and Reform Commission (NDRC). The leading group is mainly in charge of guiding and coordinating work related to the BRI.

The BRI is a grand and ambitious vision aiming to improve regional cooperation and connectivity among Asia, Europe, and Africa through a comprehensive network of ports, roads, railways, and trading hubs, thereby reviving ancient overland and maritime trade routes (Xinhua, 2015). The emergence of the BRI is of inter-generational significance and attracted considerable attention from the international community. In March 2015, the "Vision and proposed actions outlined on jointly building a Silk Road Economic Belt and 21st Century Maritime Silk Road" was issued by the NDRC, the Ministry of Foreign Affairs (MOFA), and the Ministry of Commerce (MOFCOM) of the People's Republic of China (PRC), with authorization of the State Council. Connecting the Asia-Pacific economic circle in the east with the European economic circle in the west, the BRI is currently the longest economic corridor with the greatest potential in the world (Nalbantoglu, 2017; Xinhua, 2017).

The Chinese government has released a number of official documents and statements encouraging Chinese companies to invest abroad with good policies

DOI: 10.4324/9781003302445-3

34 *The Belt and Road Initiative and CSR*

and practices in BRI host countries. The major guidelines and action plans governing the Chinese multinational enterprises (MNEs) participating in the BRI are summarized in Table 3.1.

The BRI marks a new era in which MNEs originating from China are beginning to take primary responsibility for driving global flows of FDI. By the end of 2020, China had signed 200 cooperation documents for joint construction of

Table 3.1 Guidelines and action plans governing the Chinese MNEs participating in the BRI

Guidelines and action plans	Issuing department	Year
Vision and Actions on Jointly Building Silk Road Economic Belt and 21st Century Maritime Silk Road[1]	National Development and Reform Commission (NDRC), Ministry of Foreign Affairs (MOFA), Officials of the Ministry of Commerce (MOFCOM)	2015
Building the Belt and Road: Concepts, Practices and China's Contributions[2]	NDRC, MFA, MOFCOM	2017
Guiding Opinions on Promoting the Construction of Green One Belt One Road[3]	NDRC, MFA, MOFCOM, Ministry of Environmental Protection (MEP)	2017
Vision for Maritime Cooperation under the Belt and Road Initiative[4]	NDRC, State Oceanic Administration (SOA)	2017
The Belt and Road Ecological and Environmental Cooperation Plan[5]	NDRC, MFA, MOFCOM, MEP	2017
Vision and Actions on Agriculture Cooperation in Jointly Building Silk Road Economic Belt and 21st Century Maritime Silk Road[6]	NDRC, MFA, MOFCOM	2017
Vision and Actions on Energy Cooperation in Jointly Building Silk Road Economic Belt and 21st Century Maritime Silk Road[7]	NDRC, National Energy Board (NEB)	2017
Action Plan on Development of Belt and Road Sports Tourism (2017–2020)[8]	China National Tourism Administration and General Administration of Sport of China	2017
Ministry of Culture's Action Plan on Belt and Road Culture Development (2016–2020)[9]	Ministry of Culture (MOC)	2017
Education Action Plan for the Belt and Road Initiative[10]	Ministry of Education (MOE)	2017
Guiding Principles on Financing the Development of the Belt and Road[11]	MOF	2017
Measures for the Administration of Overseas Investment of Enterprises[12]	NDRC	2018
Action Plan on Belt and Road Standard Connectivity (2018–2020)[13]	The Office of the Leading Group for the Belt and Road Initiative	2018

the BRI, involving 141 countries and 31 international organizations (Belt and Road Portal, 2021). From 2013 to 2019, China's total imports and exports of goods to and from BRI countries increased from USD1.04 trillion to USD1.34 trillion (Belt and Road Portal, 2021). In 2019, its total trade in goods with 138 BRI countries reached USD1.90 trillion, accounting for 41.5% of its total global trade in goods. From 2013 to 2019, non-financial direct investment by Chinese enterprises in BRI countries exceeded USD100 billion, with an average annual growth rate of 4.4% (Belt and Road Portal, 2021; Gunessee & Liu, 2020).

In the related policy documents, the Chinese government encourages enterprises to undertake corresponding social responsibilities in the host countries and make due contributions in promoting local economic development, increasing employment, improving people's livelihood, and protecting the environment. In the expansion of overseas markets, the importance of CSR has become a consensus and has attracted more and more attention, from host countries and international communities, and has become an important criterion for judging enterprises' goodwill and reputation (Attig et al., 2016).

CSR and BRI: Some underlying theories

The BRI has received considerable attention from researchers, business operators, and the popular media (Morck et al., 2008). In addition to its economic contribution, the BRI is a multidimensional process interlinking local, regional, and global dimensions of social life. Among hotly debated topics on how BRI is reshaping the global competitive landscape, the CSR practices of Chinese MNEs along the Belt and Road are noteworthy but have been relatively little discussed. Despite the potential and benefits that infrastructure development along the Belt and Road can offer to host countries, many BRI projects are loaded with significant challenges and threats (Belt and Road Portal, 2017a). For example, concerns about the impact of poorly designed or implemented projects on BRI host countries are growing, with issues, including the local environment, workforce, fiscal health, and political stability among them (Belt and Road Portal, 2017b).

Stakeholders and the BRI CSR

Stakeholder theory (Freeman, 1984) is most commonly used to understand why corporations should assume CSR. From the perspective of stakeholder theory, research suggests that companies participate in CSR activities and resolve social issues while building constructive relationships with key stakeholders in order to enhance business sustainability (Sweeney & Coughlan, 2008). Stakeholders are described as "groups and individuals who may influence, or are affected by, the achievement of an organization's objectives" (Freeman, 1984, p. 54). Russo and Perrini (2010) point out that the long-term survival and achievement of businesses depend on their ability to sustain and establish relationships with stakeholders when clashing over societal and environmental issues. MNEs operating

Table 3.2 Overseas CSR actions vis-à-vis key stakeholders along the Belt and Road

Stakeholder	Actions vis-à-vis key stakeholders
Employees	Responsible human resource management
	Promote overseas employee benefits and safety
	Localized employees
Consumers	Provide safe products and services
	Respect the rights of local consumers
Community	Promote local welfare and social benefits
	Foster reciprocal relationships with the local community
Investors	Provide a fair return to international investors
Environment	Commitment to sustainable development
	Commitment to local environmental protection endeavors
Suppliers	Commitment to sustainable supply chain
	Fair trade with suppliers
	Support to local suppliers

in multiple countries face diverse stakeholders who monitor and supervise corporate behaviors in overseas markets and must deal with ethical quandaries in a variety of institutional contexts (e.g., Arens & Brouthers, 2001; Yakovleva & Vazquez-Brust, 2012). Arthaud-Day (2005) emphasizes the importance of examining the CSR strategies of MNEs from rapidly developing Asian countries.

As a result of increased globalization and stakeholder demands in host countries, Chinese MNEs have to attend to increased CSR engagements, making it much more complicated for them to conduct overseas CSR activities. Thus, for Chinese MNEs operating across national frontiers, it is insufficient to involve only stakeholders from the home country. Rather, there must be representations from a diverse variety of groups across a broad range of countries relevant to the business (Blowfield & Dolan, 2014; Crane & Matten, 2007; Wheeler et al., 2002). According to the "Vision and Actions on Jointly Building Silk Road Economic Belt and 21st-Century Maritime Silk Road", this chapter identifies six major stakeholders in BRI host countries, namely employees, customers, investors, suppliers, the community, and the environment. Table 3.2 presents CSR actions relevant to each stakeholder.

Legitimacy, isomorphism, and the BRI CSR

On the other hand, CSR is embedded in institutions (Chan & Ma, 2016; Yin & Zhang, 2012; Zhao, 2012). The economic environment and the formal and informal "rules of the game" in the institutional environment also constrain CSR practices (North, 1990). MNEs operate concurrently in various institutional contexts (Kostova & Roth, 2002; Meyer et al., 2011), making it difficult for them to organize their CSR activities internationally to gain legitimacy in host countries (Rathert, 2016). As a result, most CSR research focuses on the impact of host-country institutions on MNEs' CSR (e.g., Asmussen & Fosfuri, 2019; Marano & Kostova, 2016; Rathert, 2016). The rise of MNEs from emerging economies, which are often marked by inefficient markets, active government involvement, extensive business networking, and high uncertainty (Xu & Meyer, 2013), has heightened the importance of understanding the impact of home-country institutions (Ramamurti & Hillemann, 2018). Existing research identifies two key drivers of MNEs' CSR. On the one hand, MNEs must comply with host countries' structural pressures (Beddewela & Fairbrass, 2016; Rathert, 2016). In addition, Chinese MNEs' international expansion forces them to comply with international CSR requirements, making them subject to major international isomorphic pressures (Rathert, 2016). MNEs face a variety of structural stresses, which vary widely depending on the institutional, cultural, geographical, and economic characteristics of host countries (Beddewela & Fairbrass, 2016; Campbell, 2007).

While international pressure to conform with CSR standards may play a critical role in MNEs' CSR practices, existing literature on their CSR practices points to the importance of home-country factors. Key stakeholders in home countries, whether governmental agencies or other institutions/actors, may need to provide the initial impetus for adopting certain CSR initiatives. As a result, CSR initiatives in overseas markets may result from processes of mimetic isomorphism operating at the country level, as suggested by neo-institutional theory (DiMaggio & Powell, 1983). Mimetic behaviors are usually the result of confusion or ambiguity within the organization. Under such circumstances, "organizations appear to model themselves after similar organizations in their field that they consider to be more credible and successful" (DiMaggio & Powell, 1983, p. 152). According to narratives on the diffusion of CSR practices (Matten & Moon, 2008; Rivoli & Waddock, 2011), firms operating in restrictive environments are subject to a contagion or mimetic isomorphism effect, which results in them imitating the actions of other firms with better CSR performance. Furthermore, Aguilera et al. (2007) suggest that companies adopt CSR practices in order to be seen as legitimate by other large firms in their home countries. This is especially likely in emerging economies with oligopolistic market structures and power concentration among the largest firms.

The BRI is one of China's leading institutions for facilitating companies' active involvement in regional cooperation and globalization. It is likely to have a significant impact on Chinese firms' overseas CSR practices, as home-country institutions are expected to significantly affect firms' internationalization (Cuervo-Cazurra et al., 2018). MNEs need to respond to institutional pressures by incorporating institutional elements into their policies and behaviors in order to obtain support and legitimacy for their overseas operations. Failure to comply with institutionally accepted standards may jeopardize companies' legitimacy, and ultimately their survival (Bondy et al., 2012). BRI is proposed and led by the government and is perceived as a formal institutional force exerted on Chinese MNEs through coercive and mimetic isomorphism (Haveman, 1993; Martínez-Ferrero & García-Sánchez, 2017; Mizruchi & Fein, 1999). First, coercive isomorphism derives from political interference and institutional pressure from stakeholders on which companies depend (DiMaggio & Powell, 1983; Zamir

& Saeed, 2020). To satisfy the Chinese government and gain additional legitimacy and capital for development, Chinese enterprises must strictly adhere to BRI-related policies and incorporate social responsibility criteria into their international strategies. Second, if corporate targets such as levels of commitment to CSR are unclear or uncertain, companies may model themselves to gain credibility from other more active or legitimate companies (DiMaggio & Powell, 1983). Since recently established Chinese MNEs involved in the BRI lack overseas experience, it is unclear whether how and to what extent they should engage in CSR. The government actively encourages good CSR activities, and awareness of typical MNEs participating in the BRI will assist others in improving their own CSR to meet the initiative's requirements. For example, Chinese MNEs with excellent CSR results in the BRI are listed on official Chinese government websites and promoted as exemplars, which undoubtedly enhances their credibility and provides a model for other companies (Lau et al., 2016).[14] These mimetic forces influence imitation of good peers and mobilize capital to enhance Chinese MNEs' CSR.

According to Suchman (1995), legitimacy is a generic interpretation or inference that an entity's acts are desirable, proper, or acceptable within some socially constructed sets of norms, values, beliefs, and definitions. He distinguishes three forms of organizational legitimacy – pragmatic, moral, and cognitive – and stresses that legitimacy management is highly dependent on communication. As a result, CSR practices are critical to comprehending the foundations of companies committed to ethical behaviors and socially responsible practices. Scott (2008) further develops the notion of legitimacy from an institutional perspective and describes legitimacy as "a condition reflecting perceived consonance with relevant rules and laws, normative support, or alignment with the cultural-cognitive framework" (p. 59). Milne and Patten (2002) argue that in managing the legitimacy process, managers are faced with social demands from multiple organizations and must decide on what to make public. It is widely acknowledged that Chinese MNEs investing abroad bear the burden of their home countries' backwardness and, to some extent, illegitimacy (Miska et al., 2016). The shortcomings of their home countries' institutional and business processes, combined with news about their companies' reckless actions (e.g., the case of Foxconn and the controversy over melamine-laced milk powder that killed many infants in China), lead to the accumulation of negative judgments in host countries. In turn, "there is a reputation and legitimacy deficiency in the eyes of host country stakeholders, who have become much more circumspect as a result of ineffective or missing awareness of emerging international market multinational companies, their quality, and safety requirements, and the like" (Madhok & Keyhani, 2012, p. 31).

Through the lens of legitimacy theory, firms can resolve LOE/LOF (liability of emergingness/liability of foreignness) by attending to the demands of the host environment through various types of isomorphism (DiMaggio & Powell, 1983; Zaheer, 1995), which essentially means reducing the institutional gaps between the requirements of home and host countries. As a result, some propose that Chinese MNEs seek legitimacy by adhering to international CSR norms (Campbell et al., 2012; Gugler & Shi, 2009). Several studies identify the role of institutional pressures in MNEs' decisions to pursue CSR strategies. Meanwhile, the consequences of CSR involvement are highly dependent on the host country's legal and social background. Chinese MNEs operate in host countries with radically different political, economic, and cultural conditions from those in their home country (Marano & Kostova, 2016; Mithani, 2017b). MNEs must fulfill the myriad dynamic demands of diverse stakeholders and must deal with the LOF and possibly unfriendly voices from abroad, resulting in additional costs (Mithani, 2017b). Thus, they must make further efforts to obtain legitimacy and become incorporated into the local social environment. Furthermore, owing to their dual embeddedness, MNEs must obtain legitimacy from both home and host countries (Beddewela, 2019; Hamprecht & Schwarzkopf, 2014). Similarly, assuming CSR as a strategy for MNEs to maintain external legitimacy is well-rooted in previous literature (Bebbington et al., 2009). According to early institutional research, organizations pursue legitimacy in a given context by aligning their activities with prevailing norms and attempting to become isomorphic with the environment (Fernando & Lawrence, 2014; Gray et al., 1988).

The BRI is an innovative global cooperation scheme and Chinese MNEs are investing heavily in BRI countries and there is a significant impact on the local communities. Thus, Chinese MNEs must legitimize their corporate actions by engaging in CSR initiatives to gain the approval of local societies in host countries so as to ensure their continuing existence and legitimacy. MNEs' legitimacy also stems from the concept of the social contract (Sacconi, 2007), which consists of the local society's various expectations of how MNEs should conduct their business operations. Therefore, in order to continue operating smoothly in the BRI, Chinese MNEs must act within the bounds and norms of what local society identifies as socially responsible behavior. Given that the BRI is an ambitious expansion plan for Chinese MNEs, gaining legitimacy is highly critical, and losing it will cause enormous damage to their corporate reputation (Bebbington et al., 2008). Therefore, legitimacy theory provides a robust theoretical foundation to explain Chinese MNEs' need to disclose their CSR performance along the BRI.

Social contract, norms, and the BRI CSR

Through the lens of social contract theory, CSR can be defined as "a [social] 'contract' between society and business wherein [the] community grants a firm the license to operate, and in return, the matter meets certain obligations and behaves in an acceptable manner" (Dahlsrud, 2008, p. 10). Thus, the societies in which businesses operate implicitly require them to operate responsibly (Donaldson & Dunfee, 1999). Managers take ethical decisions because they understand that the company is part of a larger social system in which society and business coexist, and that the microsocial decisions made within organizations should be conducive to the larger social system and should meet societal standards. Thus, organizations' CSR practices represent their attempts to satisfy the agreement and educate the community about their ethical choices and activities. Drawing on social contract theory, the concept of combining local and global is present in the CSR literature. While local institutional environments must be addressed, certain values that transcend cultures (referred to as "hypernorms") moderate context-specific or micronorms to ensure that universal and local values are considered in decision-making (Aguado et al., 2017; Bondy & Starkey, 2014). Although potentially divisive and contentious in practice, social contract theory exemplifies attempts to incorporate global and local issues into decision-making, leading to a growth in policies in which the notion of "being local worldwide" (Belanger et al., 1999) is becoming more prevalent. For some companies, this illustrates the previously discussed issue of trying to be consistent across operational locations while still tailoring operations to cultural differences (Leisinger, 2005; Waddock & Bodwell, 2004). For others, the connection between global and local factors must be demonstrated, which has a greater influence on how CSR is shaped (Arthaud-Day, 2005).

The BRI aims to go beyond infrastructure development to include policy coordination, trade facilitation, financial integration, and cultural and scientific exchange (National Development and Reform Commission [NDRC], 2015). Such a huge international collaboration initiative is expected to have tremendous effects on the local society.[15] Similarly, CSR in BRI host countries is part of the social contract. Therefore, a degree of plurality is required, where Chinese MNEs and their executives are encouraged to think and behave both globally and locally. In the process of serving their own business interests, Chinese MNEs are obliged to take actions that also protect and enhance the society's interests (Dusuki & Yusof, 2008).

When treating overseas CSR along the BRI as part of the social contract, two different levels must be considered: the contract between the local society and economic entities, and the contract between MNEs' management and all stakeholders in the nations participating in the BRI (Dembinski & Fryzel, 2010). Chinese MNEs are supposed to balance universal and specific CSR concerns under their own CSR policies and subsequent procedures and take a leading role in promoting sustainable development in the BRI countries. To this extent, following social contract theory, Chinese MNEs should be responsive along the BRI. At the same time, the BRI countries' governments, enterprises, employees, and all other stakeholders are expected to benefit from the, what we call here, the "BRI social contract". Therefore, Chinese MNEs should shoulder CSR to meet the various expectations of society and related stakeholders (Moir, 2001).

Resource dependency and the BRI CSR

From the perspective of resource dependence theory (RDT), firms are open systems that are not autonomous and rely on contingencies and resources in the external environment. Since firms cannot completely manage all resources required for survival, they often depend on resources managed by external stakeholders (Salancik & Pfeffer, 1978). Firms may take proactive measures to address external stakeholders' concerns about reducing uncertainty associated with accessing critical resources (Hillman et al., 2009; Salancik & Pfeffer, 1978). As one of the main stakeholders, the government is a major source of external interdependence and uncertainty for firms (Hillman, 2005). Uncertainty and dependency derived from the government are especially important and challenging for firms in handling an emerging economy. Governments often maintain financial and regulatory tools critical to firms' survival, such as governmental subsidies, business policies, and industry development guidance (Hillman et al., 2009; Hoskisson et al., 2000). RDT suggests that an "organization may use political means to alter the state of the external economic environment" in order to manage such uncertainty (Salancik & Pfeffer, 1978, p. 190). Establishing relationships with governments is a tactic used by corporations to respond to environmental risks (Guo et al., 2014; Salancik & Pfeffer, 1978), since political ties will enable them to obtain vital resources, such as a good reputation, valuable information, favorable business policies and political legitimacy.

Through investing abroad, China has significantly improved its position in the global value chain. Major characteristics of China's MNEs include relatively their recent establishment, rapid growth, large volumes, strong governmental control, and intense focus on industries and regions (Huang et al., 2017). Their activities are primarily determined by "pull" factors, such as acquiring resources to satisfy growing demands and short supplies in domestic markets, rather than "push" factors, such as home-market limitations and labor shortages, which are more common for multinational firms from developed countries (Deng, 2004). Previous studies suggest that a key reason why many Chinese companies invest abroad is to find, retain, or develop overseas markets. Foreign factors driving the expansion of Chinese firms in China have risen rapidly over the past three decades (Wadhwa & Reddy, 2011; Zhang, 2009). These include a lack of domestic markets relative to Chinese companies' overall capabilities and aspirations, which results in increased competition from both domestic and international MNEs and additional challenges around trade protectionism (Genasci & Pray, 2008). The net effect is that more and more Chinese businesses have to set up operations abroad or open offices in foreign countries. Another reason for Chinese firms going abroad is to ensure access to natural resources, especially oil, gas, and minerals. The Chinese government has been concerned about the possibility of shortages of key resources and inputs for economic expansion owing to decades of fast economic growth, as reflected in the strategic and political motives underlying FDI by large central-government-controlled MNEs.

According to the resource-dependence viewpoint (Salancik & Pfeffer, 1978), companies seek to acquire complementary assets from external environments, including rivals in other cross-border markets, and try to acquire strategic information that is not available internally from international organizations. In return, MNEs receiving various resources from host countries and advancing and improving CSR issues in those countries are considered precursors to economic and social progress (Minor & Morgan, 2011). Such CSR advances in host countries promote firms' corporate reputation and grant legitimacy to future operations (Markusen, 2004). Similarly, Chinese MNEs frequently seek to strengthen their capacity for innovation and continuously build sustainable competitive advantages in host countries, thereby reducing their reliance on location-specific endowments (De Chiara & Russo Spena, 2011). Thus, internationalization through the BRI enables them to build international networks that bind resources, including natural, human, and capital resources. Furthermore, Chinese MNEs actively participate in the BRI to obtain complementary assets that are unavailable in their home countries through linkages, leverage, and learning strategies (Hurley et al., 2019). In this scenario, overseas markets along the BRI serve specifically as learning platforms for Chinese MNEs seeking to enhance their capabilities, contribute to organizational learning, and aid in sharing new information within networks, allowing them to improve their organizational competitiveness (Huang, 2016; Noronha & Zhang, 2023). On the other hand, since Chinese MNEs utilize various resources from the BRI host countries, they are expected to behave responsibly. Along this vein, conducting various CSR initiatives in host countries is of great strategic significance to promote sustainable development along the Belt and Road.

A theoretical framework of CSR and BRI

The following figure summarizes the importance of CSR in the BRI host countries using a theoretical lens.

According to Figure 3.1, Chinese MNEs operating in the BRI host countries face a diverse set of stakeholders and are under greater pressure to align their shareholders' interests with the expectations of those in host markets. Specifically, they need to satisfy stakeholders in host countries to acquire local legitimacy and must conform with the requirements of both the parent companies and home stakeholders in order to maintain their international operating licenses. In addition, as initiators of the BRI, Chinese MNEs are obliged to take actions that also protect and enhance the society's interests and meet the various expectations of the society and related stakeholders (Moir, 2001). Such CSR initiatives are likely to promote Chinese MNEs' international image in the global arena and create a win-win situation for both BRI host countries and China. Figure 3.1 also implies that, given the BRI's adaptability, stakeholders have incentives to advocate the institutionalization of best practices and promote high social, labor, and environmental standards in BRI ventures. A comprehensive CSR strategy would help to mitigate a number of obstacles and risks associated with BRI ventures, as well as fostering more sustainable and inclusive development outcomes for host countries.

Notably, CSR-related regulations and directives for Chinese MNEs (see "Guiding Opinions on Promoting the Construction of Green One Belt One Road and the Belt and Road Ecological and Environmental Cooperation Plan" in Table 3.1) are mainly voluntary and unlike enforceable laws and regulations, and primarily define aspirational objectives and visions in terms of sustainable developing in BRI host countries. In other words, China engages stakeholders from BRI host countries proactively through soft legislations, which ensure

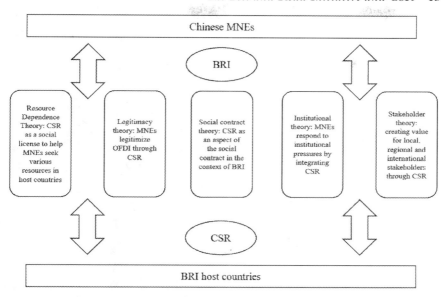

Figure 3.1 The theoretical framework incorporating CSR into the BRI.

that almost all BRI-specific laws originate from legally non-binding informal documents rather than formal treaties (Chen & Liu, 2019). The policies regulating Chinese MNEs' environmental and social impacts are still relatively weak, largely voluntary in nature, and incompatible with policies governing domestic investments. Such regulations and the ability and capacity to enforce them vary widely and are often insufficient to address CSR deficiencies. Indeed, the Chinese government does not pursue a "command and control" approach in terms of CSR in overseas markets but instead provides companies and banks with incentives for self-regulation (Fang & Nolan, 2019). Up to now, there are no international treaties or CSR requirements for MNEs in overseas host countries. Thus, there are no concrete guidelines or multi-country conventions to facilitate CSR development of MNEs across nations.

Furthermore, given that the majority of countries along the BRI are developing countries and emerging economies (Belt and Road Portal, 2021), they face many challenges from industrialization and urbanization, such as pollution and ecological destruction, and increasing demand for a faster transition to green growth (Fang & Nolan, 2019). In the absence of financial or legal penalties for non-compliance, public bodies and civil societies are likely to "name and shame" corporations to keep their voluntary undertakings accountable. Thus, this chapter argues that a more robust regulatory framework should be established for CSR reporting by Chinese MNEs in overseas markets, as the effective sustainable development of the BRI depends not only on China's commitments and priorities, but also on its capacity to sustain, enact, and execute strict CSR disclosure laws and regulations.

Notes

1 NDRC, MFA & MOFCOM (2015). *Vision and Actions on Jointly Building Silk Road Economic Belt and 21st-Century Maritime Silk Road*. Retrieved from http://www.lawinfochina.com/display.aspx?id=144&lib=dbref&SearchKeyword=&SearchCKeyword=&EncodingName=gb2312
2 NDRC, MOFCOM & MFA (2017). *Build The All Along: Idea. Practice and china's Contribution*. Retrieved from https://www.abebooks.de/servlet/BookDetailsPL?bi=22637415620&cm_sp=rec-_-pd_hw_i_1-_-bdp&reftag=pd_hw_i_1
3 NDRC, MOFCOM, MFA & MEP (2017). *Guiding Opinions on Promoting the Construction of Green "One Belt One Road"*. Retrieved from https://www.mee.gov.cn/gkml/hbb/bwj/201705/t20170505_413602.htm [only available in Chinese].
4 NDRC & SOA (2017). *Concept for Maritime Cooperation under the Belt and Road Initiative*. Retrieved from http://www.gov.cn/xinwen/2017-11/17/content_5240325.htm [only available in Chinese].
5 NDRC, MFA, MOFCOM & MEP (2017). *"One Belt One Road" Ecological Environmental Protection Cooperation Plan*. Retrieved from http://www.mee.gov.cn/gkml/hbb/bwj/201705/W020170516330272025970.pdf [only available in Chinese].
6 NDRC, MFA & MOFCOM (2017). *Vision and Actions on Agriculture Cooperation in Jointly Building Silk Road Economic Belt and 21st Century Maritime Silk Road*. Retrieved from http://cpc.people.com.cn/n/2015/0328/c64387-26764810.html
7 NDRC & NEB (2017). *Vision and Actions on Energy Cooperation in Jointly Building Silk Road Economic Belt and 21st Century Maritime Silk Road*. Retrieved from http://www.nea.gov.cn/2017-05/12/c_136277473.htm
8 China National Tourism Administration and General Administration of Sport of China (2017). *Action Plan on Development of Belt and Road Sports Tourism (2017–20)*. Retrieved from https://eng.yidaiyilu.gov.cn/wcm.files/upload/CMSydylyw/201707/201707100221023.pdf
9 MOC (2017). *Ministry of Culture's Action Plan on Belt and Road Culture Development (2016–20)*. Retrieved from https://www.yidaiyilu.gov.cn/wcm.files/upload/CMSydylgw/201703/20170301031012.pdf
10 MOE (2017). *Education Action Plan for the Belt and Road Initiative*. Retrieved from https://eng.yidaiyilu.gov.cn/zchj/qwfb/30277.htm
11 MOF (2017). *Guiding Principles on Financing the Development of the Belt and Road*. Retrieved from https://eng.yidaiyilu.gov.cn/wcm.files/upload/CMSydylyw/201705/201705160956043.pdf
12 NDRC (2018). *Measures for the Administration of Overseas Investment of Enterprises*. Retrieved from https://www.ndrc.gov.cn/fggz/lywzjw/zcfg/201712/W020190909440825920640.pdf
13 The Office of the Leading Group for the Belt and Road Initiative (2018). *Action Plan on Belt and Road Standard Connectivity (2018–20)*. Retrieved from https://www.yidaiyilu.gov.cn/zchj/qwfb/43480.htm
14 Because of their outstanding CSR performance in overseas markets, several Chinese MNEs, including the China Communications Construction Group and the National Energy Group, have repeatedly won the "Overseas CSR Model Enterprise Award" at the China CSR Communication Forum hosted by the Corporate Social Responsibility Research Center of the Chinese Academy of Social Sciences.
15 See Donleavy and Noronha (2023) for a discussion of the "phenomenon grande".

References

Aguado, R., Retolaza, J. L., & Alcañiz, L. (2017). Dignity at the level of the firm: Beyond the stakeholder approach. In M. Kostera, & M. Pirson (Eds.), *Dignity and the organization* (pp. 81–97). Palgrave Macmillan.

Aguilera, R. V., Rupp, D. E., Williams, C. A., & Ganapathi, J. (2007). Putting the S back in corporate social responsibility: A multilevel theory of social change in organizations. *Academy of Management Review, 32*(3), 836–863.

Arens, P., & Brouthers, K. D. (2001). Key stakeholder theory and state owned versus privatized firms. *Management International Review, 41*(4), 377–394.

Arthaud-Day, M. L. (2005). Transnational corporate social responsibility: A tri-dimensional approach to international CSR research. *Business Ethics Quarterly, 15*(1), 1–22.

Asmussen, C. G., & Fosfuri, A. (2019). Orchestrating corporate social responsibility in the multinational enterprise. *Strategic Management Journal, 40*(6), 894–916.

Attig, N., Boubakri, N., El Ghoul, S., & Guedhami, O. (2016). Firm internationalization and corporate social responsibility. *Journal of Business Ethics, 134*(2), 171–197.

Bebbington, J., Higgins, C., & Frame, B. (2009). Initiating sustainable development reporting: Evidence from New Zealand. *Accounting, Auditing & Accountability Journal, 22*(4), 588–625.

Bebbington, J., Larrinaga, C., & Moneva, J. M. (2008). Corporate social reporting and reputation risk management. *Accounting, Auditing & Accountability Journal, 21*(3), 337–361.

Beddewela, E. (2019). Managing corporate community responsibility in multinational corporations: Resolving institutional duality. *Long Range Planning, 52*(6), 101911.

Beddewela, E., & Fairbrass, J. (2016). Seeking legitimacy through CSR: Institutional pressures and corporate responses of multinationals in Sri Lanka. *Journal of Business Ethics, 136*(3), 503–522.

Belanger, J., Berggren, C., Bjorkman, T., & Kohler, C. (1999). *Being local worldwide: ABB and the challenge of global management*. Cornell University Press.

Belt and Road Portal. (2017a). *Guidance on promoting green belt and road*. https://eng.yidaiyilu.gov.cn/zchj/qwfb/12479.htm

Belt and Road Portal. (2017b). *The belt and road ecological and environmental cooperation plan*. https://eng.yidaiyilu.gov.cn/zchj/qwfb/13392.htm

Belt and Road Portal. (2021). *List of countries that have signed cooperation documents with China to jointly build the "Belt and Road"*. https://www.yidaiyilu.gov.cn/xwzx/roll/77298.htm

Blowfield, M., & Dolan, C. S. (2014). Business as a development agent: Evidence of possibility and improbability. *Third World Quarterly, 35*(1), 22–42.

Bondy, K., Moon, J., & Matten, D. (2012). An institution of corporate social responsibility (CSR) in multi-national corporations (MNCs): Form and implications. *Journal of Business Ethics, 111*(2), 281–299.

Bondy, K., & Starkey, K. (2014). The dilemmas of internationalization: Corporate social responsibility in the multinational corporation. *British Journal of Management, 25*(1), 4–22.

Campbell, J. L. (2007). Why would corporations behave in socially responsible ways? An institutional theory of corporate social responsibility. *Academy of Management Review, 32*(3), 946–967.

Campbell, J. T., Eden, L., & Miller, S. R. (2012). Multinationals and corporate social responsibility in host countries: Does distance matter? *Journal of International Business Studies, 43*(1), 84–106.

Chan, R. Y., & Ma, K. H. (2016). Environmental orientation of exporting SMEs from an emerging economy: Its antecedents and consequences. *Management International Review, 56*(5), 597–632.

Chen, J., & Liu, W. (2019). The belt and road strategy in international business and administration: Corporate social responsibility. In W. Liu, J. Chen, & S. Tsai (Eds.), The *belt and road strategy in international business and administration* (pp. 28–51). IGI Global.

Crane, A., & Matten, D. (2007). *Corporate social responsibility. Vol. 2: Managing and implementing corporate social responsibility.* Sage Publications.

Cuervo-Cazurra, A., Luo, Y., Ramamurti, R., & Ang, S. H. (2018). The impact of the home country on internationalization. *Journal of World Business, 53*(5), 593–604.

Dahlsrud, A. (2008). How corporate social responsibility is defined: An Analysis of 37 definitions. *Corporate Social Responsibility and Environmental Management, 15*(1), 1–13.

De Chiara, A., & Russo Spena, T. (2011). CSR strategy in multinational firms: Focus on human resources, suppliers and community. *Journal of Global Responsibility, 2*(1), 60–74.

Dembinski, P. H., & Fryzel, B. (2010). *The role of large enterprises in democracy and society.* Palgrave Macmillan.

Deng, P. (2004). Outward investment by Chinese MNCs: Motivations and implications. *Business Horizons, 47*(3), 8–16.

DiMaggio, P. J., & Powell, W. W. (1983). The iron cage revisited: Institutional isomorphism and collective rationality in organizational fields. *American Sociological Review, 48*(2), 147–160.

Donaldson, T., & Dunfee, T. W. (1999). When ethics travel: The promise and peril of global business ethics. *California Management Review, 41*(4), 45–63.

Donleavy, G., & Noronha, C. (2023). Concluding remarks: Comparative CSR and sustainability research – An axial analysis. In G. Donleavy & C. Noronha (Eds.), *Comparative CSR and sustainability: New accounting for social consequences* (pp. 380–398). Routledge.

Dusuki, A. W., & Yusof, T. F. M. T. M. (2008). The pyramid of corporate social responsibility model: Empirical evidence from Malaysian stakeholder persepective. *Management & Accounting Review, 7*(2), 29–54.

Fang, C., & Nolan, P. (Eds.). (2019). *Routledge handbook of the belt and road.* Routledge.

Fernando, S., & Lawrence, S. (2014). A theoretical framework for CSR practices: Integrating legitimacy theory, stakeholder theory and institutional theory. *Journal of Theoretical Accounting Research, 10*(1), 149–178.

Freeman, R. E. (1984). *Strategic management: A stakeholder approach.* Pitman Publishing Inc.

Genasci, M., & Pray, S. (2008). Extracting accountability: The implications of the resource curse for CSR theory and practice. *Yale Human Rights Law Journal, 37,* 50.

Gray, R., Owen, D., & Maunders, K. (1988). Corporate social reporting: Emerging trends in accountability and the social contract. *Accounting, Auditing & Accountability Journal, 1*(1), 6–20.

Gugler, P., & Shi, J. Y. (2009). Corporate social responsibility for developing country multinational corporations: Lost war in pertaining global competitiveness? *Journal of Business Ethics, 87*(1), 3–24.

Gunessee, S., & Liu, J. (2020). The economics of the belt and road initiative. In H. K. Chan, F. K. S. Chan, & D. O'Brien (Eds.), *International flows in the belt and road initiative context: business, people, history and geography* (pp. 19–59). Springer Nature Palgrave Macmillan.

Guo, H., Xu, E., & Jacobs, M. (2014). Managerial political ties and firm performance during institutional transitions: An analysis of mediating mechanisms. *Journal of Business Research, 67*(2), 116–127.

Hamprecht, J., & Schwarzkopf, J. (2014). Subsidiary initiatives in the institutional environment. *Management International Review, 54*(5), 757–778.

Haveman, H. A. (1993). Follow the leader: Mimetic isomorphism and entry into new markets. *Administrative Science Quarterly, 38*(4), 593–627.

Hillman, A. J. (2005). Politicians on the Board of Directors: Do connections affect the bottom line? *Journal of Management, 31*(3), 464-481.

Hillman, A. J., Withers, M. C., & Collins, B. J. (2009). Resource dependence theory: A review. *Journal of Management, 35*(6), 1404–1427.

Hoskisson, R. E., Eden, L., Lau, C. M., & Wright, M. (2000). Strategy in emerging economies. *Academy of Management Journal, 43*(3), 249–267.

Huang, Y. (2016). Understanding China's belt & road initiative: Motivation, framework and assessment. *China Economic Review, 40*, 314–321.

Huang, Y., Fischer, T. B., & Xu, H. (2017). The stakeholder analysis for SEA of Chinese foreign direct investment: The case of 'one belt, one road' initiative in Pakistan. *Impact Assessment and Project Appraisal, 35*(2), 158–171.

Hurley, J., Morris, S., & Portelance, G. (2019). Examining the debt implications of the belt and road initiative from a policy perspective. *Journal of Infrastructure, Policy and Development, 3*(1), 139–175.

Kostova, T., & Roth, K. (2002). Adoption of an organizational practice by subsidiaries of multinational corporations: Institutional and relational effects. *Academy of Management Journal, 45*(1), 215–233.

Lau, C., Lu, Y., & Liang, Q. (2016). Corporate social responsibility in China: A corporate governance approach. *Journal of Business Ethics, 136*(1), 73–87.

Leisinger, K. M. (2005). The corporate social responsibility of the pharmaceutical industry: Idealism without illusion and realism without resignation. *Business Ethics Quarterly, 15*(4), 577–594.

Madhok, A., & Keyhani, M. (2012). Acquisitions as entrepreneurship: Asymmetries, opportunities, and the internationalization of multinationals from emerging economies. *Global Strategy Journal, 2*(1), 26–40.

Marano, V., & Kostova, T. (2016). Unpacking the institutional complexity in adoption of CSR practices in multinational enterprises. *Journal of Management Studies, 53*(1), 28–54.

Markusen, J. R. (2004). *Multinational firms and the theory of international trade*. MIT Press.

Martínez-Ferrero, J., & García-Sánchez, I. M. (2017). Coercive, normative and mimetic isomorphism as determinants of the voluntary assurance of sustainability reports. *International Business Review, 26*(1), 102–118.

Matten, D., & Moon, J. (2008). "Implicit" and "explicit" CSR: A conceptual framework for a comparative understanding of corporate social responsibility. *Academy of Management Review, 33*(2), 404–424.

Meyer, K. E., Mudambi, R., & Narula, R. (2011). Multinational enterprises and local contexts: The opportunities and challenges of multiple embeddedness. *Journal of Management Studies, 48*(2), 235–252.

Milne, M. J., & Patten, D. M. (2002). Securing organizational legitimacy: An experimental decision case examining the impact of environmental disclosures. *Accounting, Auditing & Accountability Journal, 15*(3), 372–405.

Minor, D., & Morgan, J. (2011). CSR as reputation insurance: Primum non noncore. *California Management Review, 53*(3), 40–59.

Miska, C., Witt, M. A., & Stahl, G. K. (2016). Drivers of global CSR integration and local CSR responsiveness: Evidence from Chinese MNEs. *Business Ethics Quarterly, 26*(3), 317–345.

Mithani, M. A. (2017b). Liability of foreignness, natural disasters, and corporate philanthropy. *Journal of International Business Studies, 48*(8), 941–963.

Mizruchi, M. S., & Fein, L. C. (1999). The social construction of organizational knowledge: A study of the uses of coercive, mimetic, and normative isomorphism. *Administrative Science Quarterly, 44*(4), 653–683.

Moir, L. (2001). What do we mean by corporate social responsibility? *Corporate governance. The International Journal of Business in Society, 1*(2), 16–22.

Morck, R., Yeung, B., & Zhao, M. (2008). Perspectives on China's outward foreign direct investment. *Journal of International Business Studies, 39*(3), 337–350.

Nalbantoglu, C. (2017). One belt one road initiative: New route on China's change of course to growth. *Open Journal of Social Sciences, 5*(1), 720–726.

National Development and Reform Commission (NDRC). (2015). *Vision and actions on jointly building silk road economic belt and 21st-century Maritime Silk Road.* https://www.fmprc.gov.cn/eng/topics_665678/2015zt/xjpcxbayzlt2015nnh/201503/t20150328_705553.html

Noronha, C., & Zhang, R. (2023). Using "actor-network theory and friends" to explore CSR reporting in the information and communication technology sector under the belt and road initiative. In G. Donleavy & C. Noronha (Eds.), *Comparative CSR and sustainability: New accounting for social consequences.* pp. 162–187. Routledge.

North, D. C. (1990). *Institutions, Institutional change and economic performance.* Cambridge University Press.

Ramamurti, R., & Hillemann, J. (2018). What is "Chinese" about Chinese multinationals? *Journal of International Business Studies, 49*(1), 34–48.

Rathert, N. (2016). Strategies of legitimation: MNEs and the adoption of CSR in response to host-country institutions. *Journal of International Business Studies, 47*(7), 858–879.

Rivoli, P., & Waddock, S. (2011). "First they ignore you...": The time-context dynamic and corporate responsibility. *California Management Review, 53*(2), 87–104.

Russo, A., & Perrini, F. (2010). Investigating Stakeholder Theory and Social Capital: CSR in Large Firms and SMEs. *Journal of Business Ethics, 91*, 207–221.

Sacconi, L. (2007). A social contract account for CSR as an extended model of corporate governance (II): Compliance, reputation and reciprocity. *Journal of Business Ethics, 75*(1), 77–96.

Salancik, G. R., & Pfeffer, J. (1978). A social information processing approach to job attitudes and task design. *Administrative Science Quarterly, 23*(2), 224–253.

Scott, W. R. (2008). Approaching adulthood: The maturing of institutional theory. *Theory and Society, 37*(5), 427.

Suchman, M. C. (1995). Managing legitimacy: Strategic and institutional approaches. *Academy of Management Review, 20*(3), 571–610.
Sweeney, L., & Coughlan, J. (2008). Do different industries report corporate social responsibility differently? An investigation through the lens of stakeholder theory. *Journal of Marketing Communications, 14*(2), 113–124.
Waddock, S., & Bodwell, C. (2004). Managing responsibility: What can be learned from the quality movement? *California Management Review, 47*(1), 25–37.
Wadhwa, K., & Reddy, S. S. (2011). Foreign direct investment into developing Asian countries: The role of market seeking, resource seeking and efficiency seeking factors. *International Journal of Business and Management, 6*(11), 219.
Wheeler, D., Fabig, H., & Boele, R. (2002). Paradoxes and dilemmas for stakeholder responsive firms in the extractive sector: Lessons from the case of Shell and the Ogoni. *Journal of Business Ethics, 39*(3), 297–318.
Xinhua. (2015). *Vision and actions on jointly building silk road economic belt and 21st-century maritime silk road.* https://eng.yidaiyilu.gov.cn/qwyw/qwfb/1084.htm
Xinhua. (2017). *President Xi's speech at opening of belt and road forum.* http://news.xinhuanet.com/english/2017-05/14/c_136282982.htm
Xu, D., & Meyer, K. E. (2013). Linking theory and context: Strategy research in emerging economies since Wright et al. *Journal of Management Studies, 50*(7), 1322–1346.
Yakovleva, N., & Vazquez-Brust, D. (2012). Stakeholder perspectives on CSR of mining MNCs in Argentina. *Journal of Business Ethics, 106*(2), 191–211.
Yin, J., & Zhang, Y. (2012). Institutional dynamics and corporate social responsibility (CSR) in an emerging country context: Evidence from China. *Journal of Business Ethics, 111*(2), 301–316.
Zaheer, S. (1995). Overcoming the liability of foreignness. *Academy of Management Journal, 38*(2), 341–363.
Zamir, F., & Saeed, A. (2020). Location matters: Impact of geographical proximity to financial centers on corporate social responsibility (CSR) disclosure in emerging economies. *Asia Pacific Journal of Management, 37*(1), 263–295.
Zhang, K. H. (2009). Rise of Chinese multinational firms. *Chinese Economy, 42*(6), 81–96.
Zhao, M. (2012). CSR-based political legitimacy strategy: Managing the state by doing good in China and Russia. *Journal of Business Ethics, 111*(4), 439–460.

4 CSR Reporting and Chinese MNEs

China as a latecomer and quick learner of CSR

Although CSR is a prevalent term, it has no universally agreed definition (Matten & Moon, 2004), and therefore consensus is lacking on the basis for assessing it and relating it to the various dimensions of corporate performance (Aras & Crowther, 2009). Indeed, researchers have suggested various terms to describe CSR, including corporate citizenship, business ethics, and sustainability (Wang et al., 2010). Numerous authors have defined these concepts, which have evolved over time and are used interchangeably (Yin & Zhang, 2012). Carroll (1979), a forerunner in this field, identified four dimensions of CSR and devised a model of corporate social performance. He viewed CSR as comprising a pyramid structure of four distinct types of responsibility in the areas of economics, law, ethics, and philanthropy. Over the past few decades, the public, governments, customers, and other stakeholders have become increasingly aware of the social and environmental consequences of human activities in general, and business operations in particular.

According to the World Business Council for Sustainable Development (WBCSD, 2000), "CSR is the continuing commitment by business to behave ethically and contribute to economic development while improving the quality of life of the workforce and their families as well as the local community and society at large". Various theoretical frameworks, standards, and guidelines have been developed to capture CSR's scope and measure firms' CSR reporting, including the Global Reporting Initiative and the UN Global Compact (Spiller, 2000). Despite the development of metrics and frameworks, there is no universal agreement on which should be used to evaluate CSR reporting quality (Zhao, 2012). CSR reporting is regarded as a critical tool for enhancing CSR performance because it helps "identify strengths and shortcomings across the entire corporate responsibility continuum" and necessitates "stakeholder discourse by mapping, assessing, systematizing, and communicating what companies achieve in the field of stakeholder-related CSR" (Perrini & Vurro, 2010, p. 460). Firms can use this information to improve their CSR capabilities and resolve social and environmental concerns more comprehensively throughout their operations. Notably, CSR reporting is different from CSR initiatives that the former

DOI: 10.4324/9781003302445-4

is intended to help information users assess the impact of business operations on the environment, society, and economy (Crowther, 2000). While CSR activities are a group of activities initiated by companies to promote benefits of the various stakeholders.

Companies can also use CSR reporting to communicate with their stakeholders about their aspirations for sustainable development and CSR (Crowther, 2000). CSR reporting also enables key stakeholders to assess companies' CSR activities and reward constructive externalities, while placing pressure on companies to minimize negative ones. Although CSR reporting is becoming more common among MNEs, it has emerged in the highly ambiguous area of global socio-environmental governance, "where practices, causality, and performance are difficult to understand and map" (Wijen, 2014, p. 302). This encompasses a multitude of demands relating to CSR performance from diverse social and organizational networks, which causes uncertainty for businesses about how CSR reporting and performance are jointly evaluated (Wijen, 2014).

According to Jamali and Karam (2018), the understanding and implementation of CSR in firms in emerging economies are highly dependent on the countries' backgrounds. They suggest that, in order to understand CSR drivers in emerging markets, it is necessary to consider not only the corporate and market setting, but also the political and social structures that function outside the national business system. For example, Miska et al. (2016) investigate the gaps between global and local CSR integration in Chinese multinational corporations. They conclude that research should consider not only advanced and emerging economies, but also individual emerging economies (Miska et al., 2016), since each country is likely to have its own level of interest in CSR activities arising from social, cultural, and other factors that influence corporate behavior.

Historically, when Confucianism was prevalent in China, business organizations were seen as extensions of families, and responsibility was assumed primarily for the social group or "political family" (Fiaschi et al., 2015). From the 16th to the 18th centuries, Zen Buddhism and Daoism influenced business practices and, in combination with Confucianism, induced an honest, diligent, and charitable corporate culture (Lin, 2010). The Cultural Revolution (1966–1976) and the subsequent gradual opening of the Chinese economy challenged this approach, resulting in fundamental changes to the Chinese perceptions of CSR (Gao, 2011). The central government used to require central enterprises (CEs) and state-owned enterprises (SOEs) to provide social services to employees and their families, such as employee protection, education, and health services. These programs were delivered alongside non-profit development activities. While no explicit reference was made to CSR during that period, it has been observed that SOEs' social services amounted to the closest activity to CSR at that time (Fiaschi et al., 2015). In Confucianism, the ultimate objective of an individual is to acquire *ren* – the characteristic of being human – and to develop into a "superior person" through contributing to a harmonious society (Wang & Juslin, 2009). A similar principle has been applied to business ethics in China, where the custom is to operate profitable business based on moral principles.

That is to say, profits should come from harmonious businesses. This is the primary reason why Chinese businesses are involved "with" the society; and it is also the primary reason why businesses should engage in CSR. The pursuit of Confucian morality has led many Chinese companies to focus heavily on CSR activities at the level of a harmonious relationship between businesses and the society, while lacking attention to other stakeholders, such as the natural environment (Yu & Choi, 2016). Moreover, it is well acknowledged that the Chinese cultural framework is more relational than rule-based. Aside from managerial affiliations (a sort of personal connection), there is a type of relationship unique to the Chinese setting – state ownership – which is developed at the business level. Thus, China is widely acknowledged as a relational economy in which *guanxi* is more critical to economic success than it is in a rule-based economy (Xin & Pearce, 1996). This unique feature of Chinese organizational culture also shapes the CSR orientations of firms with different levels of governmental ties (Gu et al., 2013).

Modern CSR has roots in Western economies, where its practices have developed extensively in the last two decades. The concept has been exported to other parts of the world mainly through the activities of MNEs. Globalization and technological advancements, particularly in communication, have aided the spread of these concepts to Australasia, Asia, and the Far East, with varying degrees of success and unique challenges (Gugler & Shi, 2009). After decades of rapid economic growth, China started to face the adverse effects of swift economic development during the mid-1990s, including water resource depletion, land degradation, loss of biodiversity, and greenhouse gas emissions (Wang & Juslin, 2009). For example, many heavy industrial and manufacturing enterprises exploit the environment for short-term gains due to myopic vision, which impedes Chinese businesses' sustainable development (Zu & Song, 2009). At the beginning of the 21st century, environmental pollution resulting from urbanization and industrialization posed a severe challenge and stimulated an ecological crisis (Kahn & Yardley, 2007). Furthermore, use of under-aged workers in illegal brick kilns and iron and coal mines came under intense scrutiny from both global and local media (Tang & Li, 2009).

Along with these changes, the Chinese economy became more internationalized, as illustrated in the country joining the WTO in 2001, and increasingly vulnerable to international scrutiny, owing in no small part to criticism aimed at Chinese companies operating abroad (Lin, 2010). This propelled CSR to the top of the government's priorities, and it has been a hot topic in the Chinese academic and policy circles since 2004 (Fiaschi et al., 2015). At the same time, thanks to sellers and brand owners from developed countries from the mid-1990s to the early years of the 21st century, the Chinese companies and society started to pay attention to CSR and developed CSR implementation requirements, standards, and structures for international procurement.

Chinese businesses began to embrace CSR factory audits imposed by multinational corporations. Meanwhile, academic research on CSR burgeoned, and scholars incorporated general theoretical findings and practical experience primarily from the West to establish a theoretical framework for CSR with Chinese characteristics (Lau et al., 2016). With rapid modernization and economic growth, Chinese firms gradually shifted away from a solely profit-maximizing philosophy toward a more business-ethical philosophy (Hu et al., 2017). CSR was rapidly emerging but the concept was relatively new in China at that stage (Bai et al., 2015). Although several large MNEs introduced the concept of CSR to the Chinese public, the lack of legal enforcement and professional guidance resulted in weak implementation by most Chinese firms.

Roughly from the year 2000 to 2006, CSR began to attract widespread attention in China. The Chinese government gradually guaranteed the development of CSR at the level of the legal system. Previous studies point out that the 2002 "Conference on Labor Relations and Corporate Social Responsibility under Globalization" in Beijing resulted in China's first practical agenda for socially responsible production and marketing practices (Tang & Li, 2009). At that time, CSR was regarded as raising awareness of the need for national ratification and compliance with international conventions and agreements (Utting & Marques, 2009). In 2005, President Hu Jintao suggested the idea of "harmonious society" as a guiding principle for policymakers and the private sector. A harmonious society is one that "gives full play to modern ideas like democracy, the rule of law, fairness, justice, vitality, stability, orderliness, and harmonious coexistence between humanity and nature" (See, 2009, p. 2). This vision became synonymous with modern CSR in the Chinese Communist Party rhetoric (Lin, 2010). In 2006, the government proposed the development of a harmonious society that would include a democratic rule of law, fairness and justice, honesty and friendship, an energetic atmosphere, well-organized practices, and harmonious coexistence between human and nature. China's CSR grew rapidly in line with the country's scientific growth strategy and the "harmonious society" policy. The concept of CSR was first documented in the Company Law of the PRC in 2006. Under Article 5 of the Company Law, companies' business operations must abide by laws and regulations, observe social and commercial morality, remain honest and trustworthy, accept supervision from the government and the social public, bear social responsibility, and guarantee legal corporate protection free from infringement.

Two Chinese stock exchanges (Shenzhen and Shanghai) also took actions to promote CSR disclosures by listed firms. In 2006, the first "Guidelines for Social Responsibility of Listed Companies" were issued by the Shenzhen Stock Exchange, advocating that listed companies must actively assume social responsibility for their business operations. In 2008, the Shanghai Stock Exchange mandated certain listed companies (those listed on the Shanghai Stock Exchange Corporate Governance Index, those listed overseas, and those in the financial sector) to issue CSR reports. At the end of 2007, the State-Owned Assets Supervision and Administration Commission (SASAC) issued its "Guiding Opinions on the Implementation of Social Responsibilities of Central Enterprises" to encourage the CEs supervised by the SASAC to participate in CSR reporting, with the objective of stressing their exemplary role in enacting the government's CSR agenda, and outlining the principles and implementation of CSR measures (Gao, 2011; Lin, 2010). The introduction of relevant policies promoted the development of CSR for CEs in China. As CSR frameworks and guidelines were extended to support companies in their efforts to become more sustainable, many Chinese firms responded to these demands and implemented various sustainability initiatives in their business operations, with growing numbers implementing and disclosing CSR initiatives (Jamali et al., 2017; Tang & Tang, 2012). At the same time, Chinese enterprises began to follow Western concepts, theories, regulations, and codes of conduct for CSR (Xu & Yang, 2010).[1] In addition, many Chinese firms became more aware of the importance of CSR issues and sought recognition as responsible corporate citizens by actively undertaking CSR activities.

In summary, the Chinese government has played a critical role in promoting and influencing the country's CSR agenda and setting the boundaries of permissible CSR issues in China, while other stakeholders seem to have played only a minor role in this process (Liu & Tian, 2021). Although most government guidelines are not mandatory, they do indicate which areas are deemed to be important for corporate attention (Marquis & Qian, 2014).

In the past few decades, China has been playing an increasingly important role on the international stage and has attracted worldwide attention (Wong, 2009). Growing numbers of Chinese companies are now among the largest MNEs from developing countries, owing to the government's opening-up policies since the late 1970s. Meanwhile, excessive energy consumption due to rapid economic growth has led to a shortage of resources in China, resulting in severe ecological problems (Moon & Shen, 2010). Moreover, as Chinese companies have started to expand their business operations overseas, their labor and environmental practices in overseas markets have been challenged and examined by both domestic and global stakeholders. Thus, the increasing public attention paid to CSR issues has raised society's expectation that Chinese firms must meet local and global CSR standards while having more positive social impacts on the community. The last few decades have witnessed frequent neglect of CSR by Chinese MNEs in overseas markets. For instance, in 2006, local workers in China's Shougang Group (Steel Group) in Peru went on a three-week strike demanding a salary raise. The strike was not called off until Shougang agreed to implement a pay rise stipulated by Peruvian non-governmental organizations (NGOs). Also, at Zambia's Chambishi Copper Mine, Chinese investors were heavily criticized for their non-compliance with Zambian labor and environmental standards.

In an era of globalization, CSR reaches far beyond the interests of a single business or nation. MNEs have substantial and fundamental global impacts on all three components of the global economy – society, people, and environment – while sustainable development is a shared human interest and overarching objective. Since Chinese MNEs are increasingly competing in a global market, their business practices are progressively becoming subject to international industry regulations and standards. Their conceptualizations, practices, and reporting of CSR are shaped by complicated interactions among corporations,

NGOs, governments, and a broad spectrum of stakeholders in the Chinese society, as well as institutional pressure from both domestic and global communities. Table 4.1 summarizes the various forces affecting Chinese MNEs' overseas CSR practices.

Previous studies have raised various concerns about the CSR reporting practices of Chinese MNEs operating in overseas markets. Since the majority of Belt and Road Initiative (BRI) host countries are developing and less-developed countries, institutional voids and lack of socio-political structures and facilitators of market operations (Falkenberg & Brunsæl, 2011; Yin & Zhang,

Table 4.1 Various forces affecting overseas CSR practices of Chinese MNEs

	Overseas CSR practices of Chinese MNEs	
	Achievements	*Challenges*
Local forces	CSR is becoming more widely recognized in China, with a growing number of Chinese MNEs recognizing the definition and importance of CSR (Miska et al., 2016).	Lack of professionals, financial assistance and incentive, or punishment systems for CSR implementation in overseas markets.
	The government has established policies to encourage Chinese companies to fulfill their social responsibilities overseas.	The majority of overseas CSR regulations issued by the Chinese government are voluntary (See, 2009).
International forces	More and more Chinese MNEs are complying with international CSR standards such as GRI and ISO in overseas markets to enhance global reputation (Chen & Liu, 2019).	Trade associations, news media, international organizations, and NGOs expect better CSR performance and reporting.
	Many Chinese MNEs have joined international CSR-related alliances and participated in various sustainable development summits (Chen & Liu, 2019).	Greater accountability and transparency are expected in environmental impact information (Yang et al., 2020).
Host-country forces	Chinese MNEs' current OFDI promotes mutual benefits and win-win outcomes in host countries.[2]	Chinese MNEs' knowledge of local standards and guidelines on sustainable development needs to be enhanced (Cheng, 2016).
	The BRI emphasizes sustainable development for both host countries and China (Al-Hasni, 2019).	
	Positive spillover effect of good CSR practices by Chinese MNEs in host countries.	Institutional voids and lack of socio-political structures and facilitators of market operations in developing host countries may motivate neglect of CSR.

2012) may present both opportunities and challenges for the overseas CSR practices of Chinese MNEs. On the one hand, as "big corporations should solve big problems" (Prahalad & Hammond, 2002, p. 58), Chinese MNEs may have positive spillover effects on host countries' CSR practices while promoting economic growth through OFDI and contributing to local welfare on a par with their power and wealth (Chen & Liu, 2019; Déniz-Déniz & García-Falcón, 2002). Furthermore, the BRI does not pursue solely economic interests but is based on the principle of "Consultation, Contribution and Shared Benefits", which emphasizes sustainable development for both host countries and China (Al-Hasni, 2019). Given the pliability of the BRI, there are opportunities for all stakeholders to advocate the institutionalization of best practices and adoption of a high-road approach to social, labor, and environmental standards along the BRI. Thus, fulfilling social responsibility has become a key strategy in Chinese enterprises' internationalization. The concept of CSR also hints at public expectations of a more significant role for giant corporations in the social domain.

On the other hand, most less-developed countries along the BRI lack compulsory CSR regulations and powerful regulatory mechanisms for MNEs. In fact, previous literature suggests that emerging markets may engage in CSR practices for profit maximization (Reimann et al., 2012). For example, some developing countries strive to maintain relaxed and favorable fiscal policies and legal frameworks to promote FDI and technology transfer. However, lack of sufficiently robust fiscal policies and legal frameworks makes it hard to regulate MNEs and protect the environment and social rights (Yin & Jamali, 2016). MNEs may take advantage of the institutional void to set up low-cost production facilities that are less environmentally friendly. Thus, the above-mentioned institutional voids may motivate MNEs' neglect of CSR.

The BRI's primary aim is to build infrastructure for connectivity in Belt and Road economies (Fang & Nolan, 2019). However, environmental degradation and climate change have emerged as major global concerns (Cheng, 2016). Whether the BRI can be implemented in an environmentally friendly and sustainable manner is of international interest. Beijing has released several official documents and statements in response to increased publicity (Huang, 2016). The "Guiding Opinions on Promoting Green Construction of the Belt and Road Initiative" were published in 2017, and the idea of the "Green Belt and Road" was implemented. As the world's biggest emitter of greenhouse gases, China signed the Paris Agreement in 2016, vowing to reduce carbon emissions to combat climate change. The "Green Investment Principles for the Belt and Road Initiative" were also revealed at the second Belt and Road Forum in 2019. China's focus on sustainability for the BRI is unparalleled in Beijing's growth narratives. This suggests changing circumstances and perceptions of the sustainability-development relationship, which are rooted in China's economic circumstances and reflect the country's foreign strategy.

The BRI proposed by the Chinese government at the end of 2013 provides a rare research opportunity to examine the quality of Chinese MNEs' CSR reporting in overseas markets. The BRI has become an institution for improving bilateral and multilateral trade and investments and fostering independent and high-quality regional cooperation (Ramasamy & Yeung, 2019). Given the unprecedented scale of the BRI, academics and civil society organizations have expressed concern about its actual and potential negative environmental impacts. Most research on the BRI has so far concentrated on its geopolitical and geoeconomic ramifications, emphasizing the issue of international order (Gao, 2011; Liu & Dunford, 2016). Scholars broadly agree that the BRI will rewrite the existing geopolitical landscape if introduced as expected. However, environmental concerns have received less attention, and research on environmental governance problems and institutional frameworks that have arisen as a result of the BRI remains limited (Hughes & Scheyvens, 2020).

Institutional CSR governing Chinese MNEs

The Chinese government has released a number of official documents and statements encouraging Chinese companies to invest abroad with good policies and practices. For example, in 2006, the State Council issued its "Opinions on Encouraging and Standardizing Outward Investment Cooperation", which include nine guiding principles for Chinese overseas investment.[3] The first principle emphasizes the importance of "mutual advantage" and "win-win cooperation" with host countries. The fifth principle requires Chinese investors to obey local laws and regulations, insist on openness, fairness, and transparency in contracting projects, keep their promises, fulfill necessary social responsibilities, protect the legitimate rights and interests of local employees, pay attention to environmental resource protection, and care for and support the livability of local communities. The seventh principle emphasizes the importance of "a responsibility framework for improving healthy production" and "strengthening safety preparation".

At least two other relevant Chinese central government documents reiterate these broad concepts. In 2006, the MOFCOM and the All-China Federation of Industry and Commerce (ACFIC) jointly issued the "Opinions on Encouraging and Supporting Privately Owned Enterprises 'Going Out'", which specifically state that enterprises should be aware of their social responsibility, comply with local laws and regulations, respect local customs and habits, and realize common development through mutually beneficial cooperation.[4] In addition, in 2008, the State Council issued the "Management Measures for International Contractors", which state that Chinese contractors must comply with the laws of the countries or regions where the projects are located, uphold contracts, respect local customs and habits, stress ecological and environmental protection, and promote local economic and social development.[5] In 2009, MOFCOM released its "Management Measures for Overseas Investment", which stipulate that Chinese enterprises must recognize and comply with all applicable domestic and international laws, regulations, and policies, as well as obeying the principles of mutual benefit and win-win.[6] Furthermore, in 2010, MOFCOM, in collaboration with several other Chinese ministries, released the "Regulations on Safety

Management of Overseas Chinese-funded Enterprises and their Employees". These regulations require Chinese companies doing business abroad to take their social obligations seriously, perform well in environmental protection, address local job issues, and actively engage in public welfare projects.[7]

The major regulations and guidelines governing the CSR performance of Chinese MNEs in overseas markets are summarized in Table 4.2. All of these guidelines and opinions are applicable and critical to promoting responsible Chinese OFDI, but they are very broad in scope, provide little specific guidance, and can be difficult to translate from policy to practice. However, as an increasing number of Chinese government initiatives are providing more substantive and sector-specific guidelines on how Chinese businesses should invest responsibly, this problem may be alleviated gradually.

The official BRI guidelines, "Vision and Actions on Jointly Building Silk Road Economic Belt and Twenty-First-Century Maritime Silk Road" (hereafter "Vision and Actions"), issued by China's National Development and Reform Commission (NDRC), Ministry of Foreign Affairs (MFA), and Ministry of Commerce (MOFMOC), list five cooperation priorities, as well as the BRI's major goals of policy coordination, infrastructure connectivity, unimpeded trade, financial integration, and connecting people. Almost all of the main BRI targets inspire and require Chinese MNEs to engage actively in sustainable development in overseas markets (Fang & Nolan, 2019). For example, with regard to "unimpeded trade", the "Vision and Actions" suggest that "We support localized operation and management of Chinese companies to boost the local economy, increase local employment, improve local livelihoods, and take social responsibility for protecting local biodiversity and eco-environments". For the goal of "connecting people", the "Vision and Actions" require that "We should organize public interest activities concerning education, healthcare, poverty reduction, biodiversity and ecological protection for the benefit of the general public, and improve the production and living conditions of poverty-stricken areas along the Belt and Road". Thus, China is now stepping up its efforts to mainstream this policy model in overseas markets (Belt & Road Portal, 2017).

The Chinese government has developed a complex institutional framework for sustainable development for MNEs, especially in the context of the BRI. In addition to government-issued guidelines, industrial organizations and business networks have issued various sustainable development guidelines for overseas business operations (see Table 4.2). The BRI's two main policy documents are the "Vision and Actions", published in 2015, and the "Concept for Maritime Cooperation under the Belt and Road Initiative",[33] published in 2017 (National Development and Reform Commission, 2015; Xinhua, 2017). Both state that the BRI should increase exchanges and collaboration on environmental protection and demonstrate China's determination to improve corporate environmental governance under the initiative. Notably, CSR-related regulations and directives for Chinese MNEs are mostly voluntary and, unlike enforceable laws and regulations, they primarily define aspirational objectives and visions. In other words, China engages stakeholders from BRI host countries proactively through soft

Table 4.2 CSR regulations for Chinese MNEs

Regulation	Issuing department	Year
Guiding Policy for Industries Investing Overseas[8]	Ministry of Commerce (MOFCOM), NDRC, Ministry of Foreign Affairs (MOFA), Ministry of Finance (MOF), General Administration of Customs (GAC), State Administration of Taxation (SAT), State Administration of Foreign Exchange (SAFE)	2006
Opinions of Encouraging and Standardizing Outward Investment Cooperation[9]	State Council	2006
Opinions of Encouraging and Supporting Privately Owned Enterprises "Going Out"[10]	All-China Federation of Industry and Commerce (ACFIC), MOFCOM	2006
Guidelines for Sustainable Forest Cultivation of Chinese Enterprises Overseas[11]	State Forestry Administration (SFA), MOFCOM	2007
Management Measures for International Contractors[12]	State Council	2008
Management Measures for International Investment[13]	MOFCOM	2009
A Guide on Sustainable Overseas Forests Management and Utilization by Chinese Enterprises[14]	SFA, MOFCOM	2009
Regulations on Safety Management of Overseas Chinese-funded Enterprises and their Employees[15]	MOFCOM, MOFA, NDRC, Ministry of Public Security (MPS), SASAC, State Administration of Work Safety (SAWS), and ACFIC	2010
Guide on Social Responsibility for Chinese International Contractors[16]	China International Contractors Association (CHINCA)	2012
Guidelines on Environmental Protection for Overseas Investment and Cooperation[17]	MOFCOM, Ministry of Environmental Protection (MEP)	2013
Measures for the Administration of Overseas Investment[18]	MOFCOM	2014
Chinese Due Diligence Guidelines for Responsible Mineral Supply Chains[19]	China Chamber of Commerce for Import and Export of Metals, Minerals and Chemicals (CCCMC)	2016
Measures for the Supervision and Administration of Overseas Investments by Central Enterprises[20]	SASAC	2017
Code of Conduct for Private Enterprises' Overseas Investment and Operation[21]	NDRC, MOFMOC, People's Bank of China, MFA	2017

(Continued)

Table 4.2 CSR regulations for Chinese MNEs (Continued)

Regulation	Issuing department	Year
Guidelines for Social Responsibility in Outbound Mining Investments[22]	CCCMC	2017
Guidelines for Overseas Sustainable Infrastructure Projects of Chinese Enterprises[23]	China Association of Foreign Contractors (CAFC)	2017
Code of Conduct for Private Enterprise Foreign Investment Management[24]	NDRC	2017
Vision and Actions on Jointly Building Silk Road Economic Belt and 21st Century Maritime Silk Road[25]	NDRC, MFA, MOFCOM	2015–2017
Building the Belt and Road: Concepts, Practices, and China's Contributions[26]	NDRC, MFA, MOFCOM	
Guiding Opinions on Promoting the Construction of Green One Belt One Road[27]	NDRC, MFA, MOFCOM, MEP	
Concept for Maritime Cooperation under the Belt and Road Initiative[28]	NDRC, State Oceanic Administration (SOA)	
The Belt and Road Ecological and Environmental Cooperation Plan[29]	NDRC, MFA, MOFCOM, MEP	
Vision and Actions on Agriculture Cooperation in Jointly Building Silk Road Economic Belt and 21st Century Maritime Silk Road[30]	NDRC, MFA, MOFCOM	
Vision and Actions on Energy Cooperation in Jointly Building Silk Road Economic Belt and 21st Century Maritime Silk Road[31]	NDRC, National Energy Board (NEB)	
Measures for the Administration of Overseas Investment of Enterprises[32]	NDRC	2018

legislation, which ensures that almost all BRI-specific laws originate from legally non-binding informal documents rather than formal treaties (Wang, 2019).

In addition to its basic BRI guidelines, China has established a broader governance framework to direct and oversee investments in overseas markets. Many laws regulating the conduct and reporting of state-owned and private Chinese companies operating abroad predate the BRI. Concerns about Chinese companies' environmental activities abroad have prompted the Chinese government to establish a range of policies and measures requiring compliance with host-country laws and regulations.

There is currently no specific legislation controlling environmental issues in Chinese overseas investments (Parente et al., 2019). Several government departments have released policy recommendations outlining voluntary environmental conservation initiatives (see Table 4.2). For example, the "Guidelines on Environmental Protection for Overseas Investment and Cooperation" (2013) encourage but do not mandate, Chinese companies operating abroad to perform environmental impact assessments (EIAs), even though in China, EIAs have been legally required since 2003 for all construction projects and proposals with possible environmental impacts (Zhu & Ru, 2008). As a result, while corporations may be held liable for their future impacts within China, the Chinese government does not impose sanctions on their operations outside China. Thus, CSR regulations for Chinese MNEs in overseas markets also depend on host countries' institutional environments, laws, regulations, and the power of international and local NGOs.

Pressures on Chinese MNEs' CSR reporting

The rapid rise of Chinese MNEs around the world, as shown by how they did on the Fortune Global 500 list, their aggressive internationalization strategies, and the success of global brands like Lenovo and Huawei, shows how important their CSR practices are. The business practices of Chinese MNEs not only cause externalities for consumers, employees, and societies domestically, but also across borders.

CSR is becoming a strategic factor that affects the competitiveness of corporations and, consequently, the competitiveness of the nations or regions in which they operate. Companies are required to adhere to "international" CSR regulations in order to obtain a "passport" to the international market, which makes the firms' ability to respond to CSR regulatory constraints an increasingly crucial aspect in preserving their global competitiveness. Due to their dual embeddedness, MNEs must obtain legitimacy in both their home country and their host country (Beddewela, 2019; Hamprecht & Schwarzkopf, 2014). MNEs operate in diverse institutional environments (Cantwell et al., 2010); therefore, they must not only consider institutional pressure from their home nations but also cope with varying degrees of institutional pressure from their host countries. Additionally, CSR places Chinese MNEs in a disadvantageous position vis-à-vis their Western counterparts in global competition. Adherence to accepted CSR principles has become so common among global firms that, in order to compete successfully, MNEs from China and other transition economies may also need to adopt similar practices.

Since Chinese MNEs operate on a global scale in various institutional contexts, their reporting practices can serve as a test bed for determining the degree of standardization. In fact, due to internal constraints for consistency across multiple subsidiaries, they may serve as natural homogenization platforms for adopting and disseminating global norms and eradicating national peculiarities (Fortanier et al., 2011, p. 671). On the other hand, Chinese MNEs preserve a strong national identity and build tight ties with governments and other stakeholders in their countries of origin. In fact, China's state-owned or -controlled businesses are excellent examples of companies with demonstrable ties to domestic institutions.

In recent years, however, a number of nations have begun to view the internationalization of their own firms in certain nations as a strategic tool for achieving geopolitical and other national objectives (Li et al., 2022). China's BRI, the G-7's Build Back Better World, and the Asia-Africa Growth Corridor led by India and Japan are examples of such endeavors. In terms of institutional pressure from host nations, BRI destinations are predominantly in developing nations where CSR reporting is not frequently practiced (Attig et al., 2016; Marano & Kostova, 2016). Given the poor legal environment for CSR reporting, Chinese MNEs are striving to attain political legitimacy that is closely linked with the norms and expectations established by the Chinese government and host nations. Based on the belief that responding to government signals and exhibiting conformance with national aims is a type of non-market strategy that can achieve political legitimacy (Luo et al., 2017; Marquis & Qian, 2014), we propose the following.

The impact of Chinese MNEs' international expansion on the caliber of their CSR reports is significantly shaped by institutional pressure for CSR reporting from the home country. The Chinese central government recognizes the legitimacy and significance of the BRI, as evidenced by the country's 13th and 14th Five-Year Plans and the 2015 formation of the "Leading Group on the BRI Task" to coordinate Chinese FDI in BRI countries. Local governments (such as provincial and municipal governments) also positively respond by supporting the BRI's implementation (Chen et al., 2019; Li et al., 2019). Participating in this program by investing in BRI nations can show how a Chinese company is in line with the nation's ambitions and could enhance its ties to the national and local governments of China. In addition to SOEs that are tasked with implementing government objectives, non-state enterprises are often active in responding proactively to the call of the government in order to receive preferential treatment from various levels of government (Du & Zhang, 2018). However, China's development suffers from "a lack of clear regulations, a loose and corrupt enforcement system, and poor oversight at different levels" (Tan, 2009, p. 175). In this institutional instability, philanthropy may replace other CSR practices, including a more institutionalized and impact assessment-oriented approach to stakeholder management for Chinese MNEs. Indeed, the importance of philanthropy has been identified as a recurring theme in CSR reports of Chinese companies (Jamali & Mirshak, 2007; Tang & Li, 2009), which may be the specificity of CSR in China. On the other hand, China is striving to develop an internationally recognized system of CSR reporting standards, and the subsequent chapters in this book aim to look into the extent of "Chinese specificity" in CSR awareness, practices, and reporting among Chinese MNEs under the BRI scenario.

Notes

1 For example, major CSR-related standards and guidelines have been adopted from the West, such as SA8000, WRAP, and ISO standards, whereas a few Chinese local CSR standards such as CSC9000T are still being developed (Tang & Li, 2009).
2 White Paper on China's Peaceful Development, Information Office of the State Council, September 6, 2011.
3 State Council (2006). *Opinions on Encouraging and Regulating Foreign Investment and Cooperation of Chinese Enterprises*. Retrieved from http://www.gov.cn/ldhd/2006-10/25/content_423660.htm [only available in Chinese].
4 MOFCOM & ACFIC (2016). *Opinions on Encouraging and Supporting Private Enterprises to "Go Global"*. Retrieved from http://www.mofcom.gov.cn/aarticle/b/g/200604/20060401829430.html [only available in Chinese].
5 State Council (2008). *Regulations on the Administration of Foreign Contracted Projects, State Council Order No. 527*. Retrieved from http://www.gov.cn/flfg/2008-07/28/content_1058146.htm [only available in Chinese].
6 MOFCOM (2009). *Measures for the Administration of Overseas Investment, Ministry of Commerce Order No. 5 of 2009*. Retrieved from http://www.mofcom.gov.cn/aarticle/b/c/200903/20090306103210.html [only available in Chinese].
7 MOFCOM, MOFA, NDRC, Ministry of Public Security, SASAC, State Administration of Work Safety & ACFIC (2010). *Regulations on Security Management of Establishments and Personnel of Chinese Enterprises Abroad*. Retrieved from http://www.mofcom.gov.cn/article/b/bf/201008/20100807087099.html [only available in Chinese].
8 NDRC, MOFCOM, MOFA MOF, GAC, SAT & SAFE (2006). *Industrial Guidance Policy for Overseas Investment, NDRC Foreign Investment*. Retrieved from http://tradeinservices.mofcom.gov.cn/article/zhengce/hyfg/201710/447.html.
9 State Council (2006). *Opinions on Encouraging and Regulating Foreign Investment and Cooperation by Chinese Enterprises*. Retrieved from http://www.gov.cn/ldhd/2006-10/25/content_423660.htm [only available in Chinese].
10 MOFCOM & ACFIC (2006). *Opinions on Encouraging and Supporting Private Enterprises to "Go Global"*. Retrieved from http://www.mofcom.gov.cn/aarticle/b/g/200604/20060401829430.html [only available in Chinese].
11 SFA & MOFCOM (2007). *Guidelines for Sustainable Forest Cultivation of Chinese Enterprises Overseas*. Retrieved from http://www.mofcom.gov.cn/aarticle/b/g/200712/20071205265858.html [only available in Chinese].
12 State Council (2008). *Regulations on the Administration of Foreign Contracted Projects*. Retrieved from http://www.gov.cn/flfg/2008-07/28/content_1058146.htm [only available in Chinese].
13 MOFCOM (2009). *Measures for the Administration of Overseas Investment, Ministry of Commerce Order No. 5 of 2009*. Retrieved from http://www.mofcom.gov.cn/aarticle/b/c/200903/20090306103210.html [only available in Chinese].

64 CSR Reporting and Chinese MNEs

14 SFA & MOFCOM (2009). *Guidelines for Sustainable Management and Use of Overseas Forests by Chinese Enterprises.* Retrieved from http://www.forestry.gov.cn/portal/main/s/224/content-401396.html [only available in Chinese].
15 MOFCOM, MOFA, NDRC, Ministry of Public Security, SASAC, State Administration of Work Safety & ACFIC (2010). *Regulations on Security Management of Establishments and Personnel of Chinese Enterprises Abroad.* Retrieved from http://www.mofcom.gov.cn/article/b/bf/201008/20100807087099.html (only available in Chinese).
16 CHINCA (2012). *Guidelines on Social Responsibility in China's Foreign Contracting Industry, September 2012.* Retrieved from http://images.mofcom.gov.cn/hzs/accessory/201209/1348819602840.pdf [only available in Chinese].
17 MOFCOM & MEP (2013). *Guidelines on Environmental Protection for Outbound Investment Cooperation.* Retrieved from http://www.mofcom.gov.cn/article/b/bf/201302/20130200039930.html [only available in Chinese].
18 MOFCOM (2014). *Measures for the Administration of Overseas Investment.* Retrieved from http://www.mofcom.gov.cn/article/b/c/201409/20140900723361.shtml [only available in Chinese].
19 CCCMC (2016). *Chinese Due Diligence Guidelines for Responsible Mineral Supply Chains.* Retrieved from http://www.cccmc.org.cn/docs/2015-10/20151029133444202482.pdf [only available in Chinese].
20 SASAC (2017). *Measures for the Supervision and Administration of Overseas Investments by Central Enterprises.* Retrieved from http://www.sasac.gov.cn/n2588035/n2588320/n2588335/c4258448/content.html [only available in Chinese].
21 NDRC, MOFMOC, People's Bank of China & MFA (2017). Retrieved from https://www.ndrc.gov.cn/fggz/lywzjw/zcfg/201712/t20171218_1047049.html [only available in Chinese].
22 CCCMC (2017). *Guidelines for Social Responsibility in Outbound Mining Investments.* Retrieved from http://www.cccmc.org.cn/docs/2014-10/20141029161135692190.pdf.
23 CAFC (2017). *Guidelines for Overseas Sustainable Infrastructure Projects of Chinese Enterprises.* Retrieved from http://images.mofcom.gov.cn/csr/201706/20170622120613935.pdf.
24 CAFC (2017). *Guidelines for Overseas Sustainable Infrastructure Projects of Chinese Enterprises.* Retrieved from http://images.mofcom.gov.cn/csr/201706/20170622120613935.pdf.
25 NDRC, MFA & MOFCOM (2015). *Vision and Actions on Jointly Building Silk Road Economic Belt and 21st-Century Maritime Silk Road.* Retrieved from http://www.lawinfochina.com/display.aspx?id=144&lib=dbref&SearchKeyword=&SearchCKeyword=&EncodingName=gb2312.
26 NDRC, MOFCOM & MFA (2017). *Build The All Along: Idea. Practice and China's Contribution.* Retrieved from https://www.abebooks.de/servlet/BookDetailsPL?bi=22637415620&cm_sp=rec-_-pd_hw_i_1-_-bdp&reftag=pd_hw_i_1
27 NDRC, MOFCOM, MFA & MEP (2017). *Guiding Opinions on Promoting the Construction of Green "One Belt One Road".* Retrieved from https://www.mee.gov.cn/gkml/hbb/bwj/201705/t20170505_413602.htm [only available in Chinese].
28 NDRC & SOA (2017). *Concept for Maritime Cooperation under the Belt and Road Initiative.* Retrieved from http://www.gov.cn/xinwen/2017-11/17/content_5240325.htm [only available in Chinese].
29 NDRC, MFA, MOFCOM & MEP (2017). *"One Belt One Road" Ecological Environmental Protection Cooperation Plan.* Retrieved from http://www.mee.gov.cn/gkml/hbb/bwj/201705/W020170516330272025970.pdf [only available in Chinese].

30 NDRC, MFA & MOFCOM (2017). *Vision and Actions on Agriculture Cooperation in Jointly Building Silk Road Economic Belt and 21st Century Maritime Silk Road*. Retrieved from http://cpc.people.com.cn/n/2015/0328/c64387-26764810.html [only available in Chinese].
31 NDRC & NEB (2017). *Vision and Actions on Energy Cooperation in Jointly Building Silk Road Economic Belt and 21st Century Maritime Silk Road*. Retrieved from http://www.nea.gov.cn/2017-05/12/c_136277473.htm (only available in Chinese).
32 NDRC (2018). *Measures for the Administration of Overseas Investment of Enterprises*. Retrieved from https://www.ndrc.gov.cn/fggz/lywzjw/zcfg/201712/W020190909440825920640.pdf [only available in Chinese].
33 In order to further strengthen strategic docking and joint actions with countries along the BRI and protect the ocean and marine resources, the National Development and Reform Commission and the State Oceanic Administration formulated and issued the "Concept for Maritime Cooperation under the Belt and Road Initiative" in 2017.

References

Al-Hasni, H. (2019). The role of China's public diplomacy in promoting the belt and road initiative in Oman through communication: An examination of the integrated model of public diplomacy. *Global Media Journal*, 17(32), 1–10.

Aras, G., & Crowther, D. (2009). Corporate sustainability reporting: A study in disingenuity? *Journal of Business Ethics*, 87(1), 279–288.

Attig, N., Boubakri, N., El Ghoul, S., & Guedhami, O. (2016). Firm internationalization and corporate social responsibility. *Journal of Business Ethics*, 134, 171–197.

Bai, C., Sarkis, J., & Dou, Y. (2015). Corporate sustainability development in China: Review and analysis. *Industrial Management & Data Systems*, 115(1), 5–40.

Beddewela, E. (2019). Managing corporate community responsibility in multinational corporations: Resolving institutional duality. *Long Range Planning*, 52(6), 101911.

Belt and Road Portal. (2017). *Guidance on promoting green belt and road*. https://eng.yidaiyilu.gov.cn/zchj/qwfb/12479.htm

Cantwell, J., Dunning, J. H., & Lundan, S. M. (2010). An evolutionary approach to understanding international business activity: The co-evolution of MNEs and the institutional environment. *Journal of International Business Studies*, 41(4), 567–586.

Carroll, A. B. (1979). A three-dimensional model of corporate social responsibility. *Academy of Management Review*, 4(2), 497–505.

Chen, J., Fei, Y., Lee, P. T. W., & Tao, X. (2019). Overseas port investment policy for China's Central and local governments in the belt and road initiative. *Journal of Contemporary China*, 28(116), 196–215.

Chen, J., & Liu, W. (2019). The belt and road strategy in international business and administration: Corporate social responsibility. In W. Liu, Z. Zhang, & J. X. Chen (Eds.), *The belt and road strategy in international business and administration* (pp. 28–51). IGI Global.

Cheng, L. K. (2016). Three questions on China's "belt and road initiative". *China Economic Review*, 40, 309–313.

Crowther, D. (2000). Corporate reporting, stakeholders and the internet: Mapping the new corporate landscape. *Urban Studies*, 37(10), 1837–1848.

Déniz-Déniz, M. D. L. C., & García-Falcón, J. M. (2002). Determinants of the multinationals' social response. Empirical application to international companies operating in Spain. *Journal of Business Ethics, 38*(4), 339–370.

Du, J., & Zhang, Y. (2018). Does one belt one road initiative promote Chinese overseas direct investment? *China Economic Review, 47*, 189–205.

Falkenberg, J., & Brunsæl, P. (2011). Corporate social responsibility: A strategic advantage or a strategic necessity. *Journal of Business Ethics, 99*(1), 9–16.

Fang, C., & Nolan, P. (Eds.). (2019). *Routledge handbook of the belt and road*. Routledge.

Fiaschi, D., Giuliani, E., & Nieri, F. (2015). BRIC companies seeking legitimacy through corporate social responsibility. *UNCTAD Transnational Corporations, 22*(3), 5–42.

Fortanier, F., Kolk, A., & Pinkse, J. (2011). Harmonization in CSR reporting. *Management International Review, 51*(5), 665–696.

Gao, Y. (2011). CSR in an emerging country: A content analysis of CSR reports of listed companies. *Baltic Journal of Management, 6*(2), 263–291.

Gugler, P., & Shi, J. Y. (2009). Corporate social responsibility for developing country multinational corporations: Lost war in pertaining global competitiveness? *Journal of Business Ethics, 87*(1), 3–24.

Gu, H., Ryan, C., Bin, L., & Wei, G. (2013). Political connections, guanxi and adoption of CSR policies in the Chinese hotel industry: Is there a link. *Tourism Management, 34*, 231–235.

Hamprecht, J., & Schwarzkopf, J. (2014). Subsidiary initiatives in the institutional environment. *Management International Review, 54*(5), 757–778.

Hu, D., Ou, J., & Hu, X. (2017). On the environmental responsibility of Chinese enterprises for their FDIs in countries within the one belt and one road initiative. *The Chinese Journal of Comparative Law, 5*(1), 36–57.

Huang, Y. (2016). Understanding China's belt & road initiative: Motivation, framework and assessment. *China Economic Review, 40*, 314–321.

Hughes, E., & Scheyvens, R. (2020). Corporate social responsibility in tourism post-2015: A development first approach. In *Tourism and Sustainable Development Goals* (pp. 74–87). Routledge.

Jamali, D., & Karam, C. (2018). Corporate social responsibility in developing countries as an emerging field of study. *International Journal of Management Reviews, 20*(1), 32–61.

Jamali, D., Karam, C., Yin, J., & Soundararajan, V. (2017). CSR logics in developing countries: Translation, adaptation and stalled development. *Journal of World Business, 52*(3), 343–359.

Jamali, D., & Mirshak, R. (2007). Corporate social responsibility (CSR): Theory and practice in a developing country context. *Journal of Business Ethics, 72*(3), 243–262.

Kahn, J., & Yardley, J. (2007). As China roars, pollution reaches deadly extremes. *New York Times, 26*(8), A1.

Lau, C., Lu, Y., & Liang, Q. (2016). Corporate social responsibility in China: A corporate governance approach. *Journal of Business Ethics, 136*(1), 73–87.

Li, J., Liu, B., & Qian, G. (2019). The belt and road initiative, cultural friction and ethnicity: Their effects on the export performance of SMEs in China. *Journal of World Business, 54*(4), 350–359.

Li, J., Qian, G., Zhou, K. Z., Lu, J., & Liu, B. (2022). Belt and road initiative, globalization and institutional changes: Implications for firms in Asia. *Asia Pacific Journal of Management, 39*(3), 843–856.

Lin, L. W. (2010). Corporate social responsibility in China: Window dressing or structural change. *Berkeley Journal of International Law, 28*, 64.

Liu, W., & Dunford, M. (2016). Inclusive globalization: Unpacking China's belt and road initiative. *Area Development and Policy, 1*(3), 323–340.

Liu, L., & Tian, G. G. (2021). Mandatory CSR disclosure, monitoring and investment efficiency: Evidence from China. *Accounting & Finance, 61*(1), 595–644.

Luo, X. R., Wang, D., & Zhang, J. (2017). Whose call to answer: Institutional complexity and firms' CSR reporting. *Academy of Management Journal, 60*(1), 321–344.

Marano, V., & Kostova, T. (2016). Unpacking the institutional complexity in adoption of CSR practices in multinational enterprises. *Journal of Management Studies, 53*(1), 28–54.

Marquis, C., & Qian, C. (2014). Corporate social responsibility reporting in China: Symbol or substance. *Organization Science, 25*(1), 127–148.

Matten, D., & Moon, J. (2004). Corporate social responsibility. *Journal of Business Ethics, 54*(4), 323–337.

Miska, C., Witt, M. A., & Stahl, G. K. (2016). Drivers of global CSR integration and local CSR responsiveness: Evidence from Chinese MNEs. *Business Ethics Quarterly, 26*(3), 317–345.

Moon, J., & Shen, X. (2010). CSR in China research: Salience, focus and nature. *Journal of Business Ethics, 94*(4), 613–629.

National Development and Reform Commission. (2015). *Vision and actions on jointly building silk road economic belt and 21st-century Maritime Silk Road*. NDRC. https://www.fmprc.gov.cn/eng/topics_665678/2015zt/xjpcxbayzlt2015nnh/201503/t20150328_705553.html

Parente, R., Rong, K., Geleilate, J. M. G., & Misati, E. (2019). Adapting and sustaining operations in weak institutional environments: A business ecosystem assessment of a Chinese MNE in Central Africa. *Journal of International Business Studies, 50*(2), 275–291.

Perrini, F., & Vurro, C. (2010). Fostering social business through venture philanthropy: The role of financing in the process of new business creation. *Journal of Social Business, 1*(1), 126–154.

Prahalad, C. K., & Hammond, A. (2002). Serving the world's poor, profitably. *Harvard Business Review, 80*(9), 48–59.

Ramasamy, B., & Yeung, M. C. (2019). China's one belt one road initiative: The impact of trade facilitation versus physical infrastructure on exports. *The World Economy, 42*(6), 1673–1694.

Reimann, F., Ehrgott, M., Kaufmann, L., & Carter, C. R. (2012). Local stakeholders and local legitimacy: MNEs' social strategies in emerging economies. *Journal of International Management, 18*(1), 1–17.

See, G. (2009). Harmonious society and Chinese CSR: Is there really a link? *Journal of Business Ethics, 89*, 1–22.

Spiller, R. (2000). Ethical business and investment: A model for business and society. *Journal of Business Ethics, 27*, 149–160.

Tan, J. (2009). Institutional structure and firm social performance in transitional economies: Evidence of multinational corporations in China. *Journal of Business Ethics, 86*(2), 171–189.

Tang, L., & Li, H. (2009). Corporate social responsibility communication of Chinese and global corporations in China. *Public Relations Review, 35*(3), 199–212.

Tang, Z., & Tang, J. (2012). Stakeholder–firm power difference, stakeholders' CSR orientation, and SMEs' environmental performance in China. *Journal of Business Venturing, 27*(4), 436–455.

Utting, P., & Marques, C. (2009). The intellectual crisis of CSR. In P. Utting & J. C. Marques (Eds.), *Corporate social responsibility and regulatory governance: Towards inclusive development* (pp. 1–25). Palgrave Macmillan Publishers.

Wang, L., & Juslin, H. (2009). The impact of Chinese culture on corporate social responsibility: The harmony approach. *Journal of Business Ethics, 88*(3), 433–451.

Wang, H. (2019). China's approach to the belt and road initiative: Scope, character and sustainability. *Journal of International Economic Law, 22*(1), 29–55.

Wang, J., Qin, S., & Cui, Y. (2010). Problems and prospects of CSR system development in China. *International Journal of Business and Management, 5*(12), 128.

WBCSD. (2000). *Corporate Social Responsibility: Making good business sense.* World Business Council for Sustainable Development.

Wijen, F. (2014). Means versus ends in opaque institutional fields: Trading off compliance and achievement in sustainability standard adoption. *Academy of Management Review, 39*(3), 302–323.

Wong, L. (2009). Corporate social responsibility in China: Between the market and the search for a sustainable growth development. *Asian Business and Management, 8*(2), 129–148.

Xin, K. K., & Pearce, J. L. (1996). Guanxi: Connections as substitutes for formal institutional support. *Academy of Management Journal, 39*(6), 1641–1658.

Xinhua. (2017). *Full text of President Xi's speech at opening of Belt and Road forum.* http://www.xinhuanet.com/english/2017-05/14/c_136282982.htm

Xu, S., & Yang, R. (2010). Indigenous characteristics of Chinese corporate social responsibility conceptual paradigm. *Journal of Business Ethics, 93*(2), 321–333.

Yang, N., Wang, J., Liu, X., & Huang, L. (2020). Home-country institutions and corporate social responsibility of emerging economy multinational enterprises: The belt and road initiative as an example. *Asia Pacific Journal of Management, 39*(3), 1–39.

Yin, J., & Jamali, D. (2016). Strategic corporate social responsibility of multinational companies subsidiaries in emerging markets: Evidence from China. *Long Range Planning, 49*(5), 541–558.

Yin, J., & Zhang, Y. (2012). Institutional dynamics and corporate social responsibility (CSR) in an emerging country context: Evidence from China. *Journal of Business Ethics, 111*(2), 301–316.

Yu, Y., & Choi, Y. (2016). Stakeholder pressure and CSR adoption: The mediating role of organizational culture for Chinese companies. *The Social Science Journal, 53*(2), 226–235.

Zhao, M. (2012). CSR-based political legitimacy strategy: Managing the state by doing good in China and Russia. *Journal of Business Ethics, 111*(4), 439–460.

Zhu, D., & Ru, J. (2008). Strategic environmental assessment in China: Motivations, politics, and effectiveness. *Journal of Environmental Management, 88*(4), 615–626.

Zu, L., & Song, L. (2009). Determinants of managerial values on corporate social responsibility: Evidence from China. *Journal of Business Ethics, 88*(1), 105–117.

5 CSR Reporting in BRI Countries

Theoretical basis of Chinese MNEs' CSR reporting in BRI countries

Companies provide sustainability reports or social reports to stakeholders in order to demonstrate corporate commitment to sustainability. The World Business Council for Sustainable Development (World Business Council on Sustainable Development [WBCSD], 2002, p. 2) defines CSR reports as "public reports by corporations to provide internal and external stakeholders with an image of corporate role on activities on economic, environmental, and social dimensions". Roberts (1992) defines CSR reporting as a strategic tool for firms to manage stakeholder relationships. In other words, a firm may use its CSR disclosures to communicate with its stakeholders, since it "owes a duty to society or has a social contract" (p. 2). Previous literature indicates that stakeholders demand adequate access to information on the scope and effectiveness of firms' CSR efforts. Such CSR information is often used for decision-making by governments, investors, and customers when choosing firms to be awarded grants, invest in, or buy products from (Hou & Li, 2014).

On the other hand, BRI opens a new phase of CSR implementation for Chinese MNEs in overseas markets. The National Development and Reform Commission, Ministry of Foreign Affairs, and Ministry of Commerce of China released the "Vision and Actions on Jointly Building Silk Road Economic Belt and Twenty-First-Century Maritime Silk Road" (hereinafter "Vision and Actions"), which outlines the official guidelines for the BRI. There are five areas of cooperation in total, and the main objectives of the BRI include "policy coordination, infrastructure connectivity, unimpeded trade, financial integration and connecting people" (National Development and Reform Commission [NDRC], 2015). Nearly all of the main objectives push Chinese businesses to actively enhance their social responsibilities under the BRI. For instance, "Vision and Actions" suggests that "We support localized operation and management of Chinese companies to boost the local economy, increase local employment, improve local livelihood, and take social responsibilities in protecting local biodiversity and eco-environment". The BRI is meant to assist China to "further extend and deepen its opening-up and to boost its mutually

DOI: 10.4324/9781003302445-5

advantageous cooperation with nations in Asia, Europe, Africa, and the rest of the globe" (NDRC, 2015). The BRI views the overseas subsidiaries of Chinese MNEs involved in the BRI as its primary implementers and calls on them to uphold their CSR in order to enhance the home nation's international reputation, foster the smooth development of the BRI, and ultimately increase the mutual benefits of the BRI's participating countries. The below sub-sections will employ different theoretical foundations to explain the CSR behavior of Chinese MNEs along the Belt and Road.

Stakeholder theory

Stakeholder theory (Freeman, 1984) is the theory most commonly used to understand why corporations voluntarily disclose CSR information. From the perspective of the theory, research suggests that companies participate in CSR activities and reporting to resolve social issues and build constructive relationships with key stakeholders in order to enhance business sustainability (Sweeney & Coughlan, 2008). Stakeholders are described as "groups and individuals who may influence, or are affected by, the achievement of an organization's objectives" (Freeman, 1984, p. 54). Russo and Perrini (2010) point out that businesses' long-term survival and achievement depend on their ability to sustain and establish relationships with stakeholders when clashing over societal and environmental issues.

Chinese MNEs operating in multiple countries face diverse sets of stakeholders, who monitor and supervise corporate behavior in overseas markets, and must deal with ethical quandaries in a variety of institutional contexts. In this regard, stakeholder theory is the dominant viewpoint to research on MNEs' CSR activities (e.g., Arens & Brouthers, 2001; Yakovleva & Vazquez-Brust, 2012). Arthaud-Day (2005) emphasizes the importance of examining the CSR strategies of MNEs from rapidly developing Asian countries. Many companies have established manufacturing plants in developing countries, providing many jobs as well as other social benefits. As a result of increased globalization, stakeholder demands in host countries have increased, making it much more complicated for these MNEs to conduct overseas CSR activities. Thus, for Chinese MNEs operating across national frontiers, it is insufficient to involve only stakeholders from the home country. There must be representations from a diverse variety of groups across a broad range of countries relevant to the business (Blowfield & Dolan, 2014; Crane & Matten, 2007; Wheeler et al., 2002). As these activities may interfere with corporate decision-making, they may affect the MNEs' levels of CSR involvement and reporting. This chapter follows Papasolomou-Doukakis et al. (2005) and the BRI's two main policy documents in identifying six groups as the key stakeholders in overseas markets, namely employees, customers, investors, suppliers, the community, and the environment.[1] Based on the two main BRI policy documents, Table 5.1 presents CSR actions relevant to each cluster.

Research suggests that MNEs may use CSR to mitigate stakeholders' negative positions. According to Mithani (2017a), corporate philanthropy plays

Table 5.1 Overseas CSR actions vis-à-vis key stakeholders based on the BRI's two main policy documents

Stakeholder	Actions vis-à-vis key stakeholders
Employees	Responsible human resources management
	Promote overseas employee benefits and safety
	Localized employees
Consumers	Provide safe products and services
	Respect the rights of local consumers
Community	Promote local welfare and social benefits
	Foster reciprocal relationships with the local community
Investors	Provide a fair return to international investors
Environment	Commitment to sustainable development
	Commitment to local environment protection
Suppliers	Commitment to sustainable supply chain
	Fair trade with suppliers
	Support to local suppliers

an important role in reducing the perceived gap between local and non-local companies and thus mitigates the liability of foreignness (LOF) (Maruyama & Wu, 2015). Under the BRI scenario, the majority of BRI countries are developing countries where institutional environments are relatively weak, with limited CSR norms and practices. Groups of prominent stakeholders and the institutional environments of these countries differ from those in China. In addition, the relative weightings of stakeholder groups may vary between China and BRI countries. Aguilera and Jackson (2003) identify that cross-national institutional settings affect how different stakeholders make decisions and exert influence over firms' resources. Nevertheless, very little is known about CSR involvement and reporting in Chinese MNEs. This observation raises an important issue regarding CSR's capacity to contribute to resolving the most urgent needs of stakeholders in underprivileged areas of the world, though there is some evidence of active CSR projects in developed and emerging contexts (Baskin, 2006).

Institutional theory

According to previous research, CSR is embedded in institutions (Chan & Ma, 2016; Yin & Zhang, 2012; Zhao, 2012). The economic environment and the formal and informal "rules of the game" in the institutional environment also constrain CSR practices (North, 1990). For example, CSR relates to the institutional context because governments have incentives and put pressures on companies to engage in CSR (Sharfman et al., 2004). Social and political networks also shape CSR practices in order to foster moral motives (Aguilera et al., 2007).

MNEs operate concurrently in various institutional contexts (Kostova & Roth, 2002; Meyer et al., 2011), making it difficult for them to organize their CSR activities internationally to gain legitimacy in host countries (Rathert, 2016). As a result, most CSR research focuses on the impact of host-country institutions on MNEs' CSR (e.g., Asmussen & Fosfuri, 2019; Marano & Kostova, 2016; Rathert, 2016). The rise of MNEs from emerging economies, which are often marked by inefficient markets, active government involvement, extensive business networking, and high uncertainty (Xu & Meyer, 2013), has heightened the importance of understanding the impact of home-country institutions (Mathews, 2006; Ramamurti & Hillemann, 2018).

Existing research identifies two key drivers of MNEs' CSR. On the one hand, MNEs must comply with host countries' structural pressures (Beddewela & Fairbrass, 2016; Rathert, 2016). In addition, the global expansion of Chinese MNEs forces them to comply with international CSR requirements, making them subject to major isomorphic pressures (Rathert, 2016). MNEs face a variety of structural stresses, which vary widely depending on the institutional, cultural, geographical, and economic characteristics of host countries (Beddewela & Fairbrass, 2016). According to Brammer et al. (2009), companies investing in countries with insufficient political and civil rights tend to increase their charitable contributions, since investments in such countries are likely to trigger greater stakeholder pressure, as well as more vigorous examination of whether their strategies are ethical, or whether they are investing to exploit host-country vulnerabilities.

While international pressure to conform with CSR standards may play a critical role in MNEs' CSR reporting, existing literature on their CSR practices points to the importance of home-country factors. Key stakeholders in home countries, whether governmental agencies or other institutions/actors, may need to provide the initial impetus for adopting certain CSR initiatives. As a result, specific CSR reporting in overseas markets may result from processes of mimetic isomorphism operating at the country level, as suggested by neo-institutional theory (DiMaggio & Powell, 1983). Mimetic behaviors are usually the result of confusion or ambiguity within the organization. Under such circumstances, "organizations appear to model themselves after similar organizations in their field that they consider to be more credible and successful" (DiMaggio & Powell, 1983, p. 152). According to narratives on the diffusion of CSR practices (Matten & Moon, 2004; Rivoli & Waddock, 2011), firms operating in restrictive environments are subject to a contagion or mimetic isomorphism effect, which results in them imitating the actions of other firms in the country in terms of CSR reporting in overseas markets. Furthermore, Aguilera et al. (2007) suggest that companies adopt CSR practices in order to be seen as legitimate by other large firms in their home countries. This is especially likely in emerging economies with oligopolistic market structures and power concentration among the largest firms.

The BRI, one of China's leading institutions for facilitating companies' active involvement in regional cooperation and globalization, is likely to have a significant impact on Chinese firms' overseas CSR reporting, as home-country institutions are expected to impact significantly on firms' internationalization (Cuervo-Cazurra et al., 2018; Gao, 2011). MNEs must respond to institutional pressures by incorporating the relevant elements into their policies and behaviors in order to obtain support and legitimacy for their overseas operations. Failure to comply with institutionally accepted standards may jeopardize the companies' legitimacy, and ultimately their survival (Bondy, 2008).

The BRI is proposed and led by the government and is perceived as a formal institutional force exerted on Chinese MNEs through coercive and mimetic isomorphism (Haveman, 1993; Martínez-Ferrero & García-Sánchez, 2017; Mizruchi & Fein, 1999). First, coercive isomorphism derives from political interference and institutional pressure from stakeholders on which companies depend (DiMaggio & Powell, 1983; Zamir & Saeed, 2020). As explained in Chapter 1, under the current CSR requirements, Chinese MNEs are encouraged to disclose details of their CSR performance along the BRI. To satisfy the Chinese government and gain additional legitimacy and capital for development, Chinese enterprises must strictly adhere to BRI-related policies and incorporate social responsibility criteria into their international strategies.

Second, if corporate targets such as levels of commitment to CSR are unclear or uncertain, companies may model themselves to gain credibility from other more active or legitimate companies (DiMaggio & Powell, 1983). Since recently established Chinese MNEs involved in the BRI lack overseas experiences, it is unclear whether, how, and to what extent should they engage in CSR. The government actively encourages good CSR activities, and the awareness of typical MNEs participating in the BRI will assist others in improving their CSR to meet the BRI's requirements. For example, Chinese MNEs with excellent CSR results in the BRI are listed on official Chinese government websites and promoted as exemplars by the government, which undoubtedly enhances their credibility and provides a model[2] for other companies (Lau et al., 2016). These mimetic forces influence imitation of good peers and mobilize capital to enhance Chinese MNEs' CSR.

Legitimacy theory

According to Suchman (1995), legitimacy is a generic interpretation or inference that an entity's acts are desirable, proper, or acceptable within some socially constructed set of norms, values, beliefs, and definitions. He distinguishes three forms of organizational legitimacy – pragmatic, moral, and cognitive – and stresses that legitimacy management is highly dependent on communication. As a result, CSR reporting is critical to comprehending the foundations of companies committed to ethical behavior and socially responsible practices. Scott (2008, p. 59) further develops the notion of legitimacy from an institutional perspective and describes legitimacy as "a condition reflecting perceived consonance with relevant rules and laws, normative support, or alignment with the cultural-cognitive framework". Milne and Patten (2002) argue that in managing the legitimacy process, managers are faced with social demands from multiple organizations and must decide on what to make public.

It is widely acknowledged that Chinese MNEs investing abroad bear the burden of their home countries' backwardness and, to some extent, illegitimacy

(Miska et al., 2016). The extra burden that emerges specifically from being an emerging-economy firm has been described as the "liability of emergingness" (LOE) (Ramachandran & Pant, 2010; Madhok & Keyhani, 2012). This refers to the additional disadvantage that emerging-market MNEs appear to suffer when investing abroad compared with advanced-country multinationals. The shortcomings of their home countries' institutional and business processes, combined with news about their companies' reckless actions (for example, the case of Foxconn, and the controversy over melamine-laced milk that killed many infants in China), lead to the accumulation of negative judgments in host countries. In turn, "there is a reputation and legitimacy deficiency in the eyes of host country stakeholders, who have become much more circumspect as a result of ineffective or missing awareness of emerging international market multinational companies, their quality, and safety requirements, and the like" (Madhok & Keyhani, 2012, p. 31).

Firms can resolve LOF/LOE by attending to the demands of the host environment through various types of isomorphism (DiMaggio & Powell, 1983; Zaheer, 1995), which essentially means reducing the institutional gap between the requirements of home and host countries. As a result, some propose that Chinese MNEs seek legitimacy by adhering to international CSR norms (Campbell et al., 2012; Gugler & Shi, 2009). For example, reporting initiatives may serve Chinese MNEs' urgent need to demonstrate greater transparency in their environmental, social, and governance behavior, enabling them to communicate openly and clearly how their ethical principles, as well as projects that benefit the environment and society, are consistent with what most stakeholders would consider acceptable and desirable (Ekhator, 2014).

Several studies identify the role of institutional pressures in MNEs' decisions to pursue CSR strategies. Meanwhile, the consequences of CSR involvement and reporting are highly dependent on the host country's legal and social background. Chinese MNEs operate in host countries with radically differing political, economic, and cultural conditions from their home country (Marano & Kostova, 2016; Mithani, 2017b). MNEs must contend with the myriad dynamic demands of diverse stakeholders and must deal with the LOF and possibly unfriendly voices from abroad, resulting in additional costs (Mithani, 2017b). Thus, they must make further efforts to obtain legitimacy and become incorporated into the local social environment. Furthermore, owing to their dual embeddedness, MNEs must obtain legitimacy from both home and host countries (Beddewela, 2019). Similarly, CSR reporting as a strategy for MNEs to maintain external legitimacy is well-rooted in previous literature (Bebbington et al., 2009). According to early institutional research, organizations pursue legitimacy in a given context by aligning their activities with prevailing norms and attempting to become isomorphic with the environment (Fernando & Lawrence, 2014; Gray et al., 1988).

The BRI is an innovative global cooperation scheme which has a significant impact on local communities and Chinese MNEs are investing heavily in BRI countries. Thus, Chinese MNEs must legitimize their corporate actions by engaging in CSR reporting to gain the approval of local societies in host countries and thus ensure their continuing existence and legitimacy. MNEs' legitimacy also stems from the concept of the social contract (Sacconi, 2007), which consists of the local society's various expectations of how MNEs should conduct their business operations. Therefore, in order to continue operating smoothly, Chinese MNEs must act within the bounds and norms of what the local societies identify as socially responsible behaviors. Given that the BRI is an ambitious expansion plan for Chinese MNEs, gaining legitimacy is highly critical, and losing it will cause enormous damage to their corporate reputation (Bebbington et al., 2008). Therefore, legitimacy theory provides a robust theoretical foundation to explain Chinese MNEs' need to disclose their CSR performance along the BRI.

Social contract theory

Through the lens of social contract theory, CSR can be defined as "a [social] 'contract' between society and business wherein community grants a firm the license to operate, and in return, the matter meets certain obligations and behaves in an acceptable manner" (Dahlsrud, 2008, p. 10). Thus, the societies in which businesses operate implicitly require them to operate responsibly (Donaldson & Dunfee, 1999; Rosenfeld, 1984). Managers take ethical decisions because they understand that the company is part of a larger social system in which society and business coexist, and that the microsocial decisions made within organizations should be conducive to the larger social system and should meet societal standards. Thus, organizations' CSR reporting represents their attempts to satisfy the agreement and educate the community about their ethical choices and activities.

Drawing on social contract theory, the concept of combining local and global is present in the CSR literature (Donaldson & Dunfee, 1994). While local institutional environments must be addressed, certain values that transcend cultures (referred to as 'hyper-norms') moderate context-specific or micro-norms to ensure that universal and local values are considered in decision-making (Aguado et al., 2017; Bondy & Starkey, 2014). Although potentially divisive and contentious in practice, social contract theory exemplifies attempts to incorporate global and local issues into decision-making, leading to growth in policies in which the notion of being local worldwide is becoming more prevalent. For some companies, this illustrates the previously discussed issue of trying to be consistent across operational locations while still tailoring operations to cultural differences (Leisinger, 2005; Waddock & Bodwell, 2004). For others, the connection between global and local factors must be demonstrated, which has a greater influence on how CSR is shaped (Arthaud-Day, 2005).

The BRI aims to go beyond infrastructure development to include policy coordination, trade facilitation, financial integration, and cultural and scientific exchange (NDRC, 2015). Such a huge international collaboration initiative is expected to have tremendous effects on the local society. Similarly, CSR in BRI host countries is part of the social contract. Therefore, a degree of plurality is required, where Chinese MNEs and their executives are encouraged to think and behave both globally and locally. In the process of serving their own business interests, Chinese MNEs are obliged to take actions that also protect and enhance society's interests (Dusuki & Yusof, 2008). When treating overseas CSR along the BRI as part of the social contract, two different levels must be considered, namely the contract between local society and economic entities, and the contract between MNEs' management and all stakeholders in nations participating in the BRI (Dembinski & Fryzel, 2010). Chinese MNEs are supposed to balance universal and specific CSR concerns in their own CSR policies and subsequent procedures and take a leading role in promoting sustainable development in BRI countries. To this extent, following social contract theory, Chinese MNEs should be responsive along the BRI. At the same time, BRI countries' governments, enterprises, employees, and all other stakeholders are expected to benefit from the "BRI social contract". Therefore, Chinese MNEs should adopt CSR reporting to meet the various expectations of society and related stakeholders (Moir, 2001).

Resource dependency theory

According to resource dependency theory (RDT), firms are open systems that are not autonomous and rely on contingencies and resources in the external environment. Since firms cannot completely manage all resources required for survival, they often depend on resources managed by external stakeholders (Salancik & Pfeffer, 1978). Firms may take proactive measures to address external stakeholders' concerns about reducing uncertainty associated with accessing critical resources (Hillman et al., 2009; Salancik & Pfeffer, 1978). As one of the main stakeholders, the government is a major source of external interdependence and a major source of uncertainty for firms (Hillman, 2005). Uncertainty and dependency derived from the government are especially important and challenging for firms to handle in an emerging economy, as governments often maintain financial and regulatory tools critical to firms' survival, such as governmental subsidies, business policies, and industry development guidance (Hillman et al., 2009; Hoskisson et al., 2000). RDT suggests that an "organization may use political means to alter the state of the external economic environment" in order to manage such uncertainty (Salancik & Pfeffer, 1978, p. 190). Establishing relationships with governments is a tactic used by corporations to respond to environmental risks (Guo et al., 2014; Salancik & Pfeffer, 1978), since political ties will enable them to obtain vital resources, such as a good reputation, valuable information, favorable business policies, and political legitimacy.

Through investing abroad, China has significantly improved its position in the global value chain. Major characteristics of China's MNEs include relatively recent establishment, rapid growth, large volumes, strong governmental control, and intense focus on industries and regions (Huang et al., 2017). Their activities are primarily determined by "pull" factors, such as acquiring resources to satisfy growing demand and short supply in domestic markets, rather than "push" factors, such as home-market limitations and labor shortages, which are more common for multinational firms from developed countries (Deng, 2004). Previous studies suggest that a key reason why many Chinese companies invest abroad is to find, retain, or develop overseas markets. Foreign factors driving the expansion of Chinese firms in China have risen rapidly over the past three decades (Wadhwa & Reddy, 2011; Zhang, 2009). These include a lack of domestic markets relative to Chinese companies' overall capabilities and aspirations, which results in increased competition from both domestic and international MNEs and additional challenges around trade protectionism (Genasci & Pray, 2008). The net effect is that more and more Chinese businesses have to set up operations abroad or open offices in foreign countries. Another reason for Chinese firms going abroad is to ensure access to natural resources, especially oil, gas, and minerals. The Chinese government has been concerned about the possibility of shortages of key resources and inputs for economic expansion owing to decades of fast economic growth, as reflected in the strategic and political motives underlying Foreign Direct Investment (FDI) by large Central-Government-controlled MNEs.

According to the resource-dependence viewpoint (e.g., Salancik & Pfeffer, 1978), companies seek to acquire complementary assets from external environments, including rivals in other cross-border markets, and try to acquire strategic information from international organizations that is not available internally. In return, MNEs receiving various resources from host countries and advancing and improving CSR issues in those countries are considered precursors to economic and social progress (Minor & Morgan, 2011). Such CSR advances in host countries promote firms' corporate reputation and grant legitimacy to future operations (Markusen, 2004).

Similarly, Chinese MNEs frequently seek to strengthen their capacity for innovation and continuously build sustainable competitive advantages in host countries, thereby reducing their reliance on location-specific endowments (De Chiara & Spena, 2011). Thus, internationalization through BRI enables them to build international networks that bind resources, including natural and human capital. Furthermore, Chinese MNEs actively participate in BRI to obtain complementary resources and assets that are unavailable in their home countries, through linkages, leverage, and learning strategies (Hurley et al., 2019). In this scenario, overseas markets along the BRI serve specifically as learning platforms for Chinese MNEs seeking to enhance their capabilities, contribute to organizational learning, and aid in sharing new information within networks, allowing them to improve their organizational competitiveness (Huang, 2016). On the other hand, since Chinese MNEs utilize various resources from BRI host countries, they are expected to behave responsibly. In this vein, reporting their business footprints, as well as the various benefits to local society, is of great strategic significance along the BRI.

International strategic theory

Among many advantages of being socially responsible, one persuasive reason for addressing CSR is the "business case", or the relationship between MNEs' CSR and corporate competitiveness (Porter & Kramer, 2006). Conventional definitions of national competitiveness often focus on a country's level of economic productivity, which is defined by a variety of variables, policies, and institutions, ignoring the possibility of grounding a nation's economic competitive advantage in its social and environmental performance. The exclusion of CSR from conventional competitiveness indexes probably arises from Nobel laureate Milton Friedman's agency theory, as reported in the *New York Times* in 1970. The possibility that CSR might be a factor affecting corporate competitiveness is ruled out by this strict view of CSR ensuring shareholders' interests (Guarnieri & Kao, 2008). After decades of development, a major departure occurred with the advent of stakeholder theory, as a result of which the philosophy and scope of CSR have changed dramatically, from mere philanthropical action to so-called strategic CSR. This incorporates CSR into firms' core business operations through innovation, making CSR integral to corporate competitive strategy (Jain et al., 2017).

In its Global Competitiveness Study 2005–2006, the World Economic Forum included a chapter on climate and social problems as sources of competitive advantage. The concept of CSR as a source of competitiveness appears to be gaining momentum in international institutions, academia, and business circles. Porter further outlines how businesses can boost their long-term business prospects by combining organizations' financial and social objectives. In addition, Porter and Kramer (2003) postulate that a strategic approach to business philanthropy may align economic with social goals. According to Porter (1990), determinants of competition have two dimensions. The first relates to the macroeconomic, political, legal, and social circumstances. This dimension is required, but not necessary, for prosperity. Wealth is produced in an economy at the microeconomic level, specifically through companies' ability to produce valuable products and services in an efficient manner. The complexity and capabilities with which domestic companies or international subsidiaries compete, as well as the consistency of the microeconomic market climate in which they work, are the foundations of productivity (Porter, 1990). Previous studies have extensively demonstrated that efficient strategic management of CSR may minimize risk (Apospori et al., 2012; Husted, 2005), and that CSR programs may provide major benefits to businesses (Hillman & Keim, 2001; McWilliams & Siegel, 2001). These advantages extend beyond simply enhancing their reputation, to advancing valuable organizational capabilities (Boulouta & Pitelis, 2014). The potential competitive benefits of social impact programs have also been discussed in high-profile practitioner journals. For example, Kanter (1999) offers examples of CSR as a means of differentiating innovation, and Porter and Kramer (2002) describe how philanthropy can provide a competitive advantage in positioning.

Chinese MNEs in BRI countries are driven by the economic benefits of CSR requirements, such as better access to markets, enhanced intangible assets, and reduced risk of regulatory sanctions. In return for business restrictions, they must introduce innovative processes and technological upgrades to promote productivity and efficiency, in order to compensate for the initial costs and enable sustainable competitiveness in BRI host countries. Finally, MNEs' CSR reporting is a critical component for building corporate reputational capital. For instance, social responsibility is one of six factors on which the so-called reputation quotient (RQ) is based (Fombrun et al., 2000). From the economist's point of view, reputational returns are largely realized in the future. Thus, Chinese MNEs are advised to invest in CSR reporting to build more reputational capital, make more significant social impacts, and reap greater business benefits in the long term.

Figure 5.1 summarizes the theoretical framework of CSR reporting in BRI countries. Specifically, CSR reporting is regarded as an important aspect of the social contract between China and nations participating in the BRI, as well as between Chinese MNEs and various stakeholders. These stakeholders are from both the home country, such as government, NGOs, and investors, and the host country, such as host-country governments, as well as international stakeholders in the form of NGOs, consumers, suppliers, and communities. The rationale for conducting CSR activities in host countries is to create value for local, regional, and international stakeholders. In addition, MNEs must legitimize their actions through CSR reporting and must respond to institutional pressures by integrating CSR in host countries. Lack of legitimacy may have disastrous consequences for corporations, including loss of rights to operate, whereas high legitimacy allows companies to seek more resources (Cho & Patten, 2007; Hearit, 1995; Hybels, 1995; Patten, 2002). On the other hand, CSR serves as a social license to help MNEs seek various resources in BRI host countries, and satisfactory CSR performance is likely to enhance their reputation and competitive advantage. Similarly, damage to their reputation and stakeholder value will force MNEs to conduct more comprehensive CSR to repair and rebuild their social licenses (Parsons et al., 2014). However, legitimacy is a dynamic construct, and community expectations and institutional environments shift over time, requiring MNEs to be responsive and re-adjust their CSR strategies from time to time (Brenner & Ambos, 2013). Thus, there is a two-way relationship between Chinese MNEs and BRI host countries, as dynamic institutional pressures and feedback from stakeholders constantly shape Chinese MNEs' CSR orientations.

Why is CSR reporting along the BRI worth exploring?

Firms around the world are increasingly documenting their CSR efforts (KPMG, 2013). Formal CSR reporting began in the 1970s when larger companies in developed countries began to publish details of their CSR policies and activities in annual reports (Fifka, 2013). In response to the increasing importance and institutionalization of CSR in many countries, in the 1990s, some

80 CSR Reporting in BRI Countries

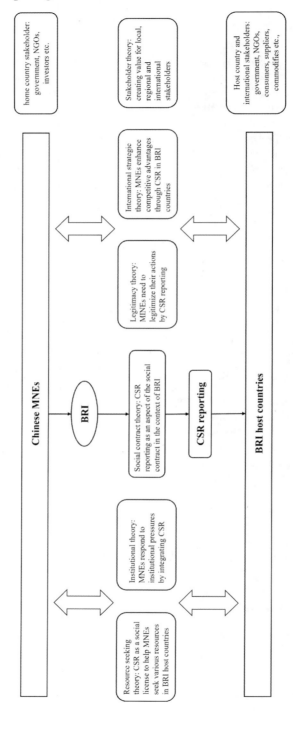

Figure 5.1 Theoretical framework of CSR reporting in the BRI countries.

Western companies started to publish standalone CSR reports (United Nations Conference on Trade and Development [UNCTAD], 2011). This trend has expanded internationally to include MNEs from developing countries that have less stringent disclosure regulations (KPMG, 2013). CSR reporting is essential to MNEs and non-market stakeholders for a variety of reasons. It communicates firms' attitudes to pertinent societal concerns (Adams & Harte, 1998; Young & Marais, 2012), and their ability to align their activities with global stakeholders' norms and aspirations (Bansal & Kistruck, 2006; Maignan & Ralston, 2002; Young & Marais, 2012). Publishing CSR reports is also regarded as an essential first step in helping firms to understand CSR and improve their CSR performance. It forces corporations to assess their social impacts and undertake efforts to improve their record in this field (UNCTAD, 2011).

The way in which Chinese MNEs have evolved raises important questions about their impact on overseas economies. Chinese enterprises have developed extensively since the "going out"[3] policy at the beginning of the 21st century (May, 2015), and lack of attention to environmental risks has been a major issue (Jenkins, 2005). Thus, given that a significant proportion of MNEs' investments from emerging sources originates from countries characterized by relatively weak legal and regulatory frameworks (Wei & Nguyen, 2017), emerging-economy firms' overseas CSR practices greatly challenge their aspirations to enter overseas markets. The responses of multinational firms from emerging economies to overseas CSR also have a significant impact on the global CSR agenda. For instance, concerns are growing about the impact of poorly conceived and executed projects on host countries within the BRI, relating to issues, such as the local environment, workforce, fiscal health, and political stability (Blanchard et al., 2017). These concerns have been especially acute for BRI projects and investments in countries where governments are unwilling or unable to assume their responsibilities (Al-Hasni, 2019). Thus, how Chinese MNEs are engaging with, defining, and implementing CSR reporting practices, especially under the BRI, will have important implications, particularly in view of growing concern about international reputational damage (Van der Merwe, 2019). Compared with developed countries, technical and economic conditions are relatively backward and supervisory systems are deficient in emerging markets. Thus, some Chinese MNEs may find loopholes and ignore CSR implementation in some least-developed countries (Cheng & Liang, 2012; Pegg, 2012). On the other hand, the concept of CSR has been "exported" to some African countries from Chinese firms and other MNEs from developed countries, yet their weak legal and institutional systems will necessitate enormous efforts in terms of CSR "education" (Tan-Mullins & Mohan, 2013). Therefore, it is of great research interest to analyze the CSR disclosures of Chinese MNEs, to track their record of CSR involvement in BRI host countries.

MNEs' CSR reporting enables key stakeholders to properly assess firms' CSR activities and reward positive externalities, while placing pressure on them to minimize negative ones (Tan-Mullins & Mohan, 2013). Several Chinese MNEs have explored practical aspects of their CSR performance. For example, in 2008,

China Iron and Steel Group released a report on its sustainable development in Africa, the first overseas CSR report issued by a Chinese enterprise; and PetroChina has released sustainable development reports on its operations in Kazakhstan, Sudan, Indonesia, and Latin America (Anyu & Dzekashu, 2019). These initiatives are excellent examples of CSR disclosures by MNEs along the BRI. Indeed, implementing the BRI requires win-win cooperation with countries along the route, in order to build communities of interest, shared destiny, and responsibility for mutual political trust, economic integration, and cultural inclusion. Thus, disclosures of overseas CSR performance are highly encouraged. On the other hand, under the BRI, China lends vast amounts of money to Africa to build infrastructure, yet it is unclear whether there are sufficient guarantees or conventions to prevent China from exploiting Africa's natural resources, such as oil (Compagnon & Alejandro, 2013; Tan-Mullins et al., 2017). Despite a rapid rise in international business literature on mushrooming Chinese MNEs (Jackson & Horwitz, 2018), relatively little is known about CSR management by Chinese firms in overseas markets. Thus, the question of what CSR initiatives Chinese MNEs are implementing and disclosing in other countries remains unanswered.

Previous literature reveals that CSR initiatives on social issues, such as reasonable labor standards with respect to equal pay, child labor, and unionization, may protect multinational firms' corporate reputations (Caves & Caves, 1996). However, most studies focus only on how MNEs from developed nations manage CSR in their home versus host countries (Surroca et al., 2013), or how they undertake CSR in developing countries (Saleh et al., 2010). For example, Engle (2007) explores the perspectives of 56 senior international business executives based in the United States on MNEs' involvement in improving host countries' human rights, standards of living, education, healthcare, and climate. The results show that all five areas are significant, with MNEs' environmental obligations being regarded as the most important. Similarly, previous studies using cases of large MNEs from developed countries, such as Walmart, Nestlé, BP, and Nike, observe divergence between what the headquarters wants, and how overseas subsidiaries act in the realm of CSR (Durand & Jacqueminet, 2015; Husted & Allen, 2006).

MNEs operating in several countries face diverse sets of stakeholders and complex ethical quandaries. Several studies articulate the role of institutional pressures in MNEs' adoption of a CSR approach (Barkemeyer & Figge, 2014). Meanwhile, CSR participation and reporting may be influenced by the MNEs' home-country background, as moral attitudes and behaviors may be affected by the cultural and legislative context of the home country (Husted & Allen, 2006; Spicer et al., 2004). As the BRI is a very large-scale international compact affecting billions of people on several continents, MNEs participating in it naturally receive greater public scrutiny from global stakeholders and the media. In addition, the BRI is one of the most influential global infrastructure development strategies adopted by developing countries, and the home countries' institutional contexts differ significantly from those in Western developed countries.

Nevertheless, little is known about the CSR reporting content of MNEs actively involved in the BRI. The existing literature tends to focus on their economic output, with limited understanding of how Chinese MNEs' current CSR reporting in BRI host countries reflects their CSR performance under the proposed "sustainable BRI". Thus, it is critical to investigate the CSR content being reported by Chinese MNEs in BRI host countries and the corresponding reporting quality, which are the main objectives of this book.

Situational factors affecting CSR reporting along the Belt and Road

Accounting for potential situational factors that may influence Chinese MNEs' CSR disclosures is essential to make sense of their CSR activities in developing countries. First of all, CSR reporting content and quality in BRI host countries vary with firm types. According to the extant literature, Chinese enterprises differ significantly from their counterparts in other countries in terms of their relatively large governmental stake, their more concentrated ownership structure, and the prevailing political connections of firms' management (Fan et al., 2007; Tian & Estrin, 2008). There are three main types of firms in China, namely central enterprises (CEs), local state-owned enterprises (SOEs), and private enterprises (PEs). CEs are directly affiliated to the State-owned Assets Supervision and Administration Commission of the State Council (SASAC) of the State Council or central ministries and commissions and are directly funded by the Central Government. There are currently 95 CEs in China. Other local SOEs are generally enterprises that state-owned capital (local SASAC) holds, participates in, or wholly owns, and whose investment behavior is determined by the will and interests of local governments. In some cases, both CEs and local SOEs are referred to as SOEs. The remaining firms are generally referred to as PEs (Milhaupt & Zheng, 2014). In summary, CEs are supervised by the Central Government, SOEs are supervised by local government, and PEs are for-profit economic organizations established or controlled by private individuals.

The importance of home-country governments in guiding and funding firms' activities is highlighted in research on emerging economies (Buckley et al., 2007; Yamakawa et al., 2008). For example, government support may compensate for lack of firm-specific advantages (Cui & Jiang, 2012). CEs and SOEs in China enjoy superior monopolistic advantages and favorable political access (Lundan, 2010). Their managers may consider the possibility of either formal or informal additional funding when making strategic decisions (Dikova et al., 2019). Furthermore, companies with a higher percentage of state ownership have easier access to government financing and can borrow capital on better terms in the open market (García-Canal & Guillén, 2008). To ensure their economic sustainability, CEs and SOEs must often depend on state support. Previous literature on government-business networks reveals that firms with strong connections with government may tend to engage more in CSR activities because of their high visibility to the state in both domestic and overseas markets (Siltaoja, 2006). This is even more critical in developing countries where the state very strongly influences business operations (Pearce & Robinson, 2000; Xin & Pearce, 1996). Investing in political legitimacy may therefore be seen as a way to minimize instability and improve the chances of survival.

A CSR-based political legitimacy strategy is a "strategic action that a company takes to create, preserve, or improve the appropriateness and desirability perceived by the state through social-environmental activities based on which the company intends to access various types of the state capital" (Zhao, 2012, p. 442). Previous literature also suggests that CEs and other SOEs may have positive impacts on CSR performance because of reciprocal firm-government relationships or government interference (Gu et al., 2013). Ownership structure has a differential effect on CSR involvement. The Chinese government is playing a growing role in establishing rules and creating standards for organizations' CSR activities (Campbell, 2007). For example, it has intervened by developing guidelines for CSR, especially in CEs and SOEs,[4] and by mandating CSR reporting. In addition, the state has issued specific CSR regulations for CEs in the context of the BRI. According to one survey, CEs employ more than 360,000 local employees in countries along with the BRI. Furthermore, 96% of SOE overseas institutions have created equal employment systems for Chinese and foreign employees, 76% of CEs have established equal employment systems for training and promotion, and 75% of CEs have also created equal employment systems for salaries and welfare (Luo et al., 2019). Similarly, Vernon (1979) argues that CEs and SOEs have many economic functions. In China, they are leading players in responses to domestic industrial policies. These firms must meet state objectives in order to gain legitimacy from their governance (Choudhury & Khanna, 2014; Wang et al., 2012). Furthermore, SOE managers' career growth and promotion are heavily influenced by their ability to meet government objectives.

Implementation of CSR reporting practices is also influenced by industry characteristics (Jackson & Apostolakou, 2010), as reports are used to gain legitimacy in the eyes of influential stakeholders (Suchman, 1995). Several studies identify industry classifications as a factor influencing corporate social and environmental disclosures (Cormier & Gordon, 2001; Hackston & Milne, 1996; Roberts, 1992). As Patten (1991) states, industry classification, like firm size, influences political visibility and may drive disclosure in order to avoid undue pressure and criticism from social activists. Etzion (2007) shows that key stakeholders are concerned with industries as discrete units of analysis in relation to CSR performance. In addition, previous literature reveals that stakeholders concerned about CSR performance usually infer industry-level behavior from individual firms' behavior, a phenomenon referred to as "reputational commons" (King & Shaver, 2001). Indeed, businesses in sectors with higher social and environmental impacts face more rigorous regulatory standards and greater demands from customers, employees, and NGOs, as well as calls for stricter accountability. Professional and industrial associations establish specific rules and regulations (Campbell, 2007) on issues such as the workplace, employment, occupational health and safety, and consultative processes, and participants in those industries are under greater obligation to their peers (Jackson & Apostolakou, 2010; Snider et al., 2003).

Companies therefore face greater coercive and normative pressures to report on CSR, as well as mimetic pressures to maintain their legitimacy. Previous research has shown that the extent of CSR risks in a given sector affects corporate reporting practices (Bebbington et al., 2008). According to Tagesson et al. (2009, p. 354), "corporations in industries whose production practices have a detrimental impact on the environment reveal and record more details than those in other industries". They find that mining, oil, and chemical companies report the most on environmental, health, and safety issues, while finance and service industries report more on philanthropic and social issues. On the other hand, firms with higher environmental and social impacts began to publish CSR reports earlier than others, such as those in financial and banking industries (Kolk & Pinkse, 2010).

It is argued that Chinese MNEs' internationalization strategies and operating environments in host countries differ significantly due to industry-related factors (Brewster et al., 2008; Nolan & Rui, 2004). Most Chinese companies participating in OFDI are in the manufacturing and construction sectors (Fang & Nolan, 2019), which have been explored extensively as standalone sectors (Aribi & Gao, 2011; Day & Woodward, 2009). Similarly, mining industries are often investigated from a legitimacy perspective because of their polluting nature (Peck & Sinding, 2003). In contrast, other relatively environmentally friendly industries, such as the information and communication technology (ICT) industry, have not been examined intensively in previous research (Holtbrügge & Dögl, 2012). Although previous studies have examined a reasonably wide range of industries for CSR reporting purposes, the CSR commitment of many other vital industries still requires attention (Khan et al., 2020). Specifically, under the BRI strategy, government and industry regulators have established various CSR reporting policies. For example, specific guidelines on due diligence and social responsibility are issued for mining companies in relation to their overseas markets.[5] Therefore, CSR reporting requirements and stakeholder concerns differ across Chinese MNEs in different industries. Furthermore, most previous empirical research on the determinants of overseas CSR reporting has focused on developed-country economies and has thus ignored factors that may be explained by studying emerging contexts such as that of Chinese MNEs. Industry-specific CSR reporting content is commonly seen in BRI host countries, which will be discussed in the chapters to follow.

Notes

1 As previously mentioned, the BRI's two main policy documents are the "Vision and Actions" and the "Concept for Maritime Cooperation under the Belt and Road Initiative".
2 Due to their outstanding CSR performance in overseas markets, several Chinese MNEs, including the China Communications Construction Group and the National Energy Group, have repeatedly won the "Overseas CSR Model Enterprise Award" at the China CSR Communication Forum hosted by the Corporate Social Responsibility Research Center of the Chinese Academy of Social Sciences.

3 The "going out" policy (also referred to as the "going global" strategy) was initiated by the Chinese government in 1999 to promote Chinese investments abroad (Salidjanova, 2011). In 2001, the Ninth National People's Congress of the PRC formally adopted the "going out" strategy as a national policy. There has been debate about what factors have driven Chinese OFDI in general, and how. Population development, urbanization, overcoming trade barriers, seeking new markets, changing monetary policies, acquiring natural resources, and acquiring brands, technology, and managerial assets are among the drivers discussed (Li, 2016; Rosen & Hanemann, 2009).
4 CEs and SOEs are under relatively strong state and party influence, with key positions being appointed by SASAC and the Communist Party (Naughton, 2008; Shi et al., 2014). Their objectives are therefore aligned with those of the state and the Communist Party and, in the last decade, have shifted from an economic growth orientation toward a combined focus on growth and a harmonious society.
5 CCCMC and OECD (2015). *Chinese Responsible Mineral Supply Chain Due Diligence Guidelines.* Retrieved from http://www.cccmc.org.cn/docs/2015-10/20151029133501092584.pdf; CCCMC (2017). *Guidelines for Social Responsibility in Outbound Mining Investments.* Retrieved from http://www.cccmc.org.cn/docs/2017-08/20170804141709355235.pdf.

References

Adams, C. A., & Harte, G. (1998). The changing portrayal of the employment of women in British banks' and retail companies' corporate annual reports. *Accounting, Organizations and Society, 23*(8), 781–812.

Aguado, R., Retolaza, J. L., & Alcañiz, L. (2017). Dignity at the level of the firm: Beyond the stakeholder approach. In M. Kostera, & M. Pirson (Eds.), *Dignity and the organization* (pp. 81–97). Palgrave Macmillan.

Aguilera, R. V., & Jackson, G. (2003). The cross-national diversity of corporate governance: Dimensions and determinants. *Academy of Management Review, 28*(3), 447–465.

Aguilera, R. V., Rupp, D. E., Williams, C. A., & Ganapathi, J. (2007). Putting the S back in corporate social responsibility: A multilevel theory of social change in organizations. *Academy of Management Review, 32*(3), 836–863.

Al-Hasni, H. (2019). The role of China's public diplomacy in promoting the belt and road initiative in Oman through communication: An examination of the integrated model of public diplomacy. *Global Media Journal, 17*(32), 1–10.

Anyu, J. N., & Dzekashu, W. G. (2019). China's enterprises in Africa: Market entry strategies, implications for capacity building, and corporate social responsibility. *Journal of Economics and Political Economy, 6*(2), 172–180.

Apospori, E., Zografos, K. G., & Magrizos, S. (2012). SME corporate social responsibility and competitiveness: A literature review. *International Journal of Technology Management, 58*(2), 10–31.

Arens, P., & Brouthers, K. D. (2001). Key stakeholder theory and state owned versus privatized firms. *MIR: Management International Review, 41*(4), 377–394.

Aribi, Z. A., & Gao, S. S. (2011). Narrative disclosure of corporate social responsibility in Islamic financial institutions. *Managerial Auditing Journal, 27*(2), 199–222.

Arthaud-Day, M. L. (2005). Transnational corporate social responsibility: A tri-dimensional approach to international CSR research. *Business Ethics Quarterly, 15*(1), 1–22.

Asmussen, C. G., & Fosfuri, A. (2019). Orchestrating corporate social responsibility in the multinational enterprise. *Strategic Management Journal*, *40*(6), 894–916.

Bansal, P., & Kistruck, G. (2006). Seeing is (not) believing: Managing the impressions of the firm's commitment to the natural environment. *Journal of Business Ethics*, *67*(2), 165–180.

Barkemeyer, R., & Figge, F. (2014). CSR in multiple environments: The impact of headquartering. *Critical Perspectives on International Business*, *10*(3), 124–151.

Baskin, J. (2006). Corporate responsibility in emerging markets. *Journal of Corporate Citizenship*, *50*(5), 635–654.

Bebbington, J., Higgins, C., & Frame, B. (2009). Initiating sustainable development reporting: Evidence from New Zealand. *Accounting, Auditing & Accountability Journal*, *22*(4), 588–625.

Bebbington, J., Larrinaga, C., & Moneva, J. M. (2008). Corporate social reporting and reputation risk management. *Accounting, Auditing & Accountability Journal*, *21*(3), 337–361.

Beddewela, E. (2019). Managing corporate community responsibility in multinational corporations: Resolving institutional duality. *Long Range Planning*, *52*(6), 101911.

Beddewela, E., & Fairbrass, J. (2016). Seeking legitimacy through CSR: Institutional pressures and corporate responses of multinationals in Sri Lanka. *Journal of Business Ethics*, *136*(3), 503–522.

Blanchard, J. M. F. (Ed.). (2017). *China's maritime Silk Road Initiative and South Asia*. Palgrave. https://link.springer.com/book/10.1007/978-981-10-5239-2

Blowfield, M., & Dolan, C. S. (2014). Business as a development agent: Evidence of possibility and improbability. *Third World Quarterly*, *35*(1), 22–42.

Bondy, K. (2008). The paradox of power in CSR: A case study on implementation. *Journal of Business Ethics*, *82*(2), 307–323.

Bondy, K., & Starkey, K. (2014). The dilemmas of internationalization: Corporate social responsibility in the multinational corporation. *British Journal of Management*, *25*(1), 4–22.

Boulouta, I., & Pitelis, C. N. (2014). Who needs CSR? The impact of corporate social responsibility on national competitiveness. *Journal of Business Ethics*, *119*(3), 349–364.

Brammer, S. J., Pavelin, S., & Porter, L. A. (2009). Corporate charitable giving, multinational companies and countries of concern. *Journal of Management Studies*, *46*(4), 575–596.

Brenner, B., & Ambos, B. (2013). A question of legitimacy? A dynamic perspective on multinational firm control. *Organization Science*, *24*(3), 773–795.

Brewster, C., Wood, G., & Brookes, M. (2008). Similarity, isomorphism or duality? Recent survey evidence on the human resource management policies of multinational corporations. *British Journal of Management*, *19*(4), 320–342.

Buckley, P. J., Clegg, L. J., Cross, A. R., Liu, X., Voss, H., & Zheng, P. (2007). The determinants of Chinese outward foreign direct investment. *Journal of International Business Studies*, *38*(4), 499–518.

Campbell, J. L. (2007). Why would corporations behave in socially responsible ways? An institutional theory of corporate social responsibility. *Academy of Management Review*, *32*(3), 946–967.

Campbell, J. T., Eden, L., & Miller, S. R. (2012). Multinationals and corporate social responsibility in host countries: Does distance matter? *Journal of International Business Studies*, *43*(1), 84–106.

Caves, R. E., & Caves, R. E. (1996). *Multinational enterprise and economic analysis*. Cambridge university press.

Chan, R. Y., & Ma, K. H. (2016). Environmental orientation of exporting SMEs from an emerging economy: Its antecedents and consequences. *Management International Review*, 56(5), 597–632.

Cheng, S., & Liang, G. (2012). Social responsibility of Chinese investment in Africa: What does it mean for EU-China cooperation on development policy towards Africa? *Trade Negotiations Insights*, 10(3), 9–11.

Cho, C. H., & Patten, D. M. (2007). The role of environmental disclosures as tools of legitimacy: A research note. *Accounting, Organizations and Society*, 32(7–8), 639–647.

Choudhury, P., & Khanna, T. (2014). Toward resource independence–Why state-owned entities become multinationals: An empirical study of India's public R&D laboratories. *Journal of International Business Studies*, 45(8), 943–960.

Compagnon, D., & Alejandro, A. (2013). China's external environmental policy: Understanding China's environmental impact in Africa and how it is addressed. *Environmental Practice*, 15(3), 220–227.

Cormier, D., & Gordon, I. M. (2001). An examination of social and environmental reporting strategies. *Accounting, Auditing & Accountability Journal*, 14(5), 587–617.

Crane, A., & Matten, D. (2007). *Corporate social responsibility. Vol. 2: Managing and implementing corporate social responsibility*. Sage Publications.

Cuervo-Cazurra, A., Luo, Y., Ramamurti, R., & Ang, S. H. (2018). The impact of the home country on internationalization. *Journal of World Business*, 53(5), 593–604.

Cui, L., & Jiang, F. (2012). State ownership effect on firms' FDI ownership decisions under institutional pressure: A study of Chinese outward-investing firms. *Journal of International Business Studies*, 43(3), 264–284.

Day, R. and Woodward, T. (2009). CSR reporting and the UK financial services sector. *Journal of Applied Accounting Research*, 10(3), 159–175.

Dahlsrud, A. (2008). How corporate social responsibility is defined: An analysis of 37 definitions. *Corporate Social Responsibility and Environmental Management*, 15(1), 1–13.

De Chiara, A., & Spena, T. R. (2011). CSR strategy in multinational firms: Focus on human resources, suppliers and community. *Journal of Global Responsibility*, 2(1), 60–74.

Dembinski, P. H., & Fryzel, B. (2010). *The role of large enterprises in democracy and society*. Palgrave Macmillan Limited.

Deng, P. (2004). Outward investment by Chinese MNCs: Motivations and implications. *Business Horizons*, 47(3), 8–16.

Dikova, D., Panibratov, A., & Veselova, A. (2019). Investment motives, ownership advantages and institutional distance: An examination of Russian cross-border acquisitions. *International Business Review*, 28(4), 625–637.

DiMaggio, P. J., & Powell, W. W. (1983). The iron cage revisited: Institutional isomorphism and collective rationality in organizational fields. *American Sociological Review*, 48(2), 147–160.

Donaldson, T., & Dunfee, T. W. (1994). Toward a unified conception of business ethics: Integrative social contracts theory. *Academy of Management Review*, 19(2), 252–284.

Donaldson, T., & Dunfee, T. W. (1999). When ethics travel: The promise and peril of global business ethics. *California Management Review*, 41(4), 45–63.

Durand, R., & Jacqueminet, A. (2015). Peer conformity, attention, and heterogeneous implementation of practices in MNEs. *Journal of International Business Studies*, 46(8), 917–937.

Dusuki, A. W., & Yusof, T. F. M. T. M. (2008). The pyramid of corporate social responsibility model: Empirical evidence from Malaysian stakeholder perspective. *Management & Accounting Review*, 7(2), 29–54.

Ekhator, E. O. (2014). Corporate social responsibility and Chinese oil multinationals in the oil and gas industry of Nigeria: An appraisal. *Cadernos de Estudos Africanos*, 28, 119–140.

Engle, R. L. (2007). Corporate social responsibility in host countries: A perspective from American managers. *Corporate Social Responsibility and Environmental Management*, 14(1), 16–27.

Etzion, D. (2007). Research on organizations and the natural environment, 1992-present: A review. *Journal of Management*, 33(4), 637–664.

Fan, J. P., Wong, T. J., & Zhang, T. (2007). Politically connected CEOs, corporate governance, and Post-IPO performance of China's newly partially privatized firms. *Journal of Financial Economics*, 84(2), 330–357.

Fang, C., & Nolan, P. (2019). *Routledge handbook of the belt and road*. London: Routledge.

Fernando, S., & Lawrence, S. (2014). A theoretical framework for CSR practices: Integrating legitimacy theory, stakeholder theory and institutional theory. *Journal of Theoretical Accounting Research*, 10(1), 149–178.

Fifka, M. S. (2013). Corporate responsibility reporting and its determinants in comparative perspective–a review of the empirical literature and a meta-analysis. *Business Strategy and the Environment*, 22(1), 1–35.

Fombrun, C. J., Gardberg, N. A., & Sever, J. M. (2000). The reputation quotient SM: A multi-stakeholder measure of corporate reputation. *Journal of Brand Management*, 7(4), 241–255.

Freeman, R. E. (1984). *Strategic management: A stakeholder approach*. Pitman Publishing Inc.

Gao, Y. (2011). CSR in an emerging country: A content analysis of CSR reports of listed companies. *Baltic Journal of Management*, 6(2), 263–291.

García-Canal, E., & Guillén, M. F. (2008). Risk and the strategy of foreign location choice in regulated industries. *Strategic Management Journal*, 29(10), 1097–1115.

Genasci, M., & Pray, S. (2008). Extracting accountability: The implications of the resource curse for CSR theory and practice. *Yale Human Rights Law Journal*, 37, 50.

Gray, R., Owen, D., & Maunders, K. (1988). Corporate social reporting: Emerging trends in accountability and the social contract. *Accounting, Auditing & Accountability Journal*, 1(1), 6–20.

Gu, H., Ryan, C., Bin, L., & Wei, G. (2013). Political connections, guanxi and adoption of CSR policies in the Chinese hotel industry: Is there a link? *Tourism Management*, 34, 231–235.

Guarnieri, R., & Kao, T. (2008). Leadership and CSR-a perfect match: How top companies for leaders utilize CSR as a competitive advantage. *People and Strategy*, 31(3), 34.

Gugler, P., & Shi, J. Y. (2009). Corporate social responsibility for developing country multinational corporations: Lost war in pertaining global competitiveness? *Journal of Business Ethics*, 87(1), 3–24.

Guo, H., Xu, E., & Jacobs, M. (2014). Managerial political ties and firm performance during institutional transitions: An analysis of mediating mechanisms. *Journal of Business Research*, 67(2), 116–127.

Hackston, D., & Milne, M. J. (1996). Some determinants of social and environmental disclosures in New Zealand companies. *Accounting, Auditing & Accountability Journal*, 9(1), 77–108.

Haveman, H. A. (1993). Follow the leader: Mimetic isomorphism and entry into new markets. *Administrative Science Quarterly*, 38(4), 593–627.

Hearit, K. M. (1995). Mistakes were made: Organizations, apologia, and crises of social legitimacy. *Communication Studies*, 46(1–2), 1–17.

Hillman, A. J. (2005). Politicians on the board of directors: Do connections affect the bottom line? *Journal of Management*, 31(3), 464–481.

Hillman, A. J., & Keim, G. D. (2001). Shareholder value, stakeholder management, and social issues: What's the bottom line? *Strategic Management Journal*, 22(2), 125–139.

Hillman, A. J., Withers, M. C., & Collins, B. J. (2009). Resource dependence theory: A review. *Journal of Management*, 35(6), 1404–1427.

Holtbrügge, D., & Dögl, C. (2012). How international is corporate environmental responsibility? A literature review. *Journal of International Management*, 18(2), 180–195.

Hoskisson, R. E., Eden, L., Lau, C. M., & Wright, M. (2000). Strategy in emerging economies. *Academy of Management Journal*, 43(3), 249–267.

Hou, S., & Li, L. (2014). Reasoning and differences between CSR theory and practice in China, the United States and Europe. *Journal of International Business Ethics*, 7(1), 19–30.

Huang, Y. (2016). Understanding China's Belt & Road Initiative: Motivation, framework and assessment. *China Economic Review*, 40, 314–321.

Huang, Y., Fischer, T. B., & Xu, H. (2017). The stakeholder analysis for SEA of Chinese foreign direct investment: The case of 'One Belt, One Road' initiative in Pakistan. *Impact Assessment and Project Appraisal*, 35(2), 158–171.

Hurley, J., Morris, S., & Portelance, G. (2019). Examining the debt implications of the Belt and Road Initiative from a policy perspective. *Journal of Infrastructure, Policy and Development*, 3(1), 139–175.

Husted, B. W. (2005). Culture and ecology: A cross-national study of the determinants of environmental sustainability. *MIR: Management International Review*, 45(3), 349–371.

Husted, B. W., & Allen, D. B. (2006). Corporate social responsibility in the multinational enterprise: Strategic and institutional approaches. *Journal of International Business Studies*, 37(6), 838–849.

Hybels, R. C. (1995). On legitimacy, legitimation, and organizations: A critical review and integrative theoretical model. *Academy of Management Proceedings*, 38(1), 241–245.

Jackson, G., & Apostolakou, A. (2010). Corporate social responsibility in Western Europe: An institutional mirror or substitute? *Journal of Business Ethics*, 94(3), 371–394.

Jackson, T., & Horwitz, F. M. (2018). Expatriation in Chinese MNEs in Africa: An agenda for research. *The International Journal of Human Resource Management*, 29(11), 1856–1878.

Jain, P., Vyas, V., & Roy, A. (2017). Exploring the mediating role of intellectual capital and competitive advantage on the relation between CSR and financial performance in SMEs. *Social Responsibility Journal*, 13(1), 1–23.

Jenkins, R. (2005). Globalization, corporate social responsibility and poverty. *International Affairs, 81*(3), 525–540.

Kanter, R. M. (1999). From spare change to real change: The social sector as beta site for business innovation. *Harvard Business Review, 77*(3), 122–123.

Khan, M., Lockhart, J., & Bathurst, R. (2020). A multi-level institutional perspective of corporate social responsibility reporting: A mixed-method study. *Journal of Cleaner Production, 265*, 121739.

King, A. A., & Shaver, J. M. (2001). Are aliens green? Assessing foreign establishments' environmental conduct in the United States. *Strategic Management Journal, 22*(11), 1069–1085.

Kolk, A., & Pinkse, J. (2010). The integration of corporate governance in corporate social responsibility disclosures. *Corporate Social Responsibility and Environmental Management, 17*(1), 15–26.

Kostova, T., & Roth, K. (2002). Adoption of an organizational practice by subsidiaries of multinational corporations: Institutional and relational effects. *Academy of Management Journal, 45*(1), 215–233.

KPMG International. (2013). *The KPMG survey of corporate responsibility reporting 2013*. KPMG. https://www.kpmg.com/Global/en/IssuesAndInsights/ArticlesPublications/corporate-responsibility/Documents/corporate-responsibility-reporting-survey-2013-execsummary.pdf

Lau, C., Lu, Y., & Liang, Q. (2016). Corporate social responsibility in China: A corporate governance approach. *Journal of Business Ethics, 136*(1), 73–87.

Leisinger, K. M. (2005). The corporate social responsibility of the pharmaceutical industry: Idealism without illusion and realism without resignation. *Business Ethics Quarterly, 15*(4), 577–594.

Li, X. (2016). The expansion of China's global hegemonic strategy: Implications for Latin America. *Journal of China and International Relations, 4*(2), 1–26.

Lundan, S. M. (2010). What are ownership advantages? *Multinational Business Review, 18*(2), 51–70.

Luo, C., Chai, Q., & Chen, H. (2019). "Going global" and FDI inflows in China: "One Belt & One Road" initiative as a quasi-natural experiment. *The World Economy, 42*(6), 1654–1672.

Madhok, A., & Keyhani, M. (2012). Acquisitions as entrepreneurship: Asymmetries, opportunities, and the internationalization of multinationals from emerging economies. *Global Strategy Journal, 2*(1), 26–40.

Maignan, I., & Ralston, D. A. (2002). Corporate social responsibility in Europe and the US: Insights from businesses' self-presentations. *Journal of International Business Studies, 33*(3), 497–514.

Marano, V., & Kostova, T. (2016). Unpacking the institutional complexity in adoption of CSR practices in multinational enterprises. *Journal of Management Studies, 53*(1), 28–54.

Markusen, J. R. (2004). *Multinational firms and the theory of international trade*. MIT press.

Martínez-Ferrero, J., & García-Sánchez, I. M. (2017). Coercive, normative and mimetic isomorphism as determinants of the voluntary assurance of sustainability reports. *International Business Review, 26*(1), 102–118.

Maruyama, M., & Wu, L. (2015). Overcoming the liability of foreignness in international retailing: A consumer perspective. *Journal of International Management, 21*(3), 200–210.

Mathews, J. A. (2006). Dragon multinationals: New players in 21st century globalization. *Asia Pacific Journal of Management*, 23(1), 5–27.

Matten, D., & Moon, J. (2004). Corporate social responsibility. *Journal of Business Ethics*, 54(4), 323–337.

May, K. (2015). Chinese agricultural overseas investment: Trends, policies and CSR. *Transnational Corporations*, 22(3), 43–74.

McWilliams, A., & Siegel, D. (2001). Profit maximizing corporate social responsibility. *Academy of Management Review*, 26(4), 504–505.

Meyer, K. E., Mudambi, R., & Narula, R. (2011). Multinational enterprises and local contexts: The opportunities and challenges of multiple embeddedness. *Journal of Management Studies*, 48(2), 235–252.

Milhaupt, C. J., & Zheng, W. (2014). Beyond ownership: State capitalism and the Chinese firm. *Georgetown Law Journal*, 103, 665.

Milne, M. J., & Patten, D. M. (2002). Securing organizational legitimacy: An experimental decision case examining the impact of environmental disclosures. *Accounting, Auditing & Accountability Journal*, 15(3), 372–405.

Minor, D., & Morgan, J. (2011). CSR as reputation insurance: Primum non noncore. *California Management Review*, 53(3), 40–59.

Miska, C., Witt, M. A., & Stahl, G. K. (2016). Drivers of global CSR integration and local CSR responsiveness: Evidence from Chinese MNEs. *Business Ethics Quarterly*, 26(3), 317–345.

Mithani, M. A. (2017a). Innovation and CSR—Do they go well together? *Long Range Planning*, 50(6), 699–711.

Mithani, M. A. (2017b). Liability of foreignness, natural disasters, and corporate philanthropy. *Journal of International Business Studies*, 48(8), 941–963.

Mizruchi, M. S., & Fein, L. C. (1999). The social construction of organizational knowledge: A study of the uses of coercive, mimetic, and normative isomorphism. *Administrative Science Quarterly*, 44(4), 653–683.

Moir, L. (2001). What do we mean by corporate social responsibility? *Corporate Governance: The International Journal of Business in Society*, 1(2), 16–22.

National Development and Reform Commission (NDRC). (2015). *Vision and actions on jointly building Silk Road economic belt and 21st-century Maritime Silk Road*. NDRC. http://en.ndrc.gov.cn/newsrelease/201503/t20150330_669367.html

Naughton, B. (2008). SASAC and rising corporate power in China. *China Leadership Monitor*, 24(2), 1–9.

Nolan, P., & Rui, H. (2004). Industrial policy and global big business revolution: The case of the Chinese coal industry. *Journal of Chinese Economic and Business Studies*, 2(2), 97–113.

North, D. C. (1990). *Institutions, institutional change and economic performance*. Cambridge University Press.

Papasolomou-Doukakis, I., Krambia-Kapardis, M., & Katsioloudes, M. (2005). Corporate social responsibility: The way forward? Maybe not! A preliminary study in Cyprus. *European Business Review*, 17(3), 263–279.

Parsons, R., Lacey, J., & Moffat, K. (2014). Maintaining legitimacy of a contested practice: How the minerals industry understands its 'social licence to operate'. *Resources Policy*, 41, 83–90.

Patten, D. M. (1991). Exposure, legitimacy, and social disclosure. *Journal of Accounting and Public Policy*, 10(4), 297–308.

Patten, D. M. (2002). The relation between environmental performance and environmental disclosure: A research note. *Accounting, Organizations and Society, 27*(8), 763–773.

Pearce, J. A. II, & Robinson, R. B. Jr. (2000). Cultivating Guanxi as a foreign investor strategy. *Business Horizons, 43*(1), 31–38.

Peck, P., & Sinding, K. (2003). Environmental and social disclosure and data richness in the mining industry. *Business Strategy and the Environment, 12*(3), 131–146.

Pegg, S. (2012). Social responsibility and resource extraction: Are Chinese oil companies different? *Resources Policy, 37*(2), 160–167.

Porter, M. E. (1990). The competitive advantage of nations. *Competitive Intelligence Review, 1*(1), 14.

Porter, M. E., & Kramer, M. R. (2002). The competitive advantage of corporate philanthropy. *Harvard Business Review, 80*(12), 56–68.

Porter, M. E., & Kramer, M. R. (2003). Corporate philanthropy: Taking the high ground. *Foundation Strategy Group, 13*(3), 1–12.

Porter, M. E., & Kramer, M. R. (2006). The link between competitive advantage and corporate social responsibility. *Harvard Business Review, 84*(12), 78–92.

Ramachandran, J., & Pant, A. (2010). The liabilities of origin: An emerging economy perspective on the costs of doing business abroad. In T. M. Devinney, T. Pedersen, L. Tihanyi (Eds.), *Advances in international management (Vol. 23: The past, present and future of international business and management* pp. 231–265). Emerald.

Ramamurti, R., & Hillemann, J. (2018). What is "Chinese" about Chinese multinationals? *Journal of International Business Studies, 49*(1), 34–48.

Rathert, N. (2016). Strategies of legitimation: MNEs and the adoption of CSR in response to host-country institutions. *Journal of International Business Studies, 47*(7), 858–879.

Rivoli, P., & Waddock, S. (2011). "First they ignore you...": The time-context dynamic and corporate responsibility. *California Management Review, 53*(2), 87–104.

Roberts, R. W. (1992). Determinants of corporate social responsibility disclosure: An application of stakeholder theory. *Accounting, Organizations and Society, 17,* 595–612.

Rosen, D. H., & Hanemann, T. (2009). *China's changing outbound foreign direct investment profile: Drivers and policy implications* (No. PB09-14). Peterson Institute for International Economics.

Rosenfeld, M. (1984). Contract and justice: The relation between classical contract law and social contract theory. *Iowa Law Review, 70,* 769–900.

Russo, A., & Perrini, F. (2010). Investigating stakeholder theory and social capital: CSR in large firms and SMEs. *Journal of Business Ethics, 91*(2), 207–221.

Sacconi, L. (2007). A social contract account for CSR as an extended model of corporate governance (II): Compliance, reputation and reciprocity. *Journal of Business Ethics, 75*(1), 77–96.

Salancik, G. R., & Pfeffer, J. (1978). A social information processing approach to job attitudes and task design. *Administrative Science Quarterly, 23*(2), 224–253.

Saleh, M., Zulkifli, N., & Muhamad, R. (2010). Corporate social responsibility disclosure and its relation on institutional ownership: Evidence from public listed companies in Malaysia. *Managerial Auditing Journal, 25*(6), 591–613.

Salidjanova, N. (2011). *Going out: An overview of China's outward foreign direct investment.* US-China Economic and Security Review Commission.

Scott, W. R. (2008). Approaching adulthood: The maturing of institutional theory. *Theory and Society*, *37*(5), 427.

Sharfman, M. P., Shaft, T. M., & Tihanyi, L. (2004). A model of the global and institutional antecedents of high-level corporate environmental performance. *Business & Society*, *43*(1), 6–36.

Shi, W., Markóczy, L., & Stan, C. V. (2014). The continuing importance of political ties in China. *Academy of Management Perspectives*, *28*(1), 57–75.

Siltaoja, M. E. (2006). Value priorities as combining core factors between CSR and reputation–a qualitative study. *Journal of Business Ethics*, *68*(1), 91–111.

Snider, J., Hill, R. P., & Martin, D. (2003). Corporate social responsibility in the 21st century: A view from the world's most successful firms. *Journal of Business Ethics*, *48*(2), 175–187.

Spicer, A., Dunfee, T. W., & Bailey, W. J. (2004). Does national context matter in ethical decision making? An empirical test of integrative social contracts theory. *Academy of Management Journal*, *47*(4), 610–620.

Suchman, M. C. (1995). Managing legitimacy: Strategic and institutional approaches. *Academy of Management Review*, *20*(3), 571–610.

Surroca, J., Tribó, J. A., & Zahra, S. A. (2013). Stakeholder pressure on MNEs and the transfer of socially irresponsible practices to subsidiaries. *Academy of Management Journal*, *56*(2), 549–572.

Sweeney, L., & Coughlan, J. (2008). Do different industries report corporate social responsibility differently? An investigation through the lens of stakeholder theory. *Journal of Marketing Communications*, *14*(2), 113–124.

Tagesson, T., Blank, V., Broberg, P., & Collin, S. O. (2009). What explains the extent and content of social and environmental disclosures on corporate websites: A study of social and environmental reporting in Swedish listed corporations. *Corporate Social Responsibility and Environmental Management*, *16*(6), 352–364.

Tan-Mullins, M., & Mohan, G. (2013). The potential of corporate environmental responsibility of Chinese state-owned enterprises in Africa. *Environment, Development and Sustainability*, *15*(2), 265–284.

Tan-Mullins, M., Urban, F., & Mang, G. (2017). Evaluating the behaviour of Chinese stakeholders engaged in large hydropower projects in Asia and Africa. *The China Quarterly*, *230*, 464–488.

Tian, L., & Estrin, S. (2008). Retained state shareholding in Chinese PLCs: Does government ownership always reduce corporate value? *Journal of Comparative Economics*, *36*(1), 74–89.

United Nations Conference on Trade and Development (UNCTAD). (2011). *Corporate governance disclosure in emerging markets: Statistical analysis of legal requirements and company practices*. UNCTAD. http://unctad.org/en/Docs/diaeed2011-d3en.pdf

Van der Merwe, J. (2019). The one belt one road initiative: Reintegrating Africa and the Middle East into China's system of accumulation. In L. Xing (Ed.), *Mapping China's 'One Belt One Road' Initiative* (pp. 197–217). Palgrave Macmillan.

Vernon, R. (1979). The product cycle hypothesis in a new international environment. *Oxford Bulletin of Economics and Statistics*, *41*(4), 255–267.

Waddock, S., & Bodwell, C. (2004). Managing responsibility: What can be learned from the quality movement? *California Management Review*, *47*(1), 25–37.

Wadhwa, K., & Reddy, S. S. (2011). Foreign direct investment into developing Asian countries: The role of market seeking, resource seeking and efficiency seeking factors. *International Journal of Business and Management*, *6*(11), 219.

Wang, C., Hong, J., Kafouros, M., & Boateng, A. (2012). What drives outward FDI of Chinese firms? Testing the explanatory power of three theoretical frameworks. *International Business Review*, *21*(3), 425–438.

Wei, Z., & Nguyen, Q. T. (2017). Subsidiary strategy of emerging market multinationals: A home country institutional perspective. *International Business Review*, *26*(5), 1009–1021.

Wheeler, D., Fabig, H., & Boele, R. (2002). Paradoxes and dilemmas for stakeholder responsive firms in the extractive sector: Lessons from the case of Shell and the Ogoni. *Journal of Business Ethics*, *39*(3), 297–318.

World Business Council on Sustainable Development (WBCSD). (2002). *Corporate social responsibility: the WBCSD's journey*. www.wbcsd.org.

Xin, K. K., & Pearce, J. L. (1996). Guanxi: Connections as substitutes for formal institutional support. *Academy of Management Journal*, *39*(6), 1641–1658.

Xu, D., & Meyer, K. E. (2013). Linking theory and context: 'Strategy research in emerging economies' after Wright et al. (2005). *Journal of Management Studies*, *50*(7), 1322–1346.

Yakovleva, N., & Vazquez-Brust, D. (2012). Stakeholder perspectives on CSR of mining MNCs in Argentina. *Journal of Business Ethics*, *106*(2), 191–211.

Yamakawa, Y., Peng, M. W., & Deeds, D. L. (2008). What drives new ventures to internationalize from emerging to developed economies? *Entrepreneurship Theory and Practice*, *32*(1), 59–82.

Yin, J., & Zhang, Y. (2012). Institutional dynamics and corporate social responsibility (CSR) in an emerging country context: Evidence from China. *Journal of Business Ethics*, *111*(2), 301–316.

Young, S., & Marais, M. (2012). A multi-level perspective of CSR reporting: The implications of national institutions and industry risk characteristics. *Corporate Governance: An International Review*, *20*(5), 432–450.

Zaheer, S. (1995). Overcoming the liability of foreignness. *Academy of Management Journal*, *38*(2), 341–363.

Zamir, F., & Saeed, A. (2020). Location matters: Impact of geographical proximity to financial centers on corporate social responsibility (CSR) disclosure in emerging economies. *Asia Pacific Journal of Management*, *37*(1), 263–295.

Zhang, K. H. (2009). Rise of Chinese multinational firms. *Chinese Economy*, *42*(6), 81–96.

Zhao, M. (2012). CSR-based political legitimacy strategy: Managing the state by doing good in China and Russia. *Journal of Business Ethics*, *111*(4), 439–460.

6 Assessment of CSR Reporting Quality along the Belt and Road

Assessment of CSR reporting quality

Since the mid-1990s, a growing social need to gauge how well the business sector is doing in relation to a range of sustainable development objectives has emerged. This rising image of corporate social responsibility (CSR) imposes unique obligations on firm management, including the need to fulfill the triple bottom line of economic, social, and environmental performance. The importance of new social dialogue formats as a contribution to business reporting, strategy formulation, and decision-making is also emphasized. As a derivative of sustainability (Zinenko et al., 2015), CSR is the modern way of managing businesses by reflecting company actions for the benefit of society, care for the natural environment, and relations with diverse stakeholder groups (Du et al., 2010). Additionally, it is a push to integrate, strengthen, and lessen harmful social and ecological effects of commercial operations on their surrounds.

In order to enable stakeholders, whose interests are connected to the reporting entities, to assess how these entities contribute to sustainable development, enterprises (or reporting organizations) are expected to report on their economic, environmental, and social performance (Tschopp & Huefner, 2015). According to Brown et al. (2009), CSR reporting is a standard requirement for socially responsible companies. It is carried out in a visible, accountable, and transparent manner utilizing CSR reporting tools (Adams & Zutshi, 2004; Toppinen et al., 2015). Companies around the world are more frequently publishing publicly accessible CSR reports to reveal how ethically they do business. Developing a high-quality CSR report may be advantageous for both a reporting company and its stakeholders. However, only reports with characteristics such as relevance, reliability, validity, and timeliness may be employed as a significant corporate communication tool and a key factor in organizations' and stakeholders' decision-making.

As CSR reporting mechanisms have grown and increased in quantity, a growing number of studies have been conducted on the topic. Researchers have been focusing on using CSR reporting frameworks (Sutantoputra, 2009), standards (Tschopp & Nastanski, 2014), and ratings and indices (Dumay et al., 2010) to assess the CSR reporting quality. Specifically, frameworks are a subset of CSR reporting systems that offer standards, programs, and best practices for CSR

DOI: 10.4324/9781003302445-6

reporting (Siew, 2015). The Global Reporting Initiative (GRI), which is frequently utilized for CSR reporting in practice, is a common example (Bernard et al., 2015). Another example would be the United Nations Global Compact (UNGC) which was established in 2000 as a set of ten principles in the areas of human rights, labor, environment, and corruption to control socially responsible conduct and reporting in commercial organizations (Fortanier et al., 2011). Standards are similar to frameworks in directing CSR reporting efforts, but they take the form of formal documentation that outlines the prerequisites for achieving social responsibility (Szczuka, 2015). For example, the International Standards Organization (ISO 26000) is gaining acceptance among global CSR reporters. ISO 26000 comprehensively addresses CSR practices in government agencies, non-profits, and enterprises (Tschopp & Nastanski, 2014). The major objective of ISO 26000 standard is to give advice for adopting and integrating social responsibility in organizations, as well as for external reporting of CSR practices. However, it should be noted that ISO 26000 is not for certification purpose. On the other hand, various ratings and indexes enable third-party verification of CSR involvement (Diez-Cañamero et al., 2020) and sustainable performance (Sharifi & Murayama, 2013). The majority of CSR indices are designed with shareholders, investors, and executives in mind (Diez-Cañamero et al., 2020). For instance, the Dow Jones Sustainability Index (DJSI) was introduced in 1999 as a global sustainability benchmark (Siew, 2015) for evaluating environmental reporting, environmental policy/management system, operational eco-efficiency, and climate strategy in commercial corporations (Angelakoglou & Gaidajis, 2015). Ratings and rankings of CSR performance, on the other hand, use a multi-stakeholder approach and are more open tools that may theoretically be utilized by any stakeholder (Diez-Cañamero et al., 2020). Additionally, this class of reporting systems can be used to evaluate the sustainability performance of communities (Searcy & Elkhawas, 2012).

Assessment of CSR reporting quality of Chinese MNEs

This chapter and the subsequent chapters adopt a mixed-methods methodology to evaluate the CSR reporting quality of Chinese multinational enterprises (MNEs) for triangulation purposes. That is to say, both quantitative and qualitative content analyses are conducted to analyze the CSR reports of Chinese MNEs that have significant involvement along the Belt and Road. Triangulation entails "using more than one process or source of data in the analysis of social phenomena" (Bryman, 2016, p. 392). Bryman observes that it has recently been described primarily in terms of utilizing a variety of data sources and methods, as opposed to Denzin's (1970) broader understanding of triangulation as including a multiplicity of investigators, theoretical viewpoints, data sources, and methods. The term "triangulation" is used in this book to refer to the process of combining different methodological approaches (in this case, quantitative and qualitative content analyses) to tackle the research questions. Unlike quantitative approaches, mixed-methods approaches have rarely been used in social and environmental studies (Vourvachis & Woodward, 2015). Balanced and objective results are thus obtained by combining these two analytical techniques.

Lack of existing research in the area and the need to analyze the current CSR reporting practices and quality of major Chinese MNEs along the Belt and Road Initiative (BRI) have led to the choice of an exploratory qualitative method combined with empirical analysis. The first step involved qualitative analysis of the CSR reports of major Chinese MNEs along the BRI from 2014 to 2021. Specifically, qualitative content analysis was conducted to analyze the various CSR themes and topics to which Chinese MNEs pay attention. This strategy involves looking for particular themes (Bryman, 2016, pp. 557–559) that then serve as a foundation for coding. The qualitative content review in this book focused on the context surrounding five CSR themes: Governance, Economy, Environment, Employment, and Social. These were divided into multiple codes corresponding with those of previous studies and relating to the reporting framework. The aims of the qualitative content analysis were to gain insights into the CSR reporting practices of Chinese MNEs along the BRI and demonstrate conceptual variations and similarities in reporting among different types of firms with different ownership structures. Empirical analysis was conducted to assess the quality of overseas CSR reporting.[1] In addition, exploratory case studies were undertaken to examine industry-specific CSR reporting content along the BRI. Figure 6.1 illustrates the methodological process adopted in this study.

The sample firms were selected from Chinese firms with significant involvement in the BRI, measured as having one or more subsidiaries in BRI countries. Specifically, Chinese MNEs are occupying an increasingly important position in the international arena. For the first time in 2020, China has more Fortune Global 500 companies than the United States, with 133 companies on the list. In 2021, a total of 143 Chinese firms made the Global 500 list, beating the second-placed

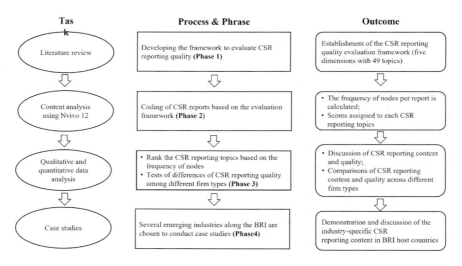

Figure 6.1 Research methodology process.

United States for the second year in a row (Xinhua, 2021). In order to better select the most representative Chinese MNEs, the sample firms included firms with the top 100 OFDI amounts according to the "Statistical Bulletin of China's Foreign Direct Investment" issued by China Enterprise Confederation and China Entrepreneur Association (China Entrepreneurs Association, 2021). In addition, firms on the Fortune 500 and Top 500 lists of Chinese companies with significant business operations in BRI countries were included. These companies represent a representative collective of Chinese MNEs with OFDI accounting for a majority amount of OFDI of all Chinese MNEs in overseas markets (China Entrepreneurs Association, 2021). The CSR disclosures of these Chinese MNEs provide us with a clear and comprehensive view of how are they approaching their social and environmental accounting practices in overseas markets. A total of 1361 CSR reports from individual companies were analyzed using NVivo 12, an advanced computer-aided content analysis program.

The GRI is viewed as one of the most authoritative reporting regulations in the social and environmental arena (Moneva et al., 2006; Wood, 2008). Specifically, the GRI Principles provide a shared language for public and private

Table 6.1 CSR report screening process

Selection layer	Selection criteria	Number of firms	Number of annual CSR reports (including CSR reports issued for particular overseas project/country, environmental reports, annual public interest reports)[2]
First	Firms with the top 100 OFDI amount in the "Statistical Bulletin of China's Foreign Direct Investment"	100	799
Second	Fortune 500 Chinese firms with significant overseas operations in BRI countries and are not included in the first layer	43	313
Third	Top 500 Chinese firms with significant overseas operations in BRI countries which are not included in the first and second layers	36	249
Total		179	1361

organizations of all sizes to report their sustainability impacts clearly and reliably. This improves global comparability and enables businesses to be more transparent and accountable. On the other hand, at the United Nations Summit on Sustainable Development held in New York in 2015, the UN issued its "Change Our World: 2030 Agenda for Sustainable Development" (hereafter referred to as the "2030 Agenda"). The 2030 Agenda established 17 Sustainable Development Goals (SDGs) and 169 targets to achieve the Millennium Development Goals (MDGs) and serves as a programmatic document to guide global sustainable development for the next 15 years (Colglazier, 2015).

In this book, other international standards were also considered, such as ISO 14000 and ISO 26000.[3] Local standards are also essential tools for leading the development of CSR reporting in China. In order to effectively guide Chinese enterprises in preparing standardized CSR reports, the CSR Research Centre of the Chinese Academy of Social Sciences (CASS) released version 1.0 of its "Guidelines for Preparing CSR Reports in China" (CASS-CSR 1.0) in 2009 and version 2.0 (CASS-CSR 2.0) in 2011. Version 4.0 was released in 2017. Table 6.2 lists out the references used to establish an evaluation framework for the CSR reporting quality of Chinese MNEs along the BRI. A total of 5 CSR themes (Governance, Economy, Environment, Employment, and Social) and 49 CSR-related topics were identified as measures. Table 6.3 presents the grouped CSR topics and themes.

Quantitative content analysis is described as "an approach to document and text analysis ... that seeks to quantify content in terms of predetermined categories in a systematic and replicable manner" (Bryman, 2016, p. 289). The first goal was to

Table 6.2 References for the establishment of the evaluation framework of CSR reporting quality of Chinese MNEs along the BRI

Compacts and initiatives	Standards	Indexes	Academic references	Documents
Global Reporting Initiative (GRI)	Sustainable Development Goals (SDGs)	Shanghai Stock Exchange CSR index	Castka and Balzarova (2008) Campopiano and De Massis (2015) Frynas and Yamahaki (2016)	Visions and Actions on Jointly Building Silk Road Economic Belt and 21st Century Maritime Silk Road
CASS-CSR 4.0	ISO 14000 Environment Quality Management System	CBN-Industrial Global Fund Social Responsibility Index	Gao (2009)	Concept for Maritime Cooperation under the Belt and Road Initiative
	ISO 26000 Social Responsibility Standard		Lock and Seele (2016)	

Table 6.3 Evaluation framework of CSR reporting quality of Chinese MNEs along the BRI

Number/Code	Evaluation base	CSR reporting subtopics	Full marks	Notes
Governance			12	
G1	GRI 102 & SDG 11,13,16,17 & CASS-CSR 4.0 G6	Stakeholder engagement	3	
G2	GRI 102 & SDG 11,13,17 & CASS-CSR 4.0 P2 G3 G4	CSR management system; supervision and evaluation mechanism of CSR activities	3	
G3	GRI 102 & SDG 11,13,17 & CASS-CSR 4.0 P3 G2	Materiality analysis of CSR issues and risk identification	3	
G4	SDG 11,13,16,17 & CASS-CSR 4.0 G5 G6	Enrollment of global sustainable development organization	3	
Economy			30	
EC1	GRI 201-1 & SDG 2,5,7,8,9 & CASS-CSR 4.0 M1.7 S1.3	Direct economic value generated and distributed to other countries or regions	3	
EC2	GRI 201-2 & SDG 13 & CASS-CSR 4.0 E1.9	Financial implications and other risks and opportunities due to climate change	3	
EC3	GRI 202-1 SDG 1,5,8 & CASS-CSR 4.0 S2.8	Ratios of standard entry level wage by gender compared to local minimum wage	3	
EC4	GRI 202-2 & SDG 8 & CASS-CSR 4.0 S1.5 S4.2 4.3	Localization of employees; promotion of local employment	3	
EC5	GRI 203-1 SDG 2,5,7,9,11 & CASS-CSR 4.0 S1 S4 M3	Infrastructure investments and services supported to local areas	3	
EC6	GRI 203-2 & SDG 1,10,17,2,3,8 & CASS-CSR 4.0 S1 S4 M3	Significant indirect economic impacts on local areas	3	
EC7	GRI 204-1 SDG 12 & CASS-CSR 4.0 S1.5 S4.2 4.4	Local suppliers	3	
EC8	GRI 205 SDG 16 & CASS-CSR 4.0 M1.3	Corruption risk assessment and anti-corruption	3	
EC9	GRI 206 & SDG 16 & CASS-CSR 4.0 M3.3 M3.7	Anti-competitive behavior and fair competition; fair trade	3	

(*Continued*)

Table 6.3 Evaluation framework of CSR reporting quality of Chinese MNEs along the BRI (Continued)

Number/Code	Evaluation base	CSR reporting subtopics	Full marks	Notes
EC10	CASS-CSR 4.0 M3.5	Protection mechanism of intellectual property rights	3	
Environment			42	
ENV1	SDG 6,7,14,15,16 & CASS-CSR 4.0 E1	Management system for environmental protection	3	
ENV2	GRI 301-2 SDG 12,8 & CASS-CSR 4.0 E2.2 2.8	Renewable materials and resources used and promotion of recycling of energy resources	3	
ENV3	GRI 301-3 SDG 12,8 & CASS-CSR 4.0 E 2.18-2.20	Reclaimed products and their packaging materials	3	
ENV4	GRI 302-1,2 SDG 12,13,7,8 & CASS-CSR 4.0 E2.24 2.25 E2.5 2.6	Energy consumption and intensity in overseas markets	3	
ENV5	GRI 302-4, 302-5 SDG 12,13,7,8 & CASS-CSR 4.0 E2.24 2.25 E2.5 2.6	Reduction of global energy consumption and energy demand for products and services	3	
ENV6	GRI 303-3,4,5 SDG 6,14 & CASS-CSR 4.0 E2.10 2.11	Global water intake, water consumption, drainage, and global water resources management in different operating areas	3	
ENV7	GRI 304-1,2 SDG 14,15,6 & CASS-CSR 4.0 E3.4	Operational sites owned, leased, managed in, or adjacent to, protected areas and areas of high biodiversity value outside protected areas; significant impacts of activities, products, and services on biodiversity	3	Not applicable for industries H, I, K
ENV8	GRI 304-3 SDG 14,15,6 & CASS-CSR 4.0 E3.3	Habitats protected or restored; Protection of the local ecological environment	3	Not applicable for industries H, I, K
ENV9	GRI 305 SDG 12,13,14,15 & CASS-CSR 4.0 E2.24 2.25	Greenhouse gas emissions and emissions of ozone-depleting substances such as nitrogen oxides (NOx), sulfur oxides (SOx), and other major gas emissions	3	Not applicable for industries H, I, K

(Continued)

Table 6.3 Evaluation framework of CSR reporting quality of Chinese MNEs along the BRI (Continued)

Number/Code	Evaluation base	CSR reporting subtopics	Full marks	Notes
ENV10	GRI 305 SDG 12,13,14,15 & CASS-CSR 4.0 E2.24 2.25	Reduction of greenhouse gases or other major gases	3	
ENV11	GRI 306-1,5 SDG 12,14,3,6 & CASS-CSR 4.0 E2.14 2.15	Drained water quality and water bodies affected by drainage and runoff	3	Not applicable for industries H, I, K
ENV12	GRI 306 SDG 12,14,15,3,6 & CASS-CSR 4.0 E2.16 2.17	Disposal, transportation, and management of pollutants and waste	3	
ENV13	GRI 308-1,2 & CASS-CSR 4.0 M3.8-3.16	Supplier environmental assessment; negative impact of the supply chain on the environment and the actions taken	3	
ENV 14	SDG 6,7,12,13, 14,15,16 & CASS-CSR 4.0 E1	Environmental compliance in overseas markets	3	
Employment			21	
EMP1	GRI 401-1,2 SDG 5,8 & CASS-CSR 4.0 S2.10	Benefits to overseas full-time employees; complete salary and welfare system	3	
EMP2	GRI 403-1,2 SDG 8 & CASS-CSR 4.0 S2.11 S3.1-3.7	Occupational health and safety management and hazard identification, risk assessment, and incident investigation	3	
EMP3	GRI 403-3,5 SDG 3,8 & CASS-CSR 4.0 S2.11	Employee occupational safety training	3	
EMP4	GRI 403-6 SDG 8 & CASS-CSR 4.0 S2.12 2.17	Promotion of employees' health; Creating a good working environment and promoting the physical and mental health of employees	3	
EMP5	GRI 404 SDG 4,5,8 & CASS-CSR 4.0 S2.14	Staff training and education for skill improvement and career development	3	
EMP6	GRI 405 SDG 10,5,8 & CASS-CSR 4.0 S2.2 2.5 2.6 2.8	Diversity of employees; gender equality	3	

(*Continued*)

Table 6.3 Evaluation framework of CSR reporting quality of Chinese MNEs along the BRI (Continued)

Number/Code	Evaluation base	CSR reporting subtopics	Full marks	Notes
EMP7	GRI 406 SDG 16,5,8 & CASS-CSR 4.0 S2.2	Anti-discrimination	3	
Social			42	
S1	GRI 407 408 409 & SDG 8 16 & CASS-CSR 4.0 S2.7	Operations and suppliers in which the right to freedom of association and collective bargaining may be at risk; operations and suppliers at significant risk for incidents of child labor; operations and suppliers at significant risk for incidents of forced or compulsory labor	3	
S2	GRI 411 SDG 1,2,4,10,11	Rights of indigenous peoples	3	Not applicable for industry H, I, K
S3	GRI 412 SDG 1,2,3,4	Human rights policy; guarantee of political rights, social rights, cultural rights, and other basic needs of employees and local residents	3	
S4	GRI 413 SDG 1,2 & CASS-CSR 4.0 S4.1	Operations with local community engagement, impact assessments, and development programs and operations with significant actual and potential negative impacts on local communities	3	
S5	GRI 414 & CASS-CSR 4.0 M3	Suppliers social assessment; CSR policies, initiatives, and requirements for suppliers	3	
S6	GRI 416 & SDG 16 & CASS-CSR 4.0 M2.1 M2.2	Product quality and safety; assessment of the impact of products and services on health and safety	3	
S7	GRI 418 & CASS-CSR 4.0 M2.13 S2.6	Privacy protection and information security of customers and employees	3	
S8	SDG 1,2,3,4,10,11 & CASS-CSR 4.0 S4.6	Community public welfare projects; Practices to benefit the local area and enhance social welfare in overseas markets	3	

(Continued)

Table 6.3 Evaluation framework of CSR reporting quality of Chinese MNEs along the BRI *(Continued)*

Number/Code	Evaluation base	CSR reporting subtopics	Full marks	Notes
S9	SDG 1,2,3,4,10,11	Promotion of cultural and educational development in overseas markets; Contribution to local social development through cultural exchanges	3	
S10	SDG 1,3,4,5 & CASS-CSR 4.0 S4.5	Promotion of rights of women, children, and other disadvantaged groups in overseas markets	3	
S11	SDG 1,2,3,4,10,11	Promotion of the health of local communities; regulating health threats, and contribution to alleviating diseases in overseas markets	3	
S12	SDG 1,2,3,4,10,11	Disaster relief and mitigation; Provision of assistance for community disaster prevention, relief, and mitigation in overseas markets	3	
S13	SDG 1,2,10 & CASS-CSR 4.0 S4.12-4.14	Contribution to poverty reduction and social development in overseas markets	3	
S14	GRI 419 SDG 16 & CASS-CSR 4.0 S1.1	Compliance with laws and regulations in overseas operations	3	

A = agriculture, forestry, animal husbandry, and fishery; B = mining; C = manufacturing; D = electricity, gas, and water; E = building and construction; F = transportation, warehousing industry; G = information and communication technology industry; H = wholesale and retail; I = finance, banking, and insurance; J = real estate; K = public facilities and social services; M = mixed. The industry classification is based on the GoldenBee Research Database on Corporate Social Responsibility Reporting in China.[4]

determine the frequency of the occurrence of specific key terms associated with the CSR themes. The themes and topics listed in Table 6.3 served as an evaluation framework for the CSR reporting quality of Chinese MNEs along the BRI. A total of five overseas CSR reporting themes with 49 overseas CSR reporting topics were thus identified. Each topic under the five themes was assigned equal weight. Since the Environment and Social themes contained more CSR reporting topics (14 each), the total weighting of these two CSR reporting themes was higher than the others. NVivo 12 was used to conduct computer-assisted content analysis. Each CSR topic in the evaluation framework represented one code in NVivo. In qualitative analysis, a code is a word or phrase that summarizes or captures the meaning of a portion of data. Coding in NVivo 12 is a method for collecting relevant materials into a container known as a node. Since more than half of the sample firms did not issue English versions of their CSR reports, the Chinese versions were used, and the Chinese language was used for coding in NVivo.

A content analysis coding system was built based on Beattie et al.'s (2004) and Krippendorff's (2013) guidelines. Expressions, clauses, and themes served as records, which could be longer or shorter than a sentence, but no more than a paragraph long (Beck et al., 2010). Each record relevant to CSR activities in BRI host countries was coded as a node under a specific code (CSR topic). A node is a set of links to information about a particular subject, event, or relationship, and the number of nodes under each CSR topic (code) per CSR report reveals the frequency of each CSR topic.

Previous literature on CSR reporting quality (Aerts & Cormier, 2009; Cormier & Magnan, 2003) used three levels (scores) for each evaluation item in the content analysis. In the current study, CSR disclosures relating to BRI countries that contain detailed descriptions and were supported by monetary amounts or figures were given three points; disclosures with substantial descriptions but not supported by monetary amounts or figures were given two points; and disclosures with general descriptions were given one point. Zero point was given if nothing was disclosed regarding a particular CSR topic in BRI countries. A list of BRI host countries is presented in Appendix 1. Throughout this book, a similar disclosure-scoring methodology was adopted, based on content analysis of disclosures on the 49 CSR-related topics under the five themes. In order to make this evaluation framework more suitable for firms in different industries, some indicators for specific industries were excluded (Day & Woodward, 2009; Gao, 2011; Kiliç et al., 2015). Overseas CSR reporting quality in BRI host countries was determined using the following formula:

$$OCSR_{quality} = \frac{\sum_i^{k_1} GOV + \sum_i^{k_2} ECO + \sum_i^{k_3} ENV + \sum_i^{k_4} EMP + \sum_i^{k_5} SOC}{3 \times (k_1 + k_2 + k_3 + k_4 + k_5)} \times 100$$

(6.1)

where k denotes the number of key indicators (see Table 6.4); $k_1 = 4$; $k_2 = 10$; $k_3 = 14$ (or 10 for industries H, I, and K); $k_4 = 7$; and $k_5 = 14$ (or 13 for industries H, I, and K). *GOV*, *ECO*, *ENV*, *EMP*, and *SOC* are the Governance, Economy, Environment, Employment, and Social dimensions, respectively.

Assessment of CSR Reporting Quality along the Belt and Road 107

Table 6.4 Illustration of assigning scores in content analysis

CSR topic	Score assigned	Illustration[5]
EC4 Localization of employees; promotion of local employment	3	We advocate a culture of respect, openness, and tolerance, adhere to the principle of "localization, specialization, and marketization of overseas employment", continue to improve the employee training mechanism, and strive to promote the localization of employees and the internationalization of the talent team. As at the end of 2018, the staff localization ratio in overseas projects reached 84.4% (China National Petroleum Corporation, 2018, p. 52).
EC4	2	BTD has always taken a proactive approach to recruit international staff and promoting the localization of overseas employees. The localization of employees helps companies gain a deeper understanding of the different cultures in each region, promote employment for the local population and contribute to the development of the local economy (BTD Auto, 2019, p.11).
EC4	1	Implementation of local hiring and procurement to promote the local community's overall social, economic, and technological advancement (Northern International, 2016, p. 14).
EMP6 Diversity of employees; gender equality	3	As at December 31, 2018, Huawei had a total of 188,000 employees worldwide. Huawei's employees come from nearly 160 countries and regions worldwide, and in China alone, there are employees of 41 nationalities. Huawei sets and holistically implements diversity goals regarding its employees' nationality, gender, age, race, and religious beliefs. Huawei strictly complies with relevant laws and regulations and international conventions worldwide to ensure fair employment for both male and female employees. In recent years, the proportion of Huawei's female employees has remained stable. Huawei focuses on the selection of female managers and helps them with their career development, with the proportion of female managers reaching 7.05% in 2018 (Huawei, 2018, p. 33).
EMP6	2	Our employees are located on all continents of the world and come from different cultural and religious backgrounds. On the one hand, we strictly abide by the relevant labor laws and regulations of the market in which we operate; on the other hand, we are committed to creating a diverse corporate culture, respecting and treating all employees fairly and impartially, and not treating them differently due to differences in gender, age, disease and race (WH Group, 2017, p. 18).
EMP6	1	Geely is committed to creating an equal, fair and harmonious working environment, focusing on cultural integration and a rejection of discrimination on the grounds of race, nationality, religion, disability, gender, education, and so on (Geely Global, 2018, p. 27).

(Continued)

108 Assessment of CSR Reporting Quality along the Belt and Road

Table 6.4 Illustration of assigning scores in content analysis (Continued)

CSR topic	Score assigned	Illustration[5]
ENV5 Reduction of global energy consumption and energy demand for products and services	3	Huawei's PowerStar energy-saving solution has been validated and delivered in many countries worldwide, including China, South Africa and Morocco. According to the South African PowerStar case study report released by the GSMA, PowerStar helped South African operators save 11.6% power on their wireless network leading equipment and 6.43 kWh of energy per day on a single base station; in Zhejiang, China PowerStar has helped operators save 12% on their wireless network main equipment, saving an estimated 26 million kWh per year in the province's wireless network; a typical network with 1,000 sites can save 1.46 million kWh per year, which is equivalent to a reduction of 1,370 tonnes of carbon emissions per year, according to estimates from existing networks (Huawei, 2018, p. 17).
ENV5	2	The new Egyptian capital project, launched in 2018, aims to solve the problems of traffic tension and air pollution in the Egyptian capital, relying on China's experience in urbanization and integrating "Chinese planning", "Chinese design", and "Chinese construction", the project will be turned into a green, livable and intelligent city, promoting the process of comprehensive urban development in Egypt and becoming a model of Sino-Egyptian cooperation (China Energy Construction Group, 2018, p. 24).
ENV5	1	LiuGong India achieves energy savings by replacing metal halide lamps with LED lamps (Liugong Group, 2019, p. 46).
S10 (Promote the rights of women, children, and other disadvantaged groups in overseas markets)	3	In order to help local people with their digital awareness and digital skills, Huawei worked with Belgian non-profit organizations: Close the Gap, UNESCO (East Africa), Kenya Computers for Schools Kenya (CFSK), Global Association for Mobile Communications Systems GSMA, Kenyan operator Safaricom to establish DigiTruck mobile digital classrooms to provide digital empowerment for remote and rural areas. Currently, Huawei's DigiTruck has been opened to five counties and townships in Kenya, and a total of 796 participants have benefited from the training program. (Huawei, 2019, p. 23).
S10	2	The company donated school books, stationeries, football balls, and other school and sports supplies to five local rural primary schools to encourage the children to study hard and live a healthy life (Shanghai Electric Power Company Limited, 2016, p. 32).
S10	1	Zijin Mining provided the opportunity for WA School of Mines students to train future mining professionals (Zijin Mining Limited, 2016, p. 26).

Assessment of CSR Reporting Quality along the Belt and Road

The data were collected and coded by one researcher. In order to check for inter-coder reliability, a second researcher conducted a similar coding process on 300 CSR reports chosen randomly from the sample. Scott's pi value was higher than 0.75, suggesting high reliability (Hayes & Krippendorff, 2007; Lombard et al., 2002; Scott, 1955).

So far, this chapter has detailed the methodology used in this study to measure the quality of CSR reports and has given examples of applications of this measurement approach. The final sample for this chapter consisted of 1361 CSR reports from 2014 to 2021. Details of the sample firms are given in Appendix 2. In addition to annual CSR reports downloaded from the selected companies' official websites, the sample also included annual public interest reports (e.g., for Alibaba), and country-specific responsibility reports, including, for example, China Communications Construction's CSR report for the Mombasa-Nairobi standard gauge railway project in Kenya. Table 6.5 presents descriptive statistics for the sample.

Panels A and B demonstrate that a majority of BRI-participating Chinese firms are with strong state ownership (either SOEs or CEs). Chinese companies primarily invest in the basic infrastructure of the BRI host countries, and the SOEs play a vital role. This is totally different from the old story of private-MNEs-dominant internationalization. This is consistent with most of the studies that SOEs serve multiple functions within the state economy and they are the primary responders to national industrial policies and act as the government's market actors (Vernon, 1979). Despite the fact that BRI is a recent idea, top state-owned Chinese contractors have been winning jobs in BRI nations starting from decades ago. For instance, Sinohydro began building hydropower dams in Laos in the late 1990s, and China State Construction Engineering has been developing significant residential and commercial structures in the UAE since the early 2000s. However, private companies, lacking strong government support, have only slowly begun to start investment projects in BRI countries since the early 20th century. The fact that leading Chinese SOEs and CEs are starting from such an established position means a large portion of the Chinese MNEs with significant BRI involvement would be those with strong state ownership. Panel C demonstrates an increasing trend for CSR reporting, as the number of CSR reports increases annually. The trend in the issuance of social responsibility reports has been relatively stable since 2020. Panels D and E present the industry distribution of Chinese MNEs along the Belt and Road. Specifically, Chinese MNEs are mainly involved in manufacturing (C), electricity, gas, and water (D), construction (E), mining (B), and information and communication technology (G) in countries along the Belt and Road.

The sample of Chinese MNEs studied in this chapter is diverse with different types of ownership and a wide range of industries distribution. The time period examined started from the beginning of the BRI until 2021, which represents a long time-span. Therefore, the following chapters will slowly unfold the "painting" which consists of the CSR reporting quality and contents of the Chinese MNEs, their reporting characteristics, the situational factors affecting their reporting contents as well as those specific to certain countries.

Table 6.5 Descriptive statistics

Panel A: Firm-type distribution of sample firms

Firm type	Private enterprise (PE)	State-owned enterprise (SOE)	Central enterprise (CE)	Total
Freq.	40	81	58	179
Percent	22.35	44.69	32.96	100

Panel B: Firm-type distribution of sample CSR reports

Firm type	Private enterprise (PE)	State-owned enterprise (SOE)	Central enterprise (CE)	Total
Freq.	262	586	513	1361
Percent	19.25	43.05	37.70	100

Panel C: Year distribution of sample CSR reports

Year	2014	2015	2016	2017	2018	2019	2020
Freq.	146	158	174	180	183	188	175
Percent	10.73	11.60	12.78	13.23	13.45	13.81	12.86

Year	2021	Total
Freq.	157	1361
Percent	11.54	100

Panel D: Industry distribution of sample firms

	A	B	C	D	E	F	Total
Freq.	3	8	68	16	15	14	179
Percent	1.68	4.47	37.98	8.94	8.38	7.26	100

	G	H	I	J	K	M	
Freq.	13	1	12	7	5	17	
Percent	7.82	0.59	6.70	3.91	2.79	9.50	

Panel E: Industry distribution of sample CSR reports

	A	B	C	D	E	F	Total
Freq.	16	103	509	132	119	86	1361
Percent	1.17	7.58	37.41	9.72	8.75	6.32	

	G	H	I	J	K	M	
Freq.	103	8	74	44	39	128	
Percent	7.58	0.58	5.44	3.21	2.82	9.43	

A = agriculture, forestry, animal husbandry, and fishery; B = mining; C = manufacturing; D = electricity, gas, and water; E = building and construction; F = transportation, warehousing industry; G = information technology industry; H = wholesale and retail; I = finance, banking, and insurance; J = real estate; K = public facilities and social services; M = mixed.

Appendix

Appendix 1: List of BRI host countries

Africa (46 countries)		European (27 countries)	
Algeria	Mali	Albania	Serbia
Angola	Mauritania	Austria	Slovakia
Botswana	Morocco	Bosnia	Slovenia
Benin	Mozambique	Belarus	Ukraine
Burundi	Namibia	Bulgaria	
Cameroon	Niger	Croatia	
Cape Verde	Nigeria	Cyprus	
Chad	Congo	Czech Republic	
Democratic Republic of the Congo	Rwanda	Estonia	
Comoros	Senegal	Greece	
Djibouti	Seychelles	Hungary	
Equatorial Guinea	Sierra Leone	Italy	
Egypt	Somalia	Latvia	
Ethiopia	South Africa	Lithuania	
Gabon	South Sudan	Luxembourg	
Ghana	Sudan	Malta	
Guinea	Tanzania	Moldova	
Côte d'Ivoire	Gambia	Montenegro	
Kenya	Togo	North Macedonia	
Lesotho	Tunisia	Poland	
Liberia	Uganda	Portugal	
Libya	Zambia	Romanian	
Madagascar	Zimbabwe	Russia	
Oceania (12 countries, 2 regions)	**America (19 countries)**	**Asia (38 countries, 2 regions)**	
Cook Islands	Antigua and Barbuda	Afghanistan	Myanmar
Fiji	Barbados	Armenia	Nepal
Kiribati	Bolivia	Azerbaijan	Oman
Federated States of Micronesia	Chile	Bahrain	Pakistan
New Zealand	Costa Rica	Bangladesh	Philippines
Niue	Cuba	Brunei	Qatar
Papua New Guinea	Commonwealth of Dominica	Cambodia	Saudi Arabia
Samoa	Dominica	Timor-Leste	Singapore
Solomon Islands	Ecuador	Georgia	Korea
Tonga	El Salvador	Indonesia	Sri Lanka
Vanuatu	Grenada	Iran	Syria
	Guyana	Iraq	Tajikistan
	Jamaica	Kazakhstan	Thailand
	Panama	Kuwait	Turkey
	Peru	Kyrgyzstan	U.A.E
	Suriname	Laos	Uzbekistan
	Trinidad and Tobago	Lebanon	Viet Nam
	Uruguay	Malaysia	Yemen
	Venezuela	Maldives	Hong Kong S.A.R
		Mongolia	Macau S.A.R

Appendix 2: Sample firm list

Number	Firm name	Firm type	Industry
1	Huawei	PE	G
2	Tcl	PE	C
3	Alibaba	PE	G
4	BYD	PE	C
5	Country Garden	PE	J
6	Chenming Paper	PE	C
7	Oceanwide	PE	M
8	Fuyao Group	PE	C
9	Fosun International	PE	M
10	Fosun Pharma	PE	C
11	Haida group	PE	A
12	Haier Electronics	PE	C
13	Hainan Airlines	PE	M
14	Hai Liang Group	PE	C
15	China Fortune Land Development	PE	J
16	Geely Group	PE	C
17	Jdcom	PE	C
18	JinkoSolar	PE	D
19	Lens Technology	PE	C
20	Lenovo	PE	G
21	Liugong Machinery	PE	C
22	Shandong Lutai Holding Group	PE	C
23	Midea	PE	C
24	SANY Group	PE	C
25	STO Express	PE	K
26	SF Express	PE	K
27	Suning	PE	H
28	Tencent	PE	G
29	Trina solar	PE	C
30	China Tianying (CNTY)	PE	K
31	Wanda Group	PE	M
32	Vanke Group	PE	J
33	WH Group Limited	PE	C
34	New Hope Liuhe	PE	A
35	YTO Express	PE	F
36	Yuntianhua Group	PE	C
37	Zhejiang Longsheng Group	PE	M
38	CHINT	PE	C
39	Zhongtian Technology	PE	G
40	ZTO Express	PE	F
41	Beijing Enterprises	SOE	C
42	Xiamen C&D Co., Ltd	SOE	J
43	China International Marine Containers	SOE	F
44	China Life Insurance Company	SOE	I
45	Industrial and Commercial Bank of China	SOE	I
46	China Development Bank	SOE	I
47	China Merchants Bank	SOE	I

Assessment of CSR Reporting Quality along the Belt and Road

48	Gezhouba Group	SOE	E
49	China Metallurgical Group Corporation	SOE	E
50	People's Insurance Company of China	SOE	I
51	GAC Group	SOE	C
52	China Construction Technology Group	SOE	E
53	China South Industries Group Corporation	SOE	C
54	Harbin Electric	SOE	C
55	Anshan Iron & Steel	SOE	C
56	Baosteel	SOE	C
57	NORINCO International	SOE	E
58	Baic Motor Corporation	SOE	C
59	Dongfeng Motor	SOE	C
60	Fiberhome Communications	SOE	G
61	Gree Electric	SOE	C
62	Industrial and Commercial Bank of China	SOE	I
63	Bright Dairy	SOE	C
64	Bright Food	SOE	M
65	Guangdong Port and Shipping Group	SOE	F
66	Guangzhou Automobile	SOE	C
67	Guangdong Rising Holdings	SOE	M
68	Guangxin Holdings	SOE	M
69	South China Airlines	SOE	F
70	Air China	SOE	F
71	State Nuclear Power Technology Corporation	SOE	D
72	Guotai Junan Securities	SOE	I
73	Conch Group	SOE	C
74	Hisense	SOE	C
75	HBIS Group	SOE	C
76	China Hi-Tech Group Corporation	SOE	C
77	Hengyi Petrochemic	SOE	C
78	Huafa group	SOE	J
79	Huaneng Power International	SOE	D
80	China Construction Bank	SOE	I
81	Anhui Jianghuai Automobile	SOE	C
82	Goldwind Technology	SOE	D
83	Agricultural Bank of China	SOE	I
84	Chery Automobile	SOE	C
85	Shaanxi Coal and Chemical Industry	SOE	B
86	Shanghai International Port	SOE	F
87	Shanghai Electric Power	SOE	D
88	Shanghai Electric	SOE	D
89	Shanghai Construction	SOE	E
90	SAIC Motor	SOE	C
91	Shenzhen Kaifa Technology	SOE	G
92	Shenhua Energy	SOE	D

93	Shougang Corporation	SOE	C
94	Taiyuan iron and steel	SOE	C
95	TBEA	SOE	C
96	Tianma Microelectronics	SOE	G
97	Tongling Nonferrous	SOE	C
98	Sinotrans & CSC	SOE	F
99	Wanhua Chemical	SOE	C
100	Weichai Power	SOE	C
101	Metallurgical Science and Engineering	SOE	E
102	Yuexiu Group	SOE	M
103	Guangdong group	SOE	M
104	Changan Automobile	SOE	C
105	Yangtze Optical Fibre And Cable Company	SOE	C
106	Shanghai Zhenhua Heavy Industry	SOE	C
107	Sinoma Construction	SOE	E
108	China CAMC Engineering	SOE	E
109	China Shipbuilding Industry Corporation	SOE	C
110	China National Technical Import and Export Corporation	SOE	E
111	China Road and Bridge	SOE	E
112	China Wuyi Co,Ltd.	SOE	J
113	Shenzhen Zhongjin Lingnan Nonfemet Company	SOE	C
114	CITIC group	SOE	M
115	CITIC Bank	SOE	I
116	CITIC Heavy Industry	SOE	C
117	ZTE Corporation	SOE	G
118	Bank of China	SOE	I
119	COSCO Shipping	SOE	F
120	COSCO SHIPPING Energy Transportation	SOE	D
121	Zijin Mining	SOE	B
122	Overseas Chinese Town Enterprises	CE	J
123	China Resources Group	CE	M
124	Xinxing Cathay International Group	CE	C
125	FAWVW Automobile	CE	C
126	Angang	CE	C
127	Baowu Steel	CE	C
128	Ordnance Equipment Group	CE	C
129	China Chengtong	CE	M
130	China Telecom	CE	G
131	Dongfang Electric	CE	C
132	Eastern Airlines	CE	F
133	Dongfeng Motor	CE	C
134	National Power Investment	CE	D
135	State Grid Corporation of China	CE	D
136	National Development Investment	CE	I
137	National Energy Group	CE	D
138	Aerospace Science and Industry	CE	C

Assessment of CSR Reporting Quality along the Belt and Road 115

139	China National Gold Group	CE	B
140	Central Academy of Mechanical Sciences	CE	C
141	China Unicom	CE	G
142	China Minmetals	CE	M
143	China Merchants Steamship Company	CE	M
144	CRRC Corporation Limited	CE	C
145	Sinosteel	CE	C
146	China Guangdong Nuclear Power	CE	D
147	China Ordnance Industry	CE	C
148	China Shipbuilding Corporation	CE	C
149	China State Shipbuilding Corporation	CE	C
150	China Datang Corporation	CE	D
151	China Power Construction	CE	E
152	China Electronics Information Industry Group	CE	G
153	China Aviation Industry	CE	C
154	China Aerospace Science and Technology Corporation	CE	C
155	China National Aviation Fuel Corporation	CE	F
156	China Huadian Corporation	CE	D
157	China Huaneng Group	CE	D
158	China National Chemical Corporation	CE	C
159	China National Machinery Industry Corporation	CE	M
160	China National Building Materials Group	CE	C
161	China Construction Technology	CE	E
162	China State Construction Engineering	CE	E
163	China Energy Conservation and Environmental Protection Group	CE	K
164	Aluminum Corporation of China	CE	B
165	China Energy Construction Corporation	CE	E
166	China National Petroleum	CE	B
167	China General Technology	CE	M
168	China West Electric	CE	D
169	China Mobile	CE	G
170	China Ocean Shipping Group	CE	F
171	China National Offshore Oil Corporation	CE	B
172	China Chemistry	CE	C
173	China Communications Construction	CE	E
174	China Oil and Food Import and Export Corporation	CE	A
175	China Tourism Group	CE	K
176	China Nonferrous Mining Group	CE	B
177	Sinopec Group	CE	B
178	China Railway Engineering Corporation	CE	F
179	COSCO	CE	F

Notes

1 Content analysis has been widely adopted in corporate disclosure studies (Guthrie et al., 2004) because it allows repeatability and valid inferences from data according to their context (Krippendorff, 2013).
2 For example, the China National Petroleum Corporation published the project-specific CSR report in Burma, in 2017, for the China-Myanmar Oil and Gas Pipeline Project; State Grid Corporation of China issued the country-specific (Brazil) CSR Report in Rio de Janeiro, Brazil, in 2019, disclosing in detail the company's business development history in Brazil, its active fulfillment of CSR and environmental protection obligations as well as its endeavors to promote the benefits of local people. China Petroleum & Chemical Corporation publishes the white paper on environmental protection on an annual basis and Alibaba issues an annual public interest report in addition to CSR reports to specifically demonstrate its endeavors on promoting social welfare.
3 ISO 14000 is a set of environmental management guidelines designed to assist organizations in (a) minimizing how their activities impact adversely on the environment, (b) complying with relevant rules, legislation, and other environmentally oriented criteria, and (c) continuously improving both these aspects. ISO 26000 is an international standard designed to assist organizations in assessing and responding to social responsibility in ways that are relevant and significant to their mission and vision, activities and procedures, clients, staff, societies, communities, and other stakeholders, as well as to their environmental impact.
4 https://goldenbee.applysquare.com/retrieval/list
5 The content analysis is based on the Chinese version of sample CSR reports, as most of the sample firms do not have corresponding English version CSR reports.

References

Adams, C., & Zutshi, A. (2004). Corporate social responsibility: Why business should act responsibly and be accountable. *Australian Accounting Review*, 14(34), 31–39.

Aerts, W., & Cormier, D. (2009). Media legitimacy and corporate environmental communication. *Accounting, Organizations and Society*, 34(1), 1–27.

Angelakoglou, K., & Gaidajis, G. (2015). A review of methods contributing to the assessment of the environmental sustainability of industrial systems. *Journal of Cleaner Production*, 108, 725–747.

Beattie, V., McInnes, B., & Fearnley, S. (2004). A methodology for analysing and evaluating narratives in annual reports: A comprehensive descriptive profile and metrics for disclosure quality attributes. *Accounting Forum*, 28(3), 205–236.

Beck, A. C., Campbell, D., & Shrives, P. J. (2010). Content analysis in environmental reporting research: Enrichment and rehearsal of the method in a British–German context. *The British Accounting Review*, 42(3), 207–222.

Bernard, S., Abdelgadir, S., & Belkhir, L. (2015). Does GRI reporting impact environmental sustainability? An industry-specific analysis of CO_2 emissions performance between reporting and non-reporting companies. *Journal of Sustainable Development*, 8(9), 190–205.

Brown, H. S., De Jong, M., & Lessidrenska, T. (2009). The rise of the global reporting initiative: A case of institutional entrepreneurship. *Environmental Politics*, 18(2), 182–200.

Bryman, A. (2016). *Social research methods*. Oxford University Press.

BYD Auto. (2019). *Annual CSR report.* BYD. https://en.byd.com/wp-content/uploads/2021/06/BYD_CSR_2019.pdf
Campopiano, G., & De Massis, A. (2015). Corporate social responsibility reporting: A content analysis in family and non-family firms. *Journal of Business Ethics, 129*(3), 511–534.
Castka, P., & Balzarova, M. A. (2008). The impact of ISO 9000 and ISO 14000 on standardisation of social responsibility—An inside perspective. *International Journal of Production Economics, 113*(1), 74–87.
China Energy Construction Group. (2018). *Annual CSR report.* CECC. http://www.ceec.net.cn/col/col43953/index.html
China Entrepreneurs Association. (2021). *Announcement of the top 100 Chinese multinational corporations and multinational index 2021.* Retrieved from http://www.cec1979.org.cn/view_sy.php?id=47421
China National Petroleum Corporation. (2018). *Annual CSR report.* CNPC. http://www.cnpc.com.cn/en/csr2019/AnnualReport_list.shtml
Colglazier, W. (2015). Sustainable development agenda: 2030. *Science, 349*(6252), 1048–1050.
Cormier, D., & Magnan, M. (2003). Environmental reporting management: A continental European perspective. *Journal of Accounting and Public Policy, 22*(1), 43–62.
Day, R., & Woodward, T. (2009). CSR reporting and the UK financial services sector. *Journal of Applied Accounting Research, 10*(3), 159–175.
Denzin, N. K. (1970). *The research act in sociology.* Aldine Publishing Company.
Diez-Cañamero, B., Bishara, T., Otegi-Olaso, J. R., Minguez, R., & Fernández, J. M. (2020). Measurement of corporate social responsibility: A review of corporate sustainability indexes, rankings and ratings. *Sustainability, 12*(5), 2153.
Du, S., Bhattacharya, C. B., & Sen, S. (2010). Maximizing business returns to corporate social responsibility (CSR): The role of CSR communication. *International Journal of Management Reviews, 12*(1), 8–19.
Dumay, J., Guthrie, J., & Farneti, F. (2010). GRI sustainability reporting guidelines for public and third sector organizations: A critical review. *Public Management Review, 12*(4), 531–548.
Fortanier, F., Kolk, A., & Pinkse, J. (2011). Harmonization in CSR reporting. *Management International Review, 51*(5), 665–696.
Frynas, J. G., & Yamahaki, C. (2016). Corporate social responsibility: Review and roadmap of theoretical perspectives. *Business Ethics: A European Review, 25*(3), 258–285.
Gao, Y. (2009). Corporate social performance in China: Evidence from large companies. *Journal of Business Ethics, 89*(1), 23–35.
Gao, Y. (2011). CSR in an emerging country: A content analysis of CSR reports of listed companies. *Baltic Journal of Management, 6*(2), 263–291.
Geely Global (2018). *Annual CSR report.* Geely. http://geelyauto.com.hk/core/files/corporate_governance/tc/20180617_C.pdf
Guthrie, J., Petty, R., Yongvanich, K., & Ricceri, F. (2004). Using content analysis as a research method to inquire into intellectual capital reporting. *Journal of Intellectual Capital, 5*(2), 282–293.
Hayes, A. F., & Krippendorff, K. (2007). Answering the call for a standard reliability measure for coding data. *Communication Methods and Measures, 1*(1), 77–89.
Huawei. (2018). *Annual CSR report.* Huawei. https://www.huawei.com/cn/sustainability/sustainability-report

Huawei. (2019). *Annual CSR report*. Huawei. https://www.huawei.com/cn/sustainability/sustainability-report

Kiliç, M., Kuzey, C., & Uyar, A. (2015). The impact of ownership and board structure on corporate social responsibility (CSR) reporting in the Turkish Banking industry. *Corporate Governance, 15*(3), 357–374.

Krippendorff, K. (2013). Commentary: A dissenting view on so-called paradoxes of reliability coefficients. *Annals of the International Communication Association, 36*(1), 481–499.

Liugong Group. (2019). *Annual CSR report*. Retrieved from https://pdf.dfcfw.com/pdf/H2_AN202004291379068787_1.pdf

Lock, I., & Seele, P. (2016). The credibility of CSR (corporate social responsibility) reports in Europe. Evidence from a quantitative content analysis in 11 countries. *Journal of Cleaner Production, 122*, 186–200.

Lombard, M., Snyder-Duch, J., & Bracken, C. C. (2002). Content analysis in mass communication: Assessment and reporting of intercoder reliability. *Human Communication Research, 28*, 587–604.

Moneva, J. M., Archel, P., & Correa, C. (2006). GRI and the camouflaging of corporate unsustainability. *Accounting Forum, 30*(2), 121–137.

Northern International. (2016). *Annual CSR report*. Northern International. https://pdf.dfcfw.com/pdf/H2_AN201706010616561276_1.pdf?1496339962000.pdf

Scott, W. A. (1955). Reliability of content analysis: The case of nominal scale coding. *Public Opinion Quarterly, 19*(3), 321–325.

Searcy, C., & Elkhawas, D. (2012). Corporate sustainability ratings: An investigation into how corporations use the Dow Jones sustainability index. *Journal of Cleaner Production, 35*, 79–92.

Shanghai Electric Power Company Limited. (2016). *Annual CSR report*. Shanghai Electric Power. http://www.shanghaipower.com/shzr/shzr/201704/P020170413359857873943.pdf

Sharifi, A., & Murayama, A. (2013). A critical review of seven selected neighborhood sustainability assessment tools. *Environmental Impact Assessment Review, 38*, 73–87.

Siew, R. Y. (2015). A review of corporate sustainability reporting tools (SRTs). *Journal of Environmental Management, 164*, 180–195.

Sutantoputra, A. W. (2009). Social disclosure rating system for assessing firms' CSR reports. *Corporate Communications: An International Journal, 14*(1), 34–48.

Szczuka, M. (2015). Social dimension of sustainability in CSR standards. *Procedia Manufacturing, 3*, 4800–4807.

Toppinen, A., Hänninen, V., & Lähtinen, K. (2015). ISO 26000 in the assessment of CSR communication quality: CEO letters and social media in the global pulp and paper industry. *Social Responsibility Journal, 11*(4), 702–715.

Tschopp, D., & Nastanski, M. (2014). The harmonization and convergence of corporate social responsibility reporting standards. *Journal of Business Ethics, 125*, 147–162.

Tschopp, D., & Huefner, R. J. (2015). Comparing the evolution of CSR reporting to that of financial reporting. *Journal of Business Ethics, 127*(3), 565–577.

Tschopp, D., & Nastanski, M. (2014). The harmonization and convergence of corporate social responsibility reporting standards. *Journal of Business Ethics, 125*(1), 147–162.

Vernon, R. (1979). The international aspects of state-owned enterprises. *Journal of International Business Studies, 10*(3), 7–14.
Vourvachis, P., & Woodward, T. (2015). Content analysis in social and environmental reporting research: Trends and challenges. *Journal of Applied Accounting Research, 16*(2), 166–195.
WH Group. (2017). *Annual CSR report*. Retrieved from http://media-whgroup.todayir.com/201810081219271709262790_tc.pdf
Wood, D. J. (2008). Dialogue: Towards a superior stakeholder theory. *Business Ethics Quarterly, 18(2)*, 153–190.
Xinhua. (2021). *Fortune Global 500 companies rise to 143*. http://www.xinhuanet.com/english/2021-08/03/c_1310104838.htm
Zijin Mining Limited. (2016). *Annual CSR report*. Zijin Mining. http://www.zjky.cn/upload/pdfjs/web/viewer.html?file=/upload/file/2017/04/12/1363a2c-7c451440d8d21d7b884b7bf53.pdf
Zinenko, A., Rovira, M. R., & Montiel, I. (2015). The fit of the social responsibility standard ISO 26000 within other CSR instruments: Redundant or complementary? *Sustainability Accounting, Management and Policy Journal, 6*(4), 498–526.

7 CSR Reporting Contents of Chinese MNEs in BRI Host Countries

Top ten CSR reporting topics related to BRI host countries

After the BRI was announced, both Chinese and international academics started to recognize the various social and environment issue embedded in the BRI. Opinions on the initiative's social and environmental impact vary greatly among academics, with some having positive views and others having deep concerns. For instance, according to a study published in *Science*, enormous energy consumption will be required throughout the implementation of the BRI, particularly for mining and power plants, highways, bridges, and manufacturing sector workshops. Although the project is intended to contribute to global and regional prosperity, it may also contribute to growing carbon footprints (Zhang et al., 2017). China's role as a worldwide leader in climate responsibility was also acknowledged; the BRI presents a plan for global collaboration that is anticipated to stress China's leadership in climate responsibility.

Chinese MNEs operate simultaneously in multiple institutional environments along the Belt and Road, and it is a big challenge for them to coordinate their CSR practices globally to obtain legitimacy in host countries. At the same time, due to the multidimensional nature of CSR (Attig et al., 2016), Chinese MNEs may respond to institutional pressures strategically according to the trade-off between costs and benefits by paying attention to different CSR reporting contents.

This chapter first discusses Chinese MNEs' CSR reporting contents relating to BRI host countries by presenting the CSR topics that emerged from the content analysis, using exemplar quotes extracted from the analyzed CSR reports. Table 7.1 lists the top ten CSR reporting topics relating to BRI host countries, ranked by the average number of nodes[1] per CSR report, and presents some illustrative examples of the CSR topics disclosed by the sample firms.

Economic impacts along the BRI

The BRI has provided a powerful impetus for globalization by enhancing bilateral and multilateral trade and FDI ventures (Li et al., 2015). The top three overseas CSR reporting topics relate to economic impacts (EC1: Direct

DOI: 10.4324/9781003302445-7

Table 7.1 Top ten CSR reporting topics related to the BRI host countries

CSR topic	Average number of nodes per CSR report	Illustration (translated from the original in Chinese)
EC1: Direct economic value generated	7.4	"State Development and Investment Corporation has been actively employing local staff in the construction of the Kensai, OMO2 and OMO3 sugar mills in Ethiopia. Each SDIC project can bring about the employment of 4,000 sugarcane planters, and each factory can provide employment for 1,000 skilled workers. The sugar factory project could significantly increase the income of local residents and boost the regional economy. In addition, SDIC sugar factories employ local tribal elders and local personnel for project security, cleaning and sanitation, and catering services. During the civil construction and installation phase, local workers were employed to participate in the construction. The last plant, the OMO3 sugar factory, was completed and began producing sugar in October 2018. The OMO3 sugar factory is Ethiopia's most automated sugar factory, with the quickest building and commissioning times" (State Development & Investment Corp., Ltd. (SDIC), 2018, p. 87).
EC5: Infrastructure investments and services	6.5	"It is the first modern standard-gauge railway in East Africa, with a total length of 472 kilometers and is the flagship project of Kenya Vision 2030. The project is designed and constructed in accordance with China's national railway standards, sharing more competitive Chinese standards and technology with the African continent" (China Communications Construction Company, 2016, p. 11).
EC6: Significant indirect economic impacts due to climate change	6.2	"COMPLANT (a subsidiary of State Development and Investment Corporation) reached a strategic investment and cooperation agreement with Tialoc Singapore. This investment is another critical strategic deployment of SDIC in countries along the BRI. SDIC's construction projects in Africa leverage on Singapore Tialoc's technical background and manufacturing strength in the field of environmental engineering. In addition, these facilities are used in various projects along the BRI, to provide chemical, electronics, pharmaceutical, solar and other related industries along the BRI, to provide innovative environmental management, sustainable recycling and environmental protection systems" (State Development & Investment Corp., Ltd. (SDIC), 2018, p. 27).

(Continued)

Table 7.1 Top ten CSR reporting topics related to the BRI host countries (Continued)

CSR topic	Average number of nodes per CSR report	Illustration (translated from the original in Chinese)
S13: Poverty reduction and reduce inequalities	5.6	"The project team has been actively supporting community development in Tocantins with a donation of more than 2 million BRL to build community centers, wells and public facilities. The community has beautiful scenery with mango, orange and other fruit trees growing naturally in the surrounding areas. After conducting a feasibility study, the project team donated a juice factory to the community, including purchasing the facilities and machines, providing training for local workers and managers and conducting initial marketing. Factory products soon became a bit in the market, helping the community to shake off poverty" (State Grid Corporation of China, 2018, p. 58)
S8: Community public welfare projects	4.3	"The Ecuadorian rainforest area, rich in petroleum resources, is covered with unique tropical rainforest vegetation and inhabited by primitive indigenous tribes, but it is the poorest area in Ecuador. The oil region where the Andean Project is located is remote from cities, with no hospitals or basic medical facilities. China National Petroleum Corporation (CNPC) built community clinics for local indigenous people, of whom more than 8,000 people have access to basic medical services. In addition, CNPC implemented the 'Sweet Water Community' program and successively drilled 49 water wells in Gudawa, benefiting 25,000 residents in 39 villages nearby. Besides, public primary school as well as local factory built by CNPC further promote the prosperity of Gudawa" (China National Petroleum Corporation, 2016, p. 61).
EMP1: Salary and welfare system	3.1	"We've constantly striving to do amazing things at TCL. For nearly 40 years, TCL has been at the forefront of consumer technology. Our products delight millions across the world by providing premium home entertainment products, cutting edge experiences, and innovative smart solutions. If you're thinking about taking your career to the next level with a job at TCL, we'd love to find out what makes you amazing, too. TCL fully respects employees' earned income according to law. TCL provides reasonable and competitive remuneration packages, and the wage levels of employees are generally higher than the local average" (TCL, 2018, p. 41).

(Continued)

CSR Reporting Contents of Chinese MNEs in BRI Host Countries   123

Table 7.1 Top ten CSR reporting topics related to the BRI host countries (Continued)

CSR topic	Average number of nodes per CSR report	Illustration (translated from the original in Chinese)
EC4: Localization of employees	2.7	"We actively recruit and train local employees and do not discriminate against local candidates for managerial positions, providing local people with job opportunities. Professionals employed in our overseas projects involve multiple disciplines, such as exploration and development, engineering construction, international trade, accounting and human resources management, covering over 70 countries/regions. In 2019, international and local employees accounted for 84.92% of our overseas workforce" (China National Petroleum Corporation, 2019, p.56).
EMP3: Employee occupational safety training	2.4	"In all countries and regions where we operate, we have implemented an effective management system, and established a corporate-level global safety incident ownership mechanism. In addition, we have developed and enforced the EHS Absolute Rules, strengthened managers' involvement in onsite projects, and built a positive safety-first culture. These actions have minimized safety risks and protected the health and safety of our employees, subcontractors, and other partners. We have assigned great importance to operational safety, and developed a highly efficient safety management system in all areas of operations, including building a safety-first culture, manufacturing safety, working environment safety, fire control safety, food safety, road traffic safety, and engineering delivery safety" (Huawei, 2015, p. 37).
ENV1: Management system for environmental protection	2.3	"Overseas subsidiaries of the China Huadian Group always comply with the environmental laws, regulations and standards of the countries (regions) where they operate, and adhere to the concept of responsible green investment and sustainable development, developing clean energy and environmentally friendly products to provide modern energy to the world. We are committed to saving energy and resources, reducing pollutant emissions, developing a circular economy, actively addressing climate change and reducing the environmental impact of our operations" (China Huadian Corporation, 2019, pp. 52).
EMP5: Staff training and career development	1.2	"The cement plant invested by CEC in Laos is currently the largest cement manufacturing enterprise in Laos, and has maintained the No. 1 market share for many years. The company has trained 10 cement process trainees from Laos University of Science and Technology and conducted more than 30 training sessions, contributing to the cultivation of high-end talents in Laos" (Power Construction Corporation of China, 2017, p. 31).

economic value generated; EC5: Infrastructure investments and services; EC6: Significant indirect economic impacts due to climate change). Statistics indicate that a large proportion of BRI investment flows to African economies (Fang & Nolan, 2019). However, the continent faces significant challenges arising from violence and political insecurity, which continue to hamper its economic recovery. BRI countries account for a third of global GDP and commerce, and nearly two-thirds of the global population. Poverty rates, or the percentage of the population living below the poverty line (USD1.90 per day), are still high in some BRI countries: 25% in Kenya, 23% in Uzbekistan and Djibouti, and 21% in Laos (Fang & Nolan, 2019). Thus, significant investment is needed to establish the necessary infrastructure facilities to reduce transportation costs, while still providing sufficient renewable power to stimulate development. In order to support sustained development, African countries require significant amounts of Outward Foreign Direct Investment (OFDI). Therefore, disclosures about economic impacts constitute a large proportion of total overseas CSR reporting contents. Economic contributions will benefit large numbers of poor people in some BRI host countries and many other global economies, with significant positive spillover effects on global welfare.

The findings reveal another factor that accounts for the large volume of CSR disclosures relating to economic assistance. Specifically, Chinese MNEs need to develop various legitimacy-building strategies to help them to cope with the challenging environment along the BRI, as those with greater legitimacy are more likely to gain access to the markets and resources needed to prosper (Dowling & Pfeffer, 1975). However, it is also difficult for them to build legitimacy, as the economic calculus may be more complex than is immediately apparent (Fang & Nolan, 2019). Closer alignment with global trade routes (like the BRI) may also increase international competition, potentially jeopardizing local employment and industries. Furthermore, many Chinese MNEs bring their workers with them, implying that the ventures may produce fewer jobs than the host countries anticipate. Moreover, the financing needed for BRI projects may push some countries' debt to unsustainable levels.[2] Therefore, a large volume of CSR disclosures relating to direct and indirect economic impacts may help Chinese MNEs to gain legitimacy and survive and avoid significant interference from outside parties in BRI host countries (Huang, 2016).

Maximizing local people's livelihoods

In recent years, world leaders have made reducing global poverty a top priority, and a plethora of international organizations, including civil society organizations and NGOs, the United Nations and its specialized agencies, the World Bank, and others, have sought to assist the vulnerable (Seto-Pamies & Papaoikonomou, 2020). Similarly, the BRI is intended to foster well-being and contribute to poverty reduction in the regions concerned by promoting connectivity between Europe and Asia, and helping to develop trade and personal exchanges. Thus, CSR disclosures reporting reductions in poverty and inequalities under the Social CSR theme (S13: Poverty reduction and reduce inequalities; S8: Community public welfare projects) are relatively frequent.

With reference to the theoretical framework for CSR reporting in BRI countries, the political legitimacy perspective is particularly useful for grasping the institution-agency connection inherent in the BRI path. Specifically, implementation and enforcement of CSR regulations in BRI host countries are critical issues, as most are transitional economies or less-developed countries and regions (Fang & Nolan, 2019). For example, some African countries are characterized by situations in which CSR regulation enforcement is weak, the capacity of civil society organizations is lacking, and non-regulatory influences are crucial (Idemudia, 2011). Responding to and managing non-regulatory forces from various stakeholder groups affects Chinese MNEs' survival and growth. Thus, several CSR-leading Chinese MNEs are dedicated to building long-term and healthy cooperative relationships with their host countries, as well as aspiring to be good corporate citizens in local societies. BRI-related investments are projected to raise returns, with jobs faring better than capital and land owners (Fang & Nolan, 2019), and activities promoting local people's benefits are frequently disclosed in CSR reports. Moreover, engagements in promoting social welfare in BRI host countries are explicitly disclosed to address the government's request for social investments in return for business licenses and stakeholders' support in local areas (Gugler & Shi, 2009). Similarly, philanthropy is an important recurring theme in Chinese companies' CSR reports, which may be specific to China, as well as countries such as Lebanon that are institutionally challenged (Jamali & Mirshak, 2007; Kolk et al., 2010; Zhao, 2012).

On the other hand, stakeholder theory illuminates the reality of organizations' involvement in socially responsible conduct, with the view that businesses are systems of interconnected interests in which companies' and communities' activities are interdependent (Hartman et al., 2007). This theory stresses the importance of integrating societal demands and "doing the right thing" in order to create a good society (Garriga & Melé, 2004). It is relevant to this study because it states that the community has the right to obtain benefits from the firm in a responsible manner, even though the firm is an external entity that is supposed to assist in the development of the community in which it is located (Ismail et al., 2015). From the perspective of stakeholder theory, MNEs' involvement in and disclosure of community-based CSR activities are necessary not only to strengthen their competitive advantage and improve the economic status of the local needy, but also to contribute to the betterment of local communities (Jamali, 2008; Kuchinke, 2010). Thus, consistent with the findings of previous studies, involvement in social welfare-related CSR activities is a common way for Chinese firms to boost stakeholder value and corporate reputation (Singh et al., 2017; Tang & Li, 2009).

Unifying environmental safeguards

Protecting the ecosystem while encouraging economic growth is likely to be complicated under the BRI, as the initiative traverses a number of vulnerable ecosystems (Chernysheva et al., 2019). Therefore, the BRI's overall progress will depend largely on whether China lives up to its aspiration for sustainable growth (Harlan, 2020). As outlined in the BRI's Ecological and Environmental Cooperation Plan, environmental cooperation is a fundamental prerequisite for the initiative and is essential to enable China's national and regional economies to undergo green transformation (Fang & Nolan, 2019).

Table 7.1 also reveals the importance of environmental management disclosures (ENV1: Management system for environmental protection) along the BRI. Thus, in addition to the Economic and Social dimensions, overseas CSR disclosures relating to environmental management are prominent. The multi-billion-dollar project includes investments in transportation, connectivity, and energy networks in over 100 countries across Eurasia, Oceania, and Africa. Its large size has attracted the interest of the international community and raises serious questions about its potential environmental consequences (Fang & Nolan, 2019). Moreover, any major infrastructure project may be exposed to financial, social, and corruption risks. Examples include habitat destruction, environmental degradation, and elite capture. These risks may be particularly critical in BRI-participating countries, where governance tends to be relatively weak (Ascensão et al., 2018). These threats must be identified and precautions put in place to mitigate their potentially negative consequences (Fang & Nolan, 2019).

The findings of this study are supported by existing literature (Adams & Frost, 2006), which documents that the drive for businesses to "go green" is not new (Shrivastava, 1995). Although environmental principles may persuade some businesses to cultivate ecological responses (Hage & Dewar, 1973), many have already adopted "green" objectives. The Chinese government issued official guidance on promoting the concept of the "green BRI" at the first BRI Forum in 2017 (Belt and Road Portal, 2017a), which indicated that it is vital for BRI-related initiatives taking place outside China to adhere to the same environmental standards to which China aspires at home (Belt and Road Portal, 2017b). Thus, Chinese MNEs pay particular attention to disclosures on environmental governance along the BRI. With regard to institutional practices, Chinese MNEs are in an exclusive position to gain social acceptance in BRI host countries (Fang & Nolan, 2019). Similarly, increasing stakeholder pressures in China have led to transfers of socially responsible practices to the subsidiaries of Chinese MNEs along the BRI (Surroca et al., 2013). In addition, more and more Chinese MNEs are disclosing superior and greener production techniques and comprehensive environmental governance along the BRI in their CSR reports (Fang & Nolan, 2019). For example, in order to reduce dust emissions, enterprises belonging to Sinosteel in Africa have installed a new dust absorption system in all facilities, and its dust interception rate of over 98% exceeds the local statutory level (Sinosteel Corporation, 2018, p. 42). Superior environmental facilities and governance enable MNEs to emit fewer pollutants during production and give them brand image advantages when competing with local firms (Hanna, 2010).

Human-oriented principle in overseas employment

The BRI is a global development strategy that significantly influences domestic employment in host countries (Fang & Nolan, 2019). As shown in Table 7.1, CSR disclosures on overseas employment account for a significant proportion of overall CSR reporting content (EMP1: Salary and welfare system; EC4: Localization of employees; EMP3: Employee occupational safety training; EMP5: Staff training and career development). Good working conditions, employee involvement in business strategies, sharing business cultures, employee safety, training, career development, non-discrimination, and equal treatment of human resources are typical examples of issues considered essential in the CSR disclosures of Chinese MNEs along the BRI.

Huawei's CSR report discloses that approximately 64% of the personnel operating outside of China are recruited on a local basis. It is worth mentioning that in the year 2021 alone, Huawei hired over 4,000 individuals for positions at its international offices (Huawei, 2021). Outside China, Huawei is committed to recruiting local professionals and working to develop diverse staff. As stated in its CSR report, "Localization is a key focus in Huawei's global operations. We prefer to hire local professionals and provide them with a platform where they can fully realize their value. We also develop tailored models for different groups of employees to maximize their value" (Huawei, 2014, p. 30).

In addition, Chinese MNEs pay close attention to employees' career development and continuing education. For instance, Huawei offers adequate and equitable opportunities for training and promotion to global workers, assigns mentors to local employees, and provides systematic training, with more than 4000 online courses in multiple languages accessible on a range of platforms, including Huawei's own iLearning site. The company's overseas training program also includes new employee induction, specific training for non-Chinese managers, and training for senior technical specialists, all of which help workers to develop their technical skills, experience, and management capabilities.

Top ten emerging CSR reporting topics related to BRI host countries

To investigate the CSR reporting content along the BRI further, analysis was conducted on the top ten emerging overseas CSR reporting topics (with the top ten rates of increase in the average number of nodes per report from 2014 to 2021) among the sample firms. The results are presented in Table 7.2.

Environmental disclosures are an emergent CSR reporting topic in BRI countries. There are high growth rates in environment-related disclosures (56.2% for ENV1: Management system for environmental protection; 54.4% for ENV5: Reduction of global energy consumption; and 40.9% for ENV2: Renewable materials and resources used and recycling of energy resources). In view of

Table 7.2 Top ten emerging CSR reporting topics in the BRI countries

CSR topic	Increase rate of the average number of nodes per report from 2014 to 2021 (%)	Illustration (translated from the original in Chinese)
ENV1: Management system for environmental protection	56.20	"We attach great importance to environmental protection and are committed to minimizing the impact on the environment in our global businesses. In Iraq, we follow PetroChina's global safety and environmental protection culture, are committed to the harmony between human and the natural environment, strictly abide by the Iraqi government's environmental protection laws and regulations, and implement the concept of cherishing the environment throughout the entire process of oilfield construction. We strive to reduce environmental footprint and control environmental impact during overseas operation" (China National Petroleum Corporation, 2019, p. 33).
ENV5: Reduction of global energy consumption	54.40	"A green business philosophy has been established by enterprises of Sinosteel in Africa to realize energy conservation, consumption reduction, clean production through purchasing energy-saving equipment and bringing environmental protection technologies. Tubatse Chrome Minerals (Pty) Ltd. establishes a waste heat power plant to collect water vapor with a low-temperature boiler, increasing 10% of the total power supply" (Sinosteel Corporation, 2018, p. 42).
EMP6: Diversity of employees and gender equality	52.60	"TCL focuses on promoting women and localized employment to play its due role in creating local employment opportunities. TCL also strictly prohibits the employment of people under the legal working age, eliminates forced labor and resists sexual harassment in the workplace to protect the rights and interests of its employees" (TCL, 2017, p. 32).
ENV8: Protect the local ecological environment	51.70	"The Bali Phase I 3×142MW coal-fired power station project of China Huadian Overseas Branch adheres to the concept of green development and invents the circular closed coal to produce electricity on the island. The first time Indonesia has adopted a circular closed coal yard to reduce dust pollution and the emission concentrations of SO2, NOX and dust are far better than the local environmental protection requirements, with remarkable environmental effects" (China Huadian Corporation, 2018, p. 49).

(Continued)

Table 7.2 Top ten emerging CSR reporting topics in the BRI countries (Continued)

CSR topic	Increase rate of the average number of nodes per report from 2014 to 2021 (%)	Illustration (translated from the original in Chinese)
ENV7: Biodiversity impacts management	49.60	"Near the Kingfisher oilfield is the Uganda Chimpanzee Forest Reserve. CNOOC Uganda invited experts in the field of chimpanzee conservation to the site to conduct a comprehensive analysis of the possible impact of oilfield development activities on the reserve and propose countermeasures to optimize various aspects of the project. At the same time, the company developed a detailed monitoring plan during the construction and operation of the project to ensure that the chimpanzees continue their original lives in a more natural state" (China National Offshore Oil Corporation, 2021, p. 74).
EMP4: Promotion of employees' physical and mental health and create a good working environment	48.10	"SDIC organizes various cultural and sports activities to enrich employees' leisure time and promote employee's physical health. SDIC also organizes important festivals celebrating and respecting the beliefs and customs of different ethnic groups and promotes the integration of diverse cultures" (State Development & Investment Corp., Ltd. (SDIC), 2019, p. 60).
EC3: Ratios of standard entry level wage by gender compared to local minimum wage	43.60	"Tubatse Alloy (Pty) Ltd., a subsidiary of Sinosteel, adjusts remuneration packages according to the South African Labor Law and industry practices and corporate benefits. Zimasco (Pvt.) Ltd. has improved its salary and welfare system, providing employees with a salary at least USD 20/person/month higher than that of the local minimum standard (USD 275/person/month), and paid vacation benefits every year" (Sinosteel Corporation, 2018, p. 33).
ENV2: Renewable materials and resources used and recycling of energy resources	40.90	"CGN is committed to the production and supply of clean energy with zero carbon emissions, and contributes to the response to global climate change with large-scale, high-quality, efficient, and sustainable clean energy products and services" (China General Nuclear, 2019, p. 47).

(Continued)

Table 7.2 Top ten emerging CSR reporting topics in the BRI countries (Continued)

CSR topic	Increase rate of the average number of nodes per report from 2014 to 2021 (%)	Illustration (translated from the original in Chinese)
S10: Rights of women, children, and disadvantaged groups	37.60	"By the end of 2021, we have used digital technology to roll out our education programs, including DigiTruck and DigiSchool, in more than 400 schools, driving equality and quality in education. Over the past year, we have helped 32 protected areas in 25 countries protect biodiversity more efficiently. We have also developed numerous products and services that offer accessibility features for vulnerable groups such as the visually impaired, hearing impaired, and the elderly. Each month, more than 4.4 million visually impaired people and 800,000 hearing impaired people use the accessibility features on Huawei devices to benefit from an increasingly digital world" (Huawei, 2021, p. 4). "Huawei sponsors over 170 international social contribution initiatives in which it served local communities, offered tangible benefits, and positively affected socioeconomic growth. These initiatives took many forms, including assisting in resolving local problems, volunteering, promoting cultural, art, sporting, and environmental activities, and assisting the disadvantaged, including the impoverished and those with serious health issues" (Huawei, 2017, p. 63).
EC10: Protection mechanism of intellectual property rights	27.40	"Huawei follows universal IPR standards and international protocols in both domestic and overseas operations. Huawei takes a constructive, cooperative approach to resolving IPR problems across multiple channels such as cross-licensing and strategic alliances. In addition, Huawei makes long-term R&D investments and maintains a substantial IPR portfolio. As a supporter and supplier of IPR rules, we also safeguard our own IPR and respects others' IPRs globally" (Huawei, 2018, p. 12).

evidence that international affiliates are reluctant to participate in social and environmental accountability in their host countries, leading to the development of so-called pollution havens (Ascensão et al., 2018), the BRI raises questions about social and long-term environmental viability. On the other hand, unsustainable construction practices and pollution may cause social unrest and impede further investment and political cooperation (Fang & Nolan, 2019; Huang, 2016; Hughes, 2019; Saud et al., 2019).

The Chinese government is attaching greater importance to sustainable development along the BRI. Thus, increasing rates of environment-related disclosures echo SDGs 6, 12, 13, 14, and 15 and policies for sustainable development along the BRI. Specifically, these policies state that "promoting the green Belt and Road is an important endeavor to engage in global environmental governance" (Belt and Road Portal, 2017a, Section 1.2), and they stress the goal of aligning the "green BRI" with the most influential global sustainability agenda – the 2030 Agenda for Sustainable Development (Ervits, 2021; See, 2009; Shahab et al., 2019).

There is also a growing trend for Chinese MNEs to disclose CSR practices relating to biodiversity in overseas markets (growth rates of 49.6% for ENV8: Protect the local ecological environment; and 51.7% for ENV7: Biodiversity impacts management). The sheer scale of infrastructure growth envisaged under the BRI may have global effects on species and ecosystems. Furthermore, the BRI poses two specific challenges to SDGs 14 and 15: first, the cumulative impacts of projects spatially clustered along corridors; and second, the difficulty of mitigating these impacts owing to projects being transboundary and multi-jurisdictional. Thus, addressing and mitigating the combined impacts of BRI infrastructure construction on critical and endangered marine ecosystems, including coral reefs, mangrove forests, and seagrass meadows, will be a significant challenge. Most Asian countries are faced with serious environmental issues arising from unsustainable development modes and lifestyles in the past and are seeking changes toward sustainable development (Saud et al., 2019). From the resource-seeking perspective, environmental conservation should be an integral part of constructing the BRI, as the potential of the local ecosystem is key to sustainable resource seeking. In addition, environmental conservation provides a foundation for and supports green growth in BRI countries, thereby enabling legitimate and sustainable OFDI in host countries (Teo et al., 2019). Finally, environmental conservation has a synergistic impact that may boost the development of other BRI-related projects (Butt & Ali, 2020). Therefore, environmental conservation should be prioritized through long-term cooperation and OFDI to grant legitimacy and competitive advantage to Chinese MNEs.

In addition to environmental concerns, there is a growing focus on decent work and employee care among Chinese MNEs along the BRI (growth rates of 52.6% for EMP6: Diversity of employees and gender equality; 48.1% for EMP4: Promotion of employees' physical and mental health and create a good working environment; and 43.6% for EC3: Ratios of standard entry-level wage by gender compared to local minimum wage). From the perspective of stakeholder theory, employees are considered to be critical internal stakeholders (Aguinis & Glavas, 2012; Devinney, 2009). Employees contribute to focal businesses' value development by providing their knowledge and capabilities. In return, companies provide fair wages, pensions, training to help workers develop their skills and experience and social benefits, and vacations. Economic globalization, the technological revolution, climate change, and demographic restructuring are profoundly changing global labor relations. Thus, protecting the rights and interests of overseas employment is a new test for the BRI labor market. On the other hand, gender equality, an SDG of the UN 2030 Agenda, is an indispensable pathway for achieving the other SDGs (Gazzola et al., 2016). Women's economic empowerment, a prerequisite for inclusive and equitable economic growth, is essential for achieving the SDG of gender equality (Grosser, 2009). As shown in Table 7.2, there is a growing trend to report CSR initiatives promoting benefits to women and other disadvantaged people (growth rate of 37.6% for S10: Rights of women, children, and disadvantaged groups).

Finally, as more and more Chinese MNEs in the ICT industry are moving abroad, awareness of intellectual property rights (IPR) is growing. High-tech companies usually maintain enormous numbers of patents. Thus, Chinese MNEs are increasingly disclosing their IPR practices on a global basis (growth rate of 27.4% for EC10: Protection mechanism for IPR). IPRs have increasingly become a core resource for the development of national strategic capital and international competitiveness, with continued economic globalization and development of the information economy. They also provide significant support for building an innovative country and mastering development initiatives (Huang, 2016). Legal regulations and institutional frameworks relating to intellectual property in international markets are continuously evolving and changing, imposing higher standards for intellectual property growth in various countries and regions, supporting domestic IPR development, and improving international awareness. The global growth of intellectual property is aided by the rapid development of property rights. As a result, implementation of intellectual property strategies is in line with global trends and enhances IPR exchange and collaboration in the international market. It is also a condition for the international legal framework and environment governing intellectual property. Thus, implementing an intellectual property policy helps mitigate IPR infringements and effectively protects businesses' legitimate rights and interests (Zhang, 2015).[3]

CSR reporting quality in BRI host countries

The second halve of this chapter addresses the quality of CSR reporting in BRI host countries. Table 7.3 presents the overseas CSR disclosure quality of sample firms, by year in Panel A, and by firm type in Panel B. To facilitate readability, a full mark is reported in the bracket next to each CSR theme. The total score for overseas CSR reporting quality is 147. This raw score is converted into a percentage score[4] and reported in Panel B. Table 7.4 reports the scores for each CSR reporting topic (raw scores).

Table 7.3 Overseas CSR (OCSR) disclosure quality by year

	\multicolumn{6}{c}{Panel A: overseas CSR disclosure quality by year (raw score)}
	Governance (12)	Economy (30)	Environment (42)	Employment (21)	Social (42)	OCSR Total (147)
2014	4.31	11.22	14.55	6.97	12.84	49.89
2015	5.02	12.06	16.28	7.69	14.52	55.57
2016	5.20	13.75	17.66	8.04	16.24	60.89
2017	6.51	15.10	19.53	9.63	19.22	69.99
2018	6.50	15.51	19.83	10.40	22.05	74.28
2019	6.85	16.97	23.39	11.47	24.80	83.48
2020	6.88	16.64	21.51	11.19	21.22	77.44
2021	6.77	15.59	20.17	10.79	23.06	76.38

	\multicolumn{6}{c}{Panel B: overseas CSR disclosure quality by year (percentage score)}
	Governance (%)	Economy (%)	Environment (%)	Employment (%)	Social (%)	OCSR Total (%)
2014	35.88	37.40	34.65	33.19	30.57	33.94
2015	41.83	40.20	38.76	36.61	34.58	37.80
2016	43.36	45.83	42.04	38.31	38.66	41.42
2017	54.22	50.34	46.51	45.84	45.76	47.61
2018	54.19	51.70	47.21	49.51	52.49	50.53
2019	57.05	56.57	55.70	54.63	59.05	56.79
2020	57.33	55.47	51.21	53.29	50.52	52.68
2021	56.41	51.97	48.02	51.43	54.90	51.96

As shown in Table 7.3, the overall CSR reporting quality in BRI host countries is increasing. Specifically, the total CSR reporting score has increased from 33.94 to 56.79 (percentage scores). The reporting quality for each individual CSR theme is also increasing. This finding indicates that firms participating in the BRI are more likely to engage in CSR reporting and disclose higher quality information. This improving trend is consistent with previous studies suggesting that as Chinese MNEs internationalize, they use CSR reporting to conquer their LOF/LOE when entering a new market and seek legitimacy by mimicking international practices (CSR reporting) if this is what the host countries demand (Miska et al., 2016).

With regard to specific CSR themes, the quality of Chinese MNEs' CSR reporting on labor practice issues (Employment theme) is the lowest of the five themes (see Table 7.4). In particular, scores are low for EMP2: Occupational health and safety management and hazard identification, risk assessment and incident investigation, EMP5: Staff training and education for skill improvement and career development, EMP6: Diversity of employees, gender equality, and EMP7: Anti-discrimination. As a result, some facets of employee interests, including professional growth, employee health, prompt resolution of workers' issues, and caring for life problems such as work-life conflicts, require improvement. Previous research also reveals that Chinese foreign contractors have failed to resolve labor practice concerns such as safety training (Akorsu & Cooke, 2011; Halegua, 2020; Sha & Jiang, 2003).

Table 7.4 Score distribution of different CSR reporting topics (raw score)

	Governance				
	G1	G2	G3	G4	
Score	1.38	1.44	1.54	1.65	
	Economy				
	EC1	EC2	EC3	EC4	EC5
Score	2.46	2.19	1.09	1.72	2.10
	EC6	EC7	EC8	EC9	EC10
Score	2.35	1.02	0.66	0.45	0.57
	Environment				
	ENV1	ENV2	ENV3	ENV4	ENV5
Score	1.92	1.49	0.54	0.89	0.47
	ENV6	ENV7	ENV8	ENV9	ENV10
Score	1.5	1.42	1.37	1.18	1.81
	ENV11	ENV12	ENV13	ENV14	
Score	1.54	1.62	1.58	1.77	
	Employment				
	EMP1	EMP2	EMP3	EMP4	EMP5
Score	1.93	1.39	1.68	1.21	1.14
	EMP6	EMP7			
Score	1.01	1.16			
	Social				
	SC1	SC2	SC3	SC4	SC5
Score	1.35	1.28	0.93	1.09	1.01
	SC6	SC7	SC8	SC9	SC10
Score	0.97	1.33	1.86	1.59	1.67
	SC11	SC12	SC13	SC14	
Score	1.36	1.73	1.69	1.37	

In addition, the quality of CSR reporting relating to the Environment theme scored below 50 from 2014 to 2018. Compared with other CSR reporting topics, the scores were low for ENV3: Reclaimed products and their packaging materials, ENV4: Energy consumption and intensity in overseas markets, and ENV5: Reduction of global energy consumption and energy demand for products and services. Previous studies have shown the emergence of environmental issues as key criteria for project success (Alzahrani & Emsley, 2013). When undertaking construction activities, every contractor has a responsibility to protect the environment (Petrovic-Lazarevic, 2008; Shen et al., 2010). Environmental sustainability has been promoted by Chinese MNEs (Jiang & Wong, 2016); however, the activities mentioned in CSR-related reports are not promising. Despite attempts to develop higher environmental standards and implement environmental reforms, most BRI host countries still have poor and fragmented environmental policies (Fang & Nolan, 2019). As a result, Chinese MNEs should concentrate on the negative environmental consequences of construction activities along the BRI. Examples of practical steps to expose their environmental impacts in BRI host countries include performing separate environmental impact assessments, conserving water supplies, minimizing greenhouse gas and carbon emissions, reducing fuel consumption, and avoiding harm to local climate conditions.

On the other hand, the quality of disclosures relating to the Economic perspective is generally higher than for other CSR themes (apart from the Governance theme). The results in Table 7.3 echo the concern that MNEs from developing countries usually focus on the demands of the most influential stakeholders, such as the government and suppliers (Newenham-Kahindi, 2011), and thus emphasize the economic perspective in their CSR reports (Yang et al., 2020). Furthermore, previous research indicates that MNEs typically make concessions to less powerful stakeholders while prioritizing the most influential stakeholders (Alden & Davies, 2006; Hah & Freeman, 2014; López-Iturriaga & López-de-Foronda, 2011).

However, the CSR reporting quality of Chinese MNEs in BRI host countries is far from satisfactory, as the percentage scores for total CSR reporting quality are below or only marginally higher than 50 from 2014 to 2019. There appear to be two reasons for the low scores, namely inadequate awareness and lack of enforcement of CSR. These may result in the low volume of CSR information disclosures by Chinese MNEs along the BRI. First, although the Chinese government has introduced sustainable development policies into the BRI, most remain aspirational (Cheng & Ge, 2020; Rauf et al., 2018). Specifically, China communicates proactively with partners from BRI host countries through soft legislation (Fang & Nolan, 2019; Wang, 2019). It has an expanding set of BRI guidelines, but they lack critical information on implementation, disclosure, and compliance (Losos et al., 2019). Similarly, a study by the Asia Society Policy Institute shows that China's claims about the "green BRI" may differ from actual environmental practices in the field (Russel & Berger, 2019). Second, in the absence of financial or legal penalties for non-compliance, public bodies and civil society players are likely to "name and shame" corporations to keep their voluntary undertakings accountable (Renwick, 2019). Domestically, this mechanism is increasingly being used in China, where polluting industries are publicized to try to shame businesses into action, and people are encouraged to help by reporting violations (Schreurs, 2017). Despite growing awareness of the government's role in CSR promotion, governments in some developing countries participating in the BRI are less-developed and are yet to construct national policies that might help promote CSR in the region (Inekwe et al., 2020; Samy et al., 2015). Thus, citizens' awareness of and interest in corporations' environmentally or socially destructive actions are lower in distant countries than domestically (Cheng, 2016). This will be a major challenge for implementation of the BRI, since participating countries prioritize economic growth over sustainable development, allowing foreign affiliates to avoid social and environmental responsibility while focusing on financial results.

Surprisingly, starting from 2020 an interesting phenomenon has been observed. As the pandemic grew and Chinese overseas investment decreased, there has been increasing speculation regarding the BRI's viability. *The Financial Times* questioned the long-term feasibility of the initiative, citing a COVID-19-induced financial problem, a global decline in overseas investment, and opposition from the United States. The overall CSR reporting quality of 2020 and 2021 has decreased compared to 2019. As expected, the COVID-19 epidemic has substantially halted infrastructure and building projects, including several that are part of the BRI. Disruptions to global supply chains, lockdowns, and travel restrictions on foreign workers, particularly Chinese laborers who are frequently engaged on BRI projects, are among the primary causes of project suspensions and slowdowns. The pandemic has also led to an increase in unemployment in some BRI host countries. Many BRI projects are located in developing nations which are more vulnerable to the effects of the pandemic. Resumption of work in these nations primarily depends on the rate at which the infection curve flattens and the accessibility of medical and health care services. Therefore, the BRI's boost to these local economies as well as their employment appeared weak, leading to the decreasing CSR reporting quality in the area of Economy and Employment as observed in 2020 and 2021.

On the opposite, to improve its image and distract itself from the effects of the shortcomings caused by the pandemic, the Chinese government has been working extremely hard to portray itself as a role model for combating the virus. China has been swift in providing medical assistance to host countries in the form of distributing face masks, respirators, test kits, and deploying medical teams (Telias & Urdinez, 2022; Verma, 2020). This "mask diplomacy" has already yielded benefits in the country's international policy. Therefore, part of the narratives of CSR performance along the Belt and Road has been shifted to helping local communities fight the pandemic. The Alibaba Foundation and the Jack Ma Foundation, for example, have already offered medical aid to many BRI host countries (Ondoa et al., 2020; Vervoort et al., 2021). The COVID-19 manual was also released by the Jack Ma Foundation to aid nations in their struggle. Other Chinese MNEs such as Zijin Mining has announced in its CSR reports that it has provided a large amount of vaccination materials to countries and regions where its projects are located (Zijing Mining, 2021, p. 6).

Additionally, the BRI has enabled the distribution of vaccines produced domestically to emerging economies. In many parts of Asia and South America, Chinese COVID-19 vaccines currently hold the biggest market share. Additionally, these initiatives have improved China's standing abroad (Huang, 2022). Thus, although the content of CSR reporting on the social dimension has changed slightly, the overall score for the social dimension remains at a high level. In terms of Environment, since the focus of CSR has shifted to fighting the pandemic as discussed before, there are fewer environment-related disclosures. Thus, a decreased reporting quality for Environment dimension is recorded. For instance, the lockdown has interrupted many biodiversity conservations programs. In some less-developed countries, the wish to economic recovery has surpassed the environmental concerns. The relaxed NGO regulatory regime due to the pandemic may have also resulted in reduced environmental disclosures of the BRI projects.

Notes

1 For example, if the total number of nodes relating to a CSR topic is 2058, after dividing by the total number of sample CSR reports (1361), the average number of nodes per report is calculated as 2058/1361 = 1.51.
2 For example, as in Sri Lanka, countries may end up incurring more debt than they can afford in order to develop projects under the initiative (Hurley et al., 2019).
3 For example, the "Flying Pigeon" bicycle trademark was pre-registered in Indonesia, and many Chinese trademarks were squatted by foreign companies during the overseas investment process, resulting in Chinese companies losing autonomy in trademark management (Zhang, 2015).
4 For example, if the total overseas CSR reporting score is 100 for company A, then the percentage score is calculated as 100/147*100 = 68.02.

References

Adams, C. A., & Frost, G. R. (2006). The internet and change in corporate stakeholder engagement and communication strategies on social and environmental performance. *Journal of Accounting & Organizational Change*, 2(3), 281–303.

Aguinis, H., & Glavas, A. (2012). What we know and don't know about corporate social responsibility: A review and research agenda. *Journal of Management*, 38(4), 932–968.

Akorsu, A. D., & Cooke, F. L. (2011). Labour standards application among Chinese and Indian firms in Ghana: Typical or atypical. *The International Journal of Human Resource Management*, 22(13), 2730–2748.

Alden, C., & Davies, M. (2006). A profile of the operations of Chinese multinationals in Africa. *South African Journal of International Affairs*, 13(1), 83–96.

Alzahrani, J. I., & Emsley, M. W. (2013). The impact of contractors' attributes on construction project success: A post construction evaluation. *International Journal of Project Management*, 31(2), 313–322.

Ascensão, F., Fahrig, L., Clevenger, A. P., Corlett, R. T., Jaeger, J. A., Laurance, W. F., & Pereira, H. M. (2018). Environmental challenges for the belt and road initiative. *Nature Sustainability*, 1(5), 206–209.

Attig, N., Boubakri, N., El Ghoul, S., & Guedhami, O. (2016). Firm internationalization and corporate social responsibility. *Journal of Business Ethics*, 134(2), 171–197.

Belt and Road Portal. (2017a). *Guidance on promoting green belt and road*. https://eng.yidaiyilu.gov.cn/zchj/qwfb/12479.htm

Belt and Road Portal. (2017b). *The belt and road ecological and environmental cooperation plan*. https://eng.yidaiyilu.gov.cn/zchj/qwfb/13392.htm

Butt, A. S., & Ali, I. (2020). Understanding the implications of belt and road initiative for sustainable supply chains: An environmental perspective. *Benchmarking: An International Journal*, 27(9), 2631–2648.

Cheng, L. K. (2016). Three questions on China's "belt and road initiative". *China Economic Review, 40*, 309–313.

Cheng, C., & Ge, C. (2020). Green development assessment for countries along the belt and road. *Journal of Environmental Management, 263*, 110344.

Chernysheva, N. A., Perskaya, V. V., Petrov, A. M., & Bakulina, A. A. (2019). Green energy for belt and road initiative: Economic aspects today and in the future. *International Journal of Energy Economics and Policy, 9*(5), 178.

China Communications Construction Company. (2016). *Annual CSR report*. CCCC. https://www.ccccltd.cn/shzr/shzr/shzrbg/201706/P020170620377609802630.pdf

China General Nuclear. (2019). *Annual CSR report*. http://www.cgnpc.com.cn/cgn/c101047/2020-03/30/fd8d2b6d6dc04ea191b28be1d1ad5abf/files/246c0b840b414d309d01f5d00c6f3f4f.pdf

China Huadian Corporation. (2018). *Annual CSR report*. CHC. http://m.chd.com.cn/site/2mobile/list/f73fe61b6a854b9fb8c9502b4f72bc50_1.html

China Huadian Corporation. (2019). *Annual CSR report*. CHC. http://m.chd.com.cn/site/2mobile/list/f73fe61b6a854b9fb8c9502b4f72bc50_1.html

China National Offshore Oil Corporation. (2021). *Annual CSR report*. https://www.cnooc.com.cn/attach/0/43c6b4cc9f85427cbd4fc23d28563565.pdf

China National Petroleum Corporation. (2016). *Annual CSR report*. CNPC. http://www.cnpc.com.cn/en/cr2016/AnnualReport_list.shtml

China National Petroleum Corporation. (2019). *Annual CSR report*. CNPC. http://www.cnpc.com.cn/en/csr2019/AnnualReport_list.shtml

Devinney, T. M. (2009). Is the socially responsible corporation a myth? The good, the bad, and the ugly of corporate social responsibility. *Academy of Management Perspectives, 23*(3), 44–56.

Dowling, J., & Pfeffer, J. (1975). Organizational legitimacy: Social values and organizational behavior. *Pacific Sociological Review, 18*(1), 122–136.

Ervits, I. (2021). CSR reporting by Chinese and Western MNEs: Patterns combining formal homogenization and substantive differences. *International Journal of Corporate Social Responsibility, 6*(1), 1–24.

Fang, C., & Nolan, P. (Eds.). (2019). *Routledge handbook of the belt and road*. Routledge.

Garriga, E., & Melé, D. (2004). Corporate social responsibility theories: Mapping the territory. *Journal of Business Ethics, 53*(1), 51–71.

Gazzola, P., Sepashvili, E., & Pezzetti, R. (2016). CSR as a mean to promote gender equality. *Economia Aziendale Online, 7*(1), 95–99.

Grosser, K. (2009). CSR and gender equality: Women as stakeholders and the EU sustainability strategy. *Business Ethics: A European Review, 18*(3), 290–307.

Gugler, P., & Shi, J. Y. (2009). Corporate social responsibility for developing country multinational corporations: Lost war in pertaining global competitiveness? *Journal of Business Ethics, 87*(1), 3–24.

Hage, J., & Dewar, R. (1973). Elite values versus organizational structure in predicting innovation. *Administrative Science Quarterly, 18*(3), 279–290.

Hah, K., & Freeman, S. (2014). Multinational enterprise subsidiaries and their CSR: A conceptual framework of the management of CSR in smaller emerging economies. *Journal of Business Ethics, 122*(1), 125–136.

Halegua, A. (2020). Where is the belt and road initiative taking international labour rights? An examination of worker abuse by Chinese firms in Saipan. In Carrai, M. A., Defraigne, J. C., & Wouters, J. (Eds.), *The belt and road initiative and global governance*. (pp. 117–137). Edward Elgar Publishing.

Hanna, R. (2010). US environmental regulation and FDI: Evidence from a panel of US-based multinational firms. *American Economic Journal: Applied Economics*, 2(3), 158–189.

Harlan, T. (2020). Green development or greenwashing? A political ecology perspective on China's green belt and road. *Eurasian Geography and Economics*, 62(2), 1–25.

Hartman, L. P., Rubin, R. S., & Dhanda, K. K. (2007). The communication of corporate social responsibility: United States and European Union multinational corporations. *Journal of Business Ethics*, 74(4), 373–389.

Huang, Y. (2016). Understanding China's belt & road initiative: Motivation, framework and assessment. *China Economic Review*, 40, 314–321.

Huang, Y. (2022). The health silk road: How China adapts the belt and road initiative to the covid-19 pandemic. *American Journal of Public Health*, 112(4), 567–569.

Huawei. (2014). *Annual CSR report.* https://www-file.huawei.com/-/media/corp2020/pdf/sustainability/past-yeas/csr_2014_cn.pdf

Huawei. (2015). *Annual CSR report.* https://www-file.huawei.com/-/media/corporate/pdf/sustainability/2015_huawei_sustainability_report_cn_final.pdf

Huawei. (2017). *Annual CSR report.* https://www-file.huawei.com/-/media/corporate/pdf/sustainability/2017_huawei_sustainability_report_cn_final.pdf

Huawei. (2018). *Annual CSR report.* Huawei. https://www.huawei.com/cn/sustainability/sustainability-report

Huawei. (2021). *Annual CSR report.* https://www-file.huawei.com/-/media/corp2020/pdf/sustainability/sustainability-report-2021-cn.pdf

Hughes, A. C. (2019). Understanding and minimizing environmental impacts of the belt and road initiative. *Conservation Biology*, 33(4), 883–894.

Hurley, J., Morris, S., & Portelance, G. (2019). Examining the debt implications of the belt and road initiative from a policy perspective. *Journal of Infrastructure, Policy and Development*, 3(1), 139–175.

Idemudia, U. (2011). Corporate social responsibility and developing countries: Moving the critical CSR research agenda in Africa forward. *Progress in Development Studies*, 11(1), 1–18.

Inekwe, M., Hashim, F., & Yahya, S. B. (2020). CSR in developing countries – The importance of good governance and economic growth: Evidence from Africa. *Social Responsibility Journal*, 17(2), 226–242.

Ismail, M., Alias, S. N., & Rasdi, R. M. (2015). Community as stakeholder of the corporate social responsibility programme in Malaysia: Outcomes in community development. *Social Responsibility Journal*, 11(1), 109–130.

Jamali, D. (2008). A stakeholder approach to corporate social responsibility: A fresh perspective into theory and practice. *Journal of Business Ethics*, 82(1), 213–231.

Jamali, D., & Mirshak, R. (2007). Corporate social responsibility (CSR): Theory and practice in a developing country context. *Journal of Business Ethics*, 72(3), 243–262.

Jiang, W., & Wong, J. K. (2016). Key activity areas of corporate social responsibility (CSR) in the construction industry: A study of China. *Journal of Cleaner Production*, 113, 850–860.

Kolk, A., Pan, H., & van Dolen, W. (2010). Corporate social responsibility in China: An analysis of domestic and foreign retailers' sustainability dimensions. *Business Strategy & The Environment*, 19(5), 289–303.

Kuchinke, K. P. (2010). Human development as a central goal for human resource development. *Human Resource Development International*, *13*(5), 575–585.

Liang, T. (2020). Handbook of COVID-19 *prevention and treatment* (Vol. 68). https://globalce.org/downloads/Handbook_of_COVID_19_Prevention_en_Mobile.pdf.

Li, P., Qian, H., Howard, K. W., & Wu, J. (2015). Building a new and sustainable "silk road economic belt". *Environmental Earth Sciences*, *74*(10), 7267–7270.

López-Iturriaga, F. J., & López-de-Foronda, Ó (2011). Corporate social responsibility and reference shareholders: An analysis of European multinational firms. *Transnational Corporations Review*, *3*(3), 17–33.

Losos, E. C., Pfaff, A., Olander, L. P., Mason, S., & Morgan, S. (2019). *Reducing environmental risks from belt and road initiative investments in transportation infrastructure*. The World Bank Policy Research Working Paper 8718.

Miska, C., Witt, M. A., & Stahl, G. K. (2016). Drivers of global CSR integration and local CSR responsiveness: Evidence from Chinese MNEs. *Business Ethics Quarterly*, *26*(3), 317–345.

Newenham-Kahindi, A. M. (2011). A global mining corporation and local communities in the lake Victoria zone: The case of Barrick Gold multinational in Tanzania. *Journal of Business Ethics*, *99*(2), 253–282.

Ondoa, P., Kebede, Y., Loembe, M. M., Bhiman, J. N., Tessema, S. K., Sow, A., & Nkengasong, J. (2020). COVID-19 testing in Africa: Lessons learnt. *The Lancet Microbe*, *1*(3), e103–e104.

Petrovic-Lazarevic, S. (2008). The development of corporate social responsibility in the Australian construction industry. *Construction Management and Economics*, *26*(2), 93–101.

Power Construction Corporation of China. (2017). *Laos sustainability report construct a beautiful tomorrow with power and love 2017*. Power China, https://www.powerchina.cn/attach/0/80534e1639394910af822ddcfd51670a.pdf

Rauf, A., Liu, X., Amin, W., Ozturk, I., Rehman, O. U., & Sarwar, S. (2018). Energy and ecological sustainability: Challenges and panoramas in belt and road initiative countries. *Sustainability*, *10*(8), 2743.

Renwick, N. (2019). The belt and road initiative: Infrastructure and sustainable development. In *Sustainable economy and emerging markets*. Routledge.

Russel, D., & Berger, B., 2019. *Navigating the belt and road initiative*. The Asia Society Policy Institute. http://ccilc.pt/wp-content/uploads/2018/04/NAVIGATING-THE-BELT-AND-ROAD-INITIATIVE-%E2%80%93-ASIA-SOCIETY-POLICY-INSTITUTE-2019-EN.pdf

Samy, M., Ogiri, H. I., & Bampton, R. (2015). Examining the public policy perspective of CSR implementation in sub-Saharan Africa. *Social Responsibility Journal*, *11*(3), 553–572.

Saud, S., Chen, S., & Haseeb, A. (2019). Impact of financial development and economic growth on environmental quality: An empirical analysis from belt and road initiative (BRI) countries. *Environmental Science and Pollution Research*, *26*(3), 2253–2269.

Schreurs, M. (2017). Multi-level climate governance in China. *Environmental Policy and Governance*, *27*(2), 163–174.

See, G. (2009). Harmonious society and Chinese CSR: Is there really a link? *Journal of Business Ethics*, *89*, 1–22.

Seto-Pamies, D., & Papaoikonomou, E. (2020). Sustainable development goals: A powerful framework for embedding ethics, CSR, and sustainability in management education. *Sustainability*, 12(5), 1762.

Sha, K., & Jiang, Z. (2003). Improving rural labourers' status in China's construction industry. *Building Research & Information*, 31(6), 464–473.

Shahab, Y., Ntim, C. G., & Ullah, F. (2019). The brighter side of being socially responsible: CSR ratings and financial distress among Chinese state and non-state owned firms. *Applied Economics Letters*, 26(3), 180–186.

Shen, L. Y., Tam, V. W., Tam, L., & Ji, Y. B. (2010). Project feasibility study: The key to successful implementation of sustainable and socially responsible construction management practice. *Journal of Cleaner Production*, 18(3), 254–259.

Shrivastava, P. (1995). The role of corporations in achieving ecological sustainability. *Academy of Management Review*, 20(4), 936–960.

Singh, P. J., Sethuraman, K., & Lam, J. Y. (2017). Impact of corporate social responsibility dimensions on firm value: Some evidence from Hong Kong and China. *Sustainability*, 9(1532), 1–24.

Sinosteel Corporation. (2018). *Annual CSR report*. Sinosteel. http://www.sinosteel.com/module/download/downfile.jsp?filename=fa67593508354fb680acce51cf941298.pdf&classid=0

State Development & Investment Corp., Ltd. (SDIC). (2018). *Annual CSR report*. SDIC. https://www.sdic.com.cn/cn/rootimages/2020/04/15/1588495741311888.pdf

State Development & Investment Corp., Ltd. (SDIC). (2019). *Annual CSR report*. SDIC. https://www.sdic.com.cn/cn/rmtzx/qkbg/shzrbg/A01030415index_1.htm

State Grid Corporation of China. (2018). *Annual CSR report*. SGCC. http://www.sgcc.com.cn/html/files/2019-09/20/20190920152947618205277.pdf

Surroca, J., Tribó, J. A., & Zahra, S. A. (2013). Stakeholder pressure on MNEs and the transfer of socially irresponsible practices to subsidiaries. *Academy of Management Journal*, 56(2), 549–572.

Tang, L., & Li, H. (2009). Corporate social responsibility communication of Chinese and global corporations in China. *Public Relations Review*, 35(3), 199–212.

TCL. (2017). *Annual CSR report*. TCL. https://sustainability.tatachemicals.com/our-approach/our-progress/reports/

TCL. (2018). *Annual CSR report*. TCL. https://sustainability.tatachemicals.com/our-approach/our-progress/reports/

Telias, D., & Urdinez, F. (2022). China's foreign aid political drivers: Lessons from a novel dataset of mask diplomacy in Latin America during the COVID-19 pandemic. *Journal of Current Chinese Affairs*, 51(1), 108–136.

Teo, H. C., Lechner, A. M., Walton, G. W., Chan, F. K. S., Cheshmehzangi, A., Tan-Mullins, M., Chan, H. K., Sternberg, T., & Campos-Arceiz, A. (2019). Environmental impacts of infrastructure development under the belt and road initiative. *Environments*, 6(6), 72.

Verma, R. (2020). China's 'mask diplomacy' to change the COVID-19 narrative in Europe. *Asia Europe Journal*, 18(2), 205–209.

Vervoort, D., Ma, X., & Luc, J. G. (2021). COVID-19 pandemic: A time for collaboration and a unified global health front. *International Journal for Quality in Health Care*, 33(1), mzaa065.

Wang, H. (2019). China's approach to the belt and road initiative: Scope, character and sustainability. *Journal of International Economic Law*, 22(1), 29–55.

Yang, G., Huang, X., Huang, J., & Chen, H. (2020). Assessment of the effects of infrastructure investment under the belt and road initiative. *China Economic Review, 60*, 101418.

Zhang, Y. (2015). *China's emerging global businesses.* Palgrave Macmillan.

Zhang, N., Liu, Z., Zheng, X., & Xue, J. (2017). Carbon footprint of China's belt and road. *Science, 357*(6356), 1107–1107.

Zhao, M. (2012). CSR-based political legitimacy strategy: Managing the state by doing good in China and Russia. *Journal of Business Ethics, 111*(4), 439–460.

Zijing Mining. (2021). Annual *CSR report.* Zijing Mining. https://www.zijinmining.com/upload/file/2022/06/09/9b7954d122554e8ab7327852dc7d4004.pdf

8 The Impact of Ownership Types on CSR Reporting Contents and Quality

The influence of ownership type on CSR reporting of Chinese MNEs

The BRI is widely viewed as China's new geopolitical strategy for enlarging its sphere of influence, developing new standards of international economic cooperation, and advancing a new world order. The US, the EU, and some of China's close neighbors are considering their own plans for increased engagement in regional economy and security as the Chinese government and academia continue to advocate the initiative at a higher profile, furthering the public's perception of intensifying geopolitical rivalry in the Indo-Pacific region. With all the BRI investments, care needs to be taken to ensure that OFDI decisions are based on sound knowledge and solid science. In this context, CSR is seen as a link to de-escalate the relationship between companies, local governments, NGOs, and affected communities.

The Chinese CEs and SOEs have been assigned the responsibility to assist the government in achieving the BRI's strategic goals (Fang & Nolan, 2019; Huang, 2016). Specifically, they provide a significant proportion of OFDI, and the government plays an influential role in directing these investments. On the other hand, CEs and SOEs possess comparative advantages in terms of easy access to capital below market interest rates, and experiences of operating in places with similar institutions and governmental control (Quer et al., 2019). As the largest shareholder, the government supplies Chinese SOEs and CEs with vital resources and legitimacy, which are essential to their future sustainability and success. Stakeholder salience theory proposed by Mitchell et al. (1997) argues that the degree to which managers prioritize conflicting stakeholder claims is correlated favorably with the stakeholder's ability to influence the firm, the validity of the stakeholder's connection with the firm, and the urgency of the stakeholder's claim on the firm. Thus, substantial state ownership may have an impact on managerial decisions. As a result, SOEs' management prioritize their social interests over those of other companies and cater to the needs of the powerful state shareholders. Similarly, Quer et al. (2020) argue that the particularity of China's institutional environment provides CEs and SOEs with firm-specific advantages in handling the risks associated with operating in

DOI: 10.4324/9781003302445-8

countries characterized by weak governance and political and economic uncertainty. Therefore, CEs and SOEs have more resources than PEs to conduct CSR initiatives and report their CSR performance accordingly.

These findings are also supported by previous findings that many large Chinese MNEs, and especially the government-led SOEs and CEs, have had extensive experience of conducting economic activities in other countries since the 1990s (Zhang, 2009), particularly in developing countries in Africa, Asia, Latin America, and even in the Caribbean and Pacific-island nations and Pacific-island nations.[1] These countries have benefited from the BRI's assistance in improving infrastructure, ranging from transportation to electricity supply. Therefore, CEs and SOEs have more experiences of communicating effectively with the local communities and have better relationships with local governments. This also echoes the findings of previous studies that state-led FDI (by CEs and SOEs) faces legitimacy challenges in both host and home countries, and that the relevant firms mitigate such challenges by improving their CSR disclosures (Zhou et al., 2018). Faced with more and stricter criteria on OFDI by the Chinese Central Government, the CEs and SOEs are under greater pressure to expand and disclose their CSR activities in order to strengthen their operations and behave as socially responsible corporate citizens.[2] In contrast, private firms occupy a peripheral position in this "go global" movement, with less government assistance and limited resources. This inherent condition that differentiates the CEs and SOEs and the PEs may result in divergent trajectories of CSR reporting motivation and quality.

Table 8.1 presents the average CSR reporting scores (raw and percentage scores) for the five CSR reporting themes across different firm types. In general, the CEs' CSR reporting performance for most of the CSR reporting topics is better than the SOEs' and PEs' performance, while the SOEs outperform the PEs. These findings echo various governmental policies regarding CSR regulations targeted specifically at the CEs' overseas operations. In terms of CSR, the

Table 8.1 CSR disclosure quality by firm types

	Panel A: overseas CSR disclosure quality by firm types (raw score)					
	Governance (12)	Economy (30)	Environment (42)	Employment (21)	Social (42)	OCSR total (147)
CE	6.79	17.33	22.46	11.15	23.87	81.6
SOE	5.95	13.58	19.92	8.49	19.25	67.19
PE	5.31	12.89	14.97	8.91	14.58	56.66
	Panel B: overseas CSR disclosure quality by firm types (percentage score)					
	Governance (%)	Economy (%)	Environment (%)	Employment (%)	Social (%)	OCSR total (%)
CE	56.58	57.77	53.48	53.10	56.83	55.51
SOE	49.58	45.27	47.43	40.43	45.83	45.71
PE	44.25	42.97	35.64	42.43	34.71	38.54

State-owned Assets Supervision and Administration Commission of the State Council (SASAC) has set up a special office to coordinate and guide the social responsibility of SOEs. This mechanism strengthens the institutional supervision of, as well as the pressure on the state-owned and central-owned MNEs through coercive isomorphism compared to private-owned MNEs.

Table 8.2 provides a synopsis of overseas CSR disclosure quality by firm types and the results of statistical tests, enabling a straightforward comparison and analysis. A series of ANOVAs were conducted to compare the average reporting scores for different CSR themes among the three types of firms. The results reported in Table 8.2 reveal significant differences in the overseas CSR reporting scores of CEs, SOEs, and PEs. Specifically, significant differences are obtained for the Economy (F $(2,1026)$ = 5.725, $p < 0.05$), Environmental (F $(2,1026)$ = 10.885, $p < 0.001$), Employment (F $(2,1026)$ = 5.258, $p < 0.05$), and Social dimensions (F $(2,1026)$ = 14.987, $p < 0.001$) among the three types of firms. There are also significant differences in the total scores for CEs, SOEs, and PEs (F $(2,1026)$ = 8.884, $p < 0.001$). For the Governance dimension, there are no significant differences between the sample firms. In the post-hoc differences analysis, CEs perform better than SOEs and PEs on the other four CSR dimensions, and SOEs perform better than PEs on the Economy, Environment, and Social dimensions. SOEs generally perform better than PEs except the disclosure quality on the Employment dimension.

Under the BRI, mimetic pressures to improve CSR are higher for CEs and SOEs than for PEs, according to institutional theory (Zhao & Patten, 2016). For SOEs and CEs, their excellent and outstanding CSR practices are often reported in the government's official website or official media. Therefore, they are likely to be more sensitive to such isomorphic pressure compared to PEs because SOEs and CEs have similar ownership, experience, investment motivation, and financial strength to the exemplars. These mimetic forces influence Chinese MNEs to imitate successful peers and mobilize resources to improving their CSR in overseas host countries. The results are consistent with governmental documents that suggest that CEs are under greater pressure than PEs and SOEs to convey their CSR performance to international stakeholders, as they are regarded as ambassadors[3] for Chinese MNEs along the BRI. Furthermore, the CEs and SOEs and their managers are more likely to follow successful competitors because of their dependence on the government as a resource provider, and their success depends on the government's provision of resources and priorities (Coenen et al., 2021). On the other hand, without detailed regulations and institutional pressures to maximize stakeholder benefits, PEs are more likely to indulge solely in profit maximization in overseas markets, and international investors will in turn demand greater returns on their shares in those MNEs. This is an argument in favor of more stringent BRI-specific and -related policies regarding CSR reporting.

Furthermore, the results presented in Table 8.2 are consistent with a previous finding that CEs and SOEs face more vigorous scrutiny from the press, which is active in broadcasting news of corporate wrong-doings (Zheng & Zhang, 2016).

Table 8.2 Comparisons of overseas CSR disclosure quality by firm types

	CE	SOE	PE	F value	CE vs. SOE	CE vs. PE	SOE vs. PE
	Mean (SD)			Difference (post-hoc)			
GOV	6.79 (2.94)	5.95 (2.52)	5.31 (3.05)	6.79 (2.94)	n.s.	n.s.	n.s.
ECO	17.33 (3.97)	13.58 (2.53)	12.89 (2.85)	17.33 (3.97)	CE > SOE*(4.295)	CE>PE*(4.581)	SOE>PE*(4.265)
ENV	22.46 (6.93)	19.92 (4.22)	14.97 (3.57)	22.46 (6.93)	CE > SOE*(4.955)	CE>PE***(13.761)	SOE>PE***(9.464)
EMP	11.15 (7.45)	8.49 (5.12)	8.91 (4.34)	11.15 (7.45)	CE > SOE*(4.936)	n.s.	n.s.
SOC	23.87 (9.32)	19.25 (8.77)	14.58 (6.23)	23.87 (9.32)	CE > SOE***(11.657)	CE > PE***(13.974)	SOE>PE***(9.394)
TOTAL	81.60 (7.42)	67.19 (5.67)	56.66 (4.95)	81.60 (7.42)	CE > SOE***(10.658)	CE > PE***(9.957)	SOE>PE***(7.284)

*p < 0.1, **p < 0.05, ***p < 0.01. n.s. stands for not significant. The bold value is used to highlight the statistically significant items.
Note: The test for homogeneity of variance is passed; this study therefore reports the Tukey's multiple comparisons of means.

Chinese businesses operate in a political environment characterized by considerable state intervention in the economy and a relatively high level of legal uncertainty (Zhao, 2012). Frequently, they must rely on state resources for economic survival. Thus, investing in domestic political legitimacy might be seen as a means to lessen uncertainty and improve survival chances. Chinese firms follow CSR-based political legitimacy strategy, a "strategic action that a company takes to build, maintain or enhance the appropriateness and desirability perceived by the state through social-environmental activities based on which the company expects to access various forms of state resources" (Zhao, 2012, p. 442). Therefore, CEs and SOEs utilize CSR reporting to enhance their transparency and accountability, as well as to hedge against reputational risks (Kao et al., 2018). CSR disclosures relating to public welfare projects, poverty reduction, enforcement of human rights, and cultural exchange offer vivid examples of the critical role of CEs as national ambassadors along the BRI. On the other hand, previous studies also suggest that, compared with other CSR initiatives, social and community-related CSR campaigns are available to a larger number of stakeholders, resulting in an image boost at lower costs (Aray et al., 2021).

Topical analysis of CSR reporting of Chinese MNEs

The distribution of raw scores for the different CSR reporting topics and the results of ANOVAs to test for differences across firm types are presented in Table 8.3. This shows that CEs perform significantly better for most CSR reporting topics, and especially on the Social dimension. Figure 8.1 demonstrates that CEs are more concerned about CSR disclosures on the Social dimension (S8, S9, S10, and S13) than other CSR reporting topics. Previous studies observe that Chinese CEs are the biggest group of firms investing abroad under the government's guidance, providing the largest OFDI volumes (Cooke, 2014). In the process of implementing the BRI, CEs have gradually expanded from resource development and infrastructure construction to diversified industrial cooperation (Fang & Nolan, 2019). CEs, in particular, face stronger demands in terms of environmental and social issues, since they are the primary drivers of globalization among Chinese enterprises. Consequently, multinational subsidiaries of CEs invest in CSR to achieve legitimacy in their host regions. Thus, they are expected to contribute significantly to regional growth in countries with high unemployment and inadequate infrastructure and education levels (Foster-McGregor et al., 2015).

The results in Table 8.3 and Figures 8.1–8.3 also show that, compared with PEs, CEs and SOEs have significantly better reporting quality for environmental disclosures. In the initiative to create the green Silk Road, President Xi Jinping has emphasized the idea of green growth on numerous occasions, calling for in-depth eco-environmental cooperation and intense eco-environmental security (Fang & Nolan, 2019). It has been made clear in the vision and associated actions that ecological progress in investment and trade should be promoted, and cooperation should be enhanced with regard to conservation of the

Table 8.3 CSR topic-level one-way ANOVA results

Governance

Code	F value	CE	SOE	PE	CE vs. SOE	CE vs. PE	SOE vs. PE
G1	1.958	1.43	1.22	1.57	0.21	−0.14	−0.35
G2	3.982**	1.86	1.13	1.34	0.73	0.52	−0.21
G3	1.045	1.68	1.58	1.48	0.10	0.20	0.10
G4	3.284**	1.82	2.02	0.92	−0.20	0.90	1.10

Economy

Code	F value	CE	SOE	PE	CE vs. SOE	CE vs. PE	SOE vs. PE
EC1	1.253	2.74	2.34	2.21	0.4	0.53	0.13
EC2	5.984***	2.47	2.23	1.75	0.24	0.72	0.48
EC3	6.234***	1.68	0.98	0.81	0.7	0.87	0.17
EC4	5.771***	2.18	1.57	1.12	0.61	1.06	0.45
EC5	1.087	2.28	1.98	1.84	0.3	0.44	0.14
EC6	4.558***	2.54	2.13	2.08	0.41	0.46	0.05
EC7	2.541*	1.17	1.09	1.01	0.08	0.16	0.08
EC8	1.587	0.72	0.72	0.75	0	−0.03	−0.03
EC9	1.872	0.64	0.36	0.54	0.28	0.10	−0.18
EC10	5.632***	0.91	0.18	0.78	0.73	0.13	−0.60

Environment

Code	F value	CE	SOE	PE	CE vs. SOE	CE vs. PE	SOE vs. PE
ENV1	4.485***	2.36	2.11	1.57	0.25	0.79	0.54
ENV2	5.238***	1.64	1.54	1.28	0.1	0.36	0.26
ENV3	2.041	0.71	0.41	0.34	0.3	0.37	0.07
ENV4	3.997**	1.11	0.95	0.73	0.16	0.38	0.22
ENV5	1.248	0.54	0.42	0.41	0.12	0.13	0.01
ENV6	10.312***	2.21	1.71	1.12	0.50	1.09	0.59
ENV7	2.017	1.52	1.49	1.19	0.03	0.33	0.30
ENV8	8.052***	1.79	1.61	1.04	0.18	0.75	0.57
ENV9	14.455***	1.48	1.29	0.95	0.19	0.53	0.34
ENV10	3.958**	1.97	1.77	1.15	0.20	0.82	0.62
ENV11	7.452***	1.76	1.34	1.19	0.42	0.57	0.15
ENV12	1.956	1.72	1.79	1.25	−0.07	0.47	0.54
ENV13	6.524***	1.78	1.74	1.22	0.04	0.56	0.52
ENV14	4.058***	1.87	1.75	1.53	0.12	0.34	0.22

Employment

Code	F value	CE	SOE	PE	CE vs. SOE	CE vs. PE	SOE vs. PE
EMP1	1.875	2.11	1.84	1.65	0.27	0.46	0.19
EMP2	5.254***	1.24	1.41	1.81	−0.17	−0.57	−0.4
EMP3	2.015	1.74	2.16	1.27	−0.42	0.47	0.89
EMP4	1.563	1.44	1.01	0.84	0.43	0.60	0.17
EMP5	6.548***	1.16	0.74	1.34	0.42	−0.18	−0.6
EMP6	1.025	1.76	0.61	0.79	1.15	0.97	−0.18
EMP7	3.425**	1.7	0.72	1.21	0.98	0.49	−0.49

(*Continued*)

Table 8.3 CSR topic-level one-way ANOVA results (*Continued*)

				Social			
Code	F value	CE	SOE	PE	CE vs. SOE	CE vs. PE	SOE vs. PE
SC1	9.168***	1.79	1.55	0.94	0.18	0.72	0.54
SC2	8.052***	1.49	1.17	0.85	0.20	0.52	0.32
SC3	12.769***	1.15	0.91	0.44	0.25	0.71	0.46
SC4	7.415***	1.48	1.26	0.69	0.42	0.76	0.34
SC5	1.568	1.36	0.94	0.74	0.42	0.62	0.20
SC6	0.986	1.27	1.09	0.81	0.28	0.43	0.15
SC7	3.542**	1.39	1.25	1.07	0.24	0.32	0.08
SC8	6.248***	2.24	1.94	1.49	0.17	0.62	0.45
SC9	5.621***	1.93	1.62	1.23	0.27	0.66	0.39
SC10	4.561***	2.26	1.58	1.37	0.47	0.68	0.21
SC11	4.987***	1.58	1.27	1.08	0.36	0.45	0.09
SC12	3.021**	2.34	1.69	1.26	0.67	0.88	0.21
SC13	3.847**	2.02	1.62	1.47	0.47	0.59	0.12
SC14	1.014	1.57	1.36	1.14	0.22	0.38	0.16
Total	8.884***	81.60	67.19	56.66	14.41	24.94	10.53

*$p < 0.1$, **$p < 0.05$, ***$p < 0.01$. The bold value is used to highlight the statistically significant items.

environment, biodiversity, and climate change. The majority of the sample CEs are from the mining, manufacturing, utilities, and construction industries, and the primary motivation for many such CEs investing abroad is to find, retain, or develop export markets, as well as to ensure access to natural resources, particularly oil, gas, and mines (Shao & Shang, 2016; Young et al., 1996). Furthermore, according to social contract theory, businesses and the society are equal partners, each with their own set of rights and obligations, so MNEs and the society have both direct and indirect shared needs. While the former need ongoing

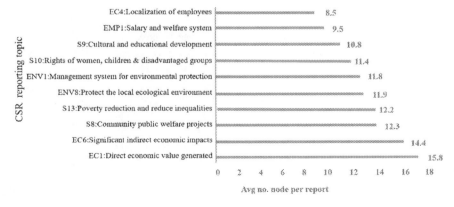

Figure 8.1 Top ten CSR reporting topics of CEs in the BRI host countries.

150 *The Impact of Ownership Types on CSR Reporting Contents and Quality*

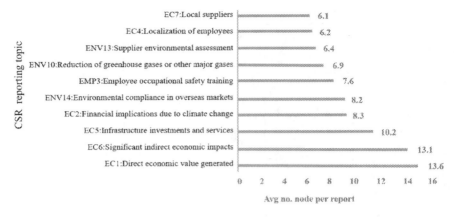

Figure 8.2 Top ten CSR reporting topics of SOEs in the BRI host countries.

services and sales from the latter, the latter may expect the former to act in a socially responsible manner because companies control vast quantities of economic and productive resources in host countries. Thus, CEs are under greater public scrutiny from both international and regional stakeholders, and in their CSR practices and disclosures, they are keen to promote stakeholder benefits in order to gain local legitimacy.

Compared with CEs and SOEs, PEs are more concerned with the Employment dimension. Table 8.3 demonstrates that PEs have better CSR reporting quality for EMP2 and EMP5, and Figure 8.3 reveals that PEs devote a large part of their CSR disclosures to the Employment dimension. On the one hand, PEs invest in the BRI seeking to identify and pursue opportunities abroad (Wadhwa & Reddy, 2011; Zhang, 2009); thus, they are more concerned about overseas market development and access to scarce resources. Employees constitute a critical asset for

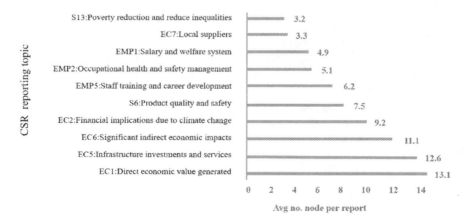

Figure 8.3 Top ten CSR reporting topics of PEs in the BRI host countries.

discovering and exploiting opportunities in the marketplace (Cooke et al., 2015; Crowther, 2018; Crowther & Seifi, 2018), and hence PEs are more concerned about CSR initiatives relating to employees. Another important aspect of PEs' CSR disclosures relates to the Economy dimension. Through transfers of knowledge and new technologies to their subsidiaries' host regions, private MNEs contribute to economic development. In this way, local firms are able to access information and technologies by forming vertical alliances with MNEs, recruiting professional workers from MNEs, and imitating MNE-introduced products, organizational processes, and technologies. By concentrating their CSR reporting on the Employment and Economy dimensions, PEs use CSR reporting as a strategic tool to boost their overseas development and market share.

However, the overseas CSR reporting scores on the Environmental and Social dimensions are far from satisfactory for PEs. Since China is becoming more environmentally conscious (Schreurs, 2017), some Chinese firms, and especially private firms, are likely to relocate inefficient and resource-intensive factories and technologies to less environmentally conscious BRI countries (Tracy et al., 2017). If host governments lower their environmental standards to attract FDI, the "pollution haven effect" will result in a "race to the bottom" (Fang & Nolan, 2019). Similarly, large MNEs, particularly those without strong public scrutiny or governmental regulation, may exploit developing host countries' cheap natural resources and labor (Alden & Davies, 2006), as PEs have lower scores on the Environment and Social dimensions. Overall, these results suggest diverse stakeholder engagements among PEs, with influential stakeholders such as international investors, local business partners, and employees receiving preferential treatment, as evidenced by higher scores on the Economy and Employment dimensions. These results go against the spirit of true normative stakeholder theory, where the equity principle remains at the heart of stakeholder management (Donaldson & Preston, 1995).

A new political-economy basis for developing CSR reporting by Chinese MNEs

There are some encouraging signs. The volume of discourse, policies, and guidelines regarding Chinese MNEs' CSR is generally increasing, demonstrating awareness by and consensus among the Chinese government and BRI host countries on the importance and necessity of CSR for Chinese companies investing there. Both local and international stakeholders are likely to welcome additional and more focused efforts to encourage CSR by Chinese MNEs. Thus, there is still much room for improvement in terms of overseas CSR reporting by all firms. Although several CEs exhibit outstanding quality in their overseas CSR reporting quality, they are not representative of all Chinese MNEs in BRI host countries.[4] While this is a crucial first move, these firms are few, and a thorough examination of the effects of the investments listed in CSR reports is urgently needed. Given that policies regulating Chinese MNEs' environmental and social impacts are still relatively weak, largely voluntary in nature, and incompatible with policies governing domestic investments, such regulations and the ability and capacity to enforce them vary widely and are often insufficient to address CSR deficiencies.[5] Furthermore, given that the majority of countries along the BRI are developing countries and emerging economies (Belt and Road Portal, 2021), they face many challenges occasioned by industrialization and urbanization, such as pollution and ecological destruction, and increasing demand for a faster transition to green growth (Fang & Nolan, 2019). According to the content analysis, Chinese MNEs would probably raise the bar for their CSR reporting in order to be seen as reliable and legitimate by those who matter in BRI host nations. We recommend that Chinese MNEs use CSR reporting for strategic purposes, such as communicating general quality, trust, and dependability and enhancing the corporate reputation. Considering that CSR communication is connected to institutional contexts and stakeholders' perceptions of a company's operations, we argue that Chinese MNEs should continuously let CSR reporting methods evolve in line with their BRI internationalization initiatives. Enhancing pertinent CSR reporting may benefit from improved environmental reporting policies and procedures for international operations. Additionally, encouraging CSR reporting could aid Chinese MNEs to better integrate into the global economy. Thus, a more robust regulatory framework should be established for CSR reporting by Chinese MNEs in overseas markets. The BRI and Sustainable Development Goals (SDGs) are mutually beneficial, but both demand a new development model that not only combines economic growth, social inclusion, and environmental protection but also suits the developing world's development context.

State ownership

From the above analysis, we can also draw some more interesting observations. First, prior studies have often argued that state ownership can both benefit and negatively impact EMNEs. To ensure socio-political and economic stability in a socialist state, SOEs are seen as essential. Instead of accommodating political differences and thereby quelling ensuing political conflicts, the Chinese government has prioritized fostering, preserving, and even imposing political harmony (Stockmann & Gallagher, 2011). In the late 1970s, the Chinese Communist Party (CCP) Central Committee began implementing the "open door" policy and reform in the societal and economic spheres, and they are still developing today. The CCP has led the reform through a recursive and gradual process known as "crossing rivers by touching the stones" (Yang & Modell, 2015), in which it learned advanced techniques from other countries, experimented with novel practices in certain industrial sectors, and then implemented relevant regulations and policies. Since the late 1980s, as an integral part of the reform, Chinese SOE sectors have undergone an unprecedented transformation via large scale but gradual processes of corporatization, privatization, and mergers and acquisitions. Some industrial sectors were also permitted to establish and run other forms of corporations, such as joint ventures, private companies, and partnerships. However, the CCP-led state government does not intend to fully adopt the Western capitalist market economy; rather, it will continue to hold a controlling stake in many SOEs in so-called strategically important sectors (Xu et al., 2014). On the one hand, when internationalizing into institutionally developed countries, EMNEs with strong state ownership face additional hurdles, such as local stakeholders' distrust in addition to a more competitive market environment (Panibratov & Michailova, 2019). On the other hand, as state ownership is frequently the outcome of a company's political ties to its home-country's government, which affects its reputation abroad (Cui & Jiang, 2012), skeptical stakeholders may believe that Chinese MNEs with significant state ownership act as political tools of Chinese foreign policy seeking to extend their international power in some BRI countries. Interestingly, prior studies have also argued that state-owned EMNEs could disclose even more CSR activities to gain legitimacy abroad and counter their "liability of stateness" (Mariotti & Marzano, 2019, p. 671). Therefore, as a means of obtaining legitimacy abroad, Chinese MNEs (such as SOEs and CEs) are more likely to declare CSR operations that ameliorate the unfavorable image of state ownership and greater scrutiny from foreign stakeholders.

Discretionary reporting for reputation

Second, the above analysis demonstrated that PEs often fail to engage in environmental disclosures. Another interesting lens to explain this result is the "fear of receiving a green lashing" (Bansal & Clelland, 2004, p. 101). Thus, some businesses decide not to disclose or under-report their environmental protection-related CSR efforts for fear of appearing hypocritical. For example, Marquis and Qian (2014) argue that businesses that are highly visible or subject to intense stakeholder scrutiny may be more likely to be accused of being hypocritical. Thus, PEs are likely to downplay their environmental CSR reporting while promoting their community-related CSR reporting to allay concerns of hypocrisy brought on by heightened stakeholder scrutiny on a global scale. Specifically, in comparison to more industrialized countries, the CSR practices of Chinese firms are generally not as advanced. Additionally, reputational worth is socially built and useful for gaining legitimacy in the form of general acceptance and public comprehension (Briscoe & Safford, 2008). Chinese MNEs may decide not to report all of their CSR efforts if they believe that particular initiatives would not be well understood or valued by stakeholders. Furthermore, given that Chinese MNEs are not known for their environmental friendliness, an overemphasis on environmental protection-related CSR reporting could be seen as unauthentic by international stakeholders. Therefore, compared to companies internationalizing to other regions of the world, Chinese MNEs expanding into BRI host countries generally prioritize reporting social and community-related activities over publicizing environmental initiatives. The findings support the notion that such communication strategies assist Chinese MNEs in avoiding reputational issues and establishing dependable relationships with stakeholders (Carlos & Lewis, 2018).

Reporting transparency and humanization

As previous chapters have pointed out, Chinese MNEs encounter difficulties when expanding internationally due to foreign stakeholders' perceptions of their native country or the risk of emergencies. For instance, in host countries with a politically unfriendly position toward the home country, mergers and acquisitions conducted by MNEs may be regarded as a danger due to the possibility of Russian official intervention (Dikova et al., 2019). Thus, while evaluating the legitimacy of Chinese MNEs, international stakeholders may engage in what is known as "adverse institutional attribution" (Ramachandran & Pant, 2010, p. 247). This is because corruption and a lack of transparency are considered to exist among Chinese firms. This unfavorable impression among international stakeholders makes it difficult for Chinese MNEs to gain and keep credibility in overseas markets. Moreover, foreign businesses must abide by local laws and ordinances, fulfill local normative obligations, and adopt local cultural norms, values, and practices according to legitimacy theory. Stakeholders in the majority of BRI countries are not paying much attention to environmental protection because they are more concerned about local employment, economic development, and industrial improvements. Nevertheless, the expansion of Chinese MNEs along the Belt and Road has caused them to be more transparent and report their CSR activities in a more explicit and thorough manner, as CSR performance plays a critical role in promoting the country's image on a global scale. The argument is supported by the data showing that Chinese MNEs are experiencing an even stronger need to engage in CSR reporting (improving scores) in BRI host countries. In doing so, Chinese MNEs are able to gain "substantial business-related benefits for the firm, in particular by supporting core business activities and thus contributing to the firm's effectiveness in accomplishing its mission" (Burke & Logsdon, 1996, p. 496) in host countries.

Another noteworthy clue drawn from the content analysis is that the disclosure contents of PEs are more diversified and flattened, while the disclosures of CEs and SOEs are more structured and "regulated". For example, many PEs strive to emphasize the employment benefits of their CSR efforts. These can be as basic as sponsoring local sports teams, advising non-governmental groups on organizational strategy or engaging employees in a fund-raising campaign for a specific charity. They also pay a lot of attention to the development of overseas talents. For instance, Huawei, in its 2021 CSR reports, stated:

> In the digital economy, digital talent plays an important role in driving digital transformations and economic growth. Huawei is committed to cultivating digital talent in the countries and regions in which it operates. In July

2021, Huawei launched its Seeds for the Future 2.0 programme. Through this updated programme, Huawei plans to invest USD150 million over the next five years to cultivate digital talent. This programme is expected to benefit over three million people. Since its launch in 2008, the Seeds for the Future programme has attracted participants from 137 countries and regions and benefited more than 12,000 students.

(Huawei, 2021, p. 95)

However, quality-of-life enhancements and increased chances for the betterment of all factory workers and the residents of their communities constitute not only moral obligations but also opportunities for businesses. From the perspective of companies, ethical behavior must be handled with reference to the local context and structured within multilateral and network partnerships in BRI host countries. The clues drawn from the emphasis on employee health and well-being by PEs highlight the importance of MNEs in building social prestige and empowering employees in host countries. For example:

We respect the backgrounds of each employee and treat employees of different nationalities, races, genders, religious beliefs and cultural backgrounds fairly and equally. We have zero tolerance for any discrimination and strive to build a diverse workforce. With diversity and equal career opportunities as our focus, we are dedicated to building a diverse and talented workforce based on each employee's skills and potential. During the reporting period, many of the new hires came from Congo, Madagascar, Pakistan, Zambia, Nigeria and other developing countries. We addressed employment issues in our host countries by adhering to local employment policies. Our local employment rate during the reporting period reached 96.04%.

(Zijing Mining, 2021, p. 52)

Honors and awards as mimetic forces

PEs are more likely to disclose contents that would earn them sustainability honors and awards. From the content analysis, we observe that Chinese MNEs, especially PEs, often devote a significant amount of effort to promoting the various awards they have received. For example, Huawei presented CSR-related honors and awards in every CSR report we examined (see Table 8.4). Researchers have already demonstrated that these awards are innovative and important; a competitor getting a CSR award is a significant event for the focus company (Morgeson et al., 2015). It is unusual for a competitor to win a CSR award because most businesses never do. When a competitor wins a CSR award, it can be disruptive for the target company because it could instantly lose social and public standing in comparison to the award winner (Rossman & Schilke, 2014). Because these awards are external indicators of the award winners' and focal firms' CSR performance and are becoming more significant in corporate strategies, competitor CSR award wins have a significant effect (Shiu & Yang, 2017). A company exists

Table 8.4 2021 Sustainability honors and awards of Huawei[6]

2021 Sustainability Honors and Awards	
Honor/Award name	Issued by
Huawei DigiTruck in Kenya: World Summit on the Information Society (WSIS) Prizes 2021 Champion Project	ITU
Nature Guardian: GSMA GLOMO for Outstanding Mobile Contribution to the UN SDGs	GSMA
Huawei RuralStar Pro: Best Mobile Innovation for Emerging Markets of GSMA GLOMO	GSMA
Best Practices for Achieving SDGs in 2021 (Protecting the Environment & Addressing Climate Change)	Global Compact Network China
Leadership Award on Climate Action	CDP
Climate A-List	CDP
FusionSolar Smart PV solution: Carbon Neutrality Actor – Climate Solver of the Year	WWF
27 Huawei subsidiaries recognized as a Top Employer	Top Employers Institute
Vodafone Health and Safety Award	Vodafone Group
Excellence in Supply Chain Development	Deutsche Telekom
Huawei India: Great Place to Work	Great Place to Work® Institute
Huawei Saudi Arabia: 2021 Sustainability Award in the Core Economic Area	King Khalid Foundation (KKF)
Huawei Bangladesh: Partner Recognition Award	bKash
Top ten Green and Low-carbon Companies	Shenzhen Emissions Exchange Co., Ltd.
Huawei Malaysia: Cyber Security Innovation of the Year	CyberSecurity Malaysia (CSM)
Huawei UAE: Cybersecurity Company of the Year and Cybersecurity CEO of the Year	UAE Cyber Security Council (CSC)

with the approval of society. If a company's operations and actions are viewed as adhering to socially accepted norms, its existence within a society is deemed legitimate. There would be a legitimacy gap between a firm's activities and what society expects if it were perceived as not adhering to societal norms in its operations. Obtaining accolades for exceptional or good CSR practices is one approach to proving good practices. If a company receives an award for good CSR efforts, the legitimacy gap between the company and society will be significantly reduced. Chinese MNEs use CSR to signal to stakeholders, such as investors and global customers, that they are able to fill institutional gaps in developing countries along the Belt and Road. Therefore, PEs are eager to implement global CSR efforts due to rising institutional pressure from local stakeholders.

Reporting influenced by party directives

In contrast, the reporting contents of SOEs and CEs are more structured, with strong intentions to reaffirm the national image. The senior executives of CEs and SOEs are specifically appointed, evaluated, and promoted by state government agencies. The governing body tasked with overseeing all significant SOEs operating in vital sectors, the SASAC, was established in 2003 (Kato & Long, 2006). In addition, executives of firms with significant state ownership hold a political position within the CCP hierarchy and receive regular training sessions organized by the Central Government agents, such as the Party School of the Central Committee of the CCP. This is a typical method to promote the intentions of the most recent ideological discourses of the CCP and subsequently implement the required actions. As a result, the majority of Chinese CEs and SOEs are required to adjust their visions and objectives in accordance with CCP discourses in the form of political leaders' discourses and documents, guiding principles issued by government authorities or the "Five-year National Development Goals" announced in the People's Congress convened by the CCP's central government (Hofman et al., 2017). In response to the national call, some leading CEs and SOEs collaborate with other MNEs to compete in the global market and are subsequently listed in leading international capital markets. Chinese CEs and SOEs have undergone transformations to adopt the governance structure of modern Western corporations, but their monopoly on core industries and the receipt of government subsidies reflect their responsibility to society at large rather than just financial success. As a result, Chinese CEs and SOEs are subject not only to national demands in terms of government requirements but also, like other multinational corporations, to international pressures and demands for more transparent and accountable operations. For example, between 2003 and 2005, a succession of political events emphasized the importance of societal harmony and sustainable development, which were formally incorporated into the national development policy in 2005. The officially declared ideas indicated a shift in the existing institutional logics in the Chinese socio-economic context from an emphasis on economic growth at all costs to a model of balanced development. A handful of SOEs initiated CSR reporting at the beginning of 2006 to confirm with the directives of the SASAC (Li & Belal, 2018).

China's motivations behind the BRI are not just to build mutually beneficial relations but rather to have the BRI be regarded as China's new geopolitical policy aimed at expanding its sphere of influence, establishing new rules of international economic cooperation and advancing a new world order. Therefore, Chinese CEs and SOEs are shouldering the responsibilities to rationalize China's global expansion and allay the negative concerns about the impacts of the BRI. For instance, using Chinese multinational contractors might expose developing nations to additional risks, such as causing their lands to become dumping grounds for obsolete Chinese technology, while local workers risk losing their jobs in their home markets. Chinese MNEs will also place projects under certain restrictions, such as allowing their contractors to select technology, utilize their equipment, and use Chinese laborers. Within the BRI, some developing countries, such as India and Indonesia, have proven to have reasonably strong project management experience. This is because of Chinese MNEs' inability to take complete control of projects, as these countries are unwilling to accept huge numbers of Chinese laborers. Other BRI nations with weaker governance include Cambodia and Pakistan. In such circumstances, China may be in a stronger position to regulate the terms and push riskier projects in these countries. Thus, we often see the following quotations from Chinese CEs describing their missions and roles along the Belt and Road:

> The company has firmly grasped the historical opportunity of the BRI, enhanced the acceleration of 'going out' and the high level of 'going up' and consolidated its position as a leader in globalization development. We have completed a huge number of landmark projects, quality projects and livelihood projects in countries and regions along the Belt and Road.
> (China Communications Construction Company, 2019, p. 18)

One of the critical drivers of CSR reporting contents comes from the political dimension for Chinese MNEs. As one of the major purposes of the BRI is to demonstrate China's global pledge, many Chinese MNEs with strong state ownership are paying particular attention to the imposition of the government's forces to initiate CSR reporting contents. These Chinese MNEs restate and reaffirm the visions and positive impacts of the BRI via CSR reporting, resembling the speech manuscript given by the Chinese government diplomat. For example:

> The Company has joined hands with the Genoa West Liguria Port Network Authority to establish an infrastructure investment platform to upgrade the port and urban infrastructure of Genoa through comprehensive strategic cooperation. At the same time, the Company also joined hands with the Italian East Adriatic Port Network Authority to carry out comprehensive cooperation on the Italian ports of Trieste and Monfalcone under the cooperation mechanism of the 'China-Europe Interconnection Platform'…. The agreement will further enhance the capacity and location of the Port of Trieste. These two agreements are also part of the BRI Cooperation Memorandum of Understanding signed between the Italian and Chinese governments to strengthen the BRI through Italy's 'Northern Port Construction' and 'Invest in Italy' programmes. The two agreements are an important reflection of the dovetailing of the BRI with Italy's 'Northern Port Construction' and 'Invest in Italy Programme'.
> (China Communications Construction Company, 2019, p. 19)

We will broaden the global network of partnerships to expand new areas of cooperation. Further upholding the concepts of mutual complementarity and mutual benefit and unswervingly following the path of 'internationalization', we will broaden our areas of energy cooperation under the BRI and the global network of partnerships. Additionally, we will raise the transnational index to contribute to the world economy, trade recovery and development. We are committed to reshaping the global industrial chain. Therefore, we will accelerate cooperation in key business areas, such as natural gas and LNG integration, shale oil and gas development and deep-water to ultra-deep-water development; intensify efforts in areas like R&D and design, marketing services and brand operations; optimise global resource allocation; and expand new areas of cooperation.

(China National Petroleum Corporation, 2020, p. 20)

Chinese MNEs with strong state ownership need to follow global demands and engage with government advocacy or state propaganda through the use of CSR reporting. It is possible that the government propagates the concepts of CSR and sustainability through internal and external means and "directs" CEs and SOEs to disseminate their CSR performance so that the ruling party can maintain its legitimacy. Given the socialist market economy ideology and total state ownership of the SOE sectors that characterize China, it is important to not undervalue the impact of governmental declarations and actions on CEs' and SOEs' behavior. For instance, when the government sends a political signal, Chinese CE and SOE leaders with heightened political sensitivity recognize the necessity and benefits of submitting a CSR report in a timely manner (Marquis & Qian, 2014; Marquis et al., 2017). This government-led initiative has inspired some CEs and SOEs to follow government policies regarding CSR reporting practices.

In summary, MNEs' contributions to the socio-economic development of developing nations have been hotly debated by academics, practitioners, and civil society organizations. By collaborating closely with host governments, MNEs play a role in alleviating poverty and fostering economic development, particularly in developing nations afflicted by extreme poverty. This requires substantial commitment from both corporations and host nations. The CSR initiatives of Chinese MNEs undoubtedly contribute to efforts to build mutual trust and socio-economic integration along the Belt and Road. However, the capacity of governments in developing nations, such as China, to demand accountability, responsibility, and openness from contemporary corporations has remained in doubt in the setting of the modern global economy. Chinese enterprises differ significantly from their counterparts in other countries in terms of the relatively large governmental stake, their more concentrated ownership structure, and the prevailing political connections among firms' management.

In this chapter, the impact of ownership structure on the CSR reporting content of Chinese MNEs is presented in detail using illustrative diagrams and figures. The impact of ownership structure on CSR reporting quality is also assessed using quantitative comparative analysis, and the findings are elaborated upon in combination with excerpts from CSR reports. The findings demonstrate ownership types significantly affect the CSR reporting contents of Chinese MNEs involved in BRI projects, as firms with different ownership types are subject to different political motivations, stakeholders' perceptions, and competition environments. The influence of governmental declarations and related actions upon CSR reporting contents is demonstrated through a new political-economy perspective, which is reshaping the why's, the how's, and the what's of Chinese MNEs, social reporting. Another important dimension influencing CSR reporting contents, which is the industry characteristics, will be explained in detail in the next chapter.

Notes

1. The "go global" strategy initiated in the 1990s resulted in many CEs and SOEs expanding overseas with strong government intervention. For example, state statistics show that the bulk of China's OFDI was made by CEs and SOEs owing to their richer resource endowment and state support (Fornés & Butt-Philip, 2009). These businesses are generally tightly regulated by the government, which ensures that their activities, both at home and abroad, remain aligned with government initiatives and national imperatives (Kolstad & Wiig, 2012).
2. Similarly, the Research Report on Chinese Overseas Enterprises' Corporate Social Responsibility states that the CEs had the highest social responsibility growth index of 42.77 overseas, with the PEs rated at only 20.93. According to the CASS (2018), in the previous three years, the CEs hired more than 360,000 local workers in BRI countries, and 99% of them did not experience any significant health or safety incidents in their activities there (CASS, 2017).
3. For example, in several working conferences held by SASAC, Li Keqiang, member of the Standing Committee of the Political Bureau of the CPC Central Committee and Premier of the State Council, gave important instructions on the role of CEs in the BRI (SASAC, 2015). SASAC strongly encourages CEs to play a leading role in enhancing China's international competitiveness. So far, 81 CEs have undertaken more than 3400 projects along the BRI, becoming an important force for transforming the BRI from concept to action (State Council Information Office, 2021).
4. Several industry-leading CEs have much higher CSR reporting scores in BRI host countries than other firms, and the standard deviation of CEs' CSR reporting quality is higher than for SOEs and PEs.
5. Indeed, the Chinese Government does not pursue a "command and control" approach in terms of CSR in overseas markets but instead provides companies and banks with incentives for self-regulation (Fang & Nolan, 2019).
6. Source: https://www-file.huawei.com/-/media/corp2020/pdf/sustainability/sustainability-report-2021-en.pdf

References

Alden, C., & Davies, M. (2006). A profile of the operations of Chinese multinationals in Africa. *South African Journal of International Affairs, 13*(1), 83–96.

Aray, Y., Dikova, D., Garanina, T., & Veselova, A. (2021). The hunt for international legitimacy: Examining the relationship between internationalization, state ownership, location and CSR reporting of Russian firms. *International Business Review, 30*(5), 101858.

Bansal, P., & Clelland, I. (2004). Talking trash: Legitimacy, impression management, and unsystematic risk in the context of the natural environment. *Academy of Management Journal, 47*(1), 93–103.

Belt and Road Portal. (2021). *List of countries that have signed cooperation documents with China to jointly build the "belt and road"*. https://www.yidaiyilu.gov.cn/xwzx/roll/77298.htm

Briscoe, F., & Safford, S. (2008). The Nixon-in-China effect: Activism, imitation, and the institutionalization of contentious practices. *Administrative Science Quarterly, 53*(3), 460–491.

Burke, L., & Logsdon, J. M. (1996). How corporate social responsibility pays off. *Long Range Planning, 29*(4), 495–502.

Carlos, W. C., & Lewis, B. W. (2018). Strategic silence: Withholding certification status as a hypocrisy avoidance tactic. *Administrative Science Quarterly*, 63(1), 130–169.

China Communications Construction Company. (2019). *Annual CSR report*. China Communications Construction Company. http://www.sasac.gov.cn/n4470048/n13461446/n14398052/n14398194/c14455192/part/14455203.pdf

China National Petroleum Corporation. (2020). *Annual CSR report*. CNPC. http://www.sinopec.com/listco/en/Resource/Pdf/2022032789.pdf

Chinese Academy of Social Science (CASS). (2017). Research Report on Corporate Social Responsibility of China: Blue Book of Corporate Social Responsibility. Social Sciences Academic Press.

Chinese Academy of Social Science (CASS). (2018). Research Report on Corporate Social Responsibility of China: Blue Book of Corporate Social Responsibility. Social Sciences Academic Press.

Coenen, J., Bager, S., Meyfroidt, P., Newig, J., & Challies, E. (2021). Environmental governance of China's belt and road initiative. *Environmental Policy and Governance*, 31(1), 3–17.

Cooke, F. L. (2014). Chinese multinational firms in Asia and Africa: Relationships with institutional actors and patterns of HRM practices. *Human Resource Management*, 53(6), 877–896.

Cooke, F. L., Wood, G., & Horwitz, F. (2015). Multinational firms from emerging economies in Africa: Implications for research and practice in human resource management. *The International Journal of Human Resource Management*, 26(21), 2653–2675.

Crowther, D. (2018). *A social critique of corporate reporting: A semiotic analysis of corporate financial and environmental reporting*. Routledge.

Crowther, D., & Seifi, S. (Eds.). (2018). *Redefining corporate social responsibility*. Emerald Group Publishing.

Cui, L., & Jiang, F. (2012). State ownership effect on firms' FDI ownership decisions under institutional pressure: A study of Chinese outward-investing firms. *Journal of International Business Studies*, 43(3), 264–284.

Dikova, D., Panibratov, A., & Veselova, A. (2019). Investment motives, ownership advantages and institutional distance: An examination of Russian cross-border acquisitions. *International Business Review*, 28(4), 625–637.

Donaldson, T., & Preston, L. E. (1995). The stakeholder theory of the corporation: Concepts, evidence, and implications. *Academy of Management Review*, 20(1), 65–91.

Fang, C., & Nolan, P. (Eds.). (2019). *Routledge handbook of the belt and road*. Routledge.

Fornés, G., & Butt-Philip, A. (2009). Chinese companies' outward internationalization to emerging countries: The case of Latin America. *Chinese Business Review*, 8(7), 13.

Foster-McGregor, N., Isaksson, A., & Kaulich, F. (2015). Foreign ownership and labour in sub-Saharan African firms. *African Development Review*, 27(2), 130–144.

Hofman, P. S., Moon, J., & Wu, B. (2017). Corporate social responsibility under authoritarian capitalism: Dynamics and prospects of state-led and society-driven CSR. *Business & Society*, 56(5), 651–671.

Huang, Y. (2016). Understanding China's Belt & Road initiative: motivation, framework and assessment. *China Economic Review*, 40, 314–321.

Huawei. (2021). *Annual CSR report*. Huawei. https://www-file.huawei.com/-/media/corp2020/pdf/sustainability/sustainability-report-2021-en.pdf

Kao, E. H., Yeh, C. C., Wang, L. H., & Fung, H. G. (2018). The relationship between CSR and performance: Evidence in China. *Pacific-Basin Finance Journal*, 51, 155–170.

Kato, T., & Long, C. (2006). Executive turnover and firm performance in China. *American Economic Review*, 96(2), 363–367.

Kolstad, I., & Wiig, A. (2012). What determines Chinese outward FDI? *Journal of World Business*, 47(1), 26–34.

Li, T., & Belal, A. (2018). Authoritarian state, global expansion and corporate social responsibility reporting: The narrative of a Chinese state-owned enterprise. *Accounting Forum*, 42(2), 199–217.

Mariotti, S., & Marzano, R. (2019). Varieties of capitalism and the internationalization of state-owned enterprises. *Journal of International Business Studies*, 50(5), 669–691.

Marquis, C., & Qian, C. (2014). Corporate social responsibility reporting in China: Symbol or substance? *Organization Science*, 25(1), 127–148.

Marquis, C., Yin, J., & Yang, D. (2017). State-mediated globalization processes and the adoption of corporate social responsibility reporting in China. *Management and Organization Review*, 13(1), 167–191.

Mitchell, R. K., Agle, B. R., & Wood, D. J. (1997). Toward a theory of stakeholder identification and salience: Defining the principle of who and what really counts. *Academy of Management Review*, 22(4), 853–886.

Morgeson, F. P., Mitchell, T. R., & Liu, D. (2015). Event system theory: An event-oriented approach to the organizational sciences. *Academy of Management Review*, 40(4), 515–537.

Panibratov, A., & Michailova, S. (2019). The role of state ownership and home government political support in Russian multinationals' internationalization. *International Journal of Emerging Markets*, 41(3), 436–450.

Quer, D., Rienda, L., & Andreu, R. (2020). FDI drivers and establishment mode choice of emerging-market MNEs: The role of state ownership. Journal of International Business Studies, 51(5), 747–769.

Quer, D., Rienda, L., Andreu, R., & Miao, S. (2019). Host country experience, institutional distance and location choice of Chinese MNEs. *Cross Cultural & Strategic Management*, 26(1), 24–45.

Ramachandran, J., & Pant, A. (2010). The liabilities of origin: An emerging economy perspective on the costs of doing business abroad. In T. M. Devinney, T. Pedersen, L. Tihanyi (Eds.), Advances in international management: Vol. 23. The past, present and future of international business and management (pp. 231–265). Emerald.

Rossman, G., & Schilke, O. (2014). Close, but no cigar: The bimodal rewards to prize-seeking. *American Sociological Review*, 79(1), 86–108.

Schreurs, M. (2017). Multi-level climate governance in China. *Environmental Policy and Governance*, 27(2), 163–174.

Shao, Y., & Shang, Y. (2016). Decisions of OFDI engagement and location for heterogeneous multinational firms: Evidence from Chinese firms. *Technological Forecasting and Social Change*, 112, 178–187.

Shiu, Y. M., & Yang, S. L. (2017). Does engagement in corporate social responsibility provide strategic insurance-like effects? *Strategic Management Journal*, *38*(2), 455–470.

State-owned Assets Supervision and Administration Commission. (SASAC). (2015). Closely integrate the "One Belt One Road" strategy and actively promote international production capacity cooperation. SASAC. http://www.gov.cn/guowuyuan/2015-06/19/content_2882041.htm.

State Council Information Office. (2021). Press conference on the economic operation of central enterprises in 2020. State Council. http://www.gov.cn/xinwen/2021-01/20/content_5581263.htm.

Stockmann, D., & Gallagher, M. E. (2011). Remote control: How the media sustain authoritarian rule in China. *Comparative Political Studies*, *44*(4), 436–467.

Tracy, E. F., Shvarts, E., Simonov, E., & Babenko, M. (2017). China's new Eurasian ambitions: The environmental risks of the silk road economic belt. *Eurasian Geography and Economics*, *58*(1), 56–88.

Wadhwa, K., & Reddy, S. S. (2011). Foreign direct investment into developing Asian countries: The role of market seeking, resource seeking and efficiency seeking factors. *International Journal of Business and Management*, *6*(11), 219.

Xu, L., Cortese, C., & Zhang, E. (2014). Ideology diffusion and the role of accounting: A Gramscian approach to understanding China's transition from 1949 to 1957. *Accounting History*, *19*(4), 434–451.

Yang, C., & Modell, S. (2015). Shareholder orientation and the framing of management control practices: A field study in a Chinese state-owned enterprise. *Accounting, Organizations and Society*, *45*, 1–23.

Young, S., Huang, C. H., & McDermott, M. (1996). Internationalization and competitive catch-up processes: Case study evidence on Chinese multinational enterprises. *MIR: Management International Review*, *36*(4), 295–314.

Zhang, K. H. (2009). Rise of Chinese multinational firms. *Chinese Economy*, *42*(6), 81–96.

Zhao, M. (2012). CSR-based political legitimacy strategy: Managing the state by doing good in China and Russia. *Journal of Business Ethics*, *111*(4), 439–460.

Zhao, N., & Patten, D. M. (2016). An exploratory analysis of managerial perceptions of social and environmental reporting in China: Evidence from state-owned enterprises in Beijing. *Sustainability Accounting, Management and Policy Journal*, *7*(1), 80–98.

Zheng, H., & Zhang, Y. (2016). Do SOEs outperform private enterprises in CSR? Evidence from China. *Chinese Management Studies*, *10*(3), 435–445.

Zhou, L., Gilbert, S., Wang, Y., Cabré, M. M., & Gallagher, K. P. (2018). Moving the green belt and road initiative: From words to actions *(Working Paper)*. Washington, DC: World Resources Institute. http://www.wri.org/publication/moving-the-green-belt.

Zijing Mining. (2021). *Annual CSR report*. Zijing Mining. https://www.zijinmining.com/upload/file/2022/06/09/9b7954d122554e8ab7327852dc7d4004.pdf.

9 Industry-specific CSR Reporting Contents in BRI Host Countries

Highlighted industries along the Belt and Road

The BRI is a huge infrastructural project running from East Asia to Europe. In 2013, President Xi Jinping of China announced the initiative and made official trips to Kazakhstan and Indonesia. The "Maritime Silk Road" and the "Overland Silk Road Economic Belt" are the two axes of the strategy. In Xi's vision, a large network of motorways, energy pipelines, railways, and border crossings would be built, and they would extend south to Pakistan, India, and the rest of Southeast Asia as well as west across the mountainous former Soviet republics. According to Xi, such a network would promote the international use of the renminbi and break the bottleneck in the Asian connection (Xi, 2017a).

President Xi best describes the BRI as follows: "China will vigorously encourage international cooperation through the Belt and Road Initiative. In doing so, we seek to accomplish policy, infrastructural, trade, financial and people-to-people connectedness, so establishing a new platform for international cooperation and generating new drivers of shared development" (Xi, 2017b, p. 61). The focus on connectivity among Belt and Road countries is both about facilitating trade and investment and thus the development of neighboring countries, as well as strategically bolstering its own energy, resources, and food security by assuming a strategic role among its most important neighbors.

The numerous concerns and challenges associated with China's domestic energy policies (i.e., energy-industrial overcapacity) as a result of the country's energy reforms are the primary drivers of China's launching of the BRI and its increasing international infrastructure and energy projects. Consequently, China has prioritized the construction of BRI-related economic, commercial, and infrastructure projects along critical energy trading and transportation lines. The Chinese government is determined to advance multimodal transportation that integrates expressways, railways, waterways, and airways, strengthening infrastructure development along the Belt and Road. In addition to enhancing connection and "physical" transport infrastructure, "soft" barriers are shifting into facilitators along the Belt and Road. For example, by providing digital and information-sharing networks, collaborative platforms, and opportunities to enhance efficiency and supply chain resilience, advancements in information and

DOI: 10.4324/9781003302445-9

digital technology and automation can aid in enhancing multimodal transport connections for host countries.

However, many BRI projects have necessitated the construction of roads and train freight lines across some of the world's most biodiverse regions. The World Wildlife Fund (WWF) has warned that the BRI might imperil 265 species, including Amur tigers, oriental white storks, and giant pandas (WWF, 2017). Narain et al. (2020) have pointed out that the BRI's corridors and other projects span some of the world's most fragile and pristine ecosystems, whose alteration would have extraordinary effects on the environment. For instance, a massive dam put in a Mekong River tributary in Cambodia and a large rail line from China to Laos resulted from deforestation and the forced relocation of thousands of families. Coal power plants in Pakistan, Kenya, Indonesia, and Serbia have triggered pollution-related demonstrations, and road and rail projects in Malaysia and elsewhere have devastated delicate ecosystems. Conservationists are vehemently opposing to a Kenyan railway that crosses Nairobi National Park and is slated to continue into Tsavo National Park, one of Africa's most significant animal sanctuaries. Similarly, Zhang and Noronha (2022) analyzed the CSR reporting of Chinese MNEs and demonstrated that they these companies not taking enough care to address the biodiversity issues resulting from various infrastructure projects along the Belt and Road.

Therefore, China has unveiled a flurry of new attempts to rebrand the BRI as a "Green Silk Road" in response to claims that the BRI is hindering the achievement of UN climate targets. In the first quarter of 2022, China's National Development and Reform Commission issued a new directive to obligate Chinese banks and MNEs to boost funding and sustainable financing standards. Chinese MNEs are highly encouraged to use green funds and launch low-carbon technologies in BRI host countries, which is also consistent with China's ultimate climate goal, which is the implementation of the UN Sustainable Development Goals (SDGs) until 2030.

According to several distinctive features of the BRI and importantly related policies, this chapter identifies several highlighted industries as the targets of analysis. They are the construction industry, mining industry, information and communication technology (ICT) industry and the banking and finance industry. Primary and secondary data for the case studies were downloaded from CSR reports, corporate websites, mass news media, and academic literature. This chapter involves a detailed documentary analysis, examining the CSR reports and CSR websites of firms in relevant industries from 2014 to 2021. Related regulations and legal documents are also examined. The sample firms are listed in Table 9.1.

The following sections will shed some light on the impacts of industry types on CSR reporting content in BRI host countries. Given that the industry distribution of the sample firms was uneven, a case study method was used to address this topic. According to Robson (2002), exploratory studies allow researchers to formulate methods for discovering real-world occurrences and

Table 9.1 Sample list in case studies

Name	Firm type	Industry
China Metallurgical Group Corporation	SOE	Construction Industry (E)
China Wu Yi	SOE	Construction Industry (E)
Shanghai Construction Group	SOE	Construction Industry (E)
Gezhouba Group	SOE	Construction Industry (E)
Zhongcai Construction Limited Company	SOE	Construction Industry (E)
China Communications Construction Group	CE	Construction Industry (E)
China National Nuclear Corporation	CE	Construction Industry (E)
China Railway Construction Corporation	CE	Construction Industry (E)
China Railway Engineering Corporation	CE	Construction Industry (E)
China National Building Material Corporation	CE	Construction Industry (E)
China Energy Engineering Corporation	CE	Construction Industry (E)
China State Construction Engineering Corporation	CE	Construction Industry (E)
China Life Insurance Company	SOE	Banking and Finance Industry (I)
Industrial and Commercial Bank of China	SOE	Banking and Finance Industry (I)
China Development Bank	SOE	Banking and Finance Industry (I)
China Merchants Bank	SOE	Banking and Finance Industry (I)
People's Insurance Company of China	SOE	Banking and Finance Industry (I)
Industrial and Commercial Bank of China	SOE	Banking and Finance Industry (I)
Guotai Junan Securities	SOE	Banking and Finance Industry (I)
China Construction Bank	SOE	Banking and Finance Industry (I)
Agricultural Bank of China	SOE	Banking and Finance Industry (I)
CITIC Bank	SOE	Banking and Finance Industry (I)
Bank of China	SOE	Banking and Finance Industry (I)
National Development Investment	CE	Banking and Finance Industry (I)
Huawei	PE	ICT Industry (G)
Alibaba	PE	ICT Industry (G)
Lenovo	PE	ICT Industry (G)
Tencent	PE	ICT Industry (G)
Zhongtian Technology	PE	ICT Industry (G)
Fiberhome Communications	SOE	ICT Industry (G)
Shenzhen Kaifa Technology	SOE	ICT Industry (G)
Tianma Microelectronics	SOE	ICT Industry (G)
ZTE Corporation	SOE	ICT Industry (G)
China Telecom	CE	ICT Industry (G)
China Unicom	CE	ICT Industry (G)
China Electronics Information Industry Group	CE	ICT Industry (G)
China Mobile	CE	ICT Industry (G)

gaining new knowledge without having to investigate the causes. Since this part of the analysis aims not to examine causality between variables but to relate observed data to pre-identified themes, it is exploratory in nature and does not conduct investigations associated with any hypothesis. By applying the theoretical framework developed in the literature review, case studies are used to explore what industry-specific external factors influence CSR reporting contents and what CSR reporting contents are specific to particular industries in BRI host countries.

Land connectively through transportation infrastructure: Construction industry

Given that a large number of BRI projects are centered on infrastructure, transportation on land is an unavoidable subject of attention. Moreover, China's internal rail reform, modernization, and development have created the largest rail sector in the world (Lin et al., 2021).

In the upcoming years, it is anticipated that the number of large construction projects, such as rails, roads, bridges, and other land developments, will increase dramatically. While it is hoped that this will stimulate economic growth, there is a risk of unintentional environmental damage associated with such initiatives (Tang, 2018; Zhu et al., 2022). The construction industry has one of the highest rates of environmental claims, and resolving those related to significant infrastructure projects has become increasingly difficult and expensive. Numerous BRI investment projects are currently taking place in biodiversity hotspots, and many infrastructure development projects are being constructed in areas of high environmental value, hence having a substantial impact on biodiversity (Atkins & Maroun, 2018; Lechner et al., 2018; Ng et al., 2020). The interconnection of transportation infrastructure enabled by railroads, highways, and bridges is one of the development focuses of the BRI. As a result, the large land area altered and the complex engineering characteristics of transportation infrastructure will inevitably impact the ecological environment. For example, the creation of infrastructure leads not only to a direct breakdown in connectivity between landscapes and ecosystems but also to secondary impacts, such as the spread of invasive alien animal and plant species, wind turbines, fires, animal deaths, pollution and microclimate alteration and creation (Cuckston, 2018; Laurila-Pant, et al., 2015; Lechner et al., 2018). Environmental consciousness is building quickly, and public awareness of the negative impacts of BRI construction projects is growing. Table 9.2 summarizes the major social and environmental risks of different types of BRI construction projects.

Infrastructure initiatives are multi-year endeavors. It is reassuring to note that almost every sample company involved in BRI land transportation projects has addressed environmental impacts in their CSR reports. For example, during the pre-construction phase of the C12 road project, China Wuyi took the initiative to communicate with local government, wildlife protection organizations, community residents, and other stakeholders to introduce the company's experience in wildlife protection during road construction and to design and optimize emergency wildlife protection plans for roads with wildlife protection needs (Kenya China Economic & Trade Association, 2019). During the construction process, China Wuyi actively listened to the suggestions of local wildlife protection organizations and appropriately adjusted the construction time

Table 9.2 Social and environmental risks of different types of land transportation projects

Project types	Social and environmental risks
Railways and roads	The area where the construction site is located might cut across one or more Key Biodiversity Areas (KBAs). The construction sites and ancillary facilities in the nearby areas take up a large amount of land, which have destroyed the vegetation and wild animals' habitats in the construction area. Construction activities could damage and affect the vegetation in and around the construction site to varying degrees. The basis for the wildlife and habitat survival of wild animals is cut off and even destroyed due to the construction of railways and roads. Construction operations fragment habitats, dividing and isolating populations. Due to the long construction period of railways and road projects, the accumulation of raw or waste materials during the construction process causes a prolonged encroachment on animal habitats or vegetation-covered areas. Emissions and waste leaking into surroundings from the construction processes may cause ground/soil contamination and water pollution in the surrounding areas. Noise pollution and frequent human activities due to construction operations have various negative impacts on the growth, development, and natural reproduction of wild animals. Human activities after project completion, such as the maintenance of railways and roads, increase the degree of disturbance to regional biodiversity and the risk of exotic species invasion. Noise from horn honking on railroads and highways can disturb the normal activities of animals. The safety guards of railroads and roads limit the range of animal activities. The ease of transportation facilitates the illegal poaching and indiscriminate logging of endangered species. Accidental deaths, such as those occurring during highway crossings, are also becoming more common. Along the construction route, indigenous people may need to be relocated. Along the construction route, indigenous people may suffer from water pollution, noise pollution, soil contamination, and dust. Accidental injury or death of employees during construction.
Bridges	The areas where construction sites are located could be important areas (such as KBAs) for the protection of marine biodiversity. Noise pollution and frequent human activities due to the construction operations have various negative impacts on the growth, development, and reproduction of wild animals in the surrounding areas. Emissions and wastes from the construction process may cause underwater and lakeshore (seashore) pollution. The light from bridges can induce migrating birds to fly low and collide with the bridge during nights of bad weather, resulting in bird mortality. In addition, vehicles travelling at high speeds on the bridge can have a negative impact on various species, especially birds. The daily operation of the bridge has negative impacts on species habitats and activities of underwater and coastal animals. The construction of the bridges affects the livelihood of local fishermen. Along the construction route, indigenous people may need to be relocated. Along the construction route, indigenous people may suffer from water pollution, noise pollution, soil contamination, and dust. Accidental injury or death of employees during construction.

(Kenya China Economic & Trade Association, 2019, p. 55). In addition, China Communications Construction Company illustrated how it is preventing biodiversity loss around its operational sites:

> During the construction process, the railroad project strictly followed Kenya's overall plan and met the requirements established by local wildlife management authorities. When passing through wildlife sanctuaries (such as Nairobi National Park and Tsavo National Park), the construction team appropriately extended the approach bridge across the river at the wildlife water source and raised the height of the bridge to facilitate animal drinking and passage.
> (China Communications Construction Company, 2015, p. 39)

> Based on the research revealing wildlife habits and migration paths, 14 animal crossings, 600 culverts and 61 bridges were installed along the Monel Railway to facilitate animal movement. All bridge-type animal passages have a clear height of 6.5 metres or more, so all animals, including giraffes, can easily pass through them.
> (China Communications Construction Company, 2017, p. 7)

In addition to this, the positive economic impact of infrastructure projects is often highlighted by Chinese multinational contractors. For example:

> In the aftermath of the COVID-19 pandemic, the Mombasa–Nairobi Standard Gauge Railway passenger and freight transport has helped ensure a more resilient and sustainable overall travel and logistics system that truly meets the passenger and freight needs of Kenya and its surrounding regions.
> (China Communications Construction Company, 2020, p. 48)

> Since entering the Guinea Dapilon–Santou Railway Project, China Railway 14th Bureau Group Co., Ltd. has constantly been exploring the incorporation of local human resources to create local employment opportunities and drive local socioeconomic benefits with the concept of 'integrating into the local community and developing together'. The Project Department has employed more than 700 locals in Guinea, with a localization rate of more than 70%, and has provided suitable jobs for some locals with disabilities. In addition, the Project Department has also provided learning opportunities for locals through staff coaching, classroom training and practical exercises.
> (China Railway Construction Corporation, 2020, p. 74)

In addition to the emphasis on economic benefits, examples of Chinese contractors working to promote the well-being of local communities were constantly mentioned. Consider the following observations:

> During the construction of the Benguela Railway in Angola, China Railway 20th Bureau Group Co., Ltd. actively explored cross-cultural management,

organized cultural exchange activities, promoted high-level visits and enhanced cultural identity. The company was included in the 'List of Most Trusted Partners' by Angolan authorities. At the 2019 Chinese Enterprise Global Image Summit, Cultural Identity in Benguela Railway Construction in Angola, submitted by the company, was awarded the 'Excellent Case for Cross-Cultural Exchanges'.

(China Railway Construction Corporation, 2019, p. 89)

Established in 1981, Public Girls, Secondary School Dutse is the only girls boarding school in Abuja, the capital of Nigeria, and has long been committed to promoting cultural exchange between China and Nigeria. It boasts a good atmosphere for broadcasting Chinese culture. On 12 September 2019, China Railway 18th Bureau Group Nigeria Engineering Co., Ltd. held an educational assistance ceremony at Public Girls, Secondary School Dutse. During the event, the company donated teaching materials and supplies to the school and offered stationery items, clothes and nutritious lunches to students. A week-long Chinese teaching activity was conducted at the school by the company, aiming to help students better understand Chinese culture, boost cultural exchange between the two countries and promote Chinese enterprises and a culture of 'going global'.

(China Railway Construction Corporation, 2019, p. 89)

During the construction process, the company donated hospitals and schools to local communities and to the Zambia AIDS Prevention and Control Foundation. Furthermore, it built wells and roads for villagers around the park.

(China National Building Materials Corporate, 2020, p. 67)

It was observed that while some Chinese MNEs noted that their infrastructure projects were located in environmentally sensitive areas, they only provided very general information about their objectives pertaining to protecting biodiversity or preventing extinction. Furthermore, aside from a small number of better performing companies, the problem of content repetition is worth noticing. However, it was observed that land infrastructure contractors have been focusing on boosting trade, increasing job creation, improving transport services, and promoting educational and health welfare around the construction sites. In terms of employment, Chinese MNEs are working hard to boost local employment. However, an increase in employment through low-skilled jobs does not represent an increase in overall local social well-being. We observed that training for higher skilled jobs and the transfer of knowledge were generally lacking in the companies studied.

There is no denying that these infrastructure projects along the BRI face a variety of risks (Chen & Liu, 2019). For instance, governments may change in the middle of the construction, local workforces in nations with strong unions may need to be handled, and locals may oppose land acquisition. Managing hazards throughout the life cycle of a project is a major task that will benefit from a renowned local partner and knowledgeable counsel from the pre-planning phase through to completion. Furthermore, the coherence and implementation of the Green BRI depend on the creation of policies and regulatory instruments that can translate the concept into actionable measures. It should be highlighted that in the absence of new powerful engines or incentives, land transportation projects will continue to pose a significant barrier to sustainable development in BRI host countries.

Green finance and sustainable BRI: Banking and finance industry

Green finance is a broad notion that has been described in a variety of ways, with no consensus having been reached. A generally cited definition of green finance from the G200's 2016 report (p. 5) is "funding investments that deliver environmental advantages for ecologically sustainable development". Green finance instruments primarily comprise green lending and green bonds. To set BRI economies on a sustainable development path, investment must shift away from greenhouse gas-, fossil fuel-, and natural resource-intensive industries and toward more resource-efficient technologies and business models. In order to achieve this green transition, the financial sector must play a crucial role (Meena, 2013). Green finance is defined as all types of investment or lending that consider environmental impact and enhance environmental sustainability (Wang & Zhi, 2016). Sustainable investment and banking, where investment and lending decisions are based on environmental screening and risk assessments to meet sustainability criteria, and insurance services cover environmental and climate risk, are important aspects of green finance (Sachs et al., 2019).

The green economy has emerged as a new engine for global economic growth, and advances in green finance and green investment have been trending (Fang & Nolan, 2019; Harlan, 2020). The challenge of balancing economic growth with long-term sustainability is universal. However, given that most emerging Asian economies' growth models have been resource- and carbon-intensive, the challenge is enormous. China is currently undergoing a crucial phase in economic structural change and transformation of its development mode. Demand for green finance, which supports long-term growth of its green industry, economy, and society, as well as international green OFDI, has risen steadily (Narain et al., 2020). Promotion of green investment and development of green finance comply with the criteria for green growth and ecological society building and also reflect sustainable and green development practices (Jian et al., 2021).

Recognizing these obstacles, the Chinese government is dedicated to developing a sustainable BRI. In 2017, four ministries of the China State Council announced jointly that sustainability has become an integral part of the BRI's advancement, and that one of China's top priorities is to strengthen the environmental management of BRI investments and establish a green financial system. The significance of green financing has since been emphasized. China's 2019 BRI progress report, for instance, recognizes that green finance should be further expanded to support the BRI's green development. The idea of green growth has run through the BRI since its inception. This has created a significant green investment and financing space, as well as greater demand for new green products and technologies (Narain et al., 2020). This potential has not yet been fully realized because the global impact of Chinese green finance remains limited (Harlan, 2020). For example, given the region's vulnerability to climate change and the need to reduce carbon emissions, massive investments in green and climate-resilient infrastructure are needed. These investments must be mindful of financial, environmental, and policy risks and may include funding from both private and public sectors, and domestic and foreign sources. Funding for long-term infrastructure in the area necessitates new approaches to mobilizing and facilitating long-term finance. In this sense, it is critical to investigate the CSR reporting contents of firms in the banking and finance industries and explore possible methods to support China's green development along the BRI.

The green economy has emerged as a new driver of economic growth on a global scale, and green finance and green investment have become fashionable (Kang et al., 2018). A new global industrial revolution has opened up novel possibilities for green growth. Two Chinese banking regulators, the People's Bank of China (hereinafter PBOC, the central bank) and the China Banking and Insurance Regulatory Commission (hereinafter CBIRC), have issued a number of policies, guidelines, and standards to strengthen the "green" characteristics of banks' green finance, particularly those pertaining to green credits and green financial bonds. If well-designed and executed, these regulatory mechanisms can improve the green performance of Chinese banks both domestically and in BRI nations; a more sustainable BRI would benefit from this development. Therefore, a comprehensive evaluation of rules is required to assess their capacity to promote a sustainable BRI. Together with several policies relating to the development of green finance (see Table 9.3), Chinese financial institutions are also actively involved in supporting the "Green BRI" initiative, which aims to improve the ecological environment and biodiversity while also reacting to climate change (Dong et al., 2018). These policies and regulations provide strong motivation for Chinese MNEs in the finance and banking industries to disclose CSR initiatives relating to green finance.

The direct and indirect economic impacts of green finance and investments are key topics in the CSR disclosures of Chinese MNEs in the banking and finance industry along the BRI. According to a survey on decarbonizing the Belt and Road, BRI countries require USD 12 trillion in green investments by 2030 in order to comply with the Paris Agreement (Cheung & Hong, 2020). Traditional governmental and philanthropic funds are incapable of meeting such a massive demand, but green finance is playing an essential role in achieving this goal. Green finance will reform current financial markets and mobilize the provision of private capital to greener industries by incentivizing "green" while restricting "brown" (polluting) industries[14] (Cheung & Hong, 2020).

According to the CSR reports of China Development Bank, in 2017, 22 large BRI ventures were completed, and new BRI loans to the value of USD 17.6 billion were extended (China Development Bank, 2017). Areas for investment

Table 9.3 Related policies for green finance in China

2007	China Banking Regulatory Commission (CBRC), People's Bank of China (PBOC), and MEP: Green Credit Policy ("Opinions on Enforcing Policies and Regulations on Environmental Protection to Prevent Credit Risk")[1]
2007	MEP and China Insurance Regulatory Commission (CIRC): Green Insurance Policy ("Guiding Opinions on Environmental Pollution Liability Insurance")[2]
2008	China Securities Regulatory Commission (CSRC) and MEP: Green Securities Policy ("Guidance Opinions on Strengthening the Oversight of Public Companies")[3]
2012	CBRC: Green Credit Guidelines[4]
2014	CBRC: Green Credit Monitoring and evaluation mechanism and Key Performance Indicators Checklist[5]
2015	PBOC: Green Financial Bond Directive and Green Bond-Endorsed Project Catalogue for Bonds Issued by Financial Institutions and Corporations[6]
2016	PBOC: Guidelines for Establishing the Green Financial System[7]
2016	NDRC and Shanghai Stock Exchange (SSE): Green Bond Guidelines[8]
2017	CSRC: Guidelines for Green Bond Issuance by Listed Companies[9]
2017	CSRC: Guidance on Supporting the Development of Green Bonds[10]
2018	Hong Kong Quality Assurance Agency: Green Finance Certification Scheme[11]
2019	Green Finance Professional Committee of China Finance Society, City of London Green Finance Initiative: Green Investment Principles (GIP) for BRI[12]
2022	Opinions on Promoting the Green Development of Belt and Road[13]

include networking, cooperation in production capacity and manufacturing facilities, financial cooperation, and development of BRI countries' overseas industrial parks. On the other hand, according to the Bank of China's CSR report, it has subsidiaries in 23 BRI countries, making it the largest Chinese bank along the Belt and Road. By the end of 2019, it had followed up on over 600 big BRI ventures and had financed approximately USD 160 billion in credit support to BRI countries. With support from the Bank of China, the Hungarian government invested in the first Bresi sovereign panda bond (Bank of China, 2019). Similarly, the Industrial and Commercial Bank of China's Luxembourg division issued the first BRI climate bond, which was valued at USD 2.15 billion and was oversubscribed by international investors. By the end of 2019, the Industrial and Commercial Bank of China had 131 branches in 21 countries and regions along the BRI, especially in Africa, the Middle East, South America, and Central and Eastern Europe, to assist in funding various BRI projects (Industrial & Commercial Bank, 2019). Table 9.4 lists the green bonds issued by major Chinese multinational banks participating in BRI-related projects (Cheung & Hong, 2020).

Furthermore, as financial institutions apply socio-economic criteria to project approval and funding, they have significant clout with businesses and governance actors (Brombal, 2018). According to the CSR report of the Export-Import Bank of China and China Development Bank, the Silk Road Fund is focusing on the development of infrastructure, resources, production capacity, and finance cooperation in BRI countries (China Development Bank, 2018). It offers financial services primarily through equity investments in various ways, including debt, fund, and credit. The Silk Road Fund has already been involved in BRI projects in a

Table 9.4 Green bond issued by major Chinese multinational banks

Issuer	Amount	Currency	Issue date	Expiry	Verification institution	Market
China Construction Bank	500 million	EUR	24/09/2018	24/10/2021	Ernst & Young	Luxembourg Green Stock Exchange
China Everbright Bank	300 million	USD	13/09/2018	19/8/2021	Sustainalytics	Hong Kong Stock Exchange
Capital Environment	250 million	USD	11/09/2018	11/09/2021	Sustainalytics	Hong Kong Stock Exchange
ICBC Asia	200 million	USD	14/06/2018	14/06/2021	HKQAA	Hong Kong Stock Exchange
Industrial and Commercial Bank of China	300 million 260 million 500 million 500 million	USD HKD USD EUR	14/06/2018 14/06/2018 11/06/2018 11/06/2018	14/06/2023 14/06/2020 11/06/2021 11/06/2023	CICERO, International Institute of Green Finance	London Stock Exchange
Bank of China	1 billion	USD	31/05/2018	31/05/2023	Ernst & Young	Hong Kong Stock Exchange
Beijing Capital Group	500 million	USD	19/03/2018	19/03/2021	Sustainalytics	Hong Kong Stock Exchange
Tianjin Rail Transit Group	630 million 400 million	RMB EUR	19/03/2018 13/03/2018	19/03/2020 22/06/2022	Sustainalytics	Luxembourg Green Exchange
CGNIC Group Co., Ltd	500 million	EUR	05/12/2017	05/12/2024	Deloitte	Euronext-Paris
Bank of China	500 million 1 billion 700 million	USD RMB EUR	22/11/2017 22/11/2017 22/11/2017	22/11/2022 22/11/2020 22/11/2020	Ernst & Young	Euronext-Paris

(Continued)

Table 9.4 Green bond issued by major Chinese multinational banks (Continued)

Issuer	Amount	Currency	Issue date	Expiry	Verification institution	Market
China Development Bank	1 billion	EUR	16/11/2017	16/11/2021	Ernst & Young	China Europe International Exchange
	500 million	USD	16/11/2017	16/11/2022		Hong Kong Stock Exchange
Industrial and Commercial Bank of China	450 million	USD	12/10/2017	12/10/2020	CICERO	Luxembourg Stock Exchange (Luxembourg Green Exchange)
Bank of China	400 million	USD	12/10/2017	12/10/2022	International Institute of Green Finance	
China Three Gorges Corporation	1.1 billion	EUR	12/10/2017	12/10/2020	Ernst & Young	Dublin Exchange
	650 million	EUR	21/06/2017	21/06/2024		
Bank of China	500 million	USD	03/11/2016	03/11/2019	Ernst & Young	London Stock Exchange
Bank of China	750 million	USD	05/07/2016	12/07/2019	Ernst & Young	Luxembourg Stock Exchange
	500 million	USD	05/07/2016	12/07/2019		
	1 billion	USD	05/07/2016	12/07/2021		
	500 million	EUR	05/07/2016	12/07/2021		
	1.5 billion	RMB	05/07/2016	12/07/2018		
GEELY	400 million	USD	26/5/2016	26/5/2021	Deloitte	London Stock Exchange
Agricultural Bank of China	400 million	USD	13/10/2015	24/7/2018	Deloitte	London Stock Exchange
	500 million	USD	13/10/2015	24/7/2020		
	600 million	RMB	13/10/2015	24/7/2017		
Xinjiang Goldwind	300 million	USD	16/07/2015	24/07/2018	DNV GL	Hong Kong Stock Exchange

variety of areas and forms, including infrastructure, resource growth, production capacity cooperation, and financial cooperation (China Development Bank, 2018). The fund also pays careful attention to the countries' environmental security during project development, minimizing harmful impacts on the local ecosystem and biology, adopting the most advanced and stringent production technology standards in conjunction with local CO_2 emission standards, and taking appropriate protective steps (Losos et al., 2019). Moreover, a report titled "Opinions and Practices for China to Promote the Development of Green Finance Along the Belt and Road" was issued jointly by the Development Research Center of the State Council and the Export-Import Bank of China. According to the report, the Export-Import Bank of China as a state-owned policy bank supports Chinese foreign trade, cross-border investment, and the BRI; however, it has the power to veto any loan application if the project does not meet environmental protection requirements. The Export-Import Bank of China continues to monitor projects after loans are made to ensure that they adhere to the social and environmental protection principles outlined in the loan contracts. Any reckless actions in any of the host nations impede Chinese MNEs from continuing to receive reliable, sizable, and affordable loans from China's policy banks, which undoubtedly has an impact on their ensuing international investment.

In the context of increasing environmental pollution, green loans and green bond issuance can help reduce carbon intensity. It has been established that the integrity of the green financial system has a beneficial effect on cleaner production; consequently, green finance may play a significant role in accelerating the transition to sustainability. Green finance can contribute to the BRI's environmental sustainability by funding "green" initiatives in host countries. In summary, sustainable infrastructure construction has emerged as a critical priority for both the planet and the BRI. Infrastructure development requires determined and forceful decisions to build ports, highways, airports, bridges, and dams in a sustainable manner, due to the construction scale, widespread effects, and technological lock-in. China has prioritized sustainable development as a key component of the BRI policy vision, and early consideration of sustainability in infrastructure development is critical to its success. Therefore, demand for green finance from both domestic and international stakeholders, as well as green finance policies issued by the government, call for more comprehensive CSR disclosures by firms in the banking and finance industry. Overall, this study demonstrates that CSR is becoming an increasingly important concern in the international banking industry, especially in the context of green finance and investment along the BRI. Specifically, the CSR reporting content of banking and finance firms focuses on providing sources of capital for "green industries" and sustainable development projects.

Digital Silk Road: Information and communication technology (ICT) industry

The "Made in China 2025" strategy aims to promote Chinese technology, standards, equipment, and engineering know-how, which can also be adopted within the BRI in competition with advanced economies attempting to do the same thing; that is to say, to win business and secure future projects based on sound benefit/cost outcomes. The sheer scope of Chinese business abroad places it in a very strong position to establish its technical norms as "global defaults" in a number of industries.

ICT encompasses a wide range of communication networks as well as the technologies that support them. The ICT sector brings together manufacturing and service businesses whose products primarily perform or enable information processing and communication via electronic means, including transmission and display. Thriving Chinese technology giants are called on to support the BRI by building various infrastructure construction projects and promoting the living standards of local people (Shen, 2018). In a joint statement issued in 2015, China's National Development and Reform Commission, Ministry of Foreign Affairs, and Ministry of Commerce formally established goals for building the "Digital Silk Road" (DSR) (Fang & Nolan, 2019). The stated goals were to establish shared technology standards among BRI host countries, and to construct and improve China's internet infrastructure (Fang & Nolan, 2019). China's DSR is essentially a combination of government programs driving domestic demand for China's technology, while also pursuing the broader goal of connecting Chinese and international technological networks. The Pakistan East African Cable, which connects Pakistan to Kenya via Djibouti, was built by Huawei Marine and funded by Hong Kong-based Tropic Science in 2017 and was a significant development of the DSR under the BRI (Ambalov & Heim, 2020). The DSR also helps Chinese exporters, including several well-known Chinese technology firms such as Huawei. DSR funding will be used to improve recipients' telecommunications networks, artificial intelligence capabilities, cloud computing, e-commerce and mobile payment systems, security technologies, smart cities, and other high-tech fields (Ambalov & Heim, 2020).

Aspects of the DSR offer additional opportunities for promoting Chinese standards and services. This is an effort to utilize "big data" to address and resolve some of the planet's sustainable development concerns. If effective, smart buildings, smart electrical grids, and smart transport logistics would assist BRI-participating economies in reducing their greenhouse gas emissions and water demands. For example, cooperation over shared standards for telecommunications, infrastructure for the "internet of things", and e-commerce offers Chinese multinational corporations tremendous prospects. Examples include the rollout of optical fiber built in China and Russia, the Beidou satellite program, which is an alternative to Global Positioning System (GPS) (currently being tested in Pakistan), and the e-commerce push in the BRI-participating economies by Alibaba and JD.com, which may allow less-developed economies to avoid the need for additional supermarket chains and shopping malls. China Telecom Corporation, China Mobile, and China Unicom are investing and collaborating with equipment suppliers such as Huawei and ZTE in the 5G space, where a race is on to establish network-appropriate standards (Tang et al., 2022). 5G will be an essential enabler for the internet of things, autonomous car operations, drones, smart cities, and other big developments. Those having the necessary intellectual property rights and network market share choose the standards for each generation. In contrast to earlier generations of mobile telephony, China is competing with the United States, South Korea, and Europe for the 5G leadership position. Millimeter wave spectrum (which is over 24 gigahertz) and Massive-Multiple-In-Multiple-Out (MMIMO), which enables hundreds of antennas and receivers to operate from a single base station as opposed to the present few, are two major components of 5G. China is well positioned for 5G trials, and Huawei is currently a leading manufacturer of mobile phone equipment.

Africa, the Middle East, and parts of Eastern Europe, Latin America, and Southeast Asia urgently need low-cost, high-quality infrastructure to extend their wireless phone networks and broadband internet coverage (Ambalov & Heim, 2020). The global infrastructure funding deficit is expected to reach nearly USD 15 trillion by 2040 (Bora, 2020). By providing or assisting in financing this essential infrastructure, DSR-related investments may help fill the gap and spark growth. Chinese MNEs are providing additional benefits to developing countries by establishing training centers and research and development programs to increase collaboration between scientists and engineers in these countries, as well as transferring technological expertise in areas such as smart cities, artificial intelligence and robotics, and renewable energy (Fang & Nolan, 2019).For example, Chinese MNEs have grown beyond basic hardware to incorporate e-governance, smart education, and digital health programs. The African Union unveiled its Smart Health Monitoring Room in 2017 using ZTE technology (ZTE, 2017).

Leading companies in the ICT industry, such as China Unicom, have expanded their scope and gone beyond infrastructure to better serve BRI-related countries and regions. According to China Unicom's CSR report, it has a total of 36 branches overseas, 16 of which have participated in countries and regions along the Belt and Road. These subsidiaries allow China Unicom to meet the needs of local markets by providing high-quality connectivity infrastructure and value-added services to businesses. In addition, the company has developed proprietary Point of Presence (PoP) covering ten major BRI countries. The submarine cable system connects 19 Belt and Road countries, while cross-border land cables link ten countries and regions (China Unicom, 2019). China Unicom also works with 277 Belt and Road operators in 64 countries to substantially reduce cross-border communications tariffs (China Unicom, 2019). In 2019, voice roaming tariffs dropped by 44% on average, while data roaming tariffs fell by 46%, helping to increase the total number of BRI roaming users by 40% and data traffic by 2.33 times. China Unicom's CSR report also mentions that it reduced its international roaming rates by eight times and lowered international settlement costs in 2019, making overseas connectivity services more accessible. Its website states that:

> China Unicom will continue to invest in global PoPs and build high-end submarine and terrestrial cable interconnection products in Europe and Asia; develop cloud services for the network to adapt to future 5G business development.

The company will enrich cloud network synergy products and launch 'cloud + network + industry application' comprehensive solutions that are tailored for specific scenarios and are flexible and cost-efficient.

Through cooperation with major international carriers and strategic shareholders, we will strengthen the sharing of network resources and innovate collaborations; and will continue to expand IDC and ICT partnerships, building a Belt and Road cooperative ecosystem

(China Unicom, 2019, p. 27).

Analysis of the CSR reports reveals that Chinese MNEs along the BRI also export Chinese-owned technological standards, in addition to enabling computing infrastructure, which has become an increasingly important element of the "going out" program as the leadership seeks to upgrade China's industrial structure. As a result of the internet's economies of scale, proprietary network standards not only yield substantial royalties but also help similar equipment manufacturers gain significant market share both domestically and internationally. Given the vast geographical area that the BRI aims to cover, this has become particularly important for its growth. For example, China Mobile has been assigned as the primary carrier of China's indigenous third-generation networking standard – TD-SCDMA – and as one of the major carriers of the China-developed 4G/5G TDLTE standard. It has actively promoted the globalization of TD-LTE, especially in BRI regions. In 2017, the company announced that 99 TD-LTE networks were being deployed in 53 countries and regions, with 39 TD-LTE networks from 21 countries and regions being deployed along the BRI routes (China Mobile, 2017).

The arrangement of Alibaba's overseas data centers also offers an interesting case for examining the enabling role of digital infrastructure in China's global expansion along the BRI. According to Alibaba's CSR report, Alibaba Cloud announced in April 2017 that its services had risen by 400% in overseas markets over the previous fiscal year, emphasizing major BRI countries (Alibaba, 2018). According to the company's vice president, its overseas expansion has paved the way and built a bridge for other Chinese companies' overseas operations, especially software companies (Yi, 2017). Alibaba Cloud asserts that helping members of its home team saves considerable logistical and operating costs by allowing these businesses to share digital resources and software as on-demand online applications. In addition, in 2018, Alibaba opened three new data centers in India, Indonesia, and Malaysia, all of which are key countries along the Belt and Road (Riccio, 2017).

In addition to these initiatives, this study further reveals that Chinese MNEs intend to disseminate their technical standards further, especially through BRI host countries. The Standardization Administration of China (SAC) has published the "Standards China Unicom Joint Construction One Belt One Road Action Plan (2018–2020)" and promotes uniform standards across a variety of technologies, including 5G, artificial intelligence, and satellite navigation systems. Chinese domestic e-payment platform, Alipay, has also started to develop direct operations through local players across BRI countries. The technology industry has had huge direct and indirect economic impacts along the BRI.

In summary, the Chinese ICT industry has aggressively marketed itself as a "boat" to assist other Chinese companies in going out and riding the wave of the BRI, in a modernized version of earlier "going out" policies. Figure 9.1 summarizes the external factors influencing the CSR reporting contents of Chinese MNEs in the ICT industry under the BRI.

Challenges ahead

The BRI is attempting to revitalize these ancient trade channels by resurrecting the cooperative spirit of the Silk Road. The BRI provides member nations with a vision of shared growth and prosperity based on five key areas: (i) policy coordination, (ii) greater connectivity, (iii) unhindered commerce, (iv) financial integration, and (v) cross-cultural exchange. The BRI has led to opportunities and challenges in many industries. For example, the ambitious BRI is composed of numerous physical cross-border connections. Thus, OFDI by Chinese MNEs in the infrastructure sector account for the majority of BRI projects related to the construction of new roads and railways. Furthermore, in the context of DSR, OFDI in ICT across the region has contributed to a surge in demand for smartphones and internet-based services in BRI host countries.

The BRI is a multi-decade program intended to enhance economic connection and collaboration among two-thirds of the world's population. As a result, the endeavor is extraordinarily complicated, and the difficulty of facilitating collaboration across more than 100 nations, ranging from emerging to developed markets, is unprecedented. While Chinese companies have experienced some early success, as the program develops in breadth, they will undoubtedly encounter an increasing number of challenges. The BRI's environmental challenges have also attracted academic interest, such as the relationship between energy consumption and carbon emissions and the effect of invasive alien species on biodiversity. These environmental issues, which have drawn widespread condemnation from both the West and BRI countries, will stigmatize the BRI and further impede its development if they are not resolved. Indeed, the possibility of physical damage to the environment has the potential to incur repair costs, and re-habitation may take place at every stage of the construction and operation of infrastructure. Stakeholder demands for project owners and contractors to act responsibly during the development of infrastructure projects and to provide evidence that all parties are capable of properly managing the primary environmental risks inherent in them have increased as a result. Failure to do so could expose the project to criticism from regulators and shareholders alike, with the relationship between the project's overall environmental performance and the project firm's reputation being a crucial factor. Thus, various social and environmental risks need to be managed throughout the entire asset ownership lifecycle. Moreover, multi-stakeholder, cross-sectoral and landscape-wide or river basin perspectives must be included as part of integrated environmental planning methodologies,

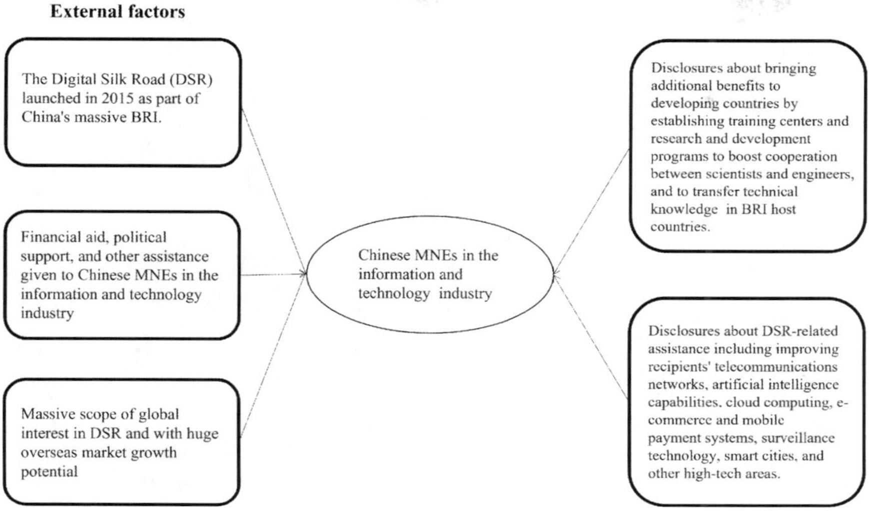

Industry-specific CSR Reporting Contents in BRI Host Countries   181

Figure 9.1 External factors influencing the CSR reporting contents of Chinese MNEs in the ICT industry.

such as strategic environmental assessments. This chapter also reveals the efforts of the banking industry regarding their vital roles in the low-carbon transition. The analysis demonstrates that these firms are taking action to finance the green transition. However, the detailed identification methods and selection criteria used by BRI projects to choose green bonds are generally not disclosed. Thus, it is recommended that Chinese banks take the lead in disclosing policies and incentives to ensure that the value of nature is incorporated into decision-making in BRI host countries.

Finally, it is suggested that the DSR is to act as a means to dispel China's technological hegemony. Over the past five years, Chinese companies, such as Huawei, have played an important role in developing global 5G technology standards and building mobile infrastructure through bodies such as the International Telecommunication Union. Other Chinese MNEs are eager to follow suit and contribute more to the global standard-setting process, which will help advance the BRI's vision of a more advanced technology stack technology stack. In this context, CSR reporting and activities will inevitably serve as important tools to legitimize Chinese MNEs in these host countries.

In summary, the three industries chosen for this study reveal typical examples of industry-specific CSR reporting content along the BRI. This chapter has also shown how CSR reporting contents vary with the nature of the industry and its position within the BRI strategy in terms of green finance to provide capital for BRI projects, increased mobility to promote BRI connectivity, and advanced technology to support BRI infrastructure. As ecological, societal, and political demands to reduce pollution have steadily increased during China's quest for

182 Industry-specific CSR Reporting Contents in BRI Host Countries

sustainable development, Chinese MNEs are expected to shoulder heavier CSR activities in BRI host countries.

Notes

1. CBRC, PBOC, & MEP. (2007). Opinions on Enforcing Policies and Regulations on Environmental Protection to Prevent Credit Risk. Retrieved from https://www.mee.gov.cn/gkml/zj/wj/200910/t20091022_172469.htm [only available in Chinese].
2. MEP & CIRC. (2007). Guiding Opinions on Environmental Pollution Liability Insurance. Retrieved from http://www.gov.cn/gongbao/content/2013/content_2396623.htm [only available in Chinese].
3. CSRC & MEP. (2008). Guidance Opinions on Strengthening the Oversight of Public Companies. Retrieved from http://www.gov.cn/gzdt/2008-02/25/content_899822.htm [only available in Chinese].
4. CBRC. (2012). Green Credit Guidelines. Retrieved from http://www.gov.cn/gongbao/content/2012/content_2163593.htm [only available in Chinese].
5. CBRC. (2014). Green Credit Monitoring & Evaluation mechanism and Key Performance Indicators Checklist. Retrieved from https://www.baidu.com/link?url=PzQSb7y-tGOjFdJeGOHH9bKDazO6ANyxRuVzfHYuSnUUxSh-TASBOBdk6NX-BLt4khB9mgMdCaBuLWIjActpEB_&wd=&eqid=9d634676005927180000000006609fd533 [only available in Chinese].
6. PBOC. (2015). Green Financial Bond Directive and Green Bond-Endorsed Project. Retrieved from http://bond.xinhua08.com/a/20160214/1608014.shtml [only available in Chinese].
7. PBOC. (2016). Guidelines for Establishing the Green Financial System. Retrieved from https://www.mee.gov.cn/gkml/hbb/gwy/201611/t20161124_368163.htm [only available in Chinese].
8. NDRC & SSE. (2016). Green Bond Guidelines. Retrieved from http://www.sse.com.cn/services/greensecurities/home/ [only available in Chinese].
9. CSRC. (2017). Guidelines for Green Bond Issuance by Listed Companies. Retrieved from http://www.csrc.gov.cn/pub/newsite/gszqjgb/zcfggszq/bmgzjgfxwj/. [only available in Chinese].
10. CSRC. (2017). Guidance on Supporting the Development of Green Bonds. Retrieved from http://www.csrc.gov.cn/pub/newsite/flb/flfg/bmgf/fx/gszj/201805/t20180515_338154.html
11. Hong Kong Quality Assurance Agency. (2018). Green Finance Certification Scheme. Retrieved from http://www.hkqaa.org/en_certservice.php?catid=26
12. Green Belt and Road Initiative Center. (2019). Retrieved from https://green-bri.org/zh-hans/%E4%B8%80%E5%B8%A6%E4%B8%80%E8%B7%AF-%E7%BB%BF%E8%89%B2%E6%8A%95%E8%B5%84%E5%8E%9F%E5%88%99%EF%BC%88gip%EF%BC%89/ The GIPs brought up in the second BRI forum could be seen as an attempt by China to set international standards and a code of best practice on green finance (Fang & Nolan, 2019).
13. NDRC. (2022). Opinions on Promoting the Green Development of Belt and Road. Retrieved from https://www.ndrc.gov.cn/xxgk/zcfb/tz/202203/t20220328_1320629.html?code=&state=123
14. Since the BRI's inception, Chinese companies have actively engaged in climate finance programs in BRI countries, helping them to adapt to and mitigate the effects of climate change. As a consequence of high climate risks, low social and economic growth levels, and extensive infrastructure building in most BRI countries, China's investment in climate finance focuses primarily on renewable energy and clean transport (rather than water and waste projects). The annual infrastructure investment deficit in the BRI area is estimated at over USD600 billion (Cheung & Hong, 2020; Fang & Nolan, 2019).

References

Alibaba Group. (2018). *Annual corporate social responsibility report*. https://esg.alibabagroup.com/ui/pdfs/Alibaba-ESG-Report-2018.pdf

Ambalov, V., & Heim, I. (2020). Investments in the Digital Silk Road. In I. Heim (Ed.), *Kazakhstan's diversification from the natural resources sector* (pp. 111–149). Palgrave Macmillan.

Atkins, J., & Maroun, W. (2018). Integrated extinction accounting and accountability: Building an ark. *Accounting, Auditing & Accountability Journal, 31*(3), 750–786.

Bank of China. (2019). *Annual corporate social responsibility report*. https://www.boc.cn/investor/ir5/202003/t20200327_17685425.html

Bora, L. Y. (2020). Challenge and perspective for Digital Silk Road. *Cogent Business & Management, 7*(1), 1804180.

Brombal, D. (2018). Planning for a sustainable Belt and Road Initiative (BRI): An appraisal of the Asian Infrastructure Investment Bank (AIIB) environmental and social safeguards. In *Normative readings of the belt and road initiative* (pp. 129–145). Springer, Cham.

Chen, J., & Liu, W. (2019). The Belt and Road strategy in international business and administration: Corporate social responsibility. In *The Belt and Road strategy in international business and administration* (pp. 28–51). IGI Global.

Cheung, F. M., & Hong, Y. Y. (Eds.). (2020). *Green finance, sustainable development and the Belt and Road Initiative*. Routledge.

China Communications Construction Company. (2015). *Annual corporate social responsibility report*. https://www.ccccltd.cn/shzr/shzr/shzrbg/201608/P020160830653823985661.pdf

China Communications Construction Company. (2017). *Annual corporate social responsibility report*. https://www.ccccltd.cn/shzr/shzr/shzrbg/201805/P020180528527052529046.pdf

China Communications Construction Company. (2020). *Annual corporate social responsibility report*. https://www.ccccltd.cn/shzr/shzr/shzrbg/202111/W020211102514820857507.png

China Development Bank. (2017). *Annual corporate social responsibility report*. https://www.climatebonds.net/files/files/China%20Development%20Bank%20Annual%20Report%20.pdf

China Development Bank. (2018). *Annual corporate social responsibility report*. http://www.cdb.com.cn/shzr/kcxfzbg/shzr_2018/

China Mobile. (2017). *Briefing on China Mobile's participation in jointly building "the Belt and Road"*. http://www.china.com.cn/zhibo/zhuanti/ch-xin-wen/2017-05/08/content_40767089.htm

China National Building Materials Corporate. (2020). *Annual corporate social responsibility report*. https://www.cnbm.com.cn/upload/files/2021/11/f2019062713464350.pdf

China Railway Construction Corporation. (2019). *Annual corporate social responsibility report*. https://www.crcc.cn/module/download/downfile.jsp?classid=0&filename=2f7f81d65cdd4d1594d867509c6c616c.pdf

China Railway Construction Corporation. (2020). *Annual corporate social responsibility report*. http://static.sse.com.cn/disclosure/listedinfo/announcement/c/new/2021-03-31/601186_20210331_10.pdf

China Unicom. (2019). *Annual CSR report*. China Unicom. http://www.chinaunicom-a.com/wcm/1/attachments/2020/3/23/1659/1584970230137.pdf

Cuckston, T. (2018). Making accounting for biodiversity research a force for conservation. *Social and Environmental Accountability Journal, 38*(3), 218–226.

Dong, L., Yang, X., & Li, H. (2018). The Belt and Road Initiative and the 2030 agenda for sustainable development: Seeking linkages for global environmental governance. *Chinese Journal of Population Resources and Environment, 16*(3), 203–210.

Fang, C., & Nolan, P. (Eds.). (2019). *Routledge handbook of the Belt and Road.* Routledge.

Harlan, T. (2020). Green development or greenwashing? A political ecology perspective on China's green Belt and Road. *Eurasian Geography and Economics, 62*(2), 1–25.

Industrial and Commercial Bank. (2019). *Annual CSR report.* ICBC. http://v.icbc.com.cn/userfiles/Resources/ICBCLTD/download/2020/2019csrcn1.pdf

Jian, J., Fan, X., & Zhao, S. (2021). The green incentives and green bonds financing under the Belt and Road Initiative. *Emerging Markets Finance and Trade*, 1–11. https://doi.org/10.1080/1540496x.2021.1887726.

Kang, L., Peng, F., Zhu, Y., & Pan, A. (2018). Harmony in diversity: Can the one belt one road initiative promote China's outward foreign direct investment. *Sustainability, 10*(9), 3264.

Kenya China Economic and Trade Association. (2019). *Chinese enterprises in Kenya social responsibility report, 2018–2019.* http://ke.mofcom.gov.cn/19cn.pdf

Laurila-Pant, M., Lehikoinen, A., Uusitalo, L., & Venesjärvi, R. (2015). How to value biodiversity in environmental management? *Ecological Indicators, 55*, 1–11.

Lechner, A. M., Chan, F. K. S., & Campos-Arceiz, A. (2018). Biodiversity conservation should be a core value of China's Belt and Road Initiative. *Nature Ecology & Evolution, 2*(3), 408–409.

Lin, Y., Qin, Y., & Xie, Z. (2021). Does foreign technology transfer spur domestic innovation? Evidence from the high-speed rail sector in China. *Journal of Comparative Economics, 49*(1), 212–229.

Losos, E. C., Pfaff, A., Olander, L. P., Mason, S., & Morgan, S. (2019). *Reducing Environmental Risks from Belt and Road Initiative Investments in Transportation Infrastructure.* The World Bank Policy Research Working Paper 8718.

Meena, R. (2013). Green banking: As initiative for sustainable development. *Global Journal of Management and Business Studies, 3*(10), 1181–1186.

Narain, D., Maron, M., Teo, H. C., Hussey, K., & Lechner, A. M. (2020). Best-practice biodiversity safeguards for Belt and Road Initiative's financiers. *Nature Sustainability, 3*(8), 650–657.

Ng, L. S., Campos-Arceiz, A., Sloan, S., Hughes, A. C., Tiang, D. C. F., Li, B. V., & Lechner, A. M. (2020). The scale of biodiversity impacts of the Belt and Road Initiative in Southeast Asia. *Biological Conservation, 248*, 108691.

Riccio, K. (2017). *Alibaba Cloud to launch data centers in India, Indonesia.* Data Center Knowledge. http://www.datacenterknowledge.com/archives/2017/06/14/alibabacloud-to-launch-data-centers-in-india-indonesia/

Robson, C. (2002). *Real world research: A resource for social scientists and practitioner-researchers.* Wiley-Blackwell.

Sachs, J., Woo, W. T., Yoshino, N., & Taghizadeh-Hesary, F. (2019). Importance of green finance for achieving sustainable development goals and energy security. In J. Sachs, W. T. Woo, N. Yoshino, Taghizadeh, & F. Hesary (Eds.), *Handbook of green finance: Energy security and sustainable development* (pp. 10–12). Springer.

Shen, H. (2018). Building a digital Silk Road? Situating the internet in China's Belt and Road Initiative. *International Journal of Communication, 12*, 19.

Tang, Z. (2018). CSR as a tool to mitigate risk for the B&R Initiative: The case of Thailand. In *Securing the belt and road initiative* (pp. 147–161). Palgrave.

Tang, Z., Shah, S. K., Ahmad, M., & Mustafa, S. (2022). Modeling consumer's switching intentions regarding 5G technology in China. *International Journal of Innovation and Technology Management, 19*(04), 2250011.

Wang, Y., & Zhi, Q. (2016). The role of green finance in environmental protection: Two aspects of market mechanism and policies. *Energy Procedia, 104*, 311–316.

WWF. (2017). *The Belt and Road Initiative: WWF recommendations and spatial analysis.* http://awsassets.panda.org/downloads/the_belt_and_road_initiative___wwf_recommendations_and_spatial_analysis___may_2017.pdf

Xi, J. (2017a). Work Together to Build the Silk Road Economic Belt and the 21st Century Maritime Silk Road, Opening speech, the Belt and Road Forum for International Cooperation, May.

Xi, J. (2017b). Secure a Decisive Victory in Building a Moderately Prosperous Society in all Respects and Strive for the Great Success of Socialism with Chinese Characteristics for a New Era, Delivered at the 19th National Congress of the Communist Party of China, 18 October.

Yi, X. (2017). Alibaba Cloud achieved scaled growth along the Belt and Road. *People's Daily.* http://ydyl.people.com.cn/n1/2017/0421/c411837-29228106.html

Zhang, R., & Noronha, C. (2022). Assessing the Nexus between cross-border infrastructure projects and extinction accounting—from the Belt and Road Initiative perspective. Social and Environmental Accountability Journal, *43*(1), 30–55.

Zhu, H., Hui, K. N. C., & Gong, Y. (2022). Uncovering the nonmarket side of internationalization: The Belt and Road Initiative and Chinese firms' CSR reporting quality. *Asia Pacific Journal of Management*, 1–29. https://doi.org/10.1007/s10490-022-09835-8

ZTE Corporation. (2017). *ZTE and Pakistan sign digital terrestrial television agreement.* ZTE. http://www.zte.com.cn/global/about/press-center/news/2017Ma-5/0515ma

10 CSR of Chinese MNEs in Developing Countries under the BRI Context

Through the Lens of Africa

Footprints of Chinese MNEs in Africa

The strategic relationship between China and African countries goes back decades. In the 1990s, the Chinese government started using provinces as a division of responsibility for investment in African countries (Tull, 2006). For many years, China has mobilized national efforts to provide a helping hand to African countries in key infrastructure projects, offering assistance in areas such as hydropower, airports, ports, railways, and other infrastructure projects. Even though the majority of the projects that have been launched are in the fields of transportation and energy, they are diverse and include international rail, intercity rail, expressways, seaports, hydropower, carbon-based power, transmission lines, water supply and sanitation (Wang & Elliot, 2014).

Africa urgently needs to improve its infrastructure (Leke et al., 2018). China is sponsoring investments and infrastructure projects that can yield long-term economic benefits essential to Africa's sustainable growth. It is becoming more challenging to maintain some of the infrastructure currently in place in Africa because it was constructed during the colonial era and is now outdated, having seen little-to-no upkeep or upgrading. The lack of political will to launch modern projects to meet urbanization-related needs is a major problem in Africa's infrastructure development. Problems of corruption have also contributed to projects having inflated costs or, in some circumstances, being abandoned. Due to the challenges associated with transporting products and services, Africa has not seen high levels of either intra-African trade or trade with the rest of the globe (Ubi-Abai & Ekere, 2018). In 2013, President Xi Jinping proposed the concept of the "China-Africa Community with a Shared Future" during his first trip to Africa. In fact, since 2000, cooperation between China and Africa has entered a stage of comprehensive deepening. The Forum on China-Africa Cooperation (FOCAC) was established in 2000, further solidifying links between China and Africa. To strengthen diplomatic, security, commerce, and investment ties between China and various African nations, the FOCAC provides a venue for consultation and cooperation procedures, which has gradually developed China-Africa cooperation from ad hoc actions to standardized, institutionalized, and sustainable China-Africa cooperation (Naidu, 2007; Taylor, 2010).

DOI: 10.4324/9781003302445-10

Urbanization in Africa is expected to grow at the fastest rate in the world (Leke et al., 2018). Over the last 10 years, China has built plenty of large reservoir power plants across Africa, including Egypt, Sudan, Ethiopia, Angola, Guinea, Uganda, Niger, Zambia, the Congo, and Zimbabwe. One of these is the Merowe Dam, the "Three Gorges of Sudan", which is 9.8 kilometers long and has a total installed capacity of 1.25 million kilowatts. It is the second largest reservoir along the Nile after Egypt's Yasvin. Furthermore, there have been significant Chinese efforts to modernize, expand, and construct new airports in Africa. For example, Chinese MNEs were named in relation to the airport upgrade projects in Angola, Ethiopia, Kenya, Nigeria, Rwanda, Senegal, and Zambia. To consolidate its geopolitical advantage in Africa, China is also building ports in Africa, including the port of Massawa in Eritrea, which has an outlet on the Red Sea; the expansion of Tamatave, the largest deep-water port in Madagascar in southeast Africa; the port of Abichamps in Guinea and the Ivory Coast on the Atlantic coast; the port of Tema, the first major port in Ghana, which is an important port in West Africa; and the major ports in Togo, Niger, Cameroon, and the Congo. African railways are also an important investment objective for China. China is funding, developing, and building railways that are revolutionizing Africa's transportation infrastructure, connecting Nairobi to Mombasa and Addis Ababa to Djibouti. These massive construction projects, which traverse safari lodges and the East African desert, are more than just remarkable architectural achievements (Foster, 2009; Gill & Reilly, 2007; Vines, 2007).

The BRI intends to link Asia, Europe, and Africa through infrastructure, trade, investment, and other forms of collaboration in the areas of education, tourism, and culture. At the Belt and Road Forum for International Cooperation (BRFIC) in May 2017, former Ethiopian Prime Minister Hailemariam Desalegn described the initiative as "the broadest and non-conflicting economic cooperation of the 21st century" (Alpha, 2017). Remarkably, the relevance and effects of this effort on Africa have received little scholarly attention or discussion to date. The BRI is a long-term program designed to improve global infrastructure connectivity and cooperation. With related efforts and projects spanning across more than 147 countries—from developed to developing to underdeveloped—it is a historic task and a challenging undertaking (Xinhua, 2022).

While a portion of China's BRI effort is focused on these particular corridors, the undertaking is actually a worldwide effort and not focused on specific geographical locales. All of Africa is heavily involved, as is Latin America. China's main goal is to finance the construction of infrastructure in the areas of transportation, power, water supply, and other industries in developing nations (Belt & Road Portal, 2017a, 2017b). President Xi made the following observations in his opening remarks at the Belt and Road Forum in Beijing in May 2017:

> Infrastructure connectivity is the foundation of development through cooperation. We should promote land, maritime, air and cyberspace connectivity, concentrate our efforts on key passageways, cities and projects and connect networks of highways, railways and sea ports .... We need to seize

opportunities presented by the new changes in the energy mix and the revolution in energy technologies to develop global energy interconnections and achieve green and low-carbon development. We should improve the trans-regional logistics network and promote connectivity among policies, rules and standards to provide institutional safeguards for enhancing connectivity.[1]

China has long valued its relations with Africa. With the BRI, China's involvement with Africa took on a new shape, with the primary goal being advancing commerce through investments in infrastructure development. Thus, the BRI is providing new inspirations for long-standing and well-established Sino-African relations. Due to colonialism and the history between Africa and the West, China's rivals for global influence have enjoyed substantial advantages in Africa. Soft power, as defined by Nye (1990), is the ability of one government to influence the desires of other nations, meaning that when utilizing this form of power, the government employs allurement rather than the conventional use of armed power and coercion to gain the support of other nations. Over the years, China has worked to strengthen its leverage over its rivals. Through the slogan of "peaceful development" (*hé píng fā zhǎn*), China has endeavored to establish itself as a peace-loving, development-focused global citizen with noble intentions in its ties with other states (Dossi, 2012). Chinese diplomats have frequently invoked this rhetoric, which has won China many allies. With its dedication to peace and economic success along the Belt and Road and among all participating governments, the initiative as a grand strategy falls fully under the sphere of peaceful development, as it is advocated.

The BRI's infrastructure development aims to match the African Union's own Agenda 2063, which is primarily focused on connecting the continent (Risberg, 2019). Both programs emphasize the need for comprehensive and people-centered development. Furthermore, both revolve around on sustainable industrialization and industrial diversification, as well as the generation of high-value-added and dignified jobs for all. According to a 2014 African Development Bank report, Africa is suffering from a significant infrastructure gap that has prevented trade, industrialization, and economic growth (George et al., 2016). The BRI presents an opportunity that Africa might strategically seize.

Africa for the BRI or the BRI for Africa: A mixed blessing?

Optimists have argued that critics of Chinese efforts in Africa are simply repeating the tales of Yellow Peril (Githaiga & Bing, 2019; Hodzi, 2018). According to a report by Mutebi, more than 10,000 Chinese companies are operating in Africa, and this has provided numerous socio-economic advantages, including jobs for locals. China's Foreign Minister Wang Yi stated that "China and Africa would undoubtedly become closer cooperative partners through cooperation fostered by the Belt and Road Initiative" during his January 2018 tour to six African nations. In contrast to the Western powers' official development assistance (ODA) paradigm, China's approach to Africa has been characterized as being more based on development cooperation (Githaiga & Bing, 2019). In addition, the development and implementation of infrastructure projects and industrial transfer in Africa have been China's primary objectives for more than a decade, well before the BRI was created. An example is the Tazara Railway, which links Tanzania to landlocked Zambia. The stated goal of this collaboration was the mutual growth of China and Africa. It is anticipated that Africa will gain a great deal from the BRI in terms of infrastructure and job development, the economic well-being of its people, and the encouragement of industrialization. In addition to boosting China's exports, the development of African infrastructure will also utilize the surplus labor force employed by China's construction enterprises (Risberg, 2019). China intends to move labor-intensive businesses, particularly manufacturing, to Africa to reduce its overcapacity and support economic reform.

However, concerns regarding China's relationship with Africa have been voiced, as this relationship has been characterized as "colonial" and one where China frequently reaps most of the benefits at the expense of less-developed host countries (Sverdrup-Thygeson, 2017). Researchers have argued that infrastructure, such as large dams, is "one of the ways in which the state actualizes sovereignty over its territory" or efforts to exert control over neighboring states (Menga & Swyngedouw, 2018; Sneddon, 2015). The Chinese investment model, as critics have noted, appears to also incorporate part exchange agreements involving oil and minerals in addition to loans and grants (Sneddon, 2015). These agreements have more of a bartering or resources-for-infrastructure feel to them. Critics of Chinese loans have also argued that because African nations have little to no diversification, the loans could cause liquidity and debt crises, leaving Africa largely dependent on China. Githaiga and Bing (2019) reported that five of China's top eight creditors in Africa have already applied for Resource for Infrastructure (R4I) loans using data from the China-Africa Research Initiative. Sudan, Nigeria, Angola, the Congo, and Ghana are among them. Angola and China agreed to the first R4I loan in 2004 in exchange for USD 2 billion in infrastructure investments, using Angola's vast petroleum reserves as security. Later, to open up additional credit lines, Angola was unable to make the payments and was forced to ask for an extension and take out new loans in 2007 and 2009 (Alves, 2013). This is thought to have had a negative impact on Angola's economic independence, as this loan structure has caused Angola to become reliant on China (Aguilar & Goldstein, 2009). However, other analysts see the BRI as a global initiative that represents Beijing's grand economic and geopolitical ambitions to challenge the status quo in the African region and around the world. Furthermore, they see the BRI as a Sinocentric project that is building on and going beyond China's "going out" strategy (Yu, 2017), which was itself a "spatial fix" to deal with China's overcapacity issue. Moreover, civil society is present and thriving in many African nations. This has resulted in civil society groups opposing numerous infrastructure projects that are believed to have negative consequences for the community. In Kenya, for example, the government had to compensate villages impacted by the Standard

Gauge Railway Line with millions of dollars to ensure that the project would proceed. Furthermore, the project had to be put on hold by the courts in some cases until compensation was fully paid. In another instance, environmentalists sued the government over the railway line that would run through Nairobi National Park, claiming that it would negatively impact the natural habitats of wildlife living there. Although the project was eventually allowed to move forward, civil societies in Kenya and many other African nations are hurdles that must be overcome, particularly by Chinese businesses that may be encountering such issues for the first time.

CSR threats of the BRI in Africa

CSR is relevant to the BRI because the mis-management of Chinese MNEs' responsibility toward the environment and society of the host countries may directly or indirectly evoke threats from local political, economic, social, and technological systems through these MNEs' interactions with stakeholders and local governments. Despite the potential benefits that various BRI corporations can provide to African host countries, BRI-related projects are laden with significant barriers and threats. Concerns are rising over the impact of poorly conceived or implemented projects on host nations, particularly on their local environment, labor force, fiscal health, and political stability. These concerns have been heightened in relation to BRI projects and investments in poor governance zones, where governments are reluctant or unable to accept their obligations. Table 10.1 summarizes the CSR threats that have resulted from the BRI and real cases in African host countries.

How does CSR assist companies in gaining legitimacy in Africa?

MNEs have two main options for gaining legitimacy: either they passively submit to isomorphic institutional pressures (DiMaggio & Powell, 1983) or they actively manage these institutional pressures by implementing specific legitimacy-seeking strategies (Kostova & Zaheer, 1999; (Pfeffer, 1987); Slangen, 2013; Suchman, 1995). In the context of the BRI, institutional pressures from host countries and legitimacy concerns from the Chinese government have influenced CSR practices among Chinese MNEs. Thus, these MNEs are proactively seeking legitimacy by engaging in CSR activities. Additionally, some examples from the real world show how taking part in the BRI might be a non-market tactic for China's political legitimacy. China Civil Engineering Construction Corporation, for instance, tweeted that "participation in the 'Belt and Road' construction is our obligation and also a development opportunity". Additionally, Wei Jianjun, the board chair of Great Wall Motor Company Limited, asserted in a BRI forum that it was the duty of Chinese automakers to make investments in other nations to advance the BRI (Great Wall Motor [GWM], 2019). Through content analysis, several themed CSR reports,

Table 10.1 The BRI threats and related CSR crisis

BRI threats	Related CSR crisis	Relevant case
Environment	Numerous infrastructure projects have generated criticisms due to their environmental impact. For example, port, railway, and industrial park projects can affect local communities and have negative environmental consequences. The host-country government's focus on growing economic development at times trumps environmental and social concerns.	Local demonstrations erupted in the area surrounding Voi, Kenya, in the fall of 2016 over a 6-kilometer elevated part of the planned Mombasa–Nairobi Standard Gauge Railway Line that was slated to pass through Nairobi National Park; as a result, the Kenyan government halted construction (Lokanathan, 2020). The construction of infrastructure leads not only to a direct reduction in connectivity between landscapes and ecosystems but also to secondary impacts, such as the spread of invasive alien animal and plant species, wind turbines, fires, animal deaths, pollution, and microclimates (Atkins et al., 2017).
Unemployment	Most jobs created by the BRI projects require no skill and are low-paying. Improved technology has a negative impact on the employment of mechanics. The hiring/inflowing of an international workforce crowds out the local skilled workforce.	In Zambia, the wealth discrepancy between the mining companies operating there and the poor local population has resulted in riots in recent years. Furthermore, the influx of international skilled workers has caused a spike in unemployment in the country's mining heartland in the process (Leslie, 2016).
Social conflicts	Social conflicts have resulted from large-scale infrastructure and mining projects' impacts on land, health, and water sources. Aboriginal conflicts have occurred due to the loss of livelihoods and forced relocation.	The bauxite boom in Guinea generated thousands of jobs, much-needed tax revenue for the government, and substantial profits for mining companies and their shareholders, but it also had significant negative effects on rural communities that are close to mining operations in terms of their ability to exercise their human rights. Mining firms have taken advantage of Guinean law's vague protection of rural land rights to expropriate ancestral farmlands without providing fair compensation or for monetary sums that are insufficient to restore the advantages communities earned from their use of the land. Communities now have less access to water for drinking, washing, and cooking due to damage to water supplies and increased demand brought on by population relocation to mining sites. Women, who are typically in charge of fetching water, are now required to go further or wait longer to get water from alternative sources. Families and medical professionals are concerned that the decreased air quality could endanger the locals' health and the environment, since the dust created by bauxite mining and transportation suffocates farmland and invades homes (HRW, 2018). In April and September 2017, riots broke out in Boké as a result of dissatisfaction over inadequate local services, specifically a lack of water and power, resentment at the rapid expansion of mining, and broader worries regarding the effects of mining on local populations (HRW, 2018).

(Continued)

Table 10.1 The BRI threats and related CSR crisis (*Continued*)

BRI threats	Related CSR crisis	Relevant case
Corruption	Almost half of the countries in the lowest half of Transparency International's Corruption Perception Index and more than half of those in the bottom quarter are African (Victor and Leyira, 2021 Victor & Leyira, 2021). Foreign anti-bribery laws pose a potential legal risk, not only at the local level in host countries. The likelihood of corruption among government officials is expected to increase as a result of the BRI.	African nations have cancelled or postponed OBORI projects over accelerating debt worries. Some governments are too corrupt, which have caused catastrophic misappropriation of funds meant for national development. The bidding processes for some BRI projects are opaque, and bribes are often paid to local officials (Githaiga et al., 2019).

specifically targeted at African host countries, are observed and documented in the following sections.

Environmental and biodiversity conservation

Africa's exceptionally rich biodiversity and ecosystems, as well as its wealth of indigenous and local knowledge, are strategic assets for the region's sustainable development (Pomeroy, 1993; Snapp et al., 2010). Africa is one of the last places on the earth to be home to numerous large mammals. The continent's biodiversity varies significantly by region, sub-region, and country, exhibiting differences in climate and physical condition and reflecting the long and variable history of human-environmental interactions. This natural richness, accumulated over millions of years, together with the continent's wealth of indigenous and local knowledge, is a strategic asset at the heart of the region's quest for sustainable development. Africa has the opportunity to fully enjoy the benefits of having such rich biodiversity and to explore how it can be used in a sustainable way to contribute to its economic and technological development. In some parts of Africa, the indigenous or local knowledge that existed has now been lost (Darwall et al., 2009). Africa has the advantage of having a smaller ecological and carbon footprint than other parts of the world, but it may still face challenges in balancing economic growth, an increasing population and population density with the need to protect, conserve, and enhance biodiversity and the ecosystem. Rapid population growth and urbanization, inappropriate economic policies and technologies, poaching and the illegal wildlife trade, as well as socio-political and cultural pressures, have accelerated the loss of biodiversity and nature's contributions.

The BRI projects, such as mining and infrastructure construction, undoubtedly have significant environmental impacts (Hughes et al., 2020). For example, numerous hotspots for terrestrial and marine biodiversity, wilderness regions and other significant conservation areas have been traversed along the six economic corridors of the BRI. The BRI has a tendency to overstate the economic benefits of infrastructure projects while understating their detrimental environmental effects (Ascensão et al., 2018; Liu et al., 2019; Zhang & Noronha, 2022). Infrastructure projects along the Belt and Road are characterized by lengthy investment and construction cycles, a relatively high impact on the biological environment, and a significant potential risk to biodiversity. Furthermore, the majority of projects are massive undertakings with far-reaching, permanent effects on the ecosystems in the vicinity, including the deterioration of biological survival circumstances and the disruption of the biological community structure (Zhang & Noronha, 2022).

Chinese MNEs are suffering from significant legitimacy crises as a result of their projects' negative environmental impacts, as there are many voices from international stakeholders that have criticized the BRI. In response to the legitimacy threat, the Chinese government has proposed some regulations for environmental protection. In September 2018, the "Beijing Declaration on Building a Closer China-Africa Community of Destiny" issued by the FOCAC Beijing Summit points out that China and Africa should adhere to environmental friendliness, cooperate to address climate change, and protect marine biodiversity. The "Beijing Action Plan (2019–2021)" states that the China-Africa Joint Research Centers, which have been established to promote environmental technology cooperation, share opportunities for green development, and carry out extensive cooperation and exchange in areas such as biodiversity and ecosystem services, climate change, and biosecurity, should continue to receive support in their development, with a focus on scientific research cooperation. During this critical period of advancing global environmental governance, strengthening cooperation between China and Africa in the emerging field of biodiversity conservation can help to further boost global environmental governance.

Chinese MNEs have demonstrated ecological restoration efforts during the construction of the BRI projects. For instance, the Mombasa-Nairobi Standard Gauge Railway passes through the Nairobi National Park and Tsavo National Park, and the latter is the largest wildlife reserve in Kenya. To minimize its environmental impacts, China Communications Construction Company engaged in the following:

> When passing through wildlife sanctuaries (such as the Nairobi National Park, Tsavo National Park, etc.), the construction team appropriately extended the approach bridge across the river at the wildlife water source and raised the height of the bridge to facilitate animal drinking and passage.
> (China Communications Construction Company, 2015, p. 39)

> The Company vigorously promotes front-loaded green planning and advocates for ecological site selection, alignment and eco-friendly design. The Company strictly implements ecological protection and soil and water conservation measures, strengthens vegetation protection and restoration and enhances the protection of biodiversity. For example, the NEMA Railway Project Department built a new animal migration path along the Kenya National Zoo section to effectively reduce the impact of the project's operational site.
> (China Communications Construction Company, 2019, p. 45)

However, in terms of mechanism design, the FOCAC and other large China-Africa exchange platforms are more oriented toward political and economic cooperation, with less attention paid to ecological and biodiversity issues, as well as the issue of the lack of special cooperation mechanisms and platforms. In terms of implementation, biodiversity conservation is transnational, a form of public welfare and non-political in nature, and its actual operation is mostly carried out by non-governmental organizations. The number of official and civil society organizations active in biodiversity conservation does not match the amount of rich natural resources in China. Investment in biodiversity conservation in China and Africa is still relatively low, and the relevant financial institutions have mostly invested in economic areas such as infrastructure construction. Furthermore, the scale of capital investment in biodiversity conservation is relatively small. Biodiversity conservation requires long-term and continuous management, operation, and financial investment, which requires long-term planning and is slow to yield results. On the one hand, some countries in Africa are politically and socially unstable, and many biodiversity cooperation projects deal with border areas or tribal communities, which poses a threat to the sustainability of the cooperation effort. On the other hand, biodiversity cooperation involves economic industries, such as agriculture and tourism, which may hinder the interests of different local groups during implementation, thus leading to conflicts and uncontrollable risks. Thus, it is anticipated that for better CSR reporting quality, both sides (home and host countries) need to actively dovetail with the UN Convention on Biological Diversity, the AU Agenda 2063, the UN 2030 Agenda for Sustainable Development, the Paris Agreement on Climate Change, and related targets on carbon peaking and carbon neutrality to introduce priority policies and improve institutional mechanisms for corporate social and environmental disclosures.

Empowerment of women

Over the course of the last three decades, researchers and development organizations have paid increasing attention to the concept of minority empowerment (Dibie & Dibie, 2012). The United Nations, the United Nations Population Fund, and the United Nations General Assembly have all contributed to laying the groundwork for the promotion of gender equality, women's empowerment, and child protection as major approaches to achieving policy goals and development objectives (Adjei, 2015; Banerjee & Bhattacharya, 2012). For example, women's empowerment and gender equality are development goals in their own right, as embodied by the Millennium Development Goals 3 and 5 (United Nations, 2019), and the fifth of the 17 Sustainable Development Goals (SDGs). The BRI is an opportunity to promote minority rights in ways that have never been possible before and to multiply these efforts' effects in a variety of sectors, including child survival, nutrition, development, and protection, with a particular emphasis on combating child poverty. For example, the 2019 CSR report of the China Communications Construction Company offered the following example:

> More than 40,000 Kenyans worked on the Mombasa–Nairobi Standard Gauge Railway project during its construction period, with over 90% of the workforce being local. Alice was one of the many ordinary people whose lives were changed by the opening of the railway. Having studied Chinese at the Confucius Institute at Kenyatta University, she was lucky enough to be selected to be trained as a train driver on the Monterey Railway and travelled to China with six other people. After 50 days of theoretical learning and driving simulations, they were able to familiarize themselves with the structure and working principles of the locomotive and the standard procedures for driving, overhauling and maintenance. On their return to Kenya,

they practiced their skills again and again and were eventually awarded their professional induction certificates, soon after which they became the 'helmspeople' of the Monel Railway. When the railway opened, Alice became the first female train driver in Kenya's history, where she chauffeured President Kenyatta on a test train. By the end of 2019, more than 1,500 locals had become involved in the operation of the Monel Railway, allowing them to attain a better life through a good job.

(China Communications Construction Company, 2019, p. 32)

Africa possesses certain normative structures that guarantee gender equality in social, economic, and political matters. Women's rights and their standing in society are improving in many nations as a result of years of campaigning and legal improvements. However, the continent is still lagging in the achievement of the objectives outlined in various continental legal frameworks, such as the "Maputo Protocol to the African Charter on Human and Peoples' Rights on the Rights of Women in Africa" and the "African Charter on the Rights and Welfare of the Child". As a result, the rights of women and girls are not being upheld, and they have been prevented from contributing fully to society by, among other things, the underlying structural inequalities that permeate all aspects of society. From this perspective, Outward Foreign Direct Investment (OFDI) by MNEs is meaningful, as the advancement of technology and economy could assist women in realizing, enjoying, and benefiting from their rights and expand the space for empowerment. Increased education and work opportunities also help women advance their quest to break societal barriers and the glass ceiling.

Fair education

Sub-Saharan Africa has the highest rate of educational marginalization. Those between the ages of around 6 and 11 make up more than half of the school-aged children and teenagers between the ages of approximately 12 and 14 are not enrolled in schools. According to UIS data, nearly 60% of adolescents between the ages of 15 and 17 are not enrolling in school (Chikoko & Mthembu, 2020). In the absence of immediate action, the situation is sure to deteriorate as the region's school-aged population continues to grow and the demand for education rises.

The Ministry of Education of China advocated the "Education Action Plan for the Belt and Road Initiative in 2017", which went into greater depth on the role of education along the Belt and Road (Ge & Ho, 2022). The strategy explored in greater depth what concrete measures could be taken to boost educational interactions along the Belt and Road while reiterating the significance of education in achieving the BRI's goal of "people-to-people relationships". While talent development can support host countries' efforts in terms of policy coordination, infrastructure interconnection, unhindered trade, and financial integration along the routes, educational exchange can act as a bridge to foster more intimate human connections. In accordance with these overarching ideas, education projects have been launched and completed in the BRI countries over the past few years. Southeast Asia, Southern Asia, Central Asia, and Eastern Europe have seen the most activity, with recent expansion in Southern and Northern Europe, the Middle East, and Northern Africa (Peters & Zhu, 2021). These initiatives have covered a wide range of topics, including entrepreneurship education, international schools, capacity building, technical and vocational education and training, student exchanges, language and cultural education, technical and vocational education, and girls' and women's education (King, 2020). Assistance and contribution to local fair education are common CSR disclosures for Chinese MNEs in African BRI countries. For instance:

> The DigiSchool program in South Africa has helped primary school children improve their English reading and comprehension skills. As the 'Progress in International Reading Literacy Study' has pointed out, 78% of 4th graders in South Africa lack basic English reading comprehension skills during the literacy foundation phase from Grades 1 to 3. To address this challenge, Huawei launched the DigiSchool project in partnership with the local carrier Rain and the educational non-profit organisation Click Foundation. The project aims to help all children in South Africa read fluently and comprehend what they are reading by the end of Grade 3. By the end of 2021, the project had connected over 90 schools and assisted more than 50,000 students.
>
> (Huawei, 2021, p. 25)

The above are only a few examples of how Chinese MNEs are assisting governments, funders, and civil society organizations in their efforts to help the most marginalized children and youth to achieve SDG 4.

Community welfare

Chinese MNEs are expected to offer social services and welfare initiatives in less-developed countries in addition to their regular business operations. Programs for community development receive a lot of attention. Examples include the provision of education and scholarships, building roads, construction of clinics, and supply of medicines for AIDS/HIV patients in South Africa, as well as the provision of medication and immunization for malaria in Zambia. While the MNEs are taking resources from such resource-rich countries, relevant, direct, and sustained benefits are demanded from them by the communities also (Eweje, 2006; Taarup-Esbensen, 2019). The above are some examples of how Chinese MNEs contribute directly to the World Business Council for Sustainable Development's (World Business Council for Sustainable Development [WBCSD], 1998) definition[2] of social/community involvement through continuous interests in community development.

Furthermore, it is argued that MNEs have a role in global development not only through financial investment, but also through investing in human capital and providing local people with the capabilities to drive their own economic development (Lall & Narula, 2004). Similar community welfare promotion illustrations are constantly being identified throughout the content analysis. Consider the following examples of community welfare projects:

> ... the company engaged in technical repairs and the construction of seven culverts and small bridges on the road from the camp to the mine site that were damaged or not well built, levelled off the road surface for nearly 10 kilometers and deployed construction machinery for site levelling and road construction for the new school .... With the construction of the project, the company has driven local economic development and promoted the employment of residents, social donations, etc., and has increased the local economic output value to nearly 200 billion guilders. Furthermore, it has raised the income of the employed population by more than one million guilders, winning full recognition and praise from the local government and people.
> (Aluminum Corporation of China, 2019, p. 77)

> The company has set up a special community relations committee and planned community relations improvement activities starting from the preliminary design of the project. Furthermore, it has designed and planned a separate chapter on community construction. The company has prepared a Community Work Guide to understand the demands of local residents and to reduce the negative impacts of the project's construction on the community.
> (Aluminum Corporation of China, 2019, p. 77)

Community development initiatives and investments are vital for the establishment of a cordial relationship between Chinese MNEs and their host communities along the BRI host countries. MNEs have the obligations to help solve problems of public concerns. By providing social welfare initiatives for host communities, Chinese MNEs act as a surrogate for governments in African host countries that often ignore the economic and social welfare programs. The examined CSR reports have demonstrated many different ways in which Chinese MNEs can help BRI-participating economies to gain better integration within the world economy and thereby benefit more from the BRI process.

Anti-corruption

Surprisingly, there are very few instances featuring actual cases of anti-corruption in African host countries. Thus, there is obviously a lack of accountability mechanisms regarding this issue. Doğan (2021), while discussing the "Chinese-style hegemony", wrote: "Moral risks cannot be denied in the healthy implementation of environment of the BRI. The biggest moral risks are bribery and corruption. Chinese companies are blamed for paying bribes to local officials to get approval of high-cost loans and sign infrastructure projects, specifically in [some African countries]" (p. 110).

Given the sensitive nature of such an issue and the advocation of transparency in the BRI projects, there is an urgent need to ensure that such projects are not only strategically aligned with China's economic and political interests but also that proper assessments are being made to ensure that these projects will have a positive impact on the economies of the recipient countries while avoiding increasing the potential for corruption among government officials. Doğan (2021) and other authors have exposed the negative aspects of the BRI from a different (non-CSR) perspective from this book. Nevertheless, this topic will be revisited briefly in the final chapter to ensure objectiveness of our observations.

Promotion of employment

Employment promotion has been seen as an important area where Chinese MNEs could contribute to tackling unemployment and under-employment, especially those of youths, women, and people with disabilities in African countries. For instance, businesses may voluntarily follow government regulations by employing foreign workers from nearby nations, ensuring their activities result in zero liquid discharge or adhering to the government's push for "localization" when it comes to hiring, training, and developing local talents. The benefits could include an increase in operational efficiency brought on by energy savings or well-trained and content personnel. Customers may come to perceive these companies positively as good brands because they are socially or ecologically conscious:

> China Three Gorges is actively engaged in localized operations, providing employment opportunities in project countries, training local hydropower technical personnel and promoting the development of the local hydropower industry. The Isimba Hydropower Station in Uganda trains local hydropower talents, including safety engineers, environmental engineers, community coordinators, administrative assistants, medical and nursing staffs, drivers, heavy equipment operators and various types of mechanics, such as repairers and general laborers.
> (China Three Gorges Group, 2019, p. 58)

> By the end of December 2019, CNPC had 89,800 Chinese and foreign employees in the Belt and Road region, including 77,300 local and international employees, with an average localization rate of 86%. Among them, the localization rate for the oil and gas investment business exceeded 95%.
> (China National Petroleum, 2020, p. 30)

Prior studies have contended that MNEs from emerging economies may incur liabilities of origin in developed host nations, such that they may use CSR reporting to address institutional pressure from these countries (Agnihotri & Bhattacharya, 2019; Marano et al., 2017; Tashman et al., 2019). However, the majority of BRI countries are developing countries with weak institutions and less-developed economies (Belt & Road Portal, 2021). Chinese businesses may not have much origin liability when they invest in another developing nation, which is the case of south-south cooperation. The stakeholders in the host nations are accustomed to dealing with businesses that lack good corporate governance and high transparency because the institutions of these BRI developing countries are not necessarily superior or even worse than those in China (Wang et al., 2022). Additionally, the governments of these developing nations still view economic growth as their major goal on a global scale, and CSR reporting is not yet a social norm (de Villiers & van Staden, 2006; Liu et al., 2020). In these underdeveloped nations, it is unlikely that institutions requiring CSR reporting will be successfully built or implemented in the short run. Chinese businesses may nevertheless experience legitimacy issues and the burden of liabilities of origin in BRI nations for other reasons. Despite having signed bilateral investment agreements with China, BRI countries may later voice their disapproval of the BRI's non-economic goals. For example, they might be particularly concerned with the "debt trap" and the loss of sovereignty (Li et al., 2022) or even "Chinese hegemony" (Doğan, 2021). CSR might therefore be applied as a typical non-market tactic for establishing legitimacy in BRI developing nations.

The BRI and the SDGs: The way forward for Africa

Promoted as the "ideal means" by which MNEs can engage in ethical behaviors, activities labeled as "CSR activities" vary greatly, ranging from engagement activities with communities (Muthuri, 2008; Seitanidi & Ryan, 2007) to developing environmental management systems (Ingram & Frazier, 1980; Rondinelli & Berry, 2000). It has become crucial to comprehend how MNEs act politically, particularly in a state-dominated developing nation in Africa, given the recent resurgence of interest in MNEs' roles as "global political actors" (Scherer et al., 2009) who are involved in the development of a global-level CSR agenda (Detomasi, 2007; Matten & Crane, 2005; Palazzo & Scherer, 2006).

At the UN Summit in September 2015, the world leaders had adopted the "2030 Agenda for the SDGs", which became operative in 2016. Ensuring global economic growth, social inclusion and environmental sustainability are among a few of the 17 SDGs. For African nations to achieve the SDGs, economic policies and collaborations with development organizations and the private sector must be rethought. Africa has historically made a negligible contribution to world trade due to poor infrastructure, a lack of skilled labor, and low production capacity. To alleviate poverty and increase Africa's global trade competitiveness, Africans need to embrace a model of local development that optimizes their national resources. When properly utilized, Africa's abundant natural and human resources will aid in its sustained development. Furthermore, Africa needs to establish a cooperative development paradigm. China may be able to assist Africa in meeting its needs. The BRI offers a framework to strengthen the socio-economically beneficial strategic alliance between China and Africa. The FOCAC promised to "actively study the links between China's measures to create the Silk Road Economic Belt and 21st Century Maritime Silk Road and Africa's economic integration and sustainable development agenda" during President Xi's visit to South Africa (Eom et al., 2018).

The SDGs are identical to the development goals of the BRI. In fact, the BRI implemented a portion of the SDGs, and it constitutes a useful mechanism to deepen Sino-African ties, which Africa may use to substantiate its own achievement of the SDGs. Through the BRI, Africa is connected, and China has supported infrastructure projects in Africa to promote trade and national economic integration along the trading route. China is assisting Africa in achieving SGD 9 on industry, innovation, and infrastructure by establishing Economic and Trade Zones that draw investments from Chinese businesses and creating infrastructure like seaports and railways. One tangible result is that the BRI has helped African nations in closing the infrastructure gap, generating employment, acquiring skills, and fostering international integration. Growing Sino-African connections are evident from the growing Chinese presence in Africa. Furthermore, the BRI's inclusion of Africa has created possibilities for Chinese development initiatives and investments, which may help Africa achieve its 2030 Agenda goals for a socially equitable, prosperous, and secure environment.

Through the analyses conducted in this chapter, we have witnessed both the shortcomings and encouraging progress of Chinese MNEs in fulfilling their social responsibilities in Africa. The chapter also pointed out the need for host governments and NGOs to ensure that existing community relations teams and health, safety, and environment committees are adequately staffed, resourced, and trained to effectively monitor the environmental, social, and human rights impacts of infrastructure projects in Africa. Furthermore, it is believed that MNEs should fully respect local land rights, ensuring that when land is expropriated, fair compensation is paid to individuals and communities with customary land rights, and that land expropriation does not negatively impact the livelihoods of local communities. In addition, high priority needs to be given to negative ecological impacts on occupied land, such as the construction of adequate ecological compensation zones and ecological restoration areas. Given the inadequate social and environmental disclosure of the impacts of the BRI projects, it is strongly recommended that Chinese MNEs publish environmental and social impact assessment data, environmental and social management plans, and periodic environment monitoring reports translated into local languages. Furthermore, we observed a lack of effective grievance processes in most of the sample firms. There should be effective mechanisms in place so that individuals affected by the BRI projects can appeal directly to companies in addition to the government. The government, international organizations, and Chinese MNEs should provide more support to civil society organizations providing legal or advisory services to affected communities, including conducting community-level or civil-society-led parallel environmental and social impact assessments (ESIAs) and monitoring reports. These actors should also offer support for communities and individuals filing complaints through companies' grievance and accountability mechanisms.

Africa is in dire need of infrastructure development, economic transformation, and cutting-edge technology. Projects that meet these needs will promote the continent's sustainable development. The BRI offers a chance to significantly increase south-south cooperation, allowing nations to share knowledge, scale up successful initiatives, and ultimately create a greater global impact. However, the BRI is about more than just building roads and bridges. Rather, the BRI projects should not, and must not for the benefit of all humanity, bring disasters to indigenous peoples. Achieving mutual benefits and a win-win situation between China and African countries in a transparent and sustainable manner, through the guidance of the SDGs, should be the ultimate goal of the initiative.

Notes

1 Xi Jinping, "Work Together to Build the Silk Road Economic Belt and The 21st Century Maritime Silk Road" (speech, Beijing, May 14, 2017), http://news.xinhuanet.com/english/2017-05/14/c_136282982.htm
2 "A broad range of activities, including community assistance programs, supporting educational needs, fostering a shared vision of a corporation's role in the community, ensuring community health and safety, sponsorship, enabling employees to do voluntary work in the community, philanthropic giving" (WBCSD, 1998, p. 8).

References

Adjei, S. B. (2015). Assessing women empowerment in Africa: A critical review of the challenges of the gender empowerment measure of the UNDP. *Psychology and Developing Societies, 27*(1), 58–80.
Agnihotri, A., & Bhattacharya, S. (2019). CEO narcissism and internationalization by Indian firms. *Management International Review, 59*(6), 889–918.
Aguilar, R., & Goldstein, A. (2009). The chinisation of Africa: The case of Angola. *World Economy, 32*(11), 1543–1562.
Alpha, D. S. (2017). *FPA: China concludes summit to foster cooperation amongst developing countries*. Frontpage Africa. https://www.frontpageafricaonline.com/index. php/diaspora/4130-china-concludes-summit-to-foster-cooperation-amongst-developing-countries
Aluminum Corporation of China. (2019). *Corporate social responsibility report*. https://www.chalco.com.cn/whzr/shzr/202103/P020210303669510127095.pdf
Alves, A. C. (2013). Chinese economic statecraft: A comparative study of China's oil-backed loans in Angola and Brazil. *Journal of Current Chinese Affairs, 42*(1), 99–130.
Ascensão, F., Fahrig, L., Clevenger, A. P., Corlett, R. T., Jaeger, J. A., Laurance, W. F., & Pereira, H. M. (2018). Environmental challenges for the Belt and Road Initiative. *Nature Sustainability, 1*(5), 206–209.
Atkins, J., Barone, E., Maroun, W., & Atkins, B. (2017). Bee accounting and accountability in the UK. In K. Atkins, & B. Atkins (Eds.), *The business of bees: An integrated approach to bee decline and corporate responsibility* (pp. 198–211). Routledge.
Banerjee, S., & Bhattacharya, S. (2012). Food gels: Gelling process and new applications. *Critical Reviews in Food Science and Nutrition, 52*(4), 334–346.

Belt and Road Portal. (2017a). *Guidance on promoting green Belt and Road.* https://eng.yidaiyilu.gov.cn/zchj/qwfb/12479.htm

Belt and Road Portal. (2017b). *The Belt and Road ecological and environmental cooperation plan.* https://eng.yidaiyilu.gov.cn/zchj/qwfb/13392.htm

Belt and Road Portal. (2021). *List of countries that have signed cooperation documents with China to jointly build the "Belt and Road".* https://www.yidaiyilu.gov.cn/xwzx/roll/77298.htm

Chikoko, V., & Mthembu, P. (2020). Financing primary and secondary education in Sub-Saharan Africa: A systematic review of literature. *South African Journal of Education, 40*(4). https://doi.org/10.15700/saje.v40n4a2046.

China Communications Construction Company. (2015). *Corporate social responsibility report.* https://www.ccccltd.cn/shzr/shzr/shzrbg/201608/P020160830653823985661.pdf

China Communications Construction Company. (2019). *Corporate social responsibility report.* http://www.sasac.gov.cn/n4470048/n13461446/n14398052/n14398194/c14455192/part/14455203.pdf

China National Petroleum. (2020). *Corporate social responsibility report.* https://www.cnpc.com.cn/cnpc/lncbw/202005/a24b4a96b82c444092341acadb363132/files/c33308b67045489cb9d5e57ce0b9e2f9.pdf

China Three Gorges Group. (2019). *Corporate social responsibility report.* https://www.ctg.com.cn/sxjt/xxxgk/shzrl/zrbg90/index.html

Darwall, W., Smith, K., Tweddle, D., & Skelton, P. (2009). *The status and distribution of freshwater biodiversity in southern Africa.* IUCN.

De Villiers, C., & Van Staden, C. J. (2006). Can less environmental disclosure have a legitimising effect? Evidence from Africa. *Accounting, Organizations and Society, 31*(8), 763–781.

Detomasi, D. A. (2007). The multinational corporation and global governance: Modelling global public policy networks. *Journal of Business Ethics, 71*(3), 321–334.

Dibie, J., & Dibie, R. (2012). Non-governmental organizations (NGOs) and the empowerment of women in Africa. *African and Asian Studies, 11*(1–2), 95–122.

DiMaggio, P. J., & Powell, W. W. (1983). The iron cage revisited: Institutional isomorphism and collective rationality in organizational fields. *American Sociological Review, 48*(2), 147–160.

Doğan, A. (2021). *Hegemony with Chinese characteristics: From the tributary system to the Belt and Road Initiative.* Routledge.

Dossi, S. (2012). Beyond the 'cognitive iron curtain'. China's white paper on peaceful development. *The International Spectator, 47*(2), 124–126.

Eom, J., Brautigam, D., & Benabdallah, L. (2018). *The path ahead: the 7th forum on China-Africa cooperation* (No. 01/2018). Briefing paper.

Eweje, G. (2006). The role of MNEs in community development initiatives in developing countries: Corporate social responsibility at work in Nigeria and South Africa. *Business & Society, 45*(2), 93–129.

Foster, V. (2009). *Building bridges: China's growing role as infrastructure financier for Sub-Saharan Africa* (Vol. 5). World Bank Publications.

Ge, Y., & Ho, K. C. (2022). Belt and Road Initiatives: Implications for China's internationalisation of tertiary-level education. *Educational Research and Evaluation, 27*(3–4), 260–279.

George, G., Corbishley, C., Khayesi, J. N., Haas, M. R., & Tihanyi, L. (2016). Bringing Africa in: Promising directions for management research. *Academy of Management Journal, 59*(2), 377–393.

Gill, B., & Reilly, J. (2007). The tenuous hold of China Inc. in Africa. *Washington Quarterly, 30*(3), 37–52.

Githaiga, N. M., & Bing, W. (2019). Belt and Road Initiative in Africa: The impact of standard gauge railway in Kenya. *China Report, 55*(3), 219–240.

Githaiga, N. M., Burimaso, A., Wang, B., & Ahmed, S. M. (2019). The Belt and Road Initiative: Opportunities and risks for Africa's connectivity. *China Quarterly of International Strategic Studies, 5*(01), 117–141.

Great Wall Motor (GWM) Company Limited. (2019). *Corporate Social Responsibility Report*. https://res.gwm.com.cn/GwmCn/upload/2020/0506/bcd3d313397a3ca3.pdf?1796791

Hodzi, O. (2018). China and Africa: Economic growth and a non-transformative political elite. *Journal of Contemporary African Studies, 36*(2), 191–206.

HRW. Org. (2018). *"What Do We Get Out of It?" The human rights impact of bauxite mining in Guinea*. Retrieved from https://www.hrw.org/report/2018/10/04/what-do-we-get-out-it/human-rights-impact-bauxite-mining-guinea

Huawei. (2021). *Corporate social responsibility report*. https://www-file.huawei.com/-/media/corp2020/pdf/sustainability/sustainability-report-2021-en.pdf

Hughes, A. C., Lechner, A. M., Chitov, A., Horstmann, A., Hinsley, A., Tritto, A., & Douglas, W. Y. (2020). Horizon scan of the Belt and Road Initiative. *Trends in Ecology & Evolution, 35*(7), 583–593.

Ingram, R. W., & Frazier, K. B. (1980). Environmental performance and corporate disclosure. *Journal of Accounting Research, 18*(2), 614–622.

King, K. (2020). China–Africa education cooperation: From focac to Belt and Road. *ECNU Review of Education, 3*(2), 221–234.

Kostova, T., & Zaheer, S. (1999). Organizational legitimacy under conditions of complexity: The case of the multinational enterprise. *Academy of Management Review, 24*(1), 64–81.

Lall, S., & Narula, R. (2004). Foreign direct investment and its role in economic development: Do we need a new agenda? *The European Journal of Development Research, 16*(3), 447–464.

Leke, A., Chironga, M., & Desvaux, G. (2018). Africa's overlooked business revolution. McKinsey Quarterly, *14*. www.mckinsey.com/featured-insights/middle-east-andafrica/africas-overlooked-business-revolution

Leslie, A. N. (2016). Zambia and China: Workers' protest, civil society and the role of opposition politics in elevating state engagement. *African Studies Quarterly, 16*(3-4), 89–106.

Liu, H., Wang, Y., Jiang, J., & Wu, P. (2020). How green is the "Belt and Road Initiative"?–Evidence from Chinese OFDI in the energy sector. *Energy Policy, 145*, 111709.

Liu, X., Blackburn, T. M., Song, T., Li, X., Huang, C., & Li, Y. (2019). Risks of biological invasion on the Belt and Road. *Current Biology, 29*(3), 499–505.

Li, J., Van Assche, A., Li, L., & Qian, G. (2022). Foreign direct investment along the Belt and Road: A political economy perspective. *Journal of International Business Studies, 53*(5), 902–919.

Lokanathan, V. (2020). China's belt and road initiative: Implications in Africa. *Observer Research Foundation Brief, 395*, 12.

Marano, V., Tashman, P., & Kostova, T. (2017). Escaping the iron cage: Liabilities of origin and CSR reporting of emerging market multinational enterprises. *Journal of International Business Studies, 48*(3), 386–408.

Matten, D., & Crane, A. (2005). Corporate citizenship: Toward an extended theoretical conceptualization. *Academy of Management Review, 30*(1), 166–179.

Menga, F., & Swyngedouw, E. (2018). States of water. In F. Menga, & E. Swyngedouw (Eds.), *Water, technology and the nation-state* (pp. 1–18). Routledge.

Muthuri, J. N. (2008). Participation and accountability in corporate community involvement programmes: A research agenda. *Community Development Journal, 43*(2), 177–193.

Naidu, S. (2007). The forum on China-Africa cooperation (FOCAC) what does the future hold? *China Report, 43*(3), 283–296.

Nye, J. S. (1990). Soft power. *Foreign Policy, 80*, 153–171.

Palazzo, G., & Scherer, A. G. (2006). Corporate legitimacy as deliberation: A communicative framework. *Journal of Business Ethics, 66*(1), 71–88.

Peters, M. A., & Zhu, X. (2021). Education and the Belt and Road Initiative (bri). *Beijing International Review of Education, 3*(1), 1–3.

Pfeffer, J. (1987). A resource dependence perspective on interorganizational relations. In M. S. *Mizruchi & M, Schwartz. (Eds.), Intercorporate relations: The structural analysis of business* (pp. 25–55). Cambridge University Press.

Pomeroy, D. (1993). Centers of high biodiversity in Africa. *Conservation Biology, 7*(4), 901–907.

Risberg, P. (2019). The give-and-take of BRI in Africa. *New Perspectives in Foreign Policy, 17*, 43–47.

Rondinelli, D. A., & Berry, M. A. (2000). Environmental citizenship in multinational corporations: Social responsibility and sustainable development. *European Management Journal, 18*(1), 70–84.

Scherer, A. G., Palazzo, G., & Matten, D. (2009). Introduction to the special issue: Globalization as a challenge for business responsibilities. *Business Ethics Quarterly, 19*(3), 327–347.

United Nations. (2019). Sustainable development goals. United Nations. https://sdgs.un.org/goals

Seitanidi, M. M., & Ryan, A. (2007). A critical review of forms of corporate community involvement: From philanthropy to partnerships. *International Journal of Nonprofit and Voluntary Sector Marketing, 12*(3), 247–266.

Slangen, A. H. (2013). Greenfield or acquisition entry? The roles of policy uncertainty and MNE legitimacy in host countries. *Global Strategy Journal, 3*(3), 262–280.

Snapp, S. S., Blackie, M. J., Gilbert, R. A., Bezner-Kerr, R., & Kanyama-Phiri, G. Y. (2010). Biodiversity can support a greener revolution in Africa. *Proceedings of the National Academy of Sciences, 107*(48), 20840–20845.

Sneddon, L. U. (2015). Pain in aquatic animals. *The Journal of Experimental Biology, 218*(7), 967–976.

Suchman, M. C. (1995). Managing legitimacy: Strategic and institutional approaches. *Academy of Management Review, 20*(3), 571–610.

Sverdrup-Thygeson, B. (2017). The Chinese story: Historical narratives as a tool in China's Africa policy. *International Politics, 54*(1), 54–72.

Taarup-Esbensen, J. (2019). Managing risk through dependency: How do mining MNEs strategise to legitimise business continuity? *The Extractive Industries and Society, 6*(2), 489–497.

Tashman, P., Marano, V., & Kostova, T. (2019). Walking the walk or talking the talk? Corporate social responsibility decoupling in emerging market multinationals. *Journal of International Business Studies, 50*(2), 153–171.

Taylor, I. (2010). *The forum on China-Africa cooperation (FOCAC)*. Routledge.

Tull, D. M. (2006). China's engagement in Africa: Scope, significance and consequences. *The Journal of Modern African Studies, 44*(3), 459–479.

Ubi-Abai, I., & Ekere, D. (2018). Fiscal policy, monetary policy and economic growth in Sub-Saharan Africa. *MPRA Paper, 91950*, 1–19

Victor, J. I., & Leyira, C. M. (2021). Corruption perception index (CPI) and government expenditure in Sub Saharan Africa: The influence of information communication technology (ICT). *IJSSHR-International Journal of Social Science and Humanities Research, 4*(07), 54–63.

Vines, A. (2007). China in Africa: A mixed blessing? *Current History, 106*(700), 213.

Wang, F. L., & Elliot, E. A. (2014). China in Africa: Presence, perceptions and prospects. *Journal of Contemporary China, 23*(90), 1012–1032.

Wang, H., Wang, X., Zhang, X., Liu, G., Chen, W. Q., Chen, S., & Shi, L. (2022). The coupling between material footprint and economic growth in the "Belt and Road" countries. *Journal of Cleaner Production, 359*, 132110.

World Business Council for Sustainable Development (WBCSD). (1998). *Meeting changing expectations: Corporate social responsibility, world business council for sustainable development* (pp. 1–31). WBCSD.

Xinhua. (2022). *China has signed more than 200 cooperation documents with 147 countries and 32 international organizations to build "One Belt, One Road"*. http://www.gov.cn/xinwen/2022-01/19/content_5669215.htm

Yu, Z. (2017). *Opinion: How can African countries get the most from Belt and Road?* CGTN News. https://news.cgtn.com/news/3d59444d796b7a4d/share_p.html?from=timeline&isappinstalled=0

Zhang, R., & Noronha, C. (2022). Assessing the Nexus between cross-border infrastructure projects and extinction accounting—from the Belt and Road Initiative perspective. Social and *Environmental Accountability Journal, 43*(1), 30–55.

11 How China's Belt and Road Initiative Is Faring

Implications and Outlooks for Corporate Social Responsibility

A review of CSR and the BRI in this study

Over the past few decades, the CSR of MNEs has become an increasingly predominant topic in international business (Bondy et al., 2012; Muller, 2006; Rathert, 2016). MNEs operate simultaneously in multiple institutional environments, and it is a big challenge for them to coordinate their CSR practices globally to gain legitimacy in host countries. In the era of globalization and the flattening world, CSR should not be restricted to regional-level initiatives. Rather, we should also consider transnational and multinational cooperation and global CSR focused on the human community as a whole – the phenomenon *grande* (Donleavy & Noronha, 2023).

In Chapter 1 of this book, we pointed out that understanding the influence of home-country institutions has become more crucial in international business research as a result of the rise of multinational enterprises from emerging economies (EMNEs), which are typically characterized by inefficient markets, active government involvement, extensive business networking, and high uncertainty (Xu & Meyer, 2013). In fact, weakly developed institutions and government promotions may coexist in emerging economies (Hoskisson et al., 2013), and governments in emerging economies are also major promoters of and collaborators in the design and implementation of CSR programs. Furthermore, due to physical and cultural distances, it is extremely difficult to monitor and regulate the CSR activities of MNEs abroad (Strike et al., 2006).

Chapter 2 tackled the rise of the Chinese economy and Chinese MNEs. Chinese companies investing and operating abroad have internationalized more recently as compared to their Western counterparts. In the late 1990s, the Chinese government implemented a "going out" program to encourage outbound foreign investment. Since then, Chinese companies have faced a slew of labor issues and conflicts in their overseas operations which have drawn international media attention. The large-scale dispatch of Chinese workers to participate in building and development projects, as well as severe breaches of local laws and management policies, have resulted in contentious or even violent conflicts with labor unions and workers in host countries.

DOI: 10.4324/9781003302445-11

In Chapter 3, the BRI was introduced. The BRI is a large-scale initiative to improve regional integration, increase trade, and stimulate economic growth by connecting Asia with Africa and Europe through land and maritime networks along six corridors. Despite the potential opportunities and advantages of foreign investment in infrastructure construction for host countries, the BRI is fraught with significant obstacles and threats. The effects of poorly designed and implemented projects on host countries are causing increasing concern, especially regarding issues, such as the local climate, workforce, fiscal health, and political stability. These issues are particularly acute in relation to BRI ventures and investments in countries designated by the Organisation for Economic Co-operation and Development (OECD) as "weak governance zones" where "governments are reluctant or unable to assume their responsibilities" (Fang & Nolan, 2019).

The BRI serves as a roadmap for Chinese MNEs looking to expand their operations in the Belt and Road nations. Their social responsibility and performance are fundamentally distinct from that of Western international corporations. Furthermore, unlike Western corporations, Chinese MNEs' CSR initiatives are characterized by marked differences. Chinese MNEs prioritize profits above all else, yet they also adhere to the tenets of the BRI of the Chinese government. Thus, they are incentivized by different things (or inspirations) compared to Western multinational corporations. Traditionally, securing essential supplies, opening up new markets, and gaining access to low-cost production inputs have been the driving forces behind business expansion abroad. It is also the strategy used by many rising companies to achieve a competitive position internationally. The BRI compels Chinese MNEs to prioritize CSR and profit-making equally from the start of this initiative, deviating from the traditional narrative of "multi-nationalization". In other words, the notion of creating shared growth through dialogue and collaboration strengthens the foundation of cooperation.

In the Keynote Speech[1] by President Xi at the opening ceremony of the Second Belt and Road Forum for International Cooperation, he pointed out that the "golden ideals" thorough consultation, collaborative efforts, and reciprocal advantages serve to lead the BRI as it enters a "new era" of more active development. According to these golden principles, businesses must take into account the demands of diverse stakeholders when designing their overseas development strategies. Furthermore, they must adhere to sustainable development and the win-win principle when conducting business. These principles can be viewed as an international corporate endeavor supported by the government that leads to distinguished CSR performance.

In Chapter 4, we began the analysis of CSR reports and Chinese MNEs by establishing a solid theoretical foundation. The world is facing enormous challenges in securing a sustainable future. Given the circumstances of wars and the pandemic, the fulfillment of CSR in a cross-border context should be of great concern and represent an essential early step in the right direction of the revolution of CSR accounting. Emerging-economy multinational enterprises (EM-MNEs) must deal with diverse and complex host nations that have a wide range of CSR criteria. Government support in the home country is positively correlated with the internationalization of emerging-economy enterprise (Gaur et al., 2018). To earn necessary support or legitimacy, corporations must respond to institutional pressures by incorporating institutional aspects into their policies and actions; and failing to conform to such institutionalized norms of acceptability can undermine a firm's legitimacy and, by extension, its existence (Bondy, 2008). As a result, we recommend that the Chinese government pay closer attention to Chinese MNEs that are making investments in host nations with weak support for CSR and make more focused policy recommendations to boost pressures in the home country so as to fill institutional gaps in host nations.

We then entered into the main part of this book – CSR reporting in BRI countries – in Chapter 5. Since the introduction of the BRI, researchers have started to assess the environmental issues associated with its projects. Opinions of the BRI's environmental influence vary greatly among experts, with some being supportive and others expressing concerns about its negative implications. Although the BRI is intended to promote regional and global prosperity, it may also be a contributing factor to the rising carbon footprint. In addition to being a pioneer in carbon trading, China is acknowledged for its role as a global leader in climate responsibility. The BRI has offered a proposal for international cooperation intended to highlight China's leadership in this aspect. Moreover, due to their dual embeddedness, multinational corporations must acquire legitimacy from both their home and host countries (Beddewela, 2019; Hamprecht & Schwarzkopf, 2014). MNEs operate in a wide variety of institutional environments (Cantwell et al., 2010); consequently, EM-MNEs must not only consider institutional pressures from home countries but also contend with varying degrees of institutional pressure from host countries. Because young Chinese MNEs involved in the BRI lack overseas experience, it is unclear whether, how, and to what extent should Chinese MNEs participate in CSR.

Chapter 6 adopted triangulated research methods that combine content analyses, empirical tests, and case studies to demonstrate how Chinese MNEs are actively and rapidly developing CSR initiatives to achieve the envisioned "sustainable BRI". The study drew on Global Reporting Initiative (GRI) reporting standards, ISO standards, SDGs, the Chinese Academy of Social Sciences (CASS) CSR framework, and related academic literature to develop a framework for evaluating overseas MNEs' CSR reporting quality. This evaluation framework was then used to evaluate CSR reporting contents and quality. Specifically, NVivo 12 was used to conduct a computer-assisted content analysis of 1029 CSR reports published by Chinese MNEs actively investing in the BRI projects. Each data point relevant to CSR activities in the BRI host countries was coded as a node under a particular code, and the number of nodes under each CSR topic (code) per CSR report illustrated the topics' frequencies, thereby revealing the top ten CSR reporting topics. The results demonstrated that contents related to economic impacts, local people's livelihoods, unified environmental safeguards, and human-oriented principles in overseas employment appeared most frequently in the Chinese MNEs' CSR reports. Amid the hot debate regarding how the BRI is reshaping the global competitive landscape, the CSR reporting practices of Chinese MNEs along the Belt and Road are noteworthy but have received relatively little attention. The chapter has presented a unique study of Chinese MNEs' engagement in CSR reporting in BRI host countries. It contributes to the literature by establishing a theoretical framework for Chinese MNEs' overseas CSR reporting that combines stakeholder, institutional, legitimacy, resource-dependence, social contracts, and international strategic theories. This theoretical framework was used to analyze the CSR reporting performance of Chinese MNEs known to be actively involved with the BRI host countries. The results suggested that to gain support and legitimacy for their overseas operations, Chinese MNEs must respond to institutional pressures by integrating institutional elements into their policies and behaviors (Bondy, 2008). Furthermore, the chapter argued that Chinese MNEs operating in BRI host countries must address the needs of a diverse set of stakeholders and are under greater pressure to align their shareholders' interests with the expectations of those in host markets. Specifically, they must satisfy stakeholders in allowing emerging countries to acquire local legitimacy, and they must conform to the requirements of both the parent company and home-country stakeholders to maintain their international operating license. In addition, as initiators of the BRI, Chinese MNEs are obliged to take actions that protect and enhance society's interests and meet the various expectations of society and related stakeholders (Moir, 2001). Such CSR initiatives are likely to promote Chinese MNEs' international image in the global arena and create a win-win situation for both BRI host countries and China. The theoretical framework also implies that, given the BRI's adaptability, all stakeholders are incentivized to advocate for the institutionalization of best practices and promote high social, labor, and environmental standards in the BRI ventures. Such a strategy would help mitigate some obstacles and risks associated with the BRI ventures and foster more sustainable and inclusive development outcomes for host countries.

Chapter 7 further examined the CSR reporting contents published by Chinese MNEs in the BRI host countries. We determined the top ten emerging overseas CSR reporting topics of the sample firms by showing the ten highest increases in the average node numbers per report from 2014 to 2019. The results indicated that CSR disclosures related to environmental governance and biodiversity are emergent topics in the BRI countries. The BRI has raised concerns about the long-term survival of society and the world. Unsustainable building practices and emissions may trigger social unrest and hinder future investments and political cooperations. Thus, the Chinese government is emphasizing the importance of long-term growth of the BRI (Fang & Nolan, 2019). Chinese MNEs along the Belt and Road are increasingly focusing on providing decent work and employee care, as previous studies have identified employees as one of the most critical internal stakeholders. The CSR reports included in the sample also revealed an increasing trend in reporting CSR initiatives that promotes benefits for women and other disadvantaged people. Moreover, as more Chinese MNEs in the ICT industry expand abroad, CSR disclosures related to Intellectual property right (IPR) are increasing, thereby supporting domestic IPR development and promoting global awareness of IPR protection.

In terms of the CSR reporting contents and quality related to the BRI host countries, this book investigated issues surrounding Chinese Outward foreign direct investment (OFDI) in the BRI countries and highlighted opportunities and challenges posed by such investments in sustainable development in host countries. New insights have suggested that the current institutional architecture of CSR reporting for a "sustainable BRI" relies partly on voluntary corporate autonomy and a multitude of regional and transnational programs for sustainability. Thus, it is argued that the regulations and standards surrounding Chinese MNEs' CSR reporting should be strengthened, as the effective sustainable development of the BRI depends not only on China's commitments and priorities but also on its capacity to sustain, enact, and execute strict CSR disclosure laws and regulations. This book advances knowledge in this field by addressing both theoretical and practical research gaps in the current contents and quality of Chinese MNEs' overseas CSR reports in the BRI context. The theoretical framework developed to analyze the CSR reporting orientations and strategies of Chinese MNEs in the BRI host countries can serve as a guide for future studies to shed light on the CSR reporting of MNEs from emerging economies.

Chapter 8 presented an analysis of CSR reporting contents and quality among three types of firms in China, namely CEs, SOEs, and PEs. The results revealed a trend of improvement in the overall CSR reporting quality in the BRI host countries. The reporting quality of each CSR theme is also progressing, which shows that firms participating in the BRI projects are more likely to engage in CSR reporting and disclose higher quality information in their reports. The quality of disclosures related to the economic dimension is generally higher than that for other CSR themes. However, overall speaking, the quality of CSR reporting by Chinese MNEs in the BRI host countries is far from satisfactory, especially regarding topics related to labor practices and environmental sustainability. Although China has an expanding set of BRI guidelines, critical information on implementation, disclosure, and compliance is lacking. In the absence of financial or legal penalties for non-compliance, public bodies and civil society players are likely to "name and shame" corporations to keep their voluntary undertakings accountable.

In general, CEs outperformed SOEs and PEs in the majority of CSR reporting topics, while SOEs outperformed PEs. These results are consistent with some government policies on CSR regulations aimed directly at CEs' overseas operations. This study observed several factors contributing to differing CSR reporting quality. Chinese CEs and SOEs have been entrusted with the task of supporting the government the government in achieving the BRI's strategic goals. CEs and SOEs account for significant amounts of OFDI, and the government plays an influential role in directing these investments. They are inspired by the government to participate in the pilot project, and their CSR goals are aligned with governmental strategies in overseas markets. However, CEs and SOEs have the comparative advantage of having easy access to capital below market rates and experiences operating in places with similar institutions and government control. Both CEs and SOEs and their managers are more likely to follow the footsteps of successful competitors because their success depends on the government's provision of resources and the establishment of priorities. In addition, state-led FDI through CEs and SOEs faces legitimacy challenges in both host and home countries, and these firms use enhanced CSR disclosures to mitigate such issues. Faced with stricter OFDI regulation criteria from the Central Government, CEs and SOEs are under greater pressure to expand and disclose their CSR activities, whereas PEs occupy a peripheral position in this "go global" movement, as they have less government assistance and limited resources. Thus, PEs are more likely to fall into profit maximization in overseas markets which lack detailed regulations and institutional pressures to prioritize stakeholder benefits, since international investors demand greater returns on their shares. Therefore, CEs and SOEs have more resources than PEs in engaging in CSR initiatives and reporting their CSR performance accordingly.

In terms of the quality of reporting on the different CSR themes, CEs are more concerned with disclosures associated with the social dimension. Chinese CEs are the group that invests most heavily abroad with the largest volume of OFDI under the government's guidance. Thus, as the primary drivers of the globalization of Chinese enterprises, they face stronger demands in terms of environmental and social issues. CSR disclosures related to public welfare projects, poverty reduction, enforcement of human rights, and cultural exchanges are vivid examples of the critical role CEs play as national proponents along the Belt and Road. CEs and SOEs are more concerned than PEs about environmental disclosures in their CSR reports, responding to the national policy of in-depth and intense eco-environmental cooperation and security along the Belt and Road (Fang & Nolan, 2019). Compared to CEs and SOEs, PEs are more concerned with the employment dimension, to which they devote large portions of their CSR disclosure reports. In concentrating on the employment and economy dimensions, PEs use CSR as a strategic tool to boost their overseas development and market share. PEs' CSR reporting scores in the environmental and social dimensions are far from satisfactory. Large MNEs, especially those not under strong public scrutiny or governmental regulations, may exploit developing host countries' cheap and abundant natural resources and labor. Overall, the results suggest varying levels of stakeholder engagement among PEs, with influential stakeholders receiving preferential attention. Overall, this book revealed widespread trends in Chinese MNEs' CSR reporting in the context of the BRI countries. The findings showed that the contents of CSR reports vary considerably across firms and that the quality of CSR reporting in overseas markets is generally improving, with significant variations among the different types of firms studied.

The "Environmental Risk Management Initiative for China's Overseas Investment" was launched in 2018. If Chinese financial institutions and corporations embrace responsible investment practices and enhance the environmental risk management of their overseas ventures, there will be enormous potential for the "greening" of the BRI. These green development concepts are communicated and implemented by Chinese MNEs. Thus, Chapter 9 presented the results of several case studies addressing industry-specific CSR reporting practices by Chinese MNEs engaged in the BRI projects. It examined the CSR reports and websites of firms in the banking and finance, ICT, and construction industries published from 2014 to 2021. The findings showed that banking and finance firms' CSR reports focused largely on supporting China's green finance policy for the BRI. In addition, typical aspects of construction firms' CSR reports were identified in accordance with the concept of the "Green BRI" promoted by President Xi, as well as international and local policies and agreements for the sustainable development of transportation infrastructure projects. Finally, China's proposal of a Digital Silk Road is driving domestic demand for its technology while fostering the wider goal of connecting Chinese and international technological networks. In investing in BRI host countries, firms in the ICT industry have disclosed their CSR performance related to digital infrastructure and technical assistance, as well as knowledge transfer and training. The reports published by the three industries represent typical examples of industry-specific CSR reporting, which help reveal how CSR reporting contents vary with the types of industry and their positions within the BRI strategy.

Chapter 10 analyzed the CSR of Chinese MNEs in developing countries under the BRI context through the lens of Africa. As already indicated, earlier studies have contended that EMNEs may be subject to origin liability in developed host nations, allowing them to use CSR reporting to counteract institutional pressures from those countries (Marano et al., 2017; Tashman et al., 2019). However, the majority of BRI countries are developing nations with weak institutions and less-developed economies (Green Finance and Development Center, 2022). When Chinese corporations engage in projects in another developing nation, a case of south-south cooperation, they may be exposed to minimal responsibility of origin. The institutions of these BRI developing nations are not necessarily stronger or can be even worse than those in China; hence, host-country stakeholders are accustomed to interacting with corporations that lack strong corporate governance and transparency (Yang et al., 2020). Furthermore, many emerging nations are still in an economic phase where economic growth is the main national focus and CSR reporting is not yet a social norm (De Villiers & Van Staden, 2006). In addition, institutions requiring CSR reporting are unlikely to be successfully formed or enforced in underdeveloped nations. Thus, this book focused on Africa as a starting point for analyzing the CSR reporting practices of Chinese MNEs in less-developed and least-developed areas. It is expected that the political interests of the government, the perceived variations in CSR among the Belt and Road countries, and enterprises' interest will appeal to all, creating realistic demands regarding the CSR performance of Chinese firms engaging in the Belt and Road. However, there are vast differences in the systems, cultures, geographical positions, and green development statuses among the host countries, creating even bigger challenges for Chinese firms to actively engage in CSR.

The BRI at the crossroad of a world full of difficulties

This study of CSR of Chinese MNEs in the BRI represents a significant "phenomenon *grande*" (Donleavy & Noronha, 2023) and a discussion of the political economy of the phenomenon is unavoidable in order to be objective and comprehensive. The following discussion attempts to remain neutral while taking into account crucial facts that are taking place in the global scene today. However, this brief excursion should swiftly return back to the central doctrine of this book. That is to say, how CSR and CSR reporting of Chinese MNEs contribute to the BRI.

A critical notion that one must face when talking about the BRI is "hegemony". This topic becomes typically controversial especially given the dire situation of the Russian war (otherwise known as special military action) on Ukraine and the consequential energy and food crises, worldwide inflation, and the various political and economic challenges that are presented on the table for China, and of course, the rest of the world. Hegemony has been typically defined as "a type of domination based primarily on dominated people's and groups' consent rather than purely on a leader's coercion and exerted force. The term is often loosely used to indicate complete domination, but its precise definition has far more analytical power" (Houssay-Holzschuch, 2020, p. 357); while Kurtz (2001) borrowed Gramsci's neo-Marxist view that there is a dialectical relation between hegemony (consent-support) and domination (coercion-force).

Doğan (2021, pp. 79–86), in his book "*Hegemony with Chinese Characteristics*", approached the BRI as a contemporary result of China's "century of humiliation" (1839–1949) which mainly stemmed from the beginning of the Opium Wars to the Boxer Uprising, to the Japanese invasion, and to the Sino-Japanese War. Taking this perspective, the BRI can be misunderstood with China being a "revenant" or even one which is taking "revenge" on other states. We want to emphasize in our book that this is not the viewpoint we hold in the fundamental assumption when conceiving and implementing this research project, and now while penning this document.

We are more in line with Beeson and Crawford's (2022) notion of "comparative hegemony". The authors pointed out the United States' "hegemonic influence" (the Marshall Plan after winning a "good war") as comparable with the BRI of China, the nation which was "candidated" as the second biggest hegemon after its ascension into the WTO in 2001 and later becoming the world's second superpower in terms of gross domestic product (GDP). Both Doğan (2021) and Beeson and Crawford (2022) underscored China's distinctive international relations (Tributary system) theory which is based on the belief of "*Tianxia*" (*Tiān Xià*) ("all under heaven" dating back from the warring states in China [476–221 BC]). Thus, the BRI represents a new interpretation of the concept of "*bǎo jiā zhi guó ping tiān xià*" ("protecting the home, governing the state, and stabilizing the *Tianxia*"), in which the *Tianxia* has now been extended to include the routes of the Maritime Silk Road and beyond in a modern context. In other words, both the American-style hegemony (the Marshall Plan) and the Chinese-style hegemony (the BRI) were designed with regional stability and peace in mind, but international politics and economic benefits have often over-ridden ideologies.

The BRI as a "phenomenon *grande*" is extremely complicated and we will discuss briefly two main points that have made the initiative so controversial in the eyes of some political and economic observers. The first issue is the "debt trap". Liao (2021) pointed out that the "debt trap diplomacy" of the BRI in fact stems from the notion of PPP (public-private partnership) which originated from the West. Unsuccessful PPPs often result in white-elephant projects due to off-balance sheet financing and moral hazard problems. The main point is that while China is exporting debts to the Belt and Road countries, the accompanying level of governance is often not properly exported at the same time; and this brings very high risks to both China and the borrowing countries (e.g., the COVID-19 pandemic has great influence on the ability of the BRI countries to repay their huge debts to China and may result in further "debt for infrastructure" situations; and if not, "debt-restructuring" for the lender (Narang, 2021). Liao (2021) indicated that the times have now changed after a series of "ghost town" incidences, white-elephants, and the collapse of Evergrande, China's largest real estate company, and that Washington may have to adopt a new narrative on the BRI. While being optimistic, the new narrative or labeling may require quite some more time and effort before a more positive position can be attained.

In relation to the "debt trap" problem, Beeson and Crawford (2022) cited Gelpern et al. (2021) who analyzed 100 Chinese debt contracts with foreign governments and "confirmed that cancellation, acceleration, and stabilisation clauses in the contracts allow Beijing to influence the domestic and foreign policies of recipient states. More than 90% of the contracts analysed had clauses that authorised Chinese officials to 'terminate the contract and demand immediate repayment' if there was a 'significant' change in the recipient state's laws or policies". The data concerning the 100 debt contracts analyzed by the researchers which spanned from 2000 to 2020 (Gelpern et al., 2021, p. 12) have actually provided good evidences to explain gigantic business failures (e.g., Evergrande) and "push backs" by debt recipient countries (e.g., Malaysia). Therefore, the still immature "fast and flexible" approach to infrastructure debts (Beeson & Crawford, 2022) demands a core governance knot to be thoroughly untied.

The second issue which is necessary to mention here is obviously the ongoing Russian military actions on Ukraine.[2] The effects of this misfortune are far-reaching for the BRI because many African countries rely heavily on Russia in terms of military supplies (including transfer of nuclear power technology), economic aid, as well as humanitarian assistance. In return, Russia is gaining precious minerals (e.g., bauxite), strategic naval ports, and mercenary troops. As a result, given the close "informal alliance" between China and Russia, the BRI (with Africa as the initiative's biggest "involver") has become a scheme that observers see as "squeezed" in between the two countries. Maizland (2022) emphasized that while both China and Russia follow the Lenin-Marxist direction, they are pursuing different targets. While China aims to outrun the United States as the largest hegemon through "win-win" and "peaceful-rise" type of interventions such as the BRI, Russia uses provocative methods, such as (not to mention the fueling of nuclear tensions with "dirty bombs") political assassination and cyber-attacks.

The two points mentioned above, namely the "debt trap" and the "peaceful state versus rouge state approaches", are both negative to the national image of China and the BRI. This probably explains why the term BRI has been disappearing literally from President Xi's speeches as compared to the heavy use of the term "One Belt, One Road" (*Yídài Yílù*) during 2017–2019. In 2021–2022, the Ministry of Foreign Affairs of China published 80 speeches in English by Chinese leaders while 44 of them related to the BRI and 22 of these 44 called the initiative "High Quality Belt and Road Cooperation", "Belt and Road Cooperation", "Green Belt and Road", emphasizing on keywords such as "cooperations" and "partnerships" which are toward a more friendly language architecture than the word "initiative", implying a "top-down" geopolitical plan (Brînzȋă, 2022). This gesture is actually good news for CSR and the MNEs cultivating global cooperations along the Belt and Road. Unless this is greenwashing, China's new approach to the "initiative" will inject invigoration into it and put the country a step forward toward the more positive "Green Belt and Road" or "Socially Responsible Belt and Road", and further away from the negative nuance of hegemony. This is in line with Gramsci's view, "a class cannot dominate in modern conditions by merely advancing its own narrow economic interests; neither can it dominate purely through force and coercion. Rather, it must exert intellectual and moral leadership, and make alliances and compromises with a variety of forces" (Sassoon, 1991). For example, Noronha and Zhang (2023), using actor-network theory (Latour, 1987, 2005), have illustrated how technical as well as social knowledge can be transferred through CSR activities in the case of a Chinese information and communication technology MNE under the BRI in a constructive and beneficial way.

Concluding remarks

In this book focusing on Chinese outward foreign direct investment (OFDI) driven by the BRI, it is argued that Chinese MNEs undertaking OFDI in BRI host countries face legitimacy challenges in both host and home countries, which can be mitigated by CSR disclosures. The majority of prior academic research on MNEs' CSR has focused on their social responsiveness and success in developed economies, and some recent studies have provided useful insights into MNEs' CSR in the developing world, attempting to fill a critical theoretical and empirical void. The emerging-market CSR literature has focused mainly on market-based solutions, such as the bottom of the pyramid and financial market responses (Kolk & Van Tulder, 2010; Mishra & Suar, 2010; Yang et al., 2020). Thus, in relation to developing countries, perceptions of the contents and quality of MNEs' CSR reports remain unclear and underdeveloped. The literature on developing-world contexts suggests that it is difficult to examine MNEs' CSR owing to the relativity and vagueness of the data. This book takes

China's BRI as a starting point to explore the content and quality of the overseas CSR reporting of major MNEs along the Belt and Road, using a consolidated research method that combines qualitative and empirical analyses. The results showed that the contents of CSR reports are generally becoming more comprehensive and that the quality of overseas CSR reporting is improving. This book also stresses the important influence of state ownership on companies' CSR efforts and proposes that government-led MNEs (CEs and SOEs) should disclose more CSR practices to gain international credibility and mitigate their LOF (Mariotti & Marzano, 2019). However, there is still considerable room for improvement in CSR reporting quality. In addition, overseas CSR reporting contents and quality vary between firm types, and distinct industry-specific CSR reporting contents were identified along the Belt and Road.

The BRI has evolved from a concept into action, a vision into reality, and an initiative into a globally popular public good, guided by the values of attaining shared growth via discussion and collaboration. China and the countries along the Belt and Road have engaged in considerable cooperation to construct ports, trains, roads, and electricity infrastructure over the past ten years, effectively boosting the level of construction in these nations. The effective execution of CSR by Chinese MNEs along the Belt and Road is becoming an increasingly crucial aspect contributing to harmonious coexistence with the local population, sustainable development of the local economy, and overall societal advancement in host nations. However, due to differences in cultures, traditions, and social development stages, China and the BRI countries have divergent knowledge and understanding of the institutional frameworks, specific scopes, modes of implementation, and the ultimate goal of CSR, causing difficulties for Chinese enterprises attempting to fulfill their social responsibilities abroad. Not only does the gap in cognition undermine the social responsibility objective, but it also has a fundamental effect on the construction and image of a "beautiful overseas China". Although the Chinese government, the Asian Infrastructure Investment Bank, the Silk Road Fund, and other financial institutions have emphasized that Chinese enterprises must strictly fulfill their social responsibilities during the construction of the Belt and Road, neither the existing academic literature nor the actual institutional practices have provided a model for Chinese enterprises to do so.

This book was inspired by global stakeholders' growing expectation that MNEs from emerging markets must resolve the social and environmental concerns associated with their global operations (Buckley et al., 2017). As the Chinese economy has become more global and business sectors more internationalized, many Chinese MNEs are undertaking diverse international CSR reporting and principle-based initiatives, including disclosure of their social responsibility activities through relevant reports, adoption of GRI reporting standards, and adherence to the SDGs. This book explores the kinds of CSR reporting contents that Chinese MNEs are most likely to adopt in response to differing isomorphic pressures from home and host countries. In examining the contents and quality of CSR reporting related to the BRI host countries, this work highlights issues surrounding Chinese OFDI and the opportunities and challenges posed by such investments for sustainable development in the BRI countries. The theoretical framework of this book revealed that CSR reporting can be used by Chinese MNEs for strategic purposes, such as signaling overall quality, transparency and reliability, as well as to improve their corporate image in the host countries. Furthermore, this book not only reveals a range of policies and discourses on Chinese OFDI in general but also shows that these policies contain rather few and limited provisions regarding CSR in overseas markets, especially when it comes to accountability and transparency. Although some Chinese MNEs have started to publicly report CSR activities in their overseas investments or have included separate sections in their annual reports to address their CSR performance in overseas host countries, this does not seem to have become a widespread practice yet. Hence, significant challenges must be overcome if Chinese MNEs are to become a positive force for sustainable development.

Furthermore, this book demonstrates that CSR is a multidimensional concept. Chinese MNEs may respond strategically to institutional constraints according to the balance between costs and benefits. For instance, Chinese MNEs may concentrate on enhancing CSR in relation to product improvements and employee perceptions, as this may be more cost-effective for reputation enhancement than enhancing other facets of social responsibility. In addition to meeting the criteria of home-country institutions, Chinese MNEs should actively learn and meet the special demands and expectations of host nations. When operating abroad, MNEs and governments are suggested to pay more attention to the opinions of the locals and address their needs, thus demonstrating that they comprehend the significance of publicity in host nations.

Chinese MNEs need to consider how to better adapt to institutional complexity in the cross-border organizational arena. Thus, in addition to engaging in positive CSR practices that are easily reported by the media and are well-known by the public and the home and host governments, Chinese MNEs must proactively correct and reduce hidden CSR issues, such as accounting irregularities, production accidents, and environmental pollution. In reality, irresponsible behaviors will have a detrimental effect on corporate reputation in the long run. We also propose that CSR reporting strategies should be implemented in conjunction with strategies for the BRI, as CSR communications are linked to the institutional context and the expectations of stakeholders involved in the MNEs' activities. The findings also indicate that China's current policy in the BRI host countries is insufficient to ensure the sustainable development of Chinese OFDI. Although broad principles supporting CSR have been repeated in many policy documents, details of the concrete steps to be taken and compliance mechanisms are still scarce. Thus, it is suggested that Chinese MNEs should be subject to stronger CSR reporting requirements, including proper and professional third-party verification and auditing. Effective sustainable development of the BRI depends not only on China's commitments and priorities but also on its capacity to sustain, enact, and execute strict CSR disclosure laws and regulations.

In conclusion, more scholarly sequels to this book are welcomed to augment critical thoughts on the BRI. This book discusses the resurrection of the Silk

Road with the addition of modern mindsets, goals for growth, communitarian ideologies, and technologies. This research is an urgently needed endeavor, since one is also essentially attempting to comprehend the intricacy of new methods for building global ties between nations and ordinary people. Overall, this book presents theoretical implications and practical proposals for the Chinese policymakers concerning the BRI to improve Chinese MNEs' CSR, maintain a positive image abroad, and thus enhance mutual trust and regional cooperation among nations along the Belt and Road. At the same time, we have provided specific corporate governance and strategy advices and recommendations for Chinese MNEs to assist them in fulfilling their CSR obligations in both their home and host countries and gain global legitimacy as they participate in the new "Green Belt and Road Cooperations and Partnerships".

Notes

1 Full text of Keynote Speech by Xi Jinping, President of the People's Republic of China, at the Opening Ceremony of the Second Belt and Road Forum for International Cooperation, http://www.beltandroadforum.org/english/n100/2019/0426/c22-1266.html
2 As at November 27, 2022, the Office of the United Nations High Commissioner for Human Rights (OHCHR) verified a total of 6655 civilian deaths during Russia's invasion of Ukraine as of November 27, 2022. Of them, 419 were children. Furthermore, 10,368 people were reported to have been injured. However, OHCHR specified that the real numbers could be higher (Statistics Research Department, 2022). As at November 24, 2022, the Ukrainian Government estimated 85,720 losses of Russian and allied forces (Ukrainska Pravda, 2022).

References

Beddewela, E. (2019). Managing corporate community responsibility in multinational corporations: Resolving institutional duality. *Long Range Planning*, 52(6), 101911.
Beeson, M., & Crawford, C. (2022). Putting the BRI in perspective: History, hegemony and geoeconomics. *Chinese Political Science Review*, 8, 45–62, https://doi.org/10.1007/s41111-022-00210-y.
Bondy, K. (2008). The paradox of power in CSR: A case study on implementation. *Journal of Business Ethics*, 82(2), 307–323.
Bondy, K., Moon, J., & Matten, D. (2012). An institution of corporate social responsibility (CSR) in multi-national corporations (MNCs): Form and implications. *Journal of Business Ethics*, 111(2), 281–299.
Brînzǎ, A. (2022). What happened to the Belt and Road Initiative? *The Diplomat*. https://thediplomat.com/2022/09/what-happened-to-the-belt-and-road-initiative/
Buckley, P. J., Doh, J. P., & Benischke, M. H. (2017). Towards a renaissance in international business research? Big questions, grand challenges, and the future of IB scholarship. *Journal of International Business Studies*, 48(9), 1045–1064.
Cantwell, J., Dunning, J. H., & Lundan, S. M. (2010). An evolutionary approach to understanding international business activity: The co-evolution of MNEs and the institutional environment. *Journal of International Business Studies*, 41(4), 567–586.

De Villiers, C., & Van Staden, C. J. (2006). Can less environmental disclosure have a legitimising effect? Evidence from Africa. *Accounting, organizations and society,* 31(8), 763–781.

Doğan, A. (2021). *Hegemony with Chinese characteristics: From the tributary system to the Belt and Road Incentive.* Routledge.

Donleavy, G., & Noronha, C. (2023). Concluding remarks: Comparative CSR and sustainability research: An axial analysis. In G. Donleavy, & C. Noronha (Eds.), *Comparative CSR and sustainability: New accounting for social consequences* (pp. 380–398). Routledge.

Fang, C., & Nolan, P. (Eds.). (2019). *Routledge handbook of the belt and road* (pp. 213–217). Routledge.

Gaur, A. S., Ma, X., & Ding, Z. (2018). Home country supportiveness/unfavorableness and outward foreign direct investment from China. *Journal of International Business Studies,* 49(3), 324–345.

Gelpern, A., Horn, S., Morris, S., Parks, B., & Trebesch C. (2021). *How China lends: A rare look into 100 debt contracts with foreign governments.* AidDATA, Kiel Institute for the World Economy, Center for Global Development, & Peterson Institute for International Economics.

Green Finance and Development Center. (2022). *Countries of the Belt and Road Initiative (BRI).* https://greenfdc.org/countries-of-the-belt-and-road-initiative-bri/

Hamprecht, J., & Schwarzkopf, J. (2014). Subsidiary initiatives in the institutional environment. *Management International Review,* 54(5), 757–778.

Hoskisson, R. E., Wright, M., Filatotchev, I., & Peng, M. W. (2013). Emerging multinationals from mid-range economies: The influence of institutions and factor markets. *Journal of Management Studies,* 50(7), 1295–1321.

Houssay-Holzschuch, M. (2020). Hegemony. In A. Kobayashi (Ed.), *International encyclopedia of human geography* (2nd ed.), (pp. 357–362). Elsevier.

Kolk, A., & Van Tulder, R. (2010). International business, corporate social responsibility and sustainable development. *International business review,* 19(2), 119–125.

Kurtz, D. V. (2001). Hegemony: Anthropological aspects. In N. J. Smelser, & P. B. Baltes (Eds.), *International encyclopedia of the social & behavioral sciences* (pp. 6642–6645). Pergamon.

Latour, B. (1987). *Science in action: How to follow scientists and engineers through society.* Harvard University Press.

Latour, B. (2005). *Reassembling the social: Introduction to actor-network-theory.* Oxford University Press.

Liao, J. C. (2021). How BRI debts put China at risk. *The Diplomat.* https://thediplomat.com/2021/10/how-bri-debt-puts-china-at-risk/

Maizland, L. (2022). *China and Russia: Exploring ties between two authoritarian powers.* Council on Foreign Relations. https://www.cfr.org/backgrounder/china-russia-relationship-xi-putin-taiwan-ukraine

Marano, V., Tashman, P., & Kostova, T. (2017). Escaping the iron cage: Liabilities of origin and CSR reporting of emerging market multinational enterprises. *Journal of International Business Studies,* 48, 386–408.

Mariotti, S., & Marzano, R. (2019). Varieties of capitalism and the internationalization of state-owned enterprises. *Journal of International Business Studies,* 50, 669–691.

Mishra, S., & Suar, D. (2010). Does corporate social responsibility influence firm performance of Indian companies? *Journal of Business Ethics,* 95(4), 571–601.

Moir, L. (2001). What do we mean by corporate social responsibility? *Corporate Governance: The International Journal of Business in Society*, *1*(2), 16–22.

Muller, A. (2006). Global versus local CSR strategies. *European Management Journal*, *24*(2–3), 189–198.

Narang, A. (2021). Evergrande has collapsed. The next is BRI. *TFIGlobal*. https://tfiglobalnews.com/2021/10/04/evergrande-has-collapsed-the-next-is-bri/

Noronha, C., & Zhang, R. (2023). Using "actor-network theory and friends" to explore CSR reporting in the information and communication technology sector under the Belt and Road Initiative. In G. Donleavy & C. Noronha (Eds.), *Comparative CSR and Sustainability: New Accounting for Social Consequences* (pp. 162–187). Routledge.

Rathert, N. (2016). Strategies of legitimation: MNEs and the adoption of CSR in response to host-country institutions. *Journal of International Business Studies*, *47*(7), 858–879.

Sassoon, A. S. (1991). Hegemony. In T. Bottomore, L. Harris, V. G. Kierman, & R. Miliband (Eds.), *The dictionary of marxist thoughts* (2nd ed.), (pp. 229–231). Blackwell Publishing Ltd.

Statistics Research Department (2022). *Number of civilian casualties during the war in Ukraine 2022*. 27 November 2022. https://www.statista.com/statistics/1293492/ukraine-war-casualties/

Strike, V. M., Gao, J., & Bansal, P. (2006). Being good while being bad: Social responsibility and the international diversification of US firms. *Journal of International Business Studies*, *37*(6), 850–862.

Tashman, P., Marano, V., & Kostova, T. (2019). Walking the walk or talking the talk? Corporate social responsibility decoupling in emerging market multinationals. *Journal of International Business Studies*, *50*, 153–171.

Ukrainska Pravda. (2022). *War on Ukraine: Total combat losses of the Russian forces for day 260*. https://www.pravda.com.ua/eng/

Xu, D., & Meyer, K. E. (2013). Linking theory and context: 'Strategy research in emerging economies' after Wright et al. (2005). *Journal of Management Studies*, *50*(7), 1322–1346.

Yang, N., Wang, J., Liu, X., & Huang, L. (2020). Home-country institutions and corporate social responsibility of emerging economy multinational enterprises: The Belt and Road Initiative as an example. *Asia Pacific Journal of Management*, *39*, 927–965.

Index

Note: Page references in *italics* refer to figures, in **bold** refer to tables and with "n" refer to endnotes.

21st Century Maritime Silk Road 12, 33

adverse institutional attribution 7, 154
Africa: anti-corruption 198–199; biodiversity conservation 193–195; BRI 188–190, 200–202; Chinese MNEs in 186–188; community welfare 197–198; CSR assisting companies in gaining legitimacy in 190–200; CSR threats of BRI in 190; employment promotion 199–200; environmental conservation 193–195; fair education 196–197; SDGs 200–202; urbanization in 187; way forward for 200–202; women empowerment 195–196
"African Charter on the Rights and Welfare of the Child" 196
African Development Bank 188
African Union 178; Agenda 2063 188, 195; Smart Health Monitoring Room 178
agency theory 78
Agenda for Sustainable Development (2030) 131–132, 195
Aguilera, R. V. 71
Alibaba Cloud 179
Alibaba Foundation 136
Alibaba Group 23, 116n2, 177, 179
Alipay 179
All-China Federation of Industry and Commerce (ACFIC) 57
Alphabet Inc. 23
Amazon 23
anti-corruption 198–199
anti-dumping measures 26

Arthaud-Day, M. L. 36, 70
Asian Infrastructure Investment Bank 217
Asia Society Policy Institute 135
Assets Supervision and Administration Commission of the State Council (SASAC) 53, 83, 145, 157, 160n3

banking and finance industry 171–176
Bank of China 173
Beattie, V. 106
Beeson, M. 214, 215
Beidou satellite program 177
"Beijing Declaration on Building a Closer China-Africa Community of Destiny" 193–194
Belt and Road Forum for International Cooperation (BRFIC) 187
Belt and Road Initiative (BRI) 12, 30, 55–57, 207–213; for Africa 188–190; Chinese MNEs participating **34**; CSR 35–42; and CSR reporting 79–85; Ecological and Environmental Cooperation Plan 126; as Green Silk Road 147, 165; highlighted industries along 164–180; internationalization through 42; as "phenomenon *grande*" 215; policy documents 58; political economy background of 33–35; and SDGs 200–202; sustainable 171–176, 209; theoretical framework of 42–43, *43*; threats and related CSR crisis **191–192**
big data 177
Bing, W. 189

biodiversity conservation 193–195
Boxer Uprising 214
Brammer, S. J. 72
BRI host countries 111; CEs in *149*; challenges 180–182; Chinese MNEs' CSR reporting in 69–79; CSR reporting in 69–85; CSR reporting quality in 132–137; CSR reporting topics related to 120–127, **121–123**; economic impacts along BRI 120–124; emerging reporting topics 127–132, **128–130**; highlighted industries along BRI 164–180; industry-specific CSR reporting contents in 164–182; local people's livelihoods 124–125; overseas employment 127; PEs in *150*; SOEs in *150*; unifying environmental safeguards 125–126
Brown, H. S. 96
Brunswick Group 29
Bryman, A. 97
Business Week 2

Carroll, A. B. 9, 50
central enterprises (CEs) 83–84, 86n4
"Change Our World: 2030 Agenda for Sustainable Development" 100
China: Company Law 53; economic reform 27; "going out" program 207; mask diplomacy 136; Ministry of Commerce 58, 177; Ministry of Education 196; Ministry of Foreign Affairs 58, 177; National Development and Reform Commission 58, 165, 177; OFDI 19, 20–21; Open Door policy 20, 152; "peaceful development" (*hé píng fā zhǎn*) slogan 188; as quick learner of CSR 50–57; related policies for green finance in **173**; rise of economy 19–30; stages of internationalization 20–23; state-controlled economy 26; types of firms in 83
"China-Africa Community with a Shared Future" 186
China-Africa Cooperation Vision 2035 26
China-Africa Joint Research Centers 194
China-Africa Research Initiative 189
China Banking and Insurance Regulatory Commission (CBIRC) 172

China Civil Engineering Construction Corporation 190
China Communications Construction Company 169, 194, 195
China Development Bank 172, 173
China Enterprise Confederation and China Entrepreneur Association 99
China Iron and Steel Group 82
China Minmetals 21, 22
China Mobile 177, 179
China National Offshore Oil Corporation (CNOOC) 21, 22, 27
China National Petroleum Corporation 116n2
China State Construction Engineering Corporation 21
China Telecom Corporation 177
China Unicom 177, 178
China Wuyi 167
Chinese Academy of Social Sciences (CASS) CSR framework 209
Chinese Communist Party (CCP) 33, 53; Central Committee 152
Chinese hegemony 198, 200
Chinese MNEs 12–13, 19–30; in Africa 186–188; characteristics of 76–77; competitive advantages of 26–28; competitive manufacturing industries 22; and CSR reporting 54–56, **55**, 61–63, 81; CSR reporting in BRI countries 69–79; CSR reporting quality of 97–110, **100**; discretionary reporting for reputation 153–154; environmental and social impacts 43; honors/awards as mimetic forces 155–156; impact of government policies on 28; institutional CSR governing 57–61, **59–60**; international operations 22; legitimacy 74–75; motivations of 23–26; new political-economy basis for CSR reporting 151–159; OFDI 20–211; ownership type and CSR reporting of 143–147; profitability 22–23; reporting influenced by party directives 156–159; reporting transparency and humanization 154–155; state ownership 152–153; topical analysis of CSR reporting of 147–151; *see also* multinational enterprises (MNEs)
CITIC Group 21, 22
CNPC 21, 22
COFCO 21

224 *Index*

community welfare 197–198
comparative hegemony 214
competitive advantages: of Chinese MNEs 26–28; downscaling technology 27; technologies 27
competitiveness: CSR as source of 78; national 78
Confucianism 51–52
construction industry 167–171
content analysis **107–108**, 116n1; coding system 106
corporate philanthropy 70–71
corporate social responsibility (CSR) 2–3, 96, 207–213; in Asian countries 11; -based political legitimacy strategy 84; Belt and Road Initiative (BRI) 35–42; China as quick learner of 50–57; of Chinese MNEs in developing countries 186–202; companies gaining legitimacy in Africa 190–200; defined 9; disclosure quality 132, **133**, **144**; of EMNEs 9–11, 29; initiatives 12; overseas **36**; as source of competitiveness 78; theoretical framework of 42–43, *43*; threats of BRI in Africa 190; topic-level one-way ANOVA results **148–149**
COSCO 21
COVID-19 pandemic 12, 29, 136, 215; induced financial problem 136; vaccines 136
Crawford, C. 214, 215
CSR reporting: in BRI countries 69–85; and Chinese MNEs 54–56, **55**, 61–63; of Chinese MNEs, and ownership type 143–147; *vs.* CSR initiatives 50–51; defined 69; evaluation framework of **101–105**; exploring 79–83; importance of 50; industry-specific contents in BRI host countries 164–182; influenced by party directives 156–159; and MNEs 51; new political-economy basis for developing 151–159; quality, assessment of 96–97; quality in BRI host countries 132–137; quality of Chinese MNEs 97–110, **100**; role of 50–51; score distribution of topics **134**; screening process **99**; situational factors affecting 83–85; theoretical framework of *80*; topical analysis, of Chinese MNEs 147–151; topics related to BRI host countries 120–127, **121–123**; transparency and humanization 154–155

CSR Research Centre of the Chinese Academy of Social Sciences (CASS) 100
Cultural Revolution 51

Daoism 51
"debt trap" 200, 215–216
debt trap diplomacy 215
Deng Xiaoping 21, 30n1
Denzin, N. K. 97
Desalegn, Hailemariam 187
developing countries: CSR of Chinese MNEs in 186–202; *see also* emerging economies
Digital Silk Road (DSR) 176–180, 213
discretionary reporting for reputation 153–154
Doğan, A. 198–199, 214
Dow Jones Sustainability Index (DJSI) 97
Dunning, J. H. 27

eclectic theory 23
ecological civilization 29
economic impacts along BRI 120–124
The Economist 2
economy: China's, rise of 19–30; emerging (*see* emerging economies); global 2, 25, 54; green 171–172; political, of BRI 33–35; relational 52; rule-based 52; sustainable 11
Edelman Trust Barometer 7
education 196–197
emerging economies: challenges 6–8; defined 1; MNEs (*see* MNEs from emerging economies (EMNEs)); opportunities 6–8; rise of 28
emerging-economy multinational enterprises (EM-MNEs) 208–209
employment: human-oriented principle in overseas **121–123**, 127; promotion 199–200
empowerment of women 195–196
Engle, R. L. 82
environmental conservation 193–195
environmental impact assessments (EIAs) 61, 135
"Environmental Risk Management Initiative for China's Overseas Investment" 212
environmental safeguards: BRI host countries 125–126; unifying 125–126
Export-Import Bank of China 173, 176

fair education 196–197
finance: green 171–176; industry 171–176
The Financial Times 136
"Flying Pigeon" bicycle trademark 137n3
FOCAC Beijing Summit 194
Forbes 3
foreign direct investment (FDI) 77; developing countries 3; *see also* outward foreign direct investment (OFDI)
Fortune magazine 2
Forum on China-Africa Cooperation (FOCAC) 186, 194, 200
Friedman, Milton 78

Gill, B. 26
Githaiga, N. M. 189
Global Competitiveness Study 2005–2006 78
globalization 19; characterization 1; and communication 52
Global Positioning System (GPS) 177
Global Reporting Initiative (GRI) 10, 97, 99, 209
"go global" strategy 160n1
"going out" policy 86n3
Great Wall Motor Company Limited 190
Gree 22
"Green Belt and Road Cooperations and Partnerships" 219
green bond: and environmental pollution 176; as green finance instrument 171; issued by Chinese multinational banks **174–175**
"green BRI" 126, 131, 135, 213
green economy 171–172
green finance 171–176; defined 171; and green bond 171; related policies for **173**; *see also* banking and finance industry
greenwashing 11

Haier 22
hegemony: Chinese 198, 200; comparative 214; defined 214
"*Hegemony with Chinese Characteristics*" (Doğan) 214
honors/awards as mimetic forces 155–156
Huawei 5, 127, 154; iLearning site 127; sustainability honors and awards of **156**
Huawei Marine 177

Hu Jintao 53
humanization, and reporting transparency 154–155
human-oriented principle, overseas employment 127
hyper-norms 75

Industrial and Commercial Bank of China 173
information and communication technology (ICT) industry 176–180
infrastructure, transportation *see* transportation infrastructure
institutional theory 71–73
institutional voids 4, 6–7, 55–56
intellectual property rights (IPR) 132, 210–211
international business theory 26
internationalization: concepts of 19–20; defined 19; stages of 20–23; through BRI 42
International Labor Organization (ILO) Conventions 10
International Standard Organization (ISO) 10–11
international strategic theory 78–79
internet of things 177
ISO 14000 100, 116n3
ISO 26000 97, 100
isomorphism: and BRI CSR 36–39; and LOF/LOE 74

Jack Ma Foundation 136
Jackson, G. 71
Jamali, D. 51
JD.com 177
Jingdong Group 23
Johanson, J. 20

Kang, R. 20
Karam, C. 51
Kramer, M. R. 78
Krippendorff, K. 106
Kurtz, D. V. 214

land connectivity, and transportation infrastructure 167–171
land transportation projects: environmental risks of **168**; social risks of **168**
legitimacy 9–10; and BRI CSR 36–39; challenges of EMNEs 7; defined 7, 38, 73; issues and EMNEs 11; and MNEs 39; organizational 73; theory 73–75

Lenovo 22
liability of emergingness (LOE) 6, 74
liability of foreignness (LOF) 71, 74
liability of origin 6
Liao, J. C. 215
Li Keqiang 160n3
local people's livelihoods: BRI host countries 124–125; maximizing 124–125
Lundan, S. M. 27

"Made in China 2025" strategy 176
Made in China products 21
Maizland, L. 215
"Maputo Protocol to the African Charter on Human and Peoples' Rights on the Rights of Women in Africa" 196
Maritime Silk Road 164, 214
Marquis, C. 153
Marshall Plan 214
mask diplomacy 136
Merowe Dam (Sudan) 187
Meta Platforms Inc. 23
Meyer, K. E. 1
Millennium Development Goals 195
Milne, M. J. 38, 73
Ministry of Commerce of China 69
Ministry of Foreign Affairs 69
Miska, C. 51
Mitchell, R. K. 143
Mithani, M. A. 70
MNEs from emerging economies (EMNEs) 1–3; advanced technology investment 25; advantages 8; challenges 6–7; CSR of 9–11, 12, 29; internationalization of 5; legitimacy issues 11; stereotypes 4
MOFCOM 57
multinational CSR 13
multinational enterprises (MNEs) 1, 11; Chinese (*see* Chinese MNEs); and CSR reporting 51; from developed economies 4; from emerging economies 207; and legitimacy 39; rise of 72; traditional developed-market 5

Nairobi National Park 165, 190, 194
Narain, D. 165
national competitiveness 78
National Development and Reform Commission (NDRC) 33, 69
New Silk Road Economic Belt 12

New York Times 78
norms, and BRI CSR 39–40
Noronha, C. 165, 216
Nye, J. S. 188

Office of the United Nations High Commissioner for Human Rights (OHCHR) 219n2
"open door" policy 152
"Opinions and Practices for China to Promote the Development of Green Finance Along the Belt and Road" report 176
Opium Wars 214
organizational legitimacy 38, 73
Organization for Economic Co-operation and Development (OECD) 10, 208
outward foreign direct investment (OFDI) 1–2, 124, 131, 196; benefits of 4; China 19, 20–21; by Chinese MNEs 5, 24; state-controlled corporations 24; *see also* foreign direct investment (FDI)
Overland Silk Road Economic Belt 164
overseas CSR (OCSR) disclosure quality: by firm types **146**; by year **133**
overseas employment: CSR disclosures on **121–123**, 127; human-oriented principle in 127; *see also* employment
ownership: and CSR reporting of Chinese MNEs 143–147; state 152–153

Pakistan East African Cable 177
Papasolomou-Doukakis 70
Paris Agreement 56, 172, 195
Parmentola, A. 25
Patten, D. M. 38, 73, 84
Perrini, F. 35, 70
PetroChina 10, 82
philanthropy 125; corporate 70–71
Porter, M. E. 78
private enterprises (PEs) 83
product life cycle theory 20
pull factors 77
push factors 77

Qian, C. 153
Quer, D. 143

reputation, discretionary reporting for 153–154
reputational commons 84

reputation quotient (RQ) 79
resource dependence theory (RDT) 40–42, 76–77
Roberts, R. W. 69
Robson, C. 165
Russo, A. 35, 70

Samsung 5
Science 120
Scott, W. R. 73
Second Belt and Road Forum for International Cooperation 208, 219n1
"Silk Road Economic Belt" strategy 33
Silk Road Fund 173, 217
Sinochem 21
Sino-Japanese War 214
Sinopec 10
Sinosteel Corporation 126
social contract theory 75–76; and BRI CSR 39–40; defined 39
soft power 188
South-South investment 3
stakeholders 10; and BRI CSR 35–36; defined 35
stakeholder theory 70–71, 71
Standardization Administration of China (SAC) 179
"Standards China Unicom Joint Construction One Belt One Road Action Plan (2018–2020)" 179
State-Owned Assets Supervision and Administration Commission (SASAC) 53, 83, 145, 157, 160n3
state-owned enterprises (SOEs) 83, 84, 86n4
state ownership 152–153
"Statistical Bulletin of China's Foreign Direct Investment" 99
Suchman, M. C. 38, 73
Supervision and Administration Commission of the State Council (SASAC) 83
sustainable BRI 171–176, 209
Sustainable Development Goals (SDGs) 152, 195; BRI and 200–202

Tagesson, T. 85
Tazara Railway 189
TCL 22
TD-LTE networks 179
Tencent Holdings Ltd 23
Tianxia 214

transportation infrastructure: Africa's 187; and BRI 167; land connectively through 167–171
triangulation 97
Tropic Science 177
Tsavo National Park 165, 194

Ukraine, Russian invasion of 214–215, 219n2
UN Convention on Biological Diversity 195
UN Environmental Program (UNEP) 11
United Nations (UN) 124, 195; 2030 Agenda for Sustainable Development 131–132, 195; General Assembly 195; Millennium Development Goals 195; Population Fund 195; Sustainable Development Goals (SDGs) 165
United Nations Global Compact (UNGC) 10, 97

Vernon, 84
"Vision and Actions on Jointly Building Silk Road Economic Belt and Twenty-First-Century Maritime Silk Road" 58

Wang Yi 188
"weak governance zones" 208
Wei, W. X. 25
Wei Jianjun 190
Wiedersheim-Paul, F. 20
women: CSR initiatives promoting benefits to 132, 210; empowerment of 195–196
World Bank 124
World Business Council for Sustainable Development (WBCSD) 50, 69, 197
World Economic Forum 78
World Trade Organization (WTO) 21, 52, 214
World Wildlife Fund (WWF) 165

Xi Jinping 12, 29–30, 33, 147, 164, 186, 201, 208, 213

Yellow Peril 188

Zen Buddhism 51
Zhang, R. 165, 216
Zhu, S. 20
Zijin Mining 10, 136

Printed in the United States
by Baker & Taylor Publisher Services